KU-720-857

# DISCOVERING ANTIQUES

*A Guide to the World of Antiques and Collectables*

**For my family**

First published in hardback in 1996 by
De Agostini Editions Limited
Griffin House
161 Hammersmith Road
London W6 8SD

This paperback edition first published in Great Britain in 1999 by
Aurum Press Ltd
25 Bedford Avenue
London WC1B 3AT

Copyright © 1999 Istituto Geografico De Agostini S.p.A.
Text copyright © 1996 Eric Knowles

All rights reserved. No part of this book may be reproduced or utilised in any
form or by any means, electronic or mechanical, including photography,
recording or by any information storage and retrieval system, without permis-
sion in writing from Aurum Press Ltd.

A catalogue record for this book is available from the British Library.

ISBN 1 85410 669 4

Publisher: Maria E. Brady

Production Co-ordinator: Deborah Pasternakiewicz

Although all reasonable care has been taken in the preparation of this book,
the Publishers cannot accept any liability for any consequences arising from
the use of the information contained herein.

Throughout this book the captions include an estimated auction house sale
price or price range for the item shown. These should be used as a guide only
as so many factors, especially condition, are involved in the pricing of antiques.

Consultants: Furniture: Tim Squire-Sanders; Silver: Loraine Turner;
Clocks: Oliver Saunders; Bears and Dolls: Sue Pearson; Toys: Leigh Gotch;
Textiles: Joanna Macfarlane; Carpets: Ian White; Collectables: Alexander
Crum-Ewing and Alexander Payne.

Caption to photograph on p.6. Clockwise from top left: French gold anchor
figure by Edmé Samson, 1880; English silver wine ewer by Richard Marlin
and Ebenezer Hall, 1883; British engraved glass magnum jug, c.1880; French
bronze and ivory "Spanish dancer," unsigned, 1930; Glasgow half-pint pewter
lidded measure, c.1870; French cast ormolu repeating carriage clock, 1850;
German bear by Steiff, c.1910, sitting in German "apple" tea caddy c.1780.
For caption to cover photographs see p.224.

Printed in Singapore by Tat Wei Printing Packaging Pte Ltd.

688442

MORAY COUNCIL
DEPARTMENT OF TECHNICAL
& LEISURE SERVICES
745.1

# Discovering
# ANTIQUES

## A Guide to the World of
## Antiques and Collectables

## ERIC KNOWLES

x

AURUM PRESS

# Contents

# Foreword

The collecting bug is highly infectious. Many of us catch it during childhood, raiding the woods for conkers, tipping the cereal packet out onto the kitchen table to find the free goody or pestering the life out of friends and relations for used stamps or unwanted foreign coins. Some of us, myself included, never find a cure. For others the magpie instinct lies dormant until an interesting something is inherited, or we take a fresh look at our possessions, find that two or three of them come under the same heading and feel compelled to add to them. You'll know you're hooked when you find yourself spending increasing amounts of your precious leisure time – and money – in single-minded pursuit of the next prize!

It is extraordinary how the interest in collecting has grown over the last ten years. Far from being a closed and stagnant world populated solely by scholarly experts, the field is shifting and expanding, with new categories and new devotees emerging every year. Weekend fairs and markets have mushroomed, television coverage has expanded and scarcely a week goes by without the publication of a new specialist book.

I have written this book for those of you making your first forays into this bustling and often bewildering world. It is the book I wish someone had written for me 25 years ago when I began to take an interest in antiques. Packed with glorious pictures, tips and up-to-the-minute prices, I hope it whets your appetite and gives you confidence. I have never bought for investment, but always because I liked a piece and it had a story to tell about where it was made and the lives of the people who made it. My early voyages of discovery developed into an enormously enjoyable career. I hope this book launches you on a journey which brings nothing but pleasure.

Finally, I would like to extend my thanks to Frances Gertler, Publishing Director at De Agostini Editions, for her endless support, her professional approach and her infectious enthusiasm, all of which made working on this book a real pleasure; and to De Agostini's talented designer, David Robinson, whose advice and calmness I greatly value. I would also like to express my gratitude to my long-time trusted friend and brilliant wordsmith, the indomitable Fiona Malcolm, for her perseverance, clear-sighted vision and dedication. I am grateful, too, to all my friends and colleagues for their generous help in the preparation of this book, especially to the consultants listed on page 2 and to all those who gave advice or information, or lent their treasured objects to be photographed; they are mentioned by name on page 224.

Eric Knowles

# Introduction

To praise experienced dealers or collectors on their "good eye and keen nose" is probably the highest compliment you could pay them. It is an acknowledgment that many years of hard work have paid off and that they have accumulated a fund of knowledge which has earned them the respect of their peers.

Only very few collectors set out to become world authorities, however. Most have neither the time nor the resources to devote themselves to studying a subject full-time, but acquiring some knowledge and a good eye is, without doubt, the best ammunition with which to start a collection.

Firstly, it is worth reminding yourself that even the great experts started out with only their enthusiasm and a thirst for knowledge. Don't be tempted to spend money to begin with, unless it is on a good reference book or two. Without any "feel" for objects, it is only too easy to make expensive mistakes, but a good range of books will earn their keep, however expensive the initial outlay may seem.

However well read you become, though, books can never compensate for hands-on experience. The more you can handle objects and study their distinguishing features, the more of an instinct you will develop for knowing when something is good, bad or indifferent. You will often hear experts use the expressions "right" and "wrong" as they examine a piece. Their skills of observation take them through a step-by-step routine of inspection. One aspect of construction or decoration might tell them all they need to know, but quite often they need to run through the lot before pronouncing!

Whatever you are looking at, to begin with stand back from it and ask yourself if the general proportions and overall lines look right. This will obviously apply more to larger objects such as furniture, longcase clocks or certain pieces of silver than to fob watches or snuff boxes, but it is a good general starting point. If a piece is made up of different sections, ask yourself if they started life together or if one section was added to another at a later point. If a piece of silver looks odd, perhaps it started life as something plain and elegant and was embossed during the 19th century, or was changed from one object to another by the addition of a spout or lid.

Examine the patina of wood, the nature of ceramic bodies (is it hard- or soft-paste porcelain, stoneware or earthenware?), the colour of metals (and this applies to glass as well as silver and bronze) and the quality of modelling and painting. Once you have seen a crisply modelled porcelain flower and looked at areas of beautifully soft gilding, you will be quick to spot its clumsily formed counterpart and lines of harsh, mirror-bright gilding. Once you have covered the more general aspects of a piece, you will be able to move on to more specific areas such as marks, styles and palettes attributable to particular factories or craftsmen.

You will also soon learn to tell the difference between something made by hand before the age of mechanization and something with the perfect and uniform lines that only a machine could achieve. You will find yourself picking up on the slight irregularities and imperfections often found on hand-made pieces such as specks of dirt from the floor of the kiln on the base of porcelain, turned wooden bowls forming circles which are not quite true, a variation in the thickness of veneers or the slight roughness left by the pontil rod when it was broken off the base of an 18th-century wine glass.

A knowledge of styles and periods will also help you to date pieces and set the appropriate alarm bells ringing. A porcelain trinket box painted with female figures wearing costume featuring bustles, for instance, cannot be 18th century because the bustle was not invented until the 19th century. English ceramics marked "Made In England" on the base cannot be earlier than 1902, and neither can anything English marked with a registration diamond be earlier than 1840. The wine cooler, the sideboard and the teapoy were 18th-century inventions, so don't let anyone try to convince you they are selling 17th-century examples of either object.

Get to know one or two specialist dealers who run either antiques shops or galleries. Those worth their salt will be happy for you to examine the stock providing they feel reassured that you will handle with care, and they are usually a fund of useful information. A canny specialist will be quick to spot your genuine interest and work out that while you may only be looking in the short term, a few months down the line you could become a valued customer.

The auction house is another great "hands on" learning environment with experts there to answer questions when goods are on view before a sale. You can browse and touch and any advice will be a good mixture of history and common sense. You will learn not only about an object's origins, but by exactly how much an area of damage or restoration affects the value. Invest in the catalogue to help identify pieces and get an idea of values, and you will be left alone to examine the lots for as long as you please, providing you turn up during official viewing times. Like the dealer, the auction house expert hopes to woo you as a client. If you want the chance to handle the very best quality objects, go to views at the top salerooms and don't be in the slightest bit intimidated by the opulent surroundings. Competition between salerooms is fierce and each wants you to be impressed by the service offered.

Even if you have scarcely left the starting post, don't rule out joining the society or collectors' club relating to your particular interest. For the most part, keen collectors gravitate towards each other. The need to share knowledge and enthusiasm is irresistible and belonging to one can be a good way to learn. Most hold regular meetings and issue a newsletter. Some organise tours, visits and holidays with a learning theme. Be prepared to pay an annual subscription, but fees are usually low.

Becoming a friend of a local or national museum is another good way to meet like-minded people and gain regular access, often at a discount, to exhibitions and special views. Unlike the shop or saleroom, however, in museums you can generally look but not touch.

However you decide to go about developing the instinct which tells you when to buy and when to walk away, don't get so bogged down in the learning process that the fun goes out of it. If the books become a chore, put them away for a while. If, after an hour or two of examining lots at a saleroom, everything begins to look the same, walk away. When you come back, perhaps a week or a month later, you may be surprised how much has already sunk in. You are on your way to becoming a discerning collector.

## Where to Buy and Sell

### Buying at Auction

Auction houses can seem mysterious and daunting institutions, but rest assured, they are in the business of buying and selling and could not survive without maintaining a good relationship with their clients. If any aspect of their procedure seems intimidating, sit in on several sales before you become a potential buyer until you feel comfortable. A good sale taken by an experienced auctioneer who knows how to handle the room is as entertaining as a trip to the theatre. It won't be long before the atmosphere rubs off on you and you become smitten by the auction bug! Salerooms both large and small usually advertise forthcoming sales in the national or local press, or in specialist magazines. They also often produce free sales calendars so that you can make a note of those that interest you over several months.

A catalogue is produced for each sale with each item or group of items (known as lots) allocated a number and a description. At some small, weekly auctions such as those held in farm outbuildings or hired halls, this can consist simply of a photocopied sheet handed out as you arrive, but at the larger houses, you should expect to pay anything from £5 to £20 for an illustrated catalogue.

Stated in the catalogue will be the viewing time for the sale, when the items are displayed for potential buyers to look at and handle. Check the times carefully and confirm them by telephone, particularly if a journey is involved. Printing errors do slip through occasionally! Allow yourself plenty of time to view: viewing should be relaxed and unhurried. Examine pieces very carefully for damage or restoration and don't be afraid to ask questions. If you cannot get to the view, the larger houses will supply condition reports over the telephone, but there is no real substitute for handling the goods yourself. Read the wording relating to the objects you are interested in very carefully and satisfy yourself completely that the pieces are exactly what you want before you set yourself a limit on how high you are prepared to bid to secure them.

If you can't face bidding yourself, or if you can't get to the sale, most auction houses will provide a free and confidential bidding service when a commission clerk will act for you. If you are bidding and the lots you are interested in are towards the end of the sale, ask how many lots per hour the auctioneer is expected to sell. The average is 80 to 140, so you can time your arrival, but remember that you will have to register, giving your personal and bank details before being issued with a numbered card or "paddle" and going into the saleroom.

If you intend to spend a significant amount, it is advisable to let the accounts department know at least 24 hours before the sale so that they can get the necessary guarantees from your bank that the funds are in place. Don't forget to add 10 or 15 % for commission onto the hammer price, plus VAT on the commission, to arrive at the final price you will have to pay per item. If you want to be able to walk away with your pieces, cash is the best method of payment, otherwise you will have to make a return journey to pick up the goods once your cheque has cleared, an enormous inconvenience if the saleroom is some distance from home. Terms and conditions of sale are usually laid out at the front of the catalogue, including a clause stating that you can return any object you have bought within a certain time limit if you can prove without doubt that it is a forgery.

Bidding techniques vary enormously, from the slightest nod of the head to the firm raising of the "paddle," but it is a complete myth that a slight gesture will result in you becoming the unwitting owner of a valuable and unwanted object. An auctioneer will always confirm that the final bid is definite, often by pointing to where the last bid came from or announcing that the bid is "on my left" or "at the back" before bringing down the hammer. Initially, it is best to make your bid absolutely clear by raising your card or "paddle." Remember too that the auctioneer is there to achieve the best prices possible for the sellers so set yourself a top limit before you make a single bid and try not to get carried away by making that extra bid which can so easily turn into two or three. Far better to lose a piece than to find yourself having to pay much more for it than you can afford.

If you are successful, you may be able to "clear" your item or items while the sale is still in progress, or you may have to wait until the final lot has been offered. Most auction houses offer at least seven days free storage if you are waiting for a cheque to clear. After that, you will find yourself paying storage charges on a per lot, per day basis. If you are buying furniture, find out if it should be collected from the saleroom or from a furniture store some distance away where the pieces are taken either later on sale day or the following day. When the piece or pieces are handed over, check them carefully in front of a member of staff to make sure they are in the same condition as they were when you viewed them, then take them home and enjoy them.

## Selling at Auction

If you have a piece you want to sell and you don't know its value, taking it to an auction house is the best policy. Not only will your item be valued free of charge, but it is in the saleroom's interest to get the best price for it at auction. The higher the price realised, the more commission they will earn. Where you decide to take your property depends to a large extent on what you are going to sell. The larger, metropolitan salerooms are not, as a rule, interested in general household effects, but you may be able to achieve a better price for a rare piece of antique porcelain at one of the top houses than a small, provincial auction room.

It is often a good idea initially to send photographs of your object to several houses asking for an indication of its value, but the estimates they give should always be confirmed by an expert who is able to examine the piece properly. It is always better to make a proper

appointment with the relevant expert rather than just turning up at the counter on the off-chance that he or she will be able to see you. If you are selling a substantial amount of property, or a collection which the experts think may be worth a good deal of money, they will make the journey to you to give a valuation. The service is free, although if you live a fair distance away, the saleroom may charge the experts' travelling expenses.

The expert will give you a potential auction value for your object and also recommend a price under which it cannot be sold, known as the protective reserve. The piece may then be sold within a week at a small auction house, but you are much more likely to have to wait a month for it to be included in a catalogue, or several months if it is to be included in one of perhaps only three specialist sales in a year.

Before you allow your property to be "taken in" for sale, ask exactly what charges you will be paying and don't be embarrassed to jot them down so that you can work out exactly what sort of money you are likely to come away with once you have paid seller's commission (usually 10%), insurance costs whilst the object is waiting to come up for sale (usually 1 to 1.5% of the hammer price, levied after the sale), a handling charge of £1–2 per lot and illustration costs. The last is always agreed prior to production of the catalogue. The higher value the object, the more cost effective it is to sell at auction, particularly if the saleroom implements a minimum commission charge which may be higher than 10% of the sale price of your item.

In return for entering into a contract with the saleroom, they are obliged to present a true and fair description of your property in a catalogue, along with an estimate of its value. They should also announce the auction in all the relevant local, national or trade publications. The top houses will also have immediate access to an international network of dealers, collectors and museums who will be alerted to any objects or collections of great interest.

Should your piece sell, how quickly you receive your money depends on how long it takes the saleroom to receive payment from the buyer, but expect to wait an average of one week to a month.

## Buying from and Selling to Antiques Shops

In common with any commercial enterprise, the world of antiques dealing attracts the good, the bad and the indifferent. Fortunately, the majority of dealers are highly reputable, knowledgeable individuals who work hard to maintain the good relationship they have with existing clients and are keen to attract new collectors.

There are many collectors who will only buy pieces through one or two dealers whom they trust and respect and who, in many cases, become valued friends. Once you have built up a good relationship with a friendly dealer, he or she will go to endless trouble to find the pieces they know you are looking for and buying in this way is usually a relaxed process involving none of the pressures bidding at auction can hold.

If you have never bought or sold from an antiques shop, contact the professional organisations to which the best dealers belong; they carry out a strict selection procedure before admitting members. These include the BADA (British Antiques Dealers' Association) and LAPADA (London and Provincial Antiques Dealers' Association) in Great Britain and NAADAAI (National Antique and Art Dealers' Association of America Incorporated) in the United States. Once you have the members list, you can select those who seem to hold the type of stock which interests you. Check their opening times before you make a visit since dealers are often out buying first thing in the morning or may spend part of the day attending auction views or sales.

Take your time looking and ask for advice, but remember that supplies of time and patience will not be endless. You may see them beginning to run out if you make several trips to the shop, spend a considerable time looking, handling the stock and asking questions, but always leave empty handed. Once you have reached a decision to buy, don't feel shy about trying to persuade the dealer to reduce the price by a small percentage. Most expect it and make allowances in the prices they ask. Make sure you get a written receipt stating exactly what the object is, its date, authenticity and any known history (called its provenance). If it is in pristine condition, ask the dealer to note this down too, so that you have some come back if you later find that areas have been restored, or even that the piece is not genuine.

Before selling to a dealer, you must have a good idea of what your property is worth. You won't have to worry about the deductions auction houses make in the way of commission, minimum charges and insurance: the price you agree will be the sum you receive, but an auction house can safeguard your object from selling below a certain price, whereas once the dealer has handed you the money and a receipt for your object, it belongs to him. Reputable dealers, however, are keen to offer a fair price. In fact, many complain that they invariably pay more for buying something privately than at auction. Some may offer to display your object in the shop and then take a 10 or 20% commission once it has sold. Most pay cash when buying and will ask you to sign a book which can be checked by the police at any time. They need some assurance that the piece is legally yours to sell. In these uncertain times, dealers must protect their credibility and minimize any risk of prosecution.

## Second-hand and Charity Shops

Time was when many of the objects being sold today as collectables formed part of the stock of second-hand shops. This is the environment in which to use your imagination and powers of intuition to predict what part of today's junk will become tomorrow's antiques. There is also the thrill of the chase as you walk through the door because there is still the chance you might find the odd thing of real value which has gone unnoticed by the staff, who may not have any specialized knowledge. The chances are, however, that the proprieter is pretty clued up; real bargains are few and far between these days. Much stock comes from house clearances and anything of great value is sold separately. Don't expect receipts or guarantees, or to be able to return something if it turns out to be a dud! If you buy something from a charity shop which turns out to be valuable and you decide to sell it on, it is up to you and your conscience whether or not you decide to split the profit with them.

## Antiques Fairs and Markets

The quality of antiques fairs and markets varies dramatically from a few stalls in a village or church hall once a month to vast open air events or prestigious annual gatherings in top hotels attended by dealers from all over the world. Many reputable and experienced individuals choose to operate at fairs and markets to avoid the cost and responsibility of shop premises. Naturally, some venues attract dishonest traders who are there to make a quick profit and disappear, so when you come to do business, always ask for a card which should list at least a name and telephone and/or fax number.

At some of the top events which last for several days you may find the first day is devoted to the trade but this is unusual. A good deal of trading goes on between dealers in the early hours as they unload their stock so it is a good idea to arrive early. Bear in mind, however, that no matter how strong your torch, clever restoration can only be seen in daylight. Expect to pay slightly less than you would in a shop, but ask for a written receipt.

If you go with property to sell, make sure it is securely wrapped, take your time walking around and only approach stallholders who sell the same sort of objects. Unwrapping and rewrapping is very time consuming so targeting the right dealers might save you a lot of work. Again, make sure you know the value of your property before you offer it for sale. At some of the smaller events, it can be worth paying for a pitch and selling your own goods. It can also be fun!

### Car Boot Sales

The car boot sale has become one of the most popular forms of weekend entertainment on both sides of the Atlantic. They range in size from several dozen stalls in a local school playground to several acres of land in the countryside. The larger, more rural ones tend not to operate during winter months, but local newsapers carry announcements of forthcoming sales usually one week in advance, although few include a contact telephone number. In larger towns and cities, many now take place in multi-storey car parks under cover. Head for one of these if it looks like rain. The boot sale is the environmentally friendly way of getting rid of your unwanted clutter, and what may be rubbish to you might give someone else enormous pleasure. If you are selling, arrive early, preferably by 6 am. Take a strong torch and be prepared to deal with a particularly persistent and voracious type of small time dealer who has a tendency to dive into the boot of your car before you have had a chance to unpack your goods. It may suit you to do a deal and sell him or her a large proportion of what you have, but if you are determined to sell to the public, you will have to stand your ground and tell them firmly to leave you alone to unpack. Be prepared to haggle or be haggled with whether you are buying or selling. This is often the place to find the collectables of the future, but bear in mind that the dealers get there early and know just what to look for, and that most people these days know the value of their goods. Always take cash with you, preferably in small denominations and avoid second-hand electrical goods. You risk being swooped on by trading standards officers for selling them and being electrocuted if you buy them.

### Societies and Swap Meets

This is not the environment in which to search for a bargain. You will be dealing with people who have an equivalent or greater knowledge than you. They may simply want to upgrade their collection by selling one or two less treasured pieces in order to buy one coveted item. This is probably the most low key and discreet way to buy and sell your pieces, so much so that in many cases societies frown upon any commercial transactions taking place at meetings and bar dealers from becoming members. That said, many members of the various collectors' societies do buy and sell amongst themselves, but you must know the value of what you are selling and buying and be able to recognise a fair price, a fair swap or a combination of the two. The primary purpose of these meetings is to promote knowledge, so don't wade in. Get to know the people first and let discretion and subtlety be your watchwords.

### Publications

Various antiques magazines, either weekly trade papers or monthly glossies, include buying and selling columns. One or two provide a free service, but most charge by the word or line and disclaim any liability for the property advertised. If you follow up these sorts of advertisements, be prepared to make a journey to inspect the goods and get a receipt when you hand over your money. To avoid a wasted trip, ask as many questions as you can over the telephone about age, condition, restoration and repair. If you are selling you must be prepared to let people into your home to look at what is on offer and to give a receipt.

Bear in mind that dealers, too, use these columns as a way of buying and selling. Also, if you buy something and then suspect that it might have been stolen goods, you should contact your local police station who will put you in touch with organizations which hold lists of stolen property along with illustrations of the items.

## Insurance

Items of lesser value are usually covered by your general contents insurance. Above a certain value, however, it becomes essential to have your property valued professionally for insurance purposes. Contact someone who is a licensed appraiser or a member of the Incorporate Society of Valuers and Auctioneers. Some auction houses have their own valuations departments and will send a representative to your home to carry out the valuation. Some charge a set fee for the service, others levy a percentage of the total value of the property and some auctioneers will return a percentage of the charge if they are allowed to sell the property within a year of the valuation taking place. It is really important that you clarify the charges before you allow the work to begin. A professional valuation can be most worthwhile since each object will then be properly identified, listed, dated, valued and recorded photographically. With lower value items, make your own list and photograph them so that you can prove you did own them if they are stolen. The insurance valuation will always take into the account the retail cost of replacement and will be at least 20 – 50% more than you would be able to sell the pieces for at auction. Insurance values on jewellery can often be double the estimated auction value.

## Display

Most collectors derive a great deal of enjoyment from displaying their pieces to best advantage, but before you decide what to invest in, it is as well to consider the amount of space you can devote to a collection. If you live in a studio flat, best avoid developing a passion for old lawnmowers or juke boxes. Similarly, a carefully chosen selection of thimbles will be lost on a small set of shelves mounted on the wall of a large room.

It's often a good idea to take a theme and build on it, using many of the things you already own as a starting point, and displaying pieces which complement them. If you are drawn to the 1920s and 1930s, you are unlikely to try to marry the bright, geometric ceramics of the period with 17th-century oak furniture, just as you would avoid displaying 18th-century porcelain in an interior otherwise filled with cheap and cheerful artefacts from the 1950s.

Safety and maintenance are major considerations. Collectors often dedicate one locked room to a collection, creating a retreat where they can quietly enjoy their subject, and, most importantly, keep pieces in the correct conditions away from the hurly burly of family life. Small children, large dogs and fragile precious possessions do not make good bedfellows, so you should display anything breakable well out of the way of small, sticky fingers and large wagging tails.

It is inevitable that pieces will deteriorate displayed in the wrong conditions, but you will find many of these aspects covered at the beginning of each chapter. If your home is a light, sunny place, open-plan and with large windows on all sides, then you will have to take great care. Paintings, furniture and textiles are vulnerable to the bleaching effects of strong light. Strong mesh curtains can do a lot to minimize the damaging effects, and a humidifier (or at least several bowls of water kept constantly topped up) is a wise investment when antique furniture and central heating come together.

Ivories, tortoiseshell, horn, treen and lacquer are all vulnerable to extremes of temperature, and are liable to crack if the atmosphere becomes too dry. Once lacquer and tortoiseshell lose their original sheen, they become almost impossible to restore, so tea caddies and the like should never be lit from above with strong bulbs which give off heat. It is now possible to install special cold lighting which comes close to natural daylight. Textiles, too, benefit from this treatment, although it is kindest to display tapestries, samplers, fans and costumes in dimly lit surroundings and for short periods only.

There are numerous companies which manufacture display units tailored to particular types of objects. Small, wall-mounted, glazed cabinets are ideal for Oriental snuff bottles, scent bottles, small enamel boxes and other objects of vertu. Original printer's trays, the printing blocks removed, provide dozens of little shelves and ledges on which to display miniatures and are advertised in the back of many specialist magazines. Watch and coin collectors often use specimen drawers to hold their collections, and plans chests, with deep, narrow drawers, are the ideal place to store textiles which are not on display, as well as prints, drawings and maps.

Furniture is often the supporting act, drawing out and enhancing other pieces. A cabinet lined with blue or black watered silk or velvet sets off silver perfectly, and silver gilt looks even richer against a dark red background. A pair of Georgian silver candlesticks placed on a sideboard or a collection of Staffordshire figures arranged on the various tiers of a 19th-century whatnot looks impressive and appropriate. Doll and teddy bear collectors, who like to arrange their girls and boys in a life-like way, often use miniature furniture such as chairs and chests of drawers, as well as prams, highchairs and even rocking-horses contemporary with their treasures, as a way of displaying them.

Collections have a habit of sprouting rapidly, often much to their creators' surprise. Display and storage can then pose a problem. One gentleman in the United States allowed his obsession with cigarette lighters to flourish to such a degree that, ultimately, he photographed every example he owned and packed them away for safekeeping in bank vaults. His display now consists of a neat row of photograph albums on a shelf. I hope few of you will be driven to such extremes.

# Styles & Periods

| | STYLE | BRITISH PERIOD | FRENCH PERIOD |
|---|---|---|---|
| 1560 | | | |
| 1570 | | Elizabethan (Elizabeth I, 1558–1603) | Renaissance (to 1610) |
| 1580 | | | |
| 1590 | Gothic (c.1558–1625) | | |
| 1600 | | | |
| 1610 | | Jacobean (James I, 1603–25) | |
| 1620 | | | Louis XIII (1610–43) |
| 1630 | | Carolean (Charles I, 1625–49) | |
| 1640 | | | |
| 1650 | | Cromwellian (Commonwealth, 1649–60) | |
| 1660 | Baroque (c.1620–1700) | Restoration (Charles II, 1660–85) | |
| 1670 | | | Louis XIV (1643–1715) |
| 1680 | | Restoration (James II, 1685–88) | |
| 1690 | | William & Mary (1688–94) | |
| 1700 | | William III (1694–1702) | |
| 1710 | | Queen Anne (1702–14) | |
| 1720 | | Early Georgian (George I, 1714–27) | Régence (1715–23) |
| 1730 | Rococo (c.1695–1760) | | |
| 1740 | | Mid-Georgian (George II, 1727–60) | |
| 1750 | | | Louis XV (1723–74) |
| 1760 | | | |
| 1770 | | | |
| 1780 | Neo-classical (c.1755–1805) | Late Georgian (George III, 1760–1811) | Louis XVI (1774–93) |
| 1790 | | | |
| 1800 | | | Directoire (1793–99) |
| 1810 | Empire (c.1799–1815) | | Empire (1799–1815) |
| 1820 | Regency (c.1812–30) | Regency (Prince Regent, 1811–20; George IV, 1820–30) | Restauration (1815–30) |
| 1830 | | William IV (1830–37) | Louis Philippe (1830–48) |
| 1840 | | | |
| 1850 | Revival (c.1830–80) | | 2nd Empire (1848–70) |
| 1860 | | Victorian (Victoria, 1837–1901) | |
| 1870 | | | |
| 1880 | | | |
| 1890 | Arts & Crafts (c.1880–1900) | | |
| 1900 | | | 3rd Republic (1871–1940) |
| 1910 | Art Nouveau (c.1890–1914) | Edwardian (Edward VII, 1901–10) | |
| 1920 | | George V (1910–36) | |
| 1930 | Art Deco (c.1920–40) | Edward VIII (1936) | |
| 1940 | | George VI (1936–52) | |

| GERMAN PERIOD | UNITED STATES PERIOD | KEY EVENTS | |
|---|---|---|---|
| | | | 1560 |
| | | 1564: Birth of William Shakespeare | 1570 |
| | | | 1580 |
| | Pre-Colonial (to 1625) | 1588: Defeat of the Spanish Armada | 1590 |
| Renaissance (to 1650) | | 1600: British East India Company established | 1600 |
| | | | 1610 |
| | | | 1620 |
| | | 1626: Founding of New Amsterdam (becomes New York in 1664) | 1630 |
| | | | 1640 |
| | | 1649–60: English Civil War | 1650 |
| | Early Colonial (1625–1700) | | 1660 |
| Renaissance/Baroque (1650–1700) | | | 1670 |
| | | 1685: Revocation of the Edict of Nantes results in mass emigration of Huguenots from France | 1680 |
| | | 1687: Isaac Newton's *Principia Mathematica* published | 1690 |
| | | | 1700 |
| Baroque (1700–30) | William & Mary style (1700–20) | | 1710 |
| | | 1715 and 1745: Jacobite rebellions | 1720 |
| | Queen Anne style (1720–55) | 1723: George of Hanover becomes George I of England | 1730 |
| Rococo (1730–60) | | | 1740 |
| | | | 1750 |
| | Chippendale style (1755–90) | 1755: Samuel Johnson completes *A Dictionary of the English Language* | 1760 |
| | | | 1770 |
| Neo-classicism (1760–1800) | | 1776: American Declaration of Independence | 1780 |
| | | 1789: French Revolution | 1790 |
| | Early Federal (1790–1810) | 1793–1815: Napoleonic Wars | |
| | | | 1800 |
| Empire (1800–15) | | | 1810 |
| | American Empire (1810–20) | 1815: George Stephenson invents the steam locomotive | 1820 |
| | Later Federal (1820–30s) | | |
| Biedermeier (1815–48) | | | 1830 |
| | | 1839: Invention of the first photographic plate | 1840 |
| | | 1851: The Great Exhibition, London | 1850 |
| Revivale (1830–80) | Victorian (1837–1901) | 1861–5: American Civil War | 1860 |
| | | | 1870 |
| | | 1876: The telephone was invented by Alexander Graham Bell | 1880 |
| | | | 1890 |
| Jugendstil (1880–1920) | | 1889: Building of the Eiffel Tower | 1900 |
| | Art Nouveau (c.1890–1914) | | 1910 |
| | | 1914–18: World War I | |
| | | 1917: Russian Revolution | 1920 |
| Bauhaus (1920–33) | Art Deco (c.1920–40) | 1927: Charles Lindbergh makes the first solo, nonstop transatlantic flight | 1930 |
| | | 1939–45: World War II | |
| | | | 1940 |

15

# Furniture

Throughout Europe during the Middle Ages, furniture for the majority of people consisted of a few basic, functional items. A cottage might contain a stool or two, a simple table and a wooden box in which to store a few possessions. It was not collected in any serious way until the mid-19th century and it wasn't until the early years of the 20th century that furniture began to be appreciated as a work of art in its own right rather than being catalogued only as part of the chattels when the contents of a house came up for sale.

In the early 18th century for the first time furniture began to be designed with purely decorative aspects tacked on to their practical function, and new types of furniture began to be made as customs and habits changed. Bureaux came into being as more people learnt to write, and bureau bookcases began to appear as mass printing made books cheaper and more readily available.

Formal dining rooms were established in Europe and the United States by the end of the 18th century. The sideboard was invented so that food could be served from its surface and napery and cutlery stored beneath. Dumb waiters, wine coolers and cheese coasters were created to take care of other aspects of dining. The rapidly expanding and prosperous middle class wanted to spend their increased leisure time in luxury and comfort. As a result more upholstered furniture began to be made, and glass became cheaper, enabling decorative mirrors to be produced in great quantity to reflect light. Boudoir furniture was constructed for the lady of the house and solid library pieces for the master.

These, along with the huge variety of objects made for 19th-century homes, form the bulk of the furniture collected today. The choice is vast, but more than in any other area of antiques, furniture has been changed or "improved," whether for practical or commercial reasons. Pieces have been cut down or added to, tops and bottoms separated or married up and rooms stripped of panelling to make "antique" pieces, so collectors need to be on their guard.

Some altered pieces, though, have a value in their own right, but your first task is to learn when various types of furniture first appeared (there is no such thing as a late 17th-century sideboard, for instance), and the main areas open to alteration. A knowledge of the woods used at different times and in different countries will also help. The following pages will give you some examples, but your most invaluable tool will be your own eyes. By talking to reputable dealers and viewing as many sales as you can, you will develop an instinct for a piece which is not as it once was.

*Left:* German birchwood veneer Biedermeier chest, c.1820; English mahoghany Chippendale-style chair, c.1890.

# Where to begin

Buying a piece of antique furniture is a big purchase so when deciding on your first piece take your time. Learn to be systematic and don't be afraid of handling objects, looking inside and underneath them and pulling out drawers to examine them more carefully.

## Woods

Learning to differentiate between a wide range of woods takes time. There is no magic shortcut, but, obviously, the more you look at and handle a good selection of antique furniture, the shorter your apprenticeship will be. Bear in mind that wood can be transformed in colour by insensitive restoration or by applying a dark varnish. You should make a point of inspecting the areas where the wood remains unfinished and in its natural state, remembering that cheaper woods often make up the invisible areas of a piece. Befriend a reputable local dealer and the relevant experts at an auction house. They will be happy to help you acquire the knowledge you need to become a discerning buyer.

**AMBOYNA** Tropical tightly burred wood similar to burr walnut but with an iridescent sheen. Used in Europe and the United States, mostly as a veneer during the first 40 years of the 19th century.

**ASH** Similar appearance to elm but a redder colour. Used mainly for provincial chair-making in Europe.

**BEECH** Pale, close-grained timber with great strength which is nevertheless susceptible to woodworm. Used throughout history in Europe for the framework of chair seats and for less expensive, provincial furniture.

**CHERRY** Hard, dense timber of orangey-red colour used largely for French provincial pieces and American late 18th-century furniture. Available only in narrow blocks so table tops are invariably multi-planked.

**CHESTNUT** A temperate timber which takes a good polish, similar in appearance to oak but with a softer grain. Mainly used in French and English provincial furniture. Available in wide blocks.

**EBONY** An intensely black tropical hardwood which is prone to splitting when used as a veneer. Used for decorative banding by European and American furniture makers, although some 17th-century Continental pieces were totally veneered in ebony.

**ELM** Light brown timber from the temperate regions similar in look to oak but without the medullary rays (iridescent flecks) and with a more evident grain due to its faster growth. Used for Windsor chair seats in England, provincial chests of drawers, and widely used for coffins because of its large plank size.

**KINGWOOD** West Indian wood with fine, purple streaks fading quickly to tones of greyish brown on exposure to air and light. Used predominantly as a cross banding due to the availability of only very small blocks.

**LIME** Soft, finely textured, close-grained wood which is ivory white when first cut but darkens with age. It was one of the most highly prized woods for carving, since it does not split when chiselled, and was used extensively for furniture, picture frames and small sculpture. Much German and Austrian carved wooden sculpture is fashioned from lime.

**MAHOGANY** Many varieties of tropical hardwoods are grouped under the heading of mahogany. A hard, dense, reddish colour, it is found in straight planks through to finely-figured veneers. It was the most popularly used wood from the early 18th century due to its strength and its ease of importation from the West Indies and other tropical areas. It is still widely used today although by the mid-19th century, all the best trees had been felled. Modern mahogany is coarse and open-grained and bears little resemblance to its 18th-century counterpart.

**OAK** Hard, strong timber available in good plank widths and used throughout history in both Europe and America. Usually identifiable by the medullary rays which can be accentuated by the way it is cut. It is resistant to woodworm due to the tannic acids it contains which harden it. An oak beam from an old house, covered in woodworm on the surface, is invariably sound in the centre.

**PINE** and **DEAL** A widely available group of timbers used in Britain and the United States. Soft and pale, they darken with age and give off a resinous aroma when newly cut. Used for the invisible parts of furniture and where saving money was important. Provincial English and American furniture was made in solid pine but little has survived with its original painted or waxed finish.

**ROSEWOOD** Highly figured reddish timber with almost black streaks imported from Brazil, where the choicest specimens were available, and the Far East for plainer examples. When first cut, it is dark and purplish. The decorative figuring only becomes apparent after exposure to air, thus making rosewood pieces some of the hardest to repolish since the purplish colour comes through again if the surface is removed. Used mainly during the late 18th and early 19th centuries in Europe.

**SATINWOOD** Two main varieties of this yellow, iridescent timber come from the East and the West Indies. The East Indies' variety, paler and with more subtle figuring, was used at the end of the 18th century for English Sheraton-style furniture. The more vibrant West Indies' variety was used in Europe and the United States at the end of the 19th century.

**VIRGINIAN WALNUT** A hard, dense American timber similar in colour to the best mahoganies. Used in solid and veneered form for English and American furniture from the early 18th century.

**WALNUT** The most predominantly used cabinet maker's timber until the middle of the 18th century when mahogany began to be imported and it went out of fashion. It enjoyed a revival from the middle of the 19th century as a veneer in both Europe and America. It came in many forms, from plain, straight planks used in the solid for table tops and chair frames, to highly figured burrs. The best burr walnut today is used for the dashboards of Rolls Royce cars.

**YEW** Reddish brown hard wood used in solid or veneered form for much English provincial furniture, with the choicest burr veneers reserved for making tea caddies and other small items.

## Construction

Medieval chests with drop lids made before the late 15th century consisted of planks of wood simply nailed together, with iron hinges and bands supplied by the blacksmith. The development of the mortise and tenon joint in the 16th century prevented the wood from splitting around the nails. To create a strong frame which supported panels of wood, the vertical sections, known as stiles, had rectangular holes cut into them to make mortises. The tenons, similarly shaped pieces of wood jutting out from the horizontal rails, fitted into them and were held together by pegs or dowels to create a strong frame which supported panels of wood. Work of this kind was carried out by a joiner.

As furniture became more sophisticated, the cabinet maker carried out any work beyond the capabilities of the joiner. A strong, smooth carcass was constructed for a piece of case furniture, usually in pine or oak, with dovetail joints used to hold together the sides, the top, the base and the open boxes which formed the drawers. Dovetails comprise two interlocking fan-shaped tenons which make a right angled joint. The carcass was then veneered, usually by a different craftsman, but the areas which were to remain unseen were not finely finished. You will find panelled construction on the backs of late 18th-century furniture, but they will not be polished. Bow fronted chests were constructed using small pieces of timber, "block built" in the same way as laying bricks

and then smoothed to the required shape. This technique, developed in the later 18th century, was less wasteful than cutting a curve from the solid and made for much finer and more delicate lines.

The earliest drawers were usually made with two dovetails to a side, pinned for greater strength. The numbers increased and the dovetails became finer as the 18th century progressed. Check that each drawer of a piece has the same number of dovetails and has not had replacement pieces added as this affects value. Early drawers had channels cut in their sides which ran on runners set into the carcass. After c.1702, runners went underneath the drawers and ran on bearers along the inside of the carcass. Runners are prone to wear but replacements are acceptable. Seventeenth-century drawer linings are often 2cm (¾in) thick but became finer, thinning down to 0.5cm (¼in) thick by the 18th century. 17th-century drawer fronts have either simple, raised decoration or mouldings fixed to them, but became flat by the 18th century, finished off with quarter-round moulding or cock beading (a slip of rounded timber).

Nails and screws should be treated with scepticism. Do not use them alone to judge the age of a piece because they often fell out and needed replacing. You may find old nails, which were hand-cut until c.1790, on fakes and alterations, because they can be recovered from house timbers during the process of demolition and sold on. The earliest screws were made c.1675 with hand-filed threads. The spiral is very shallow and they have almost no taper or point. The slots in the top are nearly always slightly off-centre. If you are looking at a piece which was supposedly made prior to this date which contains screws, either the piece is not genuine or the screws have been added during repair or restoration.

As a general guide, old nails are more trustworthy than old screws because they fell out less easily. Screws, on the other hand, were often used to hold together furniture that was meant to be taken apart for transportation, and, inevitably, they got lost and were replaced with more modern ones as time went on.

The metal mounts on a piece of furniture can be useful guides to dating. These include hinges, handles, locks and escutcheons, but handles, particularly, are often replaced. It was one way to update something and make it more fashionable. Replacement handles are acceptable providing they are in keeping with the piece. Feet are another guide to dates but because they were more susceptible to wear than any other area of a piece, they are also often replaced. The bun feet found on late 17th- or early 18th-century furniture are almost always replacements and considered quite acceptable providing they are not passed off as original.

## Decoration

**CARVING** A natural development from whittling, paring and shaping wood with sharp tools which became progressively more sophisticated as time went on. Close-grained woods lend themselves to carving better than open-grained ones, such as oak, which does not take detail well. Original carving, on a solid piece of wood, stands proud of it because a generous amount of timber was allowed before work began. Carving added later to "improve" a piece has to eat into the existing timber of, for instance, a cabriole leg. Looking at good, original examples will help you to spot the difference. Later carving reduces the value of a piece considerably.

**VENEERS** Applying thin sheets of fine wood to a carcass of cheaper, coarser wood is an ideal way of using more expensive timber sparingly. Certain woods such as satinwood, kingwood and coromandel were used only for veneers either because the timber was scarce and expensive, or because the size of the trunks produced planks too small to be used in any other way. Walnut and mahogany were used both for veneers and for making solid pieces. 17th- and 18th-century hand-cut veneers are often up to 0.3cm (⅛in) thick. Look at them closely on areas such as the edges of cupboard doors to see how they have been applied. Cutting along the length of the log produced "straight cut" veneers, across the grain "cross cut" veneers, and slices cut transversely from branches produced circular patterned "oyster" veneers.

Successive slices opened out so that one is the mirror image of the other, and four successive slices at the top and bottom of a panel are known as "quarter" veneers. Cutting through the irregular growths from trunks or roots of trees such as walnut, ash, elm and yew produced highly decorative "burr" veneers. Modern machine-cut veneers are almost paper thin. Small sections or strips of veneer known as banding were used around the edges of drawer fronts and surfaces to complement the principal veneer. Cross banding was laid in short sections at right angles to the main veneer; straight banding was applied in one long strip along, for instance, a drawer front; and feather or herringbone banding consists of two narrow strips of diagonally banded veneers placed together to give a featherlike appearance.

Marquetry is a type of ornamental veneer made up of interlocking pieces of wood forming a pattern. The different contrasting colours of the veneers could create stunning effects of perspective and illusion. When the pattern formed is geometric, it is referred to as parquetry. This type of decoration is distinct from inlay, where small pieces of ivory, mother-of-pearl, precious metals or wood are fitted into indentations made by chiselling out the solid piece of furniture, to create patterns or pictures. Stringing involved laying narrow strips of inlay of contrasting colour into the surface of a piece to create a decorative effect.

**GILDING** Even during ancient times, wood was decorated with gold leaf, which involved rolling and hammering the precious metal until it was wafer thin. Once several layers of gesso (a composition material of whiting, linseed oil and size) had been applied to the surface of the piece, it was treated with a "mordant" to help the gold leaf adhere. On water-gilded pieces, the mordant was a mixture of red clay or "bole" with egg white and hot water. Water was then used to moisten the surface before the gold leaf was applied, often in two layers which could then be burnished. The mordant for the cheaper oil-gilding was linseed oil cooked until it solidified, mixed with ground raw sienna. The gold leaf was applied to this much stickier surface as a single layer.

**LACQUERING** and **JAPANNING** True lacquer, painstakingly applied to furniture and smaller objects in as many as 200 layers in China and Japan, is the refined sap of the *Rhus vernicifera* tree. Europeans, anxious to copy the technique as early as the late 17th century, were unable to discover this essential ingredient and began to use shellac (a resin-like substance produced by certain insects) as an imitation. As good quality Japanese lacquer was imported to Europe at this time the process began to be referred to in England as "Japanning" and this term remained. In England, japanned sheet-iron made into useful and decorative objects is known as Pontypool ware (the first factory was at Pontypool in Wales). Excellent imitations of Oriental lacquer were produced in the Low Countries, and in France the term *Vernis Martin* is used to describe the items varnished with a substance invented c.1730.

**PAINTING** Painted and stencilled furniture is fashionable today, but the modern equivalent is reviving a style in favour as long ago as the 14th and 15th century when oak furniture was first painted. At this time, the favoured medium was tempera (powdered pigment mixed with size, varnish or egg white) applied over gesso, and some of the leading Italian artists of the Renaissance carried out commissions on furniture. During the 18th century, satinwood and beech-veneered furniture was painted with borders and medallions in the Neo-classical style, and then varnished. During the 19th century, wood was painted to simulate marble, and the leading lights of the Arts and Crafts Movement decorated cabinets and cupboards. The delicacy of 18th-century painted furniture was reproduced during the early 20th century in England and these pieces, so long as they are well done, have a value in their own right.

## Fakes and Alterations

Antique furniture is either faked or altered as a way of "improving" it more than any other area covered in this book. Perfectly honest reproductions, made without any intention to deceive, have their own place in the market providing they are never aged and passed off as original.

A marriage is the term used to describe pieces which consist of two or more parts (such as bureau bookcases, dressers or chests on chests) where, for instance, the base has become separated from the top for which it was made and subsequently "married" to a different top, either from the same or a different period. Style, proportion, grain and colour should all be examined carefully. So-called "improvements" were done to make a piece more fashionable. These include removing legs or feet and replacing them with a different style to give the piece an earlier appearance and adding cross bandings and inlays to pieces that would never have been decorated in this way originally. Large unwieldy pieces are also reduced in size to make them sit more comfortably in today's smaller homes. Those reduced in depth will have fresh surfaces at the back, where they have been cut and re-made, and re-joined drawer backs. Chests reduced in width will have patched-up areas where the original lock plates have been filled in, and extra holes where the handles have also been moved.

Real forgeries are usually made from old wood which once served a different purpose. Panelling has been used to make chests, old oak floor-boards have become table tops and mahogany shop counters have provided many a wide and versatile piece of timber from which to construct furniture. Nail holes in these cases are often in the wrong place and the newly cut edges have a look which does not match the surface, despite clever staining. Forgers will often use the carcass of a badly damaged but saleable type of piece and apply to it the veneer of another less commercial item. The result will be a piece composed entirely of old timber but a complete fake. Expensive early-18th century walnut-veneered furniture is particularly prone to this type of faking. The old veneer may show signs of handle marks which have been cut out and the carcass may provide clues. A badly split inside door panel with a pristine outer surface, for instance, is cause for suspicion.

The best method for spotting fakes and alterations is to develop an eye for proportion and patina, and you will soon learn to spot an unbalanced piece. Patina is the effect that the passing of time has on the surface of a piece of timber as light, air and dust harden the wood and it changes colour. Even an expert forger finds it impossible to reproduce the beauty and warmth of good patination exactly, and once you have looked at some good, original pieces, you will be able to spot clever staining, as well as distressing and drilled "worm holes."

## Restoration and Repair

Bad polishing can result in a piece of furniture being seriously devalued. It can take over 200 years for a piece to develop a good patina but only a few minutes to strip away its history. Only undertake restoration after seeking advice from a reputable dealer or specialist. Never attempt repairs yourself, unless replacing knocked-off slips of veneer which should be done quickly since a fragment of original cross banding is easily lost and cannot be replaced. A heavily restored piece will be worth considerably less than one in good original condition and the price paid should reflect any significant alterations. Skilful repolishing is acceptable, as are minor repairs to bandings and mouldings, reupholstery and the replacement of stylistically incorrect handles with ones in keeping with the period. The tightening of joints, drawer linings and backs can be part of a sensible programme of conservation.

## Care and Maintenance

Never drag a piece across a floor as this can cause serious damage. Spray polishes contain solvents which can strip the patina, although great advances in cleaning agents have resulted in one or two suitable types being developed. Read the labels carefully and avoid over-polishing. There is no need to use a wax polish more than twice a year, followed by buffing with a soft cloth. The rest of the time, simply wipe away dust. Central heating can wreak havoc on expensive antique furniture, causing splitting and cracks. You need a humidifier to maintain the correct level of moisture in the wood. Check for woodworm every now and then. A proprietary insecticide is sufficient to deal with any slight problem.

# Chests of Drawers

A coffer with a lift-up top was a perfectly satisfactory box in which to store a few meagre possessions, but a highly impractical method of organizing more generous personal effects. Creating small parcels of storage – drawers – within the box and accessible from the front, was one of the most brilliant design solutions in the history of furniture. First made in the mid-17th century, by the 18th century chests of drawers were a common feature in the homes of the well-to-do. In the 17th century, they were mostly in walnut or oak, with small round "bun" feet; by the 18th century, mahogany was the favoured wood and feet were of bracket form. By this time construction was becoming increasingly finer. Variations evolved as the 18th century progressed, including chests-on-chests (tallboys), cabinets-on-chests, linen presses and side cabinets, and a host of elegant forms, such as the bow-front commode, which was especially popular in the United States. During the 19th century the choice of woods increased; satinwood became popular in England, blond woods, such as ash and maple were popular in Germany and France; and walnut veneers were in favour throughout southern Europe.

### GEORGE III MAHOGANY CHEST OF DRAWERS
*c.1780; 91cm (36in) high, 97cm (38in) wide;*
**£1,500–2,000**

This is a well-constructed, late Georgian chest of drawers. The mahogany is nicely coloured and, starting with the shallowest at the top, the graduation in the size of the drawers is well-proportioned, giving the piece a balanced look overall. Smaller chests such as this are more desirable than larger, more unwieldy pieces.

These aren't the original handles but they are correct for the period, if a little too smart. If you look inside the drawers, you can see that the handles were carefully replaced without leaving any disfiguring marks around the hole. You can also see the paler area around the back of the handle where the originals sat in place.

This bottom-drawer hand-made lock has the rectangular pin set off centre, a feature which indicates English construction. There are no signs that the lock has been moved – as it might have been, for example, in the process of changing the size of the drawers – and the back of the drawer looks generally undisturbed.

This is an attractive set of hand-made dovetails with the original scribe line (drawn by the cabinet maker as a guide) intact, indicating that the drawer has not been altered in size at any point in its history.

These ogee bracket feet are typical of the period and indicate that the piece may well have been made in the north of England.

# Other Chests

**▲ WALNUT CHEST OF DRAWERS**
*c.1665; 104cm (41in) wide, 107cm (42in) high;* **£1,500–2,500**
This is typical of the type of chests of drawers being made in England during the latter half of the 17th century, after the restoration of the monarchy and the repressed Commonwealth period. New designs from Holland travelled to England, encouraged by Charles II who had spent his exile on the Continent, and this architectural look became prevalent. Many examples exist in oak, but solid walnut was also available, if more expensive. These chests were often made by the same craftsmen who constructed the panelling for the great houses.

**▲ WALNUT CHEST OF DRAWERS**
*c.1730; 101.6cm (40in) wide, 104cm (41in) high;* **£1,500–2,000**
This is an example of the type of furniture which dealers and auction house experts label "honest," as it is in original condition. The genuine colour and patination of the wood and the wear to the surface show that the original veneers are still intact. It is much better to buy a simpler chest with original colour than a more elaborate example which has suffered at the hands of a zealous restorer. This is not a premium piece. The veneers are well-figured but the extra decoration is confined to simple cross bandings. A top cabinet maker would have combined the cross banding with double herringbone bandings.

**▲ OYSTER-VENEERED WALNUT CHEST**
*chest 1680s, stand 1920s; 157.5cm (62in) high, 99cm (39in) wide;*
**£3,000–4,000**
The wonderful oyster veneers found on the front and the top of this chest do not match the colour of those on the drawer of the stand, indicating that the chest started life without an accompanying stand. Fortunately, the stand can simply be scrapped and the bun feet on the very smart chest replaced without depreciating its value.

**▲ AMERICAN CHIPPENDALE-STYLE MAHOGANY SERPENTINE-FRONT CHEST OF DRAWERS**
*c.1775; 104cm (41in) high;* **£5,000–7,500**
This was the final and most elegant stage in the development of the chest of drawers before function replaced aesthetics in the early 19th century and forms became heavier. The serpentine shape was difficult to construct; these later pieces benefited from improved techniques and are less clumsy than earlier 18th-century examples.

**▲ MAHOGANY BOW-FRONTED CHEST OF DRAWERS**
*1780; 122cm (48in) wide, 96.5cm (38in) high;* **£800–1,200**
Occasionally, the top drawer of these large chests was fitted with a dressing table mirror attached to an easel, and with lidded powder compartments, a comb rack and ring rack. In this form, it served more than one function in a spare or eldest son's bedroom, whereas in the master bedroom washstands, dressing tables and chests of drawers were separate pieces of furniture. The bow front came into fashion in the United States in the 1770s and remained popular there and in Europe into the 19th century. Were this piece smaller, or in an exotic timber such as satinwood, its value would be double.

**▲ FRENCH MAHOGANY COMMODE**
*c.1820; 130cm (51in) wide, 93cm (37in) high;* **£4,000–6,000**
This French mahogany commode is fitted with three fine long drawers and flanked by free-standing columns. Its Belgian granite top is typical of French furniture of the period, as are the pillar-like mouldings at the sides. These pieces were made throughout Europe during the early 19th century, often in pale woods.

**◄ MAHOGANY CHEST-ON-CHEST**
*c.1770; 193cm (76in) high;* **£3,000**
The chest-on-chest developed during the early part of the 18th century as a progression from the chest-on-stand, giving more storage space but less elegance. 1720s examples exist but are rare and fetch in the region of £20,000. A plain late 18th-century example can be bought for around £1,000. This one has a relatively high value because of its several extra design features, including the blind fret frieze (the carved section above the top drawer of the upper chest) and the quarter columns at the corners of the upper section.

**COLLECTORS' NOTES**
• Replacement handles do not affect the value providing they are in keeping with the piece and there are no unsightly reminders of previous handles.
• If the entire frame of a chest creaks and moves, don't buy it unless it was originally a very good quality example, because the cost of repair almost always exceeds the value.
• Check that all the drawers run smoothly.
• In the 17th and 18th century backs were often left unfinished as they were not intended to be seen. This is not a sign of poor-quality work.
• Get into the habit of examining furniture methodically: the wood, the feet, the handles, and so on, and don't be afraid to take drawers out for close inspection.

**COLLECTING TIP**
Mid- to late 19th-century, and early 20th-century chests are frequently well-constructed and will give years of use. You can buy one for around £200 – less than some modern ones.

# Chairs

We take the various chairs we have in our homes completely for granted, yet 500 years ago, only the nobility and the clergy enjoyed the privilege of sitting down on a chair to eat or hold conversations. The rest of the population sat on boxes, or even the section of a log. By the 16th century the stool was commonplace, and by the 17th century it had acquired a panel back and, in some instances, open arms.

Throughout Europe wealth increased and spread during the 18th century, creating a demand for more comfortable furniture on which to spend the longer hours of leisure. Reflecting this, fully upholstered seats and shaped backs began to appear and, as more people could afford more chairs, they started to be made in sets. In the early part of the 18th century, many were constructed in walnut and have not survived the ravages of woodworm, but the great quantity of mahogany chairs that were made from 1740 onwards have often survived in good condition and are still widely available.

By the 19th century, the chair was catering for every specialist need. Invalid chairs were an innovation, as were chairs designed especially for writing at a desk. Reading chairs had book rests attached for quiet hours in the study (these have only rarely survived in their original condition) and low nursing chairs catered to the needs of those nursing small babies. In the United States rocking chairs became very popular.

**► SATINWOOD ARMCHAIR**
*c.1890; 97cm (38in) high;*
**£400–600**
Unlike the chair below, this elegant and decorative armchair, a copy of a painted Hepplewhite made as one of a set of dining chairs, has a high value as a single chair because it can stand alone. It would not look at all out of place against a wall in a bedroom, say, or a drawing room.

**◄ REGENCY MAHOGANY DINING CHAIR**
*c.1820; 84cm (33in) high;*
**£40–50**
This was so obviously made as one of a set of dining chairs that it is worth very little as a single chair because it would not easily fulfil any other role, despite being a good-looking, solid chair with turned legs and a drop-in seat. A set of six, including two armchairs, would be worth upwards of £2,500.

**◄ MAHOGANY ARMCHAIR**
*c.1760; 102cm (40in) high;* **£700–1,000**
This is a good example of a classic Chippendale-inspired design with good proportions made from dense, heavy timber. It is quite plain and severe but of such good quality and in such good condition that a set would command a premium. Thomas Chippendale was the most influential English cabinet maker of the 18th century. His designs were well-documented and consequently spawned a host of imitations.

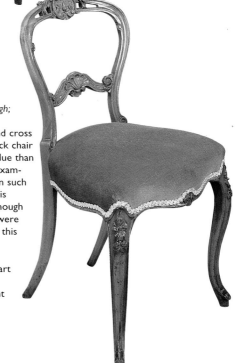

**► WALNUT BALLOON-BACK CHAIR**
*c.1850; 89cm (35in) high;*
**£50–60**
The carved top rail and cross rail on this balloon-back chair give it a little more value than the completely plain examples that were made in such numbers that a single is almost worthless. Although sturdy balloon-backs were made as dining chairs, this one – with its slender cabriole legs – would originally have been part of a drawing room or salon suite. If you want to use this type of design as a dining chair, beware of its weak construction.

## HEPPLEWHITE-STYLE DINING CHAIR
*c.1880; 94cm (37in) high;* **£300–400**
Made in England during the late 19th century as a direct copy of an 18th-century Hepplewhite chair, this is a good example of a revival piece made to a very high standard. It is both well-constructed and decorative. What gives a chair its strength are the uprights running from the top rail to the feet, and this is the first area to check. They should be constructed from one piece of timber. If you see any signs of a break, don't buy the chair. Look also for any signs that the front legs have broken off from the seat rail at some time and been mended. Be prepared to pay a great deal more for a set of chairs than the price of a single multiplied by six or eight. So many sets have been broken up over the years that any good set carries a premium. A set of eight can be worth £3,000–4,000.

## BLOCKS
The function of the blocks is to hold together the seat rails and the leg joints and prevent the chair from wobbling. The older style blocks have often been replaced by screw-in ones, but don't be put off if you discover this when inspecting the chair. It is nice to see the older blocks, but as they are not visible and don't alter the construction, they have no bearing on value.

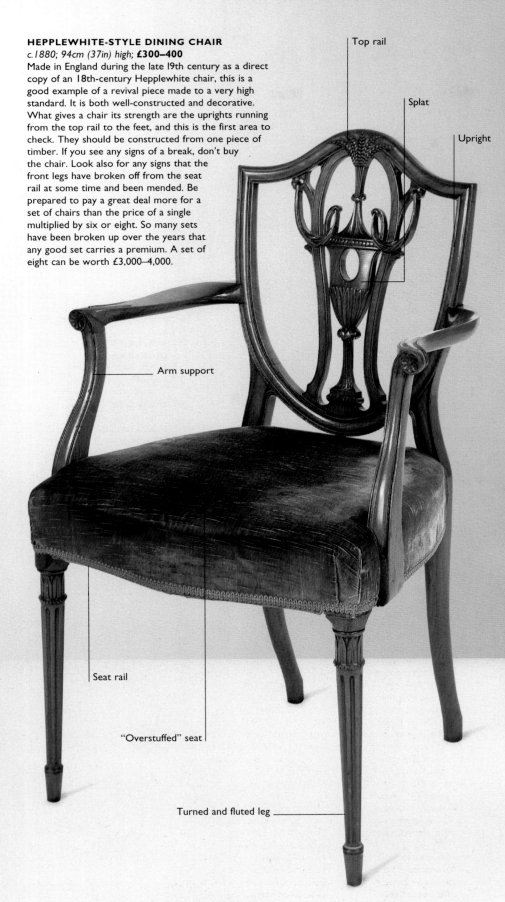

Top rail

Splat

Upright

Arm support

Seat rail

"Overstuffed" seat

Turned and fluted leg

The early 18th-century method of using glued blocks. These are sometimes secured with hand-made nails.

A later 18th-century diagonal cross brace, dropped in from the top and glued before the upholstery was applied.

The 19th-century form of corner blocks screwed to the seat rails and the method used to this day. If the screws are machine made, the piece was constructed towards the end of the 19th century.

# Other Chairs

### ◄ CHARLES II OAK CHAIR
*c.1670; 127cm (50in) high;*
**£300–400**
Early oak chairs are sought after for the wonderful dark patination that the timber acquires over the centuries, but they should be very carefully examined. Many have been thoroughly restored, and in order to be worth anything, they must be in absolutely original condition. The most stylish varieties of these chairs were made in walnut. This is an example of one that would have been made for a rich farmer rather than an aristocrat. Originally made in sets to sit around an oak refectory table, they are now only found singly or in pairs. A pair can be worth £1,500.

### ◄ LOUIS XVI GILT FAUTEUIL
*c.1780; 97cm (38in) high;*
**£800–1,200**
This is a classic example of chair design from the reign of Louis XVI (1754–93), who was content to leave the patronage of the arts (which included commissioning fine furniture) to his wife, Marie Antoinette. It incorporates the typical neo-classical features of an oval back and turned, tapered legs. The chair can be fairly accurately dated because it bears the stamp "I B Sene" showing that it was made by one of the largest families of chair makers in Paris at the time. Although it is interesting to find the name, the value of the chair depends on the quality and complexity of design.

### ◄ PAPIER-MÂCHÉ SALON CHAIR
*c.1850; 89cm (35in) high;* **£200–300**
Papier-mâché objects were first made in the Far East and introduced to France in the early 18th century. They reached England by 1760, but it was at the Great Exhibition of 1851 that they really caught the imagination of the British public, who clamoured to buy these decorative wares. When it came to making furniture, the papier-mâché was applied over a wooden frame. The critical factor in valuing pieces is the condition of the painting and gilding, which are vulnerable to wear. They are also notoriously weak and cannot be used for more than decoration in a modern home.

### ◄ MAHOGANY LADDER-BACK ARMCHAIR
*c.1770; 102cm (40in) high;*
**£500–700**
Sometimes referred to as a slat-back, this design is based on a more ornate chair popular on the Continent in the second half of the 17th century. The English took it up, probably as a result of ideas imported by Dutch craftsmen. In the United States, ladder-backs dating from the late 17th century, were again inspired by Dutch settlers. This chair, with a dished saddle leather seat, is one of a set of eight worth £4,000. Simpler examples with plainer backs had the same solid wood, saddle-cut seat as the Windsor chair.

### ► MAHOGANY SHERATON-INSPIRED ARMCHAIR
*c.1780; 97cm (38in) high;* **£250–350**
The simple, uninspired proportions of this armchair, with its total absence of carving, suggest that it might have been made by an estate carpenter who would have received an order to produce a large set of chairs, possibly at short notice, for a particular purpose. It is a good, functional chair and quite indestructible. Made from dense, solid mahogany, it is one of a set of 18 which sold recently at auction for £7,500.

**◀ ITALIAN CREAM PAINTED AND PARCEL GILT ARMCHAIR**
*1770; 125.7cm (49½in) high; £800–1,200*
Italian chairs of this period are usually larger than their northern European counterparts. This imposing armchair may once have been part of a set for dining, or for the salon. A purist would consider the neo-classical form seen here as somewhat debased. The legs are badly proportioned and the rectangular back heavy. Originally, this would probably have been upholstered in fine velvet or damask.

**▶ ENGLISH YEW WINDSOR CHAIR**
*c.1840; 104.1cm (41in) high; £600–800*
The English Windsor is a true country chair, probably first made around the area of Windsor in Buckinghamshire. It lends itself to mass production from components mostly produced on a wood-turning lathe. It went on to be made in many areas and in many forms from the beginning of the 18th century until well into the 19th century. You may come across low and high backs, pierced and solid splats, cabriole and turned legs. Yew examples are the most desirable, and all Windsor chairs have seats made of elm.

**◀ AMERICAN PAINTED WINDSOR CHAIR**
*c.1820; 127cm (50in) high; £700–1,000*
The origins of the Windsor chair are English, but their enormous popularity and the fact that they were cheap to make meant that their journey across the Atlantic was an easy one. They first appeared in the region around Philadelphia, in 1725. Their value today is determined by the originality of their black or green painted surface. A badly worn example is acceptable, but any repainting reduces the value to minimal.

**COLLECTORS' NOTES**
Before you buy either one or a set of chairs, don't simply look at them – sit on them. They will have taken, and will have to take, a good deal of use so it is very important that the basic structure is still sound. Look carefully for any repaired fractures in the back of the chair, at the point where the back runs down into the legs, and where the front legs join the seat rails. A weak structure is notoriously difficult to restore.

A modern home cannot usually accommodate a set of chairs in its original form as many started out having 14 pieces. Often the 12 side chairs and two armchairs are broken down into two sets of six side chairs with one set also having the carvers. This last will always be worth at least twice as much as a set of side chairs on their own.

If you are buying a set of 12 chairs, with a price to match, try to make sure that they are truly a set and not two sets of six chairs, closely matched. Also, check that the chairs themselves have not been made up from different pieces (a process known as scrambling): cabinet makers gave each chair frame and each drop-in seat a matching number because each one was entirely hand made and slightly different from its neighbour. If any frame number does not match that of its seat it is a sign that the two were not originally together and the structure could become weakened with use. The armchairs in most sets should be wider than the side chairs. If they are not, you may be looking at chairs to which arms have been added later to form a more commercial set.

**COLLECTING TIP**
If you are operating on a tight budget, you can still acquire a very handsome set of chairs by buying single, similar-looking examples (in the Chippendale style, for instance) for around £80 each, and then have them upholstered to match.

# Upholstered Furniture

Upholstered armchairs, which were designed as much for comfort as for basic functionality, first appeared at the end of the 17th century and by the early 18th century the wing chair, which sheltered the sitter from draughts, was well-established throughout Europe and the United States; other forms also appeared, including the bergère, with its long seat and, for comfortable reclining, settees and chaises longues.

Until the 19th century upholstered furniture was overstrung with supporting webbing fixed across the top of the seat rail. In the early 19th century, the coiled spring was developed, and after that, the webbing was fixed below the seat rail to allow room for the springs.

The demand for parlour furniture exploded during the 19th century, and upholstered furniture began to be mass produced, often at the expense of quality.

As well as a set of side chairs and a sofa, the English parlour suite often included a "His" armchair and a "Hers" easy chair without arms, whereas a Continental suite incorporated matching armchairs as well as a large centre table. The best furniture of this kind was stuffed with carefully sorted horsehair, but as demand soared and standards dropped, some late 19th-century examples derived their comfort from such diverse contents as paper and old cloth.

It is unusual to find old chairs with their original upholstery, although sympathetic restorers will have used a replacement material similar to what was used originally. It can be difficult to check the condition of upholstered chairs, but some dealers keep photographs of the piece before any restoration work was carried out showing that the frame was sound, without woodworm or splits. As with other types of furniture, don't forget to try the chair or settee for comfort before buying it.

◄ **GEORGIAN MAHOGANY LIBRARY ARMCHAIR**
*c.1760; 106.7cm (42in) high;* **£1,500–2,000**
The Georgian library chair is a later version of the wing-back chair. It was used in all the less formal rooms, such as the salon and the morning room. This chair has been badly upholstered. The sprung seat should be removed to give it a cleaner line and highlight the frame, and damask or 18th-century needlework would be a more sympathetic covering. The arms are over-stuffed and the seat should be webbed.

◄ **QUEEN ANNE WING-BACK ARMCHAIR**
*1720; 140cm (55in) high;* **£5,000–7,000**
Queen Anne's reign ended in 1714 but this style of chair continued to be made throughout the 18th century, with cabriole legs giving way to square tapered legs as the century progressed. The features that help identify this as an early example are the bold scallop shells and plain pad feet on the cabriole legs, and the outcurved arms which were to become more linear by 1740. The value of chairs is affected by the upholstery. If the chair is completely original, which is rare, it will sell for as much as £60,000–80,000. This one has been sympathetically reupholstered using hand-made needlework contemporary with the time the chair was made.

► **ITALIAN GILTWOOD SOFA**
*c.1760; 165cm (65in) long;* **£3,000–4,000**
This type of sofa was not constructed entirely for domestic comfort. Whereas in England at this time upholstered furniture was commissioned for personal use, on the Continent there was no equivalent of the middle class or of a stratum of society between the gentry and those who ran their estates. Society ran on formal lines and the furniture was made for strict social gatherings. This sofa would have been part of a much larger suite comprising up to six sofas, 24 chairs and matching stools. A common feature of these pieces is the unfinished back, as they were placed permanently against the walls of a room.

### ◄ REGENCY MAHOGANY BERGÈRE

*c.1810; 96.5cm (38in) high;*
**£1,500–2,000**

Although the term "bergère" is French, it also describes English chairs of the 18th and 19th centuries with panels under the arms filled in either with cane or upholstery. Some Continental versions have upholstered sides and arms. This example has satinwood panels on the top and seat rails and a typically Regency form.

### ▲ BIEDERMEIER MAHOGANY SOFA

*c.1825; 214cm (7ft) wide;* **£800–1,200**

Made for the general buying public, rather than as exclusive pieces, much Biedermeier furniture is of simple form, as here, with sparse decoration, making it popular with today's buyers. Biedermeier furniture also represents good value for money.

### ▼ REGENCY CHAISE LONGUE

*c.1810; 198cm (78in) long;* **£3,500–4,500**

The chaise longue was inspired by images discovered at Pompeii and Herculaneum, showing recumbent diners. During the early 19th century, the form became popular after the French artist Davide showed Madame Recamier reclining on such a sofa. This example uses brass inlay in the frame. Although uncomfortable for sitting on in the normal manner, it should be remembered that many young ladies entertained reclining on a sofa wearing the free-flowing Empire line clothes of the day, also inspired by the classical originals.

### ▼ VICTORIAN MAHOGANY AND LEATHER LIBRARY ARMCHAIR

*1880; 94cm (37in) high;* **£1,000–1,500**

Without the warm, patinated and grease-stained original leather upholstery, this chair would be totally unremarkable and worth in the region of £300. Its value lies in the leather. Its other great redeeming feature is its sheer comfort. It has a perfectly moulded back and a long seat to support the legs. Beautifully made and designed to last, chairs of this type should be treated with great care and not left standing close to central heating radiators.

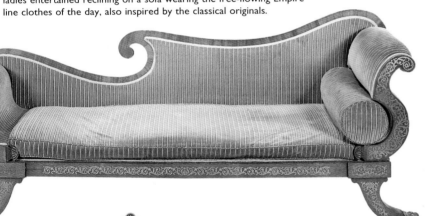

### ▲ VICTORIAN WALNUT FRAMED SOFA

*c.1870; 183cm (70in) long;* **£800–1,200**

This is the archetypal parlour sofa – one piece from what would once have been a much larger suite comprising the sofa, two armchairs and six side chairs. These suites were made from 1850 until 1920, with the style developing in keeping with the fashions of the time. They were also produced in France, Germany and the US, where Belter was the leading exponent. A large proportion of their value is determined by the quality and style of the upholstery.

### COLLECTORS' NOTES

• Check that the structural frame of the piece you are looking at is sound. Repairing it will be a major additional expense.
• The upholstery should not be a factor in the price unless you can be sure it is original. If you are buying an expensive piece that has recently been reupholstered, ask to see photographs of it before the work was done.
• Research the piece and choose fabric that is stylistically correct for its period. Don't cut corners: the wrong kind of upholstery can spoil an otherwise beautiful item.
• Have your piece reupholstered by a craftsman working to traditional methods. Only webbing and wadding were used on 18th-century furniture. Metal springs were an innovation of the 19th century.

### COLLECTING TIP

Having an antique chair or sofa properly reupholstered is well worth the time, trouble and expense. It is always more worthwhile doing this than buying a modern equivalent.

# Dining Tables

In 17th-century Europe those in positions of wealth and standing took their meals at an oak refectory table. The great majority of people, however, sat on stools by the hearth and spooned food directly from the pot hanging over the hearth into a wooden bowl. For the lowly cottager things changed little through the decades, but by the mid-18th century, many of the better-off had servants to set up a series of small drop-leaf dining tables in one room at which food was served, in the same way as in a restaurant. These tables were multipurpose, as were rooms, and could be stored against a wall when not in use.

By the end of the 18th century, in both Europe and the United States, a separate room reserved only for dining, containing a formal table surrounded by a set of chairs, was increasingly common and by the 19th century, a dining room was an established part of every newly built house. A secondary parlour or morning room, where members of the family gathered to eat breakfast and light meals became the home for breakfast tables like the one featured *right*. They were introduced at the end of the 18th century, when they were often rectangular. The round and oval versions made their appearance at the beginning of the 19th century. Most are in rosewood or mahogany, usually with a turned platform stem, as here, although some have a pedestal base with four legs.

The golden rule when buying a dining table is to sit at it first to make sure it is comfortable: of the right height and with no awkward legs getting in the way.

**WILLIAM IV MAHOGANY BREAKFAST TABLE**
*c.1835; 117cm (46in) diameter;* **£1,200–1,800**
This is a very typical example of a circular mahogany breakfast table which has not suffered any disfiguring alterations. Most of these tables were designed to seat six with the result that the rarer examples designed for eight or ten people command premium prices. Expect to pay £5,000 for an eight-seater and £15,000 for a ten-seater. These tables are ideal as a first antique dining table, especially for the smaller, modern home where space is often at a premium; they can easily be extended by covering the whole surface with a piece of protective baize and then placing over it a circular piece of plywood larger than the table top, and disguised by covering with a white tablecloth.

A dealer or auction house will up-end any dining table you are interested in so that you can examine the underside. Commonly, tops and bottoms are "married" to give a more elegant and consequently more valuable table. Any item of furniture made in two pieces is vulnerable to this type of alteration. This piece is all original, but tell-tale signs to look for include:
• traces of a different "H" frame with visible redundant screw holes and lighter marks where the original frame was fixed
• another set of redundant screw holes where the position of the brass catches may have been moved to accommodate a different sized base
• signs that the two brass catches on the block at the top of the column have been moved to accommodate a different-sized top.

Examine the top of the block for a maker's name. You often find either a stamp or a label still intact, which adds great interest and value to a piece in today's market.

The baluster column has a well-carved acanthus collar, typical of the period on this quality of table. More expensive versions have gilt metal mounts fixed to the columns to give a more sumptuous effect.

This table has a nicely figured surface created by cutting veneers from selected baulks of timber and matching them to give pleasing patterns. The join down the centre gives a butterfly effect. Cheaper tables have surfaces cut from solid pieces of plain timber, the least expensive being oak.

The triform configuration ending in nicely carved paw feet is typical of this style of table. The top and the bottom sit well together giving a balanced look overall.

33

# Other Tables

**▲ OAK GATE-LEG TABLE**
*Late 17th century; 122cm (48in) wide;* **£2,500–3,000**
Oak gate-legs were one of the most common types of table made in England, and to a certain extent in Holland, from c.1650 to 1750. Buyers should beware of the countless number of early 20th-century reproductions that exist. Size is the main factor determining price: anything larger than a six-seater commands a high premium. The complexity of the turned supports and good patination are also important. A good early 18th-century example could fetch ten times more than a poor 17th-century example.

**▲ GEORGE II MAHOGANY DROP LEAF DINING TABLE**
*c.1740; 119.5 cm (47in) wide;* **£3,000–4,000**
This is a good example of a form of table which developed from the gate-leg and was made in vast quantities in England throughout the 18th and early 19th centuries. These early ones in dense, Cuban mahogany are much sought after as long as they retain a good patina. Most have square-section or plain turned legs while this has well-drawn cabriole legs. A group of four or six of these tables were laid for dinner prior to the development of the large, central dining table.

**▲ OAK REFECTORY TABLE**
*Early 17th century; 244cm (96in) long;* **£6,000–8,000**
Oak refectory tables were made in Northern Europe over a period of about 200 years beginning c.1500, and followed a fairly standard form of a plank top, on as few as four, or as many as ten, turned legs. They were the prerogative of the wealthy, and interestingly, in some cases carved down one side only, as diners sat with their backs to the wall, facing their servants in the lower part of the Great Hall, perhaps so they could watch for any signs of insurrection!

## COLLECTORS' NOTES
• The very worst thing you can do to an antique table is to have it repolished without first taking expert advice. A badly repolished top can wipe out the history of a piece and reduce its value to a fraction of what it was with its original patina.
• Tops and bottoms should have started life together. Check for extraneous holes which serve no purpose, but show that the table has been made from two different pieces.

• On inlaid pieces, particularly Pembroke tables, check that the inlay and crossbandings are original and not later improvements done for commercial purposes.

## COLLECTING TIP
It is always preferable to buy a plain, elegant example in its original condition than a more elaborate piece which has undergone intensive restoration. You will get more pleasure from it in the long run and it will hold its value.

**▲ GEORGE II OAK LOW BOY**
*c.1740; 76cm (30in) wide;* **£2,000–3,000**
Many of these small, oak side tables, which could be used as dressing tables, were made throughout the 17th and 18th centuries. They follow the same form as their smarter brothers, usually found in veneered walnut. They have become very collectable, and unusual examples, such as this one with cabriole legs, command high prices.

▶ **GEORGE III MAHOGANY TRIPOD TABLE**
*c.1770; 66cm (26in) diameter;* **£500–700**
The tripod table was made in many forms and sizes, this being a standard example. It was used as a general occasional table, often to take the tea tray when it was brought into the drawing room. Few were made on the Continent, and those that were followed the English style. This piece is in original condition and is desirable because the top has mellowed to a rich tone. Many of these tables have replacement tops, or are a marriage between two different pieces.

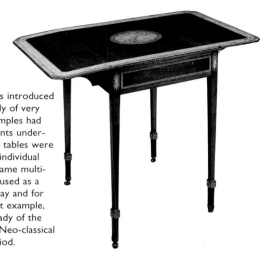

▶ **GEORGE III MAHOGANY PEMBROKE TABLE**
*1780; 74cm (29in) wide;* **£2,500–3,000**
The Pembroke table was introduced c.1750, and was originally of very heavy design. Some examples had a cupboard for condiments underneath the drawer as the tables were originally used to serve individual suppers. Later, they became multi-functional and could be used as a writing surface, for display and for the tea tray. This elegant example, probably made for the lady of the house, has many of the Neo-classical motifs typical of the period.

◀ **RARE FRENCH MAHOGANY EXTENDING DINING TABLE**
*Late 18th/early 19th century; 75cm (29in) high; 117cm (46in) deep;* **£5,000–7,000**
This French dining table is a perfect example of *La Goût Anglaise* (the English taste) which was fashionable among a small Continental elite at this time. The demi-lune ends with a rectangular centre section is typically English but the ormolu moulding around the frieze and the castors betray its Continental origin.

▼ **FRENCH RESTAURATION MAHOGANY CONSOLE TABLE**
*c.1815; 160cm (63in) wide;* **£5,000–7,000**
Console tables formed part of the interior decoration of many Continental salons, being placed around the walls alongside commodes and chairs. Classically inspired versions in mahogany were first made towards the end of the 18th century, and became heavier in design during the Empire period. During the Restauration (when Louis XVIII was restored to the French throne), the designs became more curvilinear, as in this example, but retained classical ormolu mounts.

▲ **VICTORIAN WALNUT CARD TABLE**
*c.1870; 92cm (36in) wide;* **£1,500–1,800**
The heyday of the card table with its fold-over top was the 18th century, with, in some cases, orders being placed with a cabinet maker for up to a dozen tables to be made for a large, country house. For this reason, they survive in great numbers. They always follow the style of the period in which they were made, this example being typical of the walnut furniture made during the Victorian period in England.

# Sideboards

The sideboard is very much an English invention of the 18th century. Before it came into being the serving of food in the formal dining room was done from separate pieces of furniture. These consisted of a marble or wooden topped serving table and two pedestals, one containing a lead-lined compartment where glasses were rinsed and the other a tin-lined compartment where a small charcoal burner sat below a rack on which plates were kept warm. On top of the pedestals sat urns containing cutlery; the wine cooler or cellaret was placed beneath the table.

Later in the century, as dining rooms became smaller, the pieces came together so that the pedestals were built into the serving table and became deep drawers with a central drawer for cutlery. The lead-lined drawer remained, now used for keeping wine cool. The sideboard usually had six legs. At first these were square and tapered but later turned legs became fashionable.

During the early 19th century, the pedestal sideboard came into being, with cupboards extending on either side of the central section giving extra storage space. Apart from its function as the place from which food was brought to the table, the sideboard was also where the family plate was proudly displayed. It is still a popular piece of furniture even in smaller houses where a dining area may have superseded the separate dining room. The small, elegant Georgian sideboard, with its graceful proportions, is a particularly good piece of furniture for the small, modern home.

The cellaret drawer, lined with lead, was filled with ice or cool water in which wine could be kept chilled. These drawers usually incorporate a plug in the bottom which serves as a drain hole, but if you want to use the drawer for the same purpose today, be extremely careful: most of the lead linings have corroded with age, and you don't want cold water leaking all over your antique sideboard.

**ALTERED GEORGE III MAHOGANY SIDEBOARD**
*c.1790; 99cm (39in) high, 139.7cm (55in) wide;* **£1,500–2,000**
This sideboard, although based on a late 18th-century original, has been significantly altered, probably between 1920 and 1940. The width has been greatly reduced by literally sawing sections out of the middle drawer. The shape of the end drawers has also been changed and the whole piece has been put back together with added stringing, giving the overall sideboard a strange shape. Nevertheless, in spite of the alterations, this remains an attractive and useable piece, which can still command a good price.

You can see quite plainly that this later added banding has been badly constructed. It has been put in so roughly that some of the bandings don't even line up. No 18th-century cabinet maker would have made this kind of mistake!

This is the area where you may find evidence of a brass gallery which might once have run around the back of the sideboard to support a curtain that protected the wall behind from being splashed as food was served. Not all sideboards were fitted with a gallery and if one has been removed this does not detract from the value. If the gallery is still intact, however, it does lend additional interest to the piece.

This style of small sideboard nearly always had four legs, but occasionally was constructed with six (the additional legs would be positioned as indicated here). The extra legs can be more pleasing to the eye and make the piece more desirable.

Some sideboards started life with turned legs, but square tapered legs became fashionable at the beginning of the 20th century when furniture began to be seriously collected. You can see that this leg has been altered as the timber above the join does not match that below it.

You may come across a cupboard in the side of a Georgian sideboard which once contained a commode. During the long hours of raucous drinking and merrymaking which occurred after the ladies had withdrawn, guests did not feel compelled to leave the room to answer calls of nature. The servants simply dealt with the consequences of the night's revelry during the small hours.

# Other Sideboards

## ▲ GEORGE III MAHOGANY SERPENTINE SIDEBOARD
*c.1780; 183cm (72in) wide; £6,000–8,000*

This is a particularly attractive example of the classic sideboard, made more saleable by the decorative figured veneers and fan-shaped inlays, and by the fact that it is of a size that will sit comfortably in the smaller dining area of a modern home. The serpentine form is very popular.

## ▲ GEORGE III MAHOGANY D SHAPED SIDEBOARD
*c.1800; 201cm (79in) wide; £3,000–4,000*

This has a much bulkier shape than the elegant serpentine form seen *left*, but is still an attractive piece, incorporating all the necessary features of cupboard, cellaret drawer and central napery drawer. The drawer handles at the extreme sides of the piece front dummy drawers. Although well-made, the price is held down slightly by its depth and lack of inlay.

## ▲ CHIPPENDALE REVIVAL MAHOGANY PEDESTAL SIDEBOARD
*c.1880; 214cm (84in) wide; £3,000–4,000*

During the late 19th century ornate revival styles became highly popular and this is typical of the genre. This large pedestal sideboard, of a style that would never have graced an 18th-century dining room, has had various Chippendale motifs grafted onto its bulky form, such as gadrooning, blind fretwork and rococo foliate scrolls. The price is low because its sheer size makes it impractical for the average home and because heavy pedestal ends are unpopular.

## ▲ VICTORIAN WALNUT SIDE CABINET
*c.1860; 183cm (72in) wide; £2,000–2,500*

This type of cabinet was made both on the Continent and in England, and sometimes the only way to tell them apart is to examine the locks. Although it was not necessarily used as a piece of dining room furniture in the Victorian home, and was often found in the parlour, it fits in well with today's taste for recreating a Victorian dining room. Unlike the Georgian examples, which were constructed purely for the function of dining, these were made solely for display at a time when porcelain tea services had supplanted plate.

## COLLECTORS' NOTES

• The overall original colour, proportions and appearance should be good. Decorative inlays add value.

• As well as replacing turned legs with square tapered ones (*see previous page*), another common alteration is reducing the depth of a sideboard by chopping off the overhang at the back. This affects the drawers, which originally would have run right to the back of the sideboard. Look at the back of the drawers; the dovetails may have disappeared altogether, or they may just look different from those on the front of the drawers. This affects value badly on a really good-quality piece, but actually tends to improve the saleability of one of lesser quality, as it gives it more practical, compact proportions.

• As sideboards inevitably receive a lot of hard usage, minor damage, such as small scratches or replaced sections of decoration, should not deter the prospective purchaser although, as with all furniture, the price should take account of the condition.

# Dressers

The dresser, with cupboards and drawers in the lower section and shelves above for display, developed from the 17th-century court cupboard and buffet. They are homely pieces of furniture, designed for practicality, and were usually made by local carpenters to the specification of the customer. In Britain there are many regional variants. The differences do not significantly increase desirability unless a piece is being sold in the area in which it was made. What does affect value is an unrestored polished finish, and size. Small examples are obviously more practical than some of the huge pieces which sometimes covered an entire wall of the family room. In America, the dresser was normally made of pine with painted, grained decoration. Few examples have survived in a country whose population was still highly mobile at this stage in its history.

**▶ GEORGE III OAK DRESSER**
*1770; 201cm (79in) wide, 213.5cm (84in) high;*
**£4,000–6,000**
This is a good, solid oak dresser of the late 18th century, made in the country for a farmhouse. As well as being used for storage and for serving, it provided plenty of space on which to display the family pottery and pewter plates.

**▲ OAK SIDEBOARD OR DRESSER**
*c.1750; 213.5cm (84in) wide;* **£6,000–8,000**
This is a good example of something between a sideboard and a dresser. It does not incorporate the traditional functions of a town sideboard, but in country houses with no formal dining room, it would have been used for display, serving and storage. Cabriole legs can still be seen on examples made at the end of the 18th century, although square, tapered legs were more fashionable by this time.

**◀ GEORGE III OAK DRESSER**
*c.1800; 193cm (76in) wide;*
**£2,000–3,000**
A simpler variant of the other examples shown here, this dresser was constructed with an open base with a bottom shelf on which to store large cooking pots, milk churns and flour bins. Not every dresser has a rack, and some bases have been "married" later to a rack. Always check the timber on both parts to confirm that the pairing is genuine.

**▶ GEORGE III OAK DRESSER WITH RACK**
*c.1770; 165cm (65in) wide;*
**£5,000–7,000**
**GEORGE III OAK DRESSER WITH RACK**
*c.1770; 211cm (83in) wide;*
**£3,000–4,000**
Comparing these two examples of standard late Georgian dressers is a good way to show how big is not always better: the dresser on the left is small and nicely proportioned and also has a good, rich red colour whereas the one on the right is bigger and therefore less practical as well as being paler and plainer.

# Bookcases and Display Cabinets

Whatever type of writing furniture you come across in antique shops and salerooms, you can be sure that it does not date from before the second half of the 17th century. The reason is simply that not many people (apart from a few members of the nobility and a larger number of ecclesiastics) could read and write or had possessions to display before this time. During the 18th century, literacy increased dramatically, and with it the manufacture of desks and writing tables. As more people began to own books, bookcases were more frequently added to desks to form bureau- or secretaire-bookcases, which had a flap that pulled forward to provide a writing surface. To cater for the new fashion for collecting silver and porcelain, some cabinets were made with glazed upper sections to better display these highly prized possessions. Smaller library furniture, such as revolving bookcases and library steps, which were made from the end of the 18th century, are very collectable as they can fit easily into most modern homes.

**◀ MAHOGANY BUREAU CABINET**
*c.1760; 2.28m (7ft 6in) high, 1.04m (3ft 5in) wide;*
**£3,000–3,500**
The architectural pediment on this bureau cabinet adds elegance and gives it a slight edge over other plainer examples. The carved wooden eagle was a common addition of the period, but unfortunately, in this case, does not enhance the piece because the workmanship is poor. Often, the panelled doors of the upper sections of these bookcases were removed and replaced with astragal glazing, such as that on the front of the secretaire-bookcase, *right*. It is usually possible to detect that this has been done, because astragals added later will simply be stuck to the door frame or butt up against it; original astragals would slot properly into the frame.

**▲ MAHOGANY SECRETAIRE-BOOKCASE**
*c.1780; 2.13m (7ft 4in) high, 1.24m (4ft 1in) wide;* **£2,500–3,000**
This is a standard example of a secretaire-bookcase, in common use by this date, with a flat rather than an angled front. To get to the desk section, you pull out the deep drawers and press a button on either side, which causes the front to hinge down on brass quadrants. This example is made more interesting by the elegant, curved astragals that divide the glazed bookcase section. The feet are replacements for the original, typically 18th-century, narrow outswept feet.

## COLLECTORS' NOTES

Because bureau bookcases were made in standard sizes they were easy to take apart, so many examples are marriages between different pieces from the same or even from different periods – for example, a Georgian bureau is often topped by a modern reproduction bookcase. You should therefore check:

**THE SIDES** The timber should match exactly all the way from the top to the bottom, as it should have been cut from the same plank.

**THE BASE** The plain pine carcase should be visible, as in genuine examples the top of the bureau would not have been veneered. You will have to take the bookcase off to see it, but a veneered bureau will have started life without an accompanying bookcase.

**THE MOULDING** Disguising the join between the two sections, the moulding should be on the bureau not the bookcase.

**THE DECORATION** Any cross bandings, stringings and mouldings should be in the same style on both sections.

## COLLECTING TIP

A good quality late-Victorian or Edwardian copy is a better buy than a married or poor quality 18th-century original

## DUTCH MARQUETRY BUREAU CABINET
*c.1770 with later inlay; 2.1m (7ft)
high, 1.1m (3ft 6in) wide;*
**£7,000–9,000**
In common with many pieces of
Dutch marquetry furniture, this is
not what it seems. It was made
in the 18th century as a
plain piece, and returned
to the cabinet makers in
the 19th century to be
improved and made more
commercial at a time when
ornate decoration was the
height of fashion.

These flat surfaces were
designed especially to take
a garniture of Oriental blue
and white vases. The Dutch
were fond of displaying
porcelain in this way, and
seeing this feature is one
way to attribute a piece.

Look at how badly fitting
some of these pieces of
marquetry are. The original,
thickly cut walnut or
mahogany veneers have
been stripped off and
replaced by these thin
19th-century, machine-
cut veneers with ill-fitting
designs of leaves and birds.
This was an expensive
piece of furniture when
it was made, so great care
would have been taken
with any veneers and inlay.

The interior on this is
relatively elaborate in
comparison with an English
or American equivalent.
A slide covers a well at the
centre in which all manner
of paperwork could be
stored – a standard feature
on Dutch pieces and early
English examples too. The
lock is also original.

This shows typical
18th-century Dutch
construction with side
runners and nailed joints
rather than dovetails. The
overall construction of
the carcass is invariably
crude in comparison
with English or American
work being done at the
same time.

# Other Writing Furniture

**▲ FIGURED MAHOGANY BUREAU**
*c.1770; 94cm (37in) wide;* **£2,000–3,000**
A plain example of a standard bureau can be bought for £1,000 but this is particularly desirable, and therefore more valuable, because the well-chosen and matched veneers give it such decorative appeal. The interiors at this period are usually quite simple, consisting of drawers and pigeon holes often flanking a central cupboard.

**▲ CHIPPENDALE FIGURED MAPLE SLANT-FRONT DESK**
*c.1775–1800; 112cm (44in) high;* **£4,000–5,500**
This bureau, or slant-front desk, was made during the American Chippendale period (1750–80) probably in Philadelphia. Although maple was much used earlier in the century, mahogany would have been a more common choice at this time. Its large size makes it less saleable than a smaller equivalent.

**◄ KINGWOOD BONHEUR DU JOUR**
*c.1790; 68.5cm (27in) wide;*
**£2,000–3,000**
A desk designed specifically for ladies as a boudoir piece was developed towards the end of the 18th century. It provided the perfect surface on which to pen a *billet doux* or the daily notes to the staff. The writing surface hinges forward to give more space when required and the small niche in the centre was designed to hold a favourite objet d'art or a small stack of novels. Although quite rare in exotic timbers like the kingwood shown here, plainer mahogany examples are more widely available. Fakes abound because the construction is so simple.

**▲ SATINWOOD CYLINDER BUREAU**
*c.1790; 97cm (38in) wide;* **£2,500–3,000**
Satinwood was an extremely popular timber in Europe by the end of the 18th century, as it was well-suited to the light airy interiors that replaced the heavier, more sombre architectural style fashionable earlier in the century. The interior is fitted with the standard arrangement of drawers and pigeon holes. It is missing some of its bandings and the brass castors, but with some minor and skilful restoration it would be a very pretty piece of furniture.

**COLLECTORS' NOTES**
• Desks come in such a variety of shapes and sizes, that it is most important to think about what you might need from one – for example, how many drawers or cupboards you require – rather than be seduced merely by the style of the piece.

• If you choose a bureau, look out for warping on the fall. This cannot be repaired without incurring major expense.
• A common deception is to reveneer a plain oak or mahogany pedestal desk with walnut, satinwood or bird's eye maple, in an attempt to increase the value.

**▲ MAHOGANY WRITING TABLE**
*c.1820; 124.5cm (49in) wide;* **£2,800–3,500**
A great house with a vast library may have been furnished with as many as four or five of these handsome writing tables. In a smaller establishment, such a piece would have had pride of place in the study and was used by the gentleman of the house. Writing tables are more adaptable than other writing furniture because the surface could be used for other purposes, such as to stack books or display a microscope or a globe. On this example, the well-carved supports display many of the classical features so fashionable during the Regency period in England, such as acanthus carving and paw feet.

**▶ BIEDERMEIER FRUITWOOD SECRETAIRE CHEST**
*c.1820; 104.5cm (41in) high, 108cm (42½in) wide;* **£1,500–2,500**
This handy piece of furniture looks like a chest or side table, but the top drawer pulls out to provide a writing surface. The use of fruitwood, rather than, say, mahogany, indicates that the piece is less refined than some made during this period. Its simplicity suggests that it may have been made in Scandinavia, rather than in Austria or Germany, where the Biedermeier style was given a more sophisticated interpretation.

**▲ WALNUT PEDESTAL DESK**
*c.1870; 137cm (54in) wide;* **£3,000–4,000**
This is the style of desk most commonly used in an office, as well as in a gentleman's study. They nearly always contain nine drawers at the front and a plain back. Larger examples, known as "partners' desks," have drawers in one of the pedestals and cupboards in the other. The least expensive examples were made in oak. More desirable are these walnut pieces and most sought after of all are rare pedestal desks constructed in the Far Eastern colonies in exotic timbers such as ebony and amboyna.

**▶ BIRD'S EYE MAPLE TAMBOUR DESK**
*c.1860; 122cm (48in) wide;* **£2,400–3,000**
The tambour shutter is a variant on the cylinder bureau (see *previous page*). Horizontal strips of timber are glued to a canvas back making the shutter flexible enough to concertina inside the back of the frame. A cylinder mechanism is solid wood and requires a larger, deeper space at the back of the frame where it can be stored when the shutter is open. This piece was probably a special commission, as the cupboards enclose trays which are the exact size for Admiralty charts.

**▶ MARQUETRY BUREAU PLAT**
*c.1880; 127cm (50in) wide;* **£1,800–2,500**
This type of 19th-century revivalist furniture was inspired by the Louis XVI style popular from the middle of the century. These bureaux plats were made of varying quality, something which obviously helps determine their price today. Produced in both Paris and London, there is little to choose between the two centres of manufacture. They were constructed virtually on a production line basis, with clients able to specify their preference for a different design in the marquetry panel on the surface, perhaps depicting birds rather than fruit or flowers.

# Miscellaneous Furniture

The main framework of a collection of antique furniture consists of the larger pieces such as sideboards, dining tables, bookcases and chests of drawers. If these major investments look set to break the bank balance, then collectors and would-be collectors can take comfort in the knowledge that there are great quantities of smaller pieces on the market which can enhance a room filled with more modern items. Conversely, they can be added to the major purchases after these have been made.

Not all these smaller items have to be from the same period. In fact, a variety of timbers, styles and dates usually looks more interesting. The sole criterion should be that the pieces were well made originally and have not suffered unsympathetic restoration. You would probably want to buy only one piece at a time, building up a variety over the years. In fact, if you owned all the examples illustrated on the following pages, you would be the envy of many a connoisseur of fine furniture.

**▲ MAHOGANY WHATNOT**
*c.1820; 157.5cm (62in) high;*
**£2,000–2,500**
Whatnot is the English term for a tiered stand of rectangular shelves used to display ornaments and objets d'art. The first recorded design for one is in the cost book for 1800 of a well known English firm of furniture makers, Gillow. They were made with as many as six surfaces, as in the example shown here, or as few as three, and are as useful today as during the 19th century. This piece is unusual in not having a drawer in the lower tier.

**▲ MAHOGANY DUMB WAITER**
*c.1815; 66cm (26in) diameter;*
**£1,800–2,000**
Much drinking and conversation took place in the mid- to late 18th–century dining room after the ladies had withdrawn. As diners began to require more privacy, the dumb waiter was developed so the servants could leave. Consisting of two to four tiers arranged around a central column, they were loaded with cheeses, desserts and drinks so that people could help themselves. This example is unusual in having drop leaf tiers.

**▲ POLESCREEN**
*c.1860; 152cm (60in) high;*
**£200–300**
The polescreen was made to shield a seated young lady from the heat of a roaring fire, and for this reason has ceased to be anything but a decorative piece of occasional furniture. They are therefore good value. This mahogany example still contains the original silkwork panel which would have been worked by the woman of the household. It has become common practice to remove the panel and use the base to support the surface of a tripod table.

**▲ MAHOGANY CAKE STAND**
*c.1910; 91cm (36in) high;*
**£50–100**
The ritual of afternoon tea involved the presentation of various types of sandwiches and cakes which were placed on a multi-tiered cake stand beside the lady of the house in the drawing room. Today, they are often used to display plants. Later examples were adapted so that the circular trays folded against the supports for storage.

**▲ MAHOGANY WINE COOLER**

*c.1770; 36cm (14in) wide;*
**£1,200–1,800**
The lead liner for containing iced water distinguishes this wine cooler from the cellaret (*right*). Originally, a brass tap was fitted underneath the piece to allow the water to be drained off, and some examples have retained this. A few years ago, at the height of the market, this brass-bound cooler might have fetched over £3,000.

**▼ REGENCY ROSEWOOD TEAPOY**

*c.1810; 35.5cm (14in) wide;*
**£1,000–1,500**
The original definition of a tea-poy was a small, three-legged table or stand, but over the years it has become associated with tables like this, which incorporate a container for tea or a tea caddy. They were made mainly in the early years of the 19th century.

**► REGENCY MAHOGANY WORK TABLE**

*c.1810; 35.5cm (14in) wide;* **£800–1,200**
Work tables in various forms were made from the latter part of the 18th century up to the present day. This is a standard example with a fitted drawer above a forward-sliding basket in which tapestries and other needlework in progress could be stored. Despite the fact that needlework is no longer the major leisure pursuit it once was, these work tables are still popular, and are often used as lamp stands.

**◄ MAHOGANY CELLARET**

*c.1790; 43cm (17in) wide;* **£800–1,200**
The term cellaret is usually reserved for a wine storage piece, like this one, that has no lead liner. This example is most attractive with its domed top, but it is probably less desirable because it cannot be put to any other use, unlike one with a flat top.

**▲ HUNGARIAN ASH CANTERBURY**

*c.1825; 46cm (18in) wide;* **£1,000–1,500**
The canterbury is basically a wooden stand divided into sections, designed originally to hold sheet music. It was made for around 100 years from the late 18th century until purpose-made music cabinets drove it out of fashion. The wreath and scrolls which decorate this example are typical of the classical taste of the time.

**▲ MAHOGANY BEDSIDE CABINET**

*c.1910; 33cm (13in) high;*
**£150–250**
A good 18th-century bedside cabinet can cost £700–1,000, but this is a turn-of-the-century reproduction (now acquiring age in its own right) of the English Georgian style with a gently bowed front, a single cupboard and tapering legs.

# Other Miscellaneous Furniture

▲ **OAK TOILET MIRROR**
*c.1830; 31cm (12in) wide;* **£50–80**
The toilet mirror is a practical, useful item of bedroom furniture which can sit on top of a chest of drawers or dressing table. They were made in many forms and a good quality 18th-century mahogany example can be worth up to £400, especially if it incorporates a drawer in the base. This is a simple, rectangular oak version with gilt metal screws.

▲ **MAHOGANY ARCHITECT'S TABLE**
*1780; 99cm (39in) wide;* **£1,000–1,500**
Originally, architects' tables were often commissioned by young men of taste and means who considered themselves to be amateur architects and designers in much the same way as they often elevated themselves to the position of scientist or astronomer. This one appears beautifully made, but when the surface is lowered, it is no more than a standard, plain side table, which is why the price is low. It is not considered a practical piece of furniture today, but forms a perfect surface on which to display a watercolour or a lavishly illustrated book.

◀ **PAIR OF VENETIAN BLACKAMOOR LAMP SUPPORTS**
*1900; 2m (6ft 8in) high;* **£4,000–5,000**
Blackamoor figures originated in the late 17th and early 18th centuries when black people were considered enormously exotic. In Venice, a major southern trading port where these lamp supports were made, black people from North Africa were a much more common sight than in other parts of Europe. Blackamoors come in many forms, sometimes holding trays for visiting cards, but more often as lamp supports like this. These are turn-of-the-century copies of earlier pieces but are still worth a great deal. They are very popular and consequently many modern copies exist.

◀ **REGENCY GILT CONVEX MIRROR**
*c.1810; 71cm (28in) high;* **£800–1,200**
The plate of a convex mirror bulges slightly outwards and a genuine example tends to be peculiar to the early 19th century. They were so popular, however, that many modern reproductions of poor quality have been made. Convex mirrors are usually surmounted by a carved wooden eagle in various poses. This example is a fairly standard size, but a few very large examples with 91.5cm (36in) diameter plates exist and are worth many thousands of pounds.

**◄ GOTHIC REVIVAL CHEVAL MIRROR**
*c.1850; 178cm (70in) high; 81.3cm (32in) wide;*
**£800–1,200**
Although this form of dressing mirror originated in the latter part of the 18th century, this example is inspired by the British architect and designer Augustus Pugin's rebuilding of the Houses of Parliament in England. The market for this style of furniture is fairly limited, but has grown in the past few years, and well-designed examples are fetching good prices.

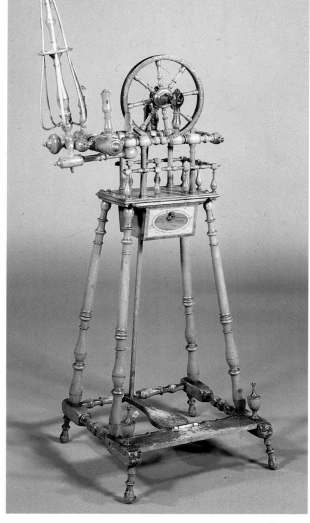

**▲ FRUITWOOD SPINNING WHEEL**
*c.1780; 96.5cm (38in) high;* **£600–800**
Far from being a tool of the cottager, this was very much a piece of drawing room or boudoir furniture, used by a wealthy lady in the spinning of silk which was then made into lace for pretty cuffs and collars. She might have pursued the art of lace-making in much the same way as her husband pored over globes and scientific instruments in the privacy of his library. In England, these examples with a pewter flywheel are often labelled "John Jameson of York."

**► CHINESE TRIPOD TABLE**
*c.1880; 62cm (24in) diam;* **£300–500**
Pieces of Chinese furniture were made in huge quantities, specifically for export to Europe. They included large and elaborate cabinets as well as smaller, useful items such as nests of tables and occasional tables like this tripod. Ornately carved in hardwood with a dragon or mythical beast design, the top has been inset with a colourful Canton porcelain plaque.

**COLLECTORS' NOTES**
• Never buy a mirror where the original worn gilding has been covered over with gold paint, as this is impossible to remove.
• Because many of these pieces are relatively simple and also extremely useful, numerous 20th-century copies exist, so buy from a reputable dealer or auction house.
• If you have a mirror with its original plate of glass which has become foxed and mottled, leave it alone rather than replace it. If the foxing bothers you, sell the piece and replace it with another containing modern glass.

**COLLECTING TIP**
As many of these items will be completing your collection of furniture, buy pieces of the same standard of craftsmanship as your larger, more expensive investments. Though small, they will all contribute to the effect of your room so it is worth getting something eyecatching.

**► NEST OF SATINWOOD OCCASIONAL TABLES**
*c.1800; 46cm (18in) wide;* **£800–1,200**
Nests of tables were developed at the end of the 18th century as rests for drinks in the drawing room. They are put to much the same purpose today which is why they are such strong, commercial antiques. They were usually made in sets of four, known as quartetto tables. This set is missing its largest table. Individual examples turn up quite regularly and can be bought for around £150, much less than a good tripod table.

# Ceramics

Ceramics (from the Greek "Keramos" meaning clay) is the generic term for a huge variety of wares under the main headings of pottery and porcelain. Both groups can be subdivided into numerous others, including bone china, stoneware and earthenware, and part of the fun is deciding what interests you and how much you can afford to spend before setting out on your treasure hunt.

The subject is complicated, but don't be put off, because of all the media open to the collector, this is the most plentiful, with something to suit every pocket. Your first task should be to familiarize yourself with the differences between the various types, so that you can distinguish between, for example, a piece of earthenware and a piece of porcelain sitting side by side. The most difficult nut to crack is telling hard- from soft-paste porcelain. It may seem like an insurmountable obstacle at the start, but every porcelain collector in the world once faced the same dilemma. Buying chipped or cracked pieces is a very good way to build up a source of reference. A badly chipped delft tile will provide the reference for looking at the body (the paste) and the glaze. Pieces of damaged Chelsea and Meissen, studied together, will help you understand the difference between soft- and hard-paste porcelain.

A good reference book on marks is invaluable, providing you bear in mind that not all marks are to be trusted. Many were faked, some as long ago as the 18th century, when English porcelain factories copied the marks of Meissen, Sèvres and other leading European makers whose wares they were seeking to emulate. Samson of Paris was the most famous copyist during the 19th century. His wares were not intended to deceive, however, and although in many cases they have been removed, some pieces still carry his own mark of crossed "S"s.

When you feel ready to start building a collection, exercise great caution. Make sure that what you are buying is genuine by doing business only with reputable dealers and auction houses. Condition is also important. A chip, a crack or an area of restoration will detract from the value of a piece, although it is possible to amass and enjoy a collection at a fraction of the normal cost by being prepared to accept slight imperfections – as long as these are reflected in the price.

Think about what you really want to buy. Does Oriental porcelain hold a great fascination, or the long and varied history of the English Staffordshire factories? Perhaps German fairings have caught your eye, or the vast array of seaside souvenir wares? I hope the following pages will give you a flavour of the beauty and variety of ceramics and start you on an exciting journey of discovery.

*Left: back left* Chinese export *famille-verte* dish, c.1720; *centre row left* Meissen figural group, c.1880; *centre* Chinese export blue and white octagonal plate, c.1760; *right* Paris porcelain vase, 1860; *front row left* German Westerwald stoneware jug commemorating Queen Mary II of England, c.1690; *right* Masons Japan pattern English jug, c.1840.

# Where to begin

When planning your initial forays into the world of ceramics collecting it is useful to learn makers' marks, but always treat them with great suspicion. A thorough knowledge of the different types of bodies will stand you in far better stead.

## The Main Ceramic Bodies: Pottery

Under the wide heading of pottery comes a variety of bodies made since the earliest times, some of which are still manufactured today.

EARTHENWARE first made when man discovered that raw clay could be dug out from the ground, shaped into a vessel and hardened by baking in a fire. A red clay, commonly known as terracotta, was also used with a few additions and fired in the same way.

STONEWARE where the clay is mixed with some kind of fusible rock and can be fired to a higher temperature than earthenware. More opaque than porcelain, it was produced from medieval times for useful wares.

SALT GLAZED STONEWARE was produced from the early 18th century in Staffordshire (*see Glazes*).

As the 18th century wore on, pottery bodies became more refined with the discovery of china clay or kaolin. It helped Josiah Wedgwood perfect both *creamware* (an opaque white body with a creamy translucent glaze) and *pearlware* (an off-white body with a blue tinted glaze).

## Porcelain

Like pottery, porcelain is made from different compositions of ingredients.

HARD-PASTE or TRUE PORCELAIN first made in China in the 8th century, consists of equal parts of china clay and a feldspathic rock also known as petuntse. The clay fuses at approximately 1700°C, the petuntse at about 1450°C. The powdered rock is mixed with the clay and fired at the lower of the two temperatures until the rock fuses to the consistency of glass to form the body of the piece. True porcelain is translucent.

SOFT-PASTE or ARTIFICIAL PORCELAIN was first made in Europe in Italy around 1575, in an attempt to emulate Oriental porcelain. Since European potters didn't know the ingredients, they experimented by mixing china clay with powdered glass, and either soapstone or bone ash.

To tell the difference between hard- and soft-paste porcelain examine chipped pieces of both types side by side. The soft-paste body is slightly porous and granular with a glassy skin of glaze. Chipped hard-paste looks more like opaque glass with a thin, glittering glaze which has fused with the body. Glazes on soft-paste tended to run and to absorb enamel colours. Enamel colours on hard-paste rest on top. Dirt will sink into the unglazed soft-paste body whereas it will wash off hard-paste.

BONE CHINA is a cross between hard- and soft-paste porcelain. The mixture contains 25% china stone, 25% china clay and 50% calcined cattle bones. More stable at high firing temperatures than soft-paste porcelain, it has lower firing costs than hard-paste porcelain.

PARIAN WARE is similar to hard-paste porcelain with a smooth, semi-matt, unglazed surface achieved by a second firing at a higher temperature than the first. Developed in the mid-19th century in Staffordshire, it was widely used for figure modelling because of its suitability for casting in moulds.

## Glazes

Most ceramic bodies are semi-porous and must be covered with a glaze to create a water-tight vessel. Glaze is primarily ground glass suspended in water with china clay added to prevent the compounds from sinking to the bottom. The pot is dipped in, allowed to dry and then fired. Glazes can be coloured, opaque or translucent.

*Lead glazes*, used from medieval times, give a translucent glaze; *tin glazes* provide a white glaze, found on pots made as long ago as 1000BC; and *salt glazes*, used in Germany and from c.1720 in Staffordshire, form a fine glassy glaze on white stoneware bodies, the best of which was considered as good as Chinese porcelain.

Coloured glazes, made from varying compositions and applied with different techniques produce a range of decoration. *Majolica glazes* were the colourful opaque lead glazes painted onto the once-fired bodies before re-firing them. *Feathered glazes* and *tortoiseshell effects* were made by layering and splashing coloured glazes onto a body before using a fine brush to create the desired effect. A *marbled glaze* on a pot was created by painting oils over coloured glazes to help trail the colours.

## Decoration

Incising patterns into the wet clay of a pot with a stick is known as *sgrafitto decoration* and was the earliest way of embellishing earthenwares. During the 17th and 18th centuries, *sgrafitto* was enhanced by painting glaze into the incised areas. *Moulded decoration* involves pre-forming pots in a mould before firing or applying pieces to them to create a moulded effect. *Slip trailing* is a form of applied decoration similar to the method used to ice a cake. Liquid slip (clay and water) is trailed onto the body to create a raised outline and provide a barrier for the different colours. *Under-glaze hand painting* was done onto the biscuit body using brushes dipped in pigments. The paint was absorbed immediately into the once-fired piece and mistakes could never be rectified. The piece was dipped in glaze and fired again. *On-glaze hand painting,* a process applied to stonewares, porcelain and earthenwares, used enamel paints which fused onto the glazed surface once the decoration was complete and the pot returned to the kiln. *Transfer-printing* was mainly used for under-glaze decoration. A design engraved onto a copper plate was filled with ink; a sheet of tissue paper absorbed the design and was then laid carefully onto the piece. This paper transfer burnt off in the kiln to leave the inked design. Perfected in the 18th century, this technique was developed for mass production in the 19th century. *Gilding* is always the final decorative process as a lower kiln temperature is needed to fire the gold leaf. For a raised effect, gold leaf was applied over raised enamels. Matt gilding could be decorated with elaborate patterns using an agate stone to burnish it and achieve contrast. This last method is called *tooled gilding*.

## Copies, Fakes and Alterations

18th-century porcelain was widely collected in the 19th century. To satisfy demand, the Paris factory of Edmé Samson, founded in 1845, produced a range of copies, now collected in their own right. All in hard-paste porcelain, they are relatively easy to identify. The glazes often pool into foot rims with a blue-grey appearance.

Marks are often misleading. Several 18th- and 19th-century manufacturers in England and Continental Europe marked wares with devices closely resembling those used at Meissen and Sèvres. Early 19th-century examples are collected in their own right, but late 19th- and early 20th-century copies have little value. 15th- and 16th-century maiolica was extensively reproduced in the late 19th century.

Treat dated pieces with suspicion. Always check that the material is correct for the type and the period. A Bow figure would not be modelled in stoneware nor a Chelsea Red Anchor plate in creamware, for instance. Some slip trailed wares bearing names of famous potters are known to have been produced during the late 19th and 20th centuries. Originals are thickly potted and irregular in shape with spontaneous decoration, whereas copies are uniform in thickness and precise in form.

During the 19th century, Chinese blue and white porcelain was often "improved" with additional on-glaze enamel decoration known as "clobbering." Some 18th-century Chinese and Sèvres porcelain was subjected to "skimming" whereby on-glaze enamels were removed so as to redecorate pieces with a more desirable design.

Pieces made in sections should be carefully examined to ensure that both the top and bottom are original and contemporary with one another.

## Restoration

When considering buying, it is important to be aware of any damage to a piece. Excessive overpainting of a defect is to be avoided as this is a prime example of bad restoration. Many collectors prefer defects to be visible and if a part is missing, visible infill is desirable.

To spot restorations look closely at the surface. A fine crazing over the body may contrast with one completely smooth area which has been restored. An ultra violet lamp, shone onto a piece in a dark room is another good test. If the surface is uniform, the piece is problem free, but should a distinct area show up darker, you are probably looking at restoration.

To detect a hairline crack, gently tap near the top rim. A bell-like tone indicates a perfect piece, but a dull, vibrating sound suggests a hairline crack in the body. This test can only be applied to flatware such as dishes and plates, not to figures or jugs. Repairs contemporary with the piece – for example Chinese porcelain teapots with replacement silver spouts – are best left alone. They indicate the high value of porcelain in the 18th century.

## Care and Maintenance

The biggest enemies of tablewares are cutlery and the effects of citrus acids from fruit which eat into on-glaze enamels. Moisture can cause problems if a bowl, for instance, is used as a plant stand. Limescale builds up on the inside and is difficult to remove. Soft-paste porcelain is particularly susceptible to extreme changes in temperature because the body and the glaze expand and contract at different rates, resulting in crazing, or, at worst, cracking and splitting.

Avoid metal plate stands at all costs. Plastic-covered or perspex stands will not cause rim chips. Dust can be removed from difficult places by using a compressed air canister with a fine jet. When washing ceramics, handle one piece at a time in a plastic bowl with a piece of foam laid in the base. Wash in warm water with washing up liquid and avoid abrasive scourers, cream cleaners, bleach and dishwashers. Dry with absorbent kitchen towel rather than a cloth towel, which can catch on applied decoration such as flower heads and leaves.

# Chinese Porcelain

The earliest Chinese porcelain was manufactured in the north of the country during the Tang dynasty (618–906). The Chinese began to export their wares as early as the 9th century, but to Southeast Asia, India and the Middle East. It was not until Portuguese explorers found their way to China in the early 16th century that Chinese porcelain was introduced to Europe, where it became very highly prized.

The finest porcelains produced during the Ming dynasty were made at the Jingdezhen potteries during the "middle" period (the 14th to the 15th century), but the demand for the wares was so great that unskilled labour was taken on to meet orders, and standards inevitably declined, with hurried decoration painted onto a body prone to chipping at the rims. There was a marked revival in quality after the rebuilding of the Jingdezhen kilns, which had been destroyed by fire in 1675. Under the Qing emperor Kangxi (1662–1722), the body became denser and whiter and the decoration more delicate and refined. The wares are usually blue and white but occasionally three or more colours were used.

By this time, trade with Europe had begun to expand and several nations had established trading posts in Canton which, apart from being a port, was a centre of porcelain production and enamelling. Along with blue and white, the palettes which found particular favour in the West were green and pink. In addition, the often eggshell-thin wares made during the reign of the emperor Yongzheng (1723–35) were decorated with extremely fine enamelling and are considered the most desirable of all 18th-century Chinese porcelain.

During the reign of the following emperor Qianlong (1736–95), massive consignments of porcelain were shipped to the West with elaborate table services which were often especially commissioned and occasionally decorated with European subjects copied faithfully by Chinese decorators from European engravings. They were sometimes painted in black and gilt (referred to as *en grisaille*), incorporating elaborate armorial crests or initials in script.

Prices were competitive and demand remained keen until the beginning of the 19th century when the huge technological advances that were made in the production of European pottery and porcelain began to have an adverse effect on trade with China. By c.1820, the quantity of Chinese porcelain exported to Europe had dwindled to a trickle.

◀ **BLUE AND WHITE VASE, KANGXI PERIOD**
*c.1710; 25.4cm (10in) high;* **£400–500**
The ladies in the painted decoration are of a type known as "Long Elizas" in English and "Lange Lyzen" in Dutch because their height and slenderness are exaggerated. The porcelain is good and white, and the foot rim cut and trimmed, a feature evident on many pieces of this time. Originals carry six character marks of the emperor Kangxi on the base, whereas 19th-century examples usually have four. Just to confuse matters, during the period this was made, the pottery sometimes put on a Ming mark in homage to the wares of the previous dynasty.

▲ **CHINESE EXPORT SAUCE BOAT**
*1770; 20.3cm (8in) long;* **£300–400**
This sauce boat, based on European silver of the period, would have formed part of one of the large and expensive dinner services exported in quantity to Europe and America during the late 18th century. The decoration is of the *famille rose* (predominantly pink) type with various gentlemen and their attendants bearing lanterns within elaborately shaped panels with outer reserves of gilt scrollwork. The foot rim is banded with a spearhead and dot motif.

▼ **CANTON VASE**
*c.1850; 20.3cm (8in) high;*
**£100–120**
This has the unmistakable palette favoured by the Canton enamellers and used to decorate an endless variety of wares during the 19th century. Vases of this type can be found up to 91.5cm (36in) high or more. The decoration consists principally of panels enclosing numerous high-born Chinese ladies and gentlemen on garden terraces or in elaborate interiors. The background is decorated with small birds and insects, often among flowering plants. This kind of vase decoration was popular well into the 20th century.

▲ **"MANDARIN" TEAPOY AND COVER**
*c.1790–1810; 15.2cm (6in) high;*
**£150–250**
This palette of iron red and black together with colourful enamels was very popular around 1800 in Europe and America. The small size of this vessel reflects the high price of tea at the time and the fact that it was bought and stored in small quantities. Around the base it has elaborate, moulded scrollwork heightened with gilt.

**STANDARD *FAMILLE ROSE* PLATE**
*c.1760; 23cm (9½in) diameter; £150–250*
The porcelain wares made in this predominantly pink (*famille rose*) palette cannot be
attributed to a particular factory but this
plate is likely to have been made in, and
exported from, Canton. This type of ware
was thinly potted and is prone to hairline
cracks. Typically, the rim is edged in brown.
Some pieces are marked on the reverse in
underglaze blue with Taoist symbols such
as an Artemesia leaf or a ribbon scroll.

The gilt detailing you can see
here on the bird is often worn
away but in this instance is in
good order, which makes the
piece more desirable. The gilding
is softer than the enamel and so
much more susceptible to wear.

This *cavetto*, or inner well, is
decorated with a narrow band
of pink *ruyi* (like a fungus head)
– something that in later
examples is replaced with a
black and gilt spearhead design.

This particular blue enamel
normally bleeds a slight
iridescence around the
outline where it meets the
white porcelain, a feature
that rarely appears on
19th-century copies.

Peonies are a popular motif on Chinese
porcelain and these are reasonably well
painted, although if you were to look at
an example of *famille rose* made during the
earlier period of Yongzheng you would
notice that the flower heads would be more
densely petalled, with finer toning of colour.

The thinness of the potting
can best be seen in the
rim, which is edged in
brown to give it slightly
greater strength.

**COLLECTORS' NOTES**
Canton pieces that were made
during the 20th century were
often marked "Made in China."
If you examine a Canton piece
which purports to be 19th
century but you can see evidence

of such a mark having been
scratched away, beware – you are
probably looking at a later copy.
    You can still build up a
colourful display of Chinese
export and Canton porcelain if
you are prepared to buy damaged

examples. Hairline cracks on
*famille rose* and *famille verte*
(mostly green) plates are often
not easily detectable and
consequently are not disfiguring.
Late 18th-century Chinese
porcelain is a dense material

impervious to moisture, so cracks
are not prone to staining, unlike
soft-paste porcelain, or the later
bone china equivalent.
    Many pieces have been
repaired using discreet rivets;
these should not be removed

# Japanese Porcelain

Before the early 17th century, all the porcelain used in Japan was imported from China, but the ruling Tokugawa Shogunate in Japan wanted to be free of the Chinese merchants and, during raids carried out on Korea, captured their native potters. They brought them back to Japan and settled them inland at Arita, which became the main area of production after 1616 when the correct type of clay was found locally.

Between the collapse of the Chinese Ming dynasty in 1644 and the establishment of the Ch'ing dynasty in 1682, many of the imperial kilns were destroyed. The main traders in Chinese wares, the Dutch, turned to Japan to replace the vast quantities of porcelain that arrived in Europe by the shipload.

By the time the Chinese had re-established their porcelain industry, the Japanese had begun to retreat into a long period of self-imposed isolation. Between the late 17th century and about 1860, only small quantities of wares were exported from Japan by Westerners who managed to retain a small trading post in Nagasaki in the south. After the reopening of trade in the 1860s, the West was flooded with Imari, Kutani and Satsuma wares and the fashion for Japanese goods took off under the banner of the Aesthetic movement.

Collectors are spoilt for choice because of the sheer volume of porcelain exported to Europe and the United States from the mid-19th century until the outbreak of the Second World War. Many of the pieces are still very affordable: if you hunt carefully you could find a 19th-century Imari vase and cover of middling size in good condition for under £100. If you become a committed collector the sky's the limit: from a Nabeshima dish for £10,000 to a rare Kakiemon bowl for £40,000. Happy hunting!

### ▼ ARITA PLATE
*c.1720; 25.5cm (10½in) diam;*
**£8,000–1,200**
Made from the 17th century on, this blue and white ware was one of the first to reach the West. Created by the same potters as Imari porcelain, the blue of the early examples is slightly blurred, becoming more controlled by the date of this dish. Pieces tend to be thickly potted and are occasionally covered in fine, spider's web crazing never found on Chinese porcelain. Shapes, including covered jars and tankards, copied European examples. Look for three, five or seven stilt marks on the base, caused by the supports on which the objects rested in the kiln.

### ▲ KAKIEMON VASE
*c.1690; 35.5cm (14in) high;*
**£4,000–5,000**
The milky white body of this vase, its matt surface and slightly greasy looking sheen, are typical of Kakiemon wares, made from the 17th century onwards. Early wares were boldly painted with landscapes, flowers, shrubs and birds on branches; decoration became more refined during the 18th century. This piece is typically restrained, using a palette of turquoise, iron red, green, lavender, blue and yellow enamels painted on the glaze. Some later pieces also use a brownish purple. Rims of plates and bowls are edged in brown.

### ▲ SATSUMA VASE
*c.1890; 23cm (9¼in) high;*
**£1,500–2,000**
The Satsuma range of densely painted, richly gilded buff-coloured earthenware, exemplifed by this vase, has a clear to slightly yellowy glaze, often with a fine crackle. Decoration is applied over the glaze. Most pieces were made after 1880. The best, signed on the base with a seal mark, come from Kyoto. Beautifully dressed women and samurai are often depicted, as well as naturalistic bird and flower scenes like those here. Quality varies greatly, but prices have risen steadily in the last ten years.

### ▲ HIRADO VASE
*c.1840; 30.5cm (12in) high;*
**£1,200–1,500**
A chalky white body with a soft, satiny glaze characterizes these high-quality blue and white wares made in the mid- and late 18th and 19th centuries at the Mikawachi kilns for the lords of Hirado, an island near Arita. The most desirable pieces were produced around 1840, as was this vase, and consist mainly of ornamental wares. The pure white clay lent itself to intricate piercing and finely carved detail on cricket cages, lanterns and finely modelled figures of children and animals subtly decorated with blue.

## IMARI JAR AND COVER
*1880; 63.5cm (25in) high;*
**£2,500–3,500**

Painted with a striking palette of iron red, blue and gilt, Imari wares were made in Arita from c.1700, but shipped to Europe from the port of Imari – hence the name. An instant success in the West, the patterns (originally based on textiles) were copied by many English and Continental factories during the 18th century and by Samson of Paris during the 19th century. Among the most popular pieces with collectors are the garnitures, comprising three lidded vases and a pair of trumpet vases. Vases with vertical ribbing tend to be 19th-century.

Wisteria was a popular flower in the West so Japanese decorators frequently used it as a decorative motif.

Cranes were a favourite emblem of 19th-century Japanese porcelain; the design very much echoes that found on Chinese fabrics and brocades.

This deep orange/red is almost the colour of ripe tomatoes and is several shades deeper than on the earlier wares.

The porcelain body of this piece is a very pure white. On 18th-century Imari, look out for a bluish/green tinge to the body.

It is common for 19th-century pieces to be decorated with figures. Here, strong use is made of gilding.

This blending of dark and pale blue in one area is very much a feature of 19th-century pieces. On an 18th-century example, the two shades would be used separately.

Formalized decoration around the base tends to predominate on 19th-century wares.

### LOOK FOR
- Brown rims on the edge of plates or vases – a sign of quality.
- Figural subjects, animals, birds or insects, which all add value to the piece.
- Quality enamelwork, often evident in border designs
- Pieces that bear a mark

### AVOID
- Worn gilding.
- Scratched enamels and interiors.
- Wares which have been used for fruit and become damaged by their acids.
- Blistered glazes, black speckling or any disfiguring of the decoration

### VALUE NOTE
In real terms the market for Japanese porcelain was at a high 15 years ago. Since then demand appears to have dropped and prices have fallen.

### COLLECTORS' TIP
Look out for better-quality eggshell services and vases, made c.1900–25 by such companies as Noritake and Samurai China. Prices are still low: vast quantities were made and much has survived, stored safely in display cabinets owing to its fragility. Quality varies enormously, but every piece is hand-painted

# Maiolica, Faïence and Delft

Technically, maiolica, faïence and delft are the same type of earthenware covered with a tin enamel glaze (glass opacified by the addition of tin oxide) but each looks quite different by virtue of where it was made and the style in which it was decorated. Maiolica was made in Italy, faïence in France, Germany and Spain, and delft in Holland and England.

The very earliest tin glazes were used on Babylonian brick reliefs around 1000 BC, but the technique then disappeared, not emerging again until about the 8th century, when it was rediscovered by Persian potters, who spread their ideas through their conquests along the northern coast of Africa, into Spain and on to Italy by way of the island of Maiorca (now Majorca), hence the name maiolica. The work done in Italy during the Renaissance was pre-eminent, from centres in Venice in the north to Sicily in the south.

The technique passed into France over the Pyrenees, but didn't become established until later, when the work being done at Faenze in Italy influenced potters at Lyon and gave the French version its name. Later still, in the 17th century, several potteries sprang up in the Dutch town of Delft on the site of breweries destroyed by fire. The Dutch dominated the scene during the 17th and early 18th centuries, their style and decoration emulating imported wares from China. They took their ideas to England at the end of the 16th century and potteries soon began to grow in London where chargers were made, backed in lead glaze apart from the wells, which were tin glazed. English delft spread after 1640, promoted by King Charles I, although its production suffered a lull during the Commonwealth period. By the beginning of the 18th century, however, there were thriving factories in London, Bristol, Liverpool, Dublin and Belfast. All these centres benefited from having ready export markets in America.

Towards the end of the 18th century, new types of bodies such as creamware, began to be developed in Staffordshire and soon affected the production of tin-glazed wares all over Europe. The Dutch carried on making delft, but also began importing English goods. The French industry was adversely affected by the Revolution, and in Italy the manufacture of porcelain and creamware began to supersede that of maiolica.

▼ **PAIR OF DUTCH DELFT FLOWER VASES**
*1740; 25.4cm (10in) high;*
**£1,200–1,800 the pair**
Delft was such an important centre for tin-glazed earthenware in Holland that the name became synonymous with all pieces made in both Holland and England. At first, potters copied Chinese wares but later moved on to silver and metalware shapes. This distinctive goblet shape with heavy scroll handles is typical of Dutch work of the period, as is the blue and white decoration.

▲ **ENGLISH DELFT COMMEMORATIVE PLATE**
*1738; 23cm (9in) diameter;*
**£4,000–6,000**
Dated subjects in English delftware are always at a premium and this plate has the added interest of being inscribed in memory of Queen Caroline, the wife of King George II (1727–60). It also made a statement of loyalty at a time of political unrest. The Jacobite Rebellion – when "Bonnie Prince Charlie" returned to try to reclaim the crown lost by his grandfather, James II – was brewing and was not finally suppressed until 1745 at the Battle of Culloden.

▲ **VENETIAN MAIOLICA DRUG JAR**
*c.1550; 25.4cm (10in) high;*
**£600–800**
These pots were used primarily by apothecaries and you often see them labelled in Latin with the names of their original contents. This distinctive style of decoration with a portrait medallion painted with the head of a classical warrior and the strong cobalt blue and mustard yellow, indicate that it was made in the Venice area, as does the top heavy or *alberello* shape. The flaking of the glaze around the base and the rim shows that the glaze sits on top of a brown earthenware body.

▲ **FRENCH FAÏENCE PLATE**
*1760; 24cm (9½in) diameter;*
**£120–180**
This plate shows that pottery can be decorated to the same high standard as porcelain. The flower sprays, the central tulip and the trailing daisies are skilfully painted, and the colours are typical of French faïence. The artist has taken care to apply a line of brown around the rim, as in much Oriental porcelain. The shape follows the design of silver of the period. The plate was made at a time when French porcelain manufacture was monopolised by the Sèvres factory.

## CASTELLI PLATE
*c.1740; 30.5cm (12in) diameter;*
**£1,200–1,800**
This is an example of maiolica decoration at its most elaborate. The artist is making the subject absolutely clear and demonstrating the breadth of his skill. The central figure is emblematic of the season of summer. The soft palette of pale blue and yellow is typical of the work done at Castelli, as is the active, busy subject matter and the high quality of the painting.

Despite being from the 18th century, this type of scroll work is very much in the style of the Renaissance. The plate was probably commissioned by a Cardinal: you can see his armorial here, surmounted by a Cardinal's hat. These borders often incorporate mythical beasts or grotesques. They are also often chipped because the tin glaze sits on top of the body and is vulnerable.

Here the three months of the summer are symbolized, not only by the central figure in all his magnificence and strength, but by these smaller symbols of Cancer, Leo and Virgo, painted within circular panels.

### COLLECTORS' NOTES
Together with early Florentine wares of relatively simple form and decoration, the finely executed *istoriato* plates (story plates, often depicting a scene from antiquity or a biblical text) decorated by the artists of Urbino are the most sought after. Collectors of these tin-glazed wares are more tolerant of chips and cracks than collectors of later pottery and porcelain, because the glaze sits on top of the body and is particularly vulnerable.

### COLLECTING TIP
18th-century maiolica is still relatively affordable. A pair of good Castelli plaques, decorated with figures set within country landscapes or classical ruins, can be bought for a sum in the region of £2,000–3,000, whereas an earlier *istoriato* plate made in Urbino, Deruta, Palermo or Venice could cost as much as £20,000–30,000.

# 18th-Century Continental Porcelain

When the first Chinese porcelain began to arrive in Europe during the Middle Ages, it caused enormous excitement. European potters began trying to imitate it in the late 16th century, after royalty and the aristocracy had formed significant collections of Oriental wares. The first artificial porcelain was made in Italy c.1575 under the patronage of the Grand Duke of Tuscany, a brief experiment which stood unrepeated until a more successful attempt took place in France at the end of the 17th century in Rouen.

The French were content to work with soft-paste and numerous factories sprang up in the early years of the 18th century, including those at Chantilly (1725), Mennecy (1734) and later at St. Cloud (1764), using the Orient as their source of inspiration. But in Germany, the Elector of Saxony's passion for Japanese and Chinese porcelain made him determined to find the formula for true porcelain and control its manufacture.

His dream was realized when Johann Friedrich Bottger, an alchemist imprisoned by the Elector when he failed to make gold from lead and copper to finance the Elector's foreign wars, developed the first successful hard-paste bodies by 1709. The Meissen factory was established in 1710 and its wares became wildly fashionable throughout Europe.

The secret spread and factories opened in Vienna, Hochst and Furchstenberg. Towards the end of the 18th century, hard-paste porcelain was being manufactured all over Europe, but Sèvres had taken over as the leader in fashion by about 1757 under the protection of King Louis XV whose edicts ensured that the manufacture of porcelain was suppressed elsewhere in France.

Successful factories also operated in Holland, Italy and Denmark during the 18th century. The work done in soft-paste at Capodimonte from 1743–59 is legendary. Many of the smaller factories, whose wares are now highly sought after, were fairly short-lived, unable by the end of the century to compete with some of the new, cheaper-to-produce bodies such as creamware developed by Josiah Wedgwood in England.

**◄ MEISSEN FIGURE OF A LADY OF THE ORDER OF THE PUG DOGS**
*1745; 29cm (11½in) high;* **£7,000**
18th-century Meissen figures are generally the most sought after, and this exquisite example was modelled by the factory's master himself, Johann Joachim Kandler. Made in hard-paste, the porcelain is a stark white and the detailing crisp because the glaze fuses perfectly with the body, allowing for much clearer definition. The pug dog relates to the secret friendly society of which it became the symbol. The lady is modelled on Johanne Charlotte, Princess of Anhalt-Dessau who governed the independent German state, the Bishopric of Herford.

**▲ PORCELAIN SUCRIER AND COVER**
*1795; 15cm (6in) high;* **£250**
This piece was made at one of a number of factories that began making hard-paste porcelain in the Paris area after deposits of kaolin were found there in 1768. They flouted the Royal edicts which stated that porcelain could only legally be manufactured at Sèvres and got away with it because they were protected by important members of the aristocracy. The bodies are a stark white and the shapes are in the neoclassical style. The gilding is thin and wears easily. Originally, this knop would have been completely gilded.

**▲ FRANKENTHAL TEA BOWL AND SAUCER**
*c.1770; cup 5.5cm (2¼in) high, saucer 14cm (5½in) in diameter;* **£1,300**
The Frankenthal factory started manufacture under the direction of Paul-Antoine Hannong under the patronage of Elector Karl Theodor in 1755. The body is a fine, white hard-paste which declined in quality after 1774, and the glaze is slightly grey and grainy. This tea bowl and saucer is from a service entitled "Goldchinesien," showing figures and landscapes richly painted in gold. Delicate flower painting, chinoiserie scenes, and landscapes featuring classical ruins are also typical.

**► SÈVRES CREAM JUG**
*1770, 7.5cm (3in) high;* **£500**
Sèvres soft-paste porcelain has a creamy white body which does not reflect much light but shines from within. These soft, colourful enamels sink into the underlying glaze so they look perfectly fused with the body. The gilding is very skilled, matching the quality of the decoration, and the shape is quite novel.

## MEISSEN TEAPOT
*c.* 1770; 12.7cm (5in) high;
**£600–800**
The shape of this delightful, well-balanced teapot with its four bulbous lobes (known as *quatre-lobed*) is distinctly German. The spout extends away from the body in the same proportions as the handle, which is of a type that can be found on English teapots from a slightly later date.

Just as on the flowers, a faint shadow has been painted down the length of the centipede to create a three-dimensional effect. These insects were always beautifully painted and anatomically correct. They were often positioned so as to disguise any underlying blemishes caused by firing on an otherwise perfect body.

The gold paste was actually mixed with honey before being applied, which gave this wonderful bronzed effect. It has survived in good condition and is relatively restrained compared with that on earlier Meissen teapots. The elaborate lattice and cell design on the spout with the trailing husk pattern was popular during this classical revival period.

Applied with very fine brush strokes, the quality of this painting is superb. If you look closely, you can see that the artist has tried to create a three-dimensional effect by adding a faint shadow around the edge of the sprays. These European flowers painted on porcelain are usually referred to as *Deutsche Blumen*.

Unglazed bases like this tend to be a feature of 18th-century Meissen. The true hard-paste porcelain body did not absorb moisture, but an English soft-paste porcelain equivalent had to be glazed. So hard was the porcelain that it was difficult to get the famous crossed swords mark to adhere to the unglazed biscuit body – one of the reasons why, as here, the mark is often faint.

### COLLECTORS' NOTES
• Much 18th-century English porcelain is unmarked but the reverse is true of Continental pieces, so buy a marked example if at all possible

• Try to buy pieces that retain as much of their original gilding as possible.
• Look for good detailed figural decoration, especially set within all-over landscapes rather than

• Decoration depicting specific professions and events, such as harbour scenes and battles, is more highly sought after than decoration showing more general, idyllic pastoral

### COLLECTING TIP
If you're prepared to accept thin gilding, the Paris factories still offer very good value for money, and the neo-classical shapes sit well in a contem-

# 18th-Century English Porcelain

The English passion for the ritual of tea drinking, first introduced after the Restoration in about 1660, is responsible for many of the beautiful 18th-century porcelain pieces produced there. In the mid-17th century, the East India Company ships, loaded with fine hard-paste porcelain teawares exported from China, arrived at British ports on a regular basis. The rustic, thickly potted goods produced by English potters could not compete with these delicate tea bowls and pots, so feverish experiments with paste began, at first in an effort to rival the Chinese, and then the Continental porcelain that had started to arrive. The useful tea- and tablewares were made to rival the former (the Bow factory was often referred to as New Canton) and the ornamental wares, such as the figures, were made to emulate Meissen and Nymphenburg.

From the mid-1740s, factories at Bow, Chelsea, Worcester and Derby, among many others in England, were producing artificial or soft-paste porcelain. The granular consistency was difficult to fire and expensive in comparison with pottery, so pieces tended to be small. Many of the shapes followed those manufactured in silver. In fact, Nicholas Sprimont, one of the founders of the Chelsea factory, started out as a silversmith.

It was William Cookworthy, an eminent citizen of Plymouth, who perfected the formula for hard-paste porcelain in England. He patented it in 1768 and production began soon afterwards. Finding the running of the factory too heavy a load on his own, Cookworthy moved it to Bristol, where his friend and business partner Richard Champion could play a more active role. In 1774, Cookworthy retired and Champion took over.

1784 is a highly significant date in the history of English ceramics. Parliament passed the Communication Act which reduced the duty paid on tea from 119 percent to 12½ percent, ending the profitability of smuggling it. Tea became available to a much wider range of people, and the demand for pots and cups in which to serve the drink exploded. Added to this, Greek- and Roman-inspired decoration eclipsed the fashion for things Oriental. By 1798, the East India Company had reduced its imports of Chinese porcelain to almost nothing.

**▲ CHELSEA CAULIFLOWER TUREEN AND COVER**
*Red Anchor period (1752–57); 12.7cm (5in) high;* **£1,000**
Chelsea produced a range of novelty tureens and covers, including life-size rabbits as well as birds and other animals and vegetables. It was founded in 1745 by Nicholas Sprimont and Charles Gouyn, a silversmith and a jeweller. The works were bought in 1770 by William Duesbury of Derby who continued to run them until 1784. Red Anchor, so-called after the mark on the base, is considered to be the finest period in the factory's history. Other periods are the incised-triangle and raised-anchor periods, 1745–52, and the gold-anchor period, 1759–69.

**▲ CHAMPION'S BRISTOL CREAM JUG**
*c.1780; 10cm (4in) high;* **£300**
This cream jug came from the only factory making hard-paste porcelain in England until the patent was sold to the Newhall factory in 1781. The small sprigs of flowers sparsely decorating the body are quite typical, as are the ribbon-tied laurel garland around the neck in a distinctive clear, bright green, and the pronounced ear-shaped handle. The body is a translucent white, covered with a clear, greyish glaze.

**◄ DERBY FIGURE OF DIANA**
*c.1775; 30.5cm (12in) high;* **£800**
The earliest figures made at Derby date from around 1752–3 and are known as "dry edge" figures because the lower edge of the base was wiped free of glaze. This later example is quite thickly glazed and painted with enamels. The floral bocage applied to the base and to one side of the figure is quite typical of the factory. Pieces also exhibit distinctive patch marks on the base showing where they were supported in the kiln.

**▲ WORCESTER TANKARD**
*c.1775; 17.8cm (7in) high;* **£500**
Made during the first period at the factory under Dr John Wall, this is typically thinly potted and decorated to the very highest standards. The arrangement of flower sprays and garlands, with the central urn in the neo-classical style of the late 18th century, is a hallmark of the factory, as are the enamel colours of green, puce, iron red and pink. The intricate gilding stands out strongly against the underglaze bands of blue around the rim and the base of the tankard.

## WORCESTER CREAM JUG
*1770; 5cm (2in) high;* **£1,000**

It is hard to believe that this beautifully proportioned piece of fragile porcelain was made to be used, but it was. Covered with an even, colourless glaze with a slightly greenish tint, it is thinly potted, as was often the case with the small wares produced by the Worcester factory in the late 18th century.

The factory at Worcester was founded by Benjamin Lund in 1752, using moulds bought from an earlier factory at Bristol. The early pieces were painted with Chinese-inspired scenes and made to compete with the vast quantities of imports from China. Worcester used a paste containing soapstone, which gave the factory a commercial edge because their teawares could withstand boiling water.

**COLLECTORS' NOTES**
• Get to grips with the difference betweeen the porous, granular look of soft-paste sandwiched between a thick, glassy glaze and the dense, white glassiness of hard-paste where the glaze is fused with the body.
• Learn to recognise the various marks of the factories.
• Different factories favoured particular enamels, which helps with identification – for example, a distinctive green is often found on Derby leaf and flower decoration; a peculiar blue is evident on Bow figures; and a vibrant underglaze cobalt blue is seen on Longton Hall figures.

**LOOK FOR**
• Pieces in pristine condition, wherever possible.
• Well-defined facial expression.
• Skilful floral decoration.

**AVOID**
• Unsympathetic restoration work, which pays no attention to the original.

**COLLECTING TIP**
Later Derby figures and decorated teawares from the Caughley pottery in Shropshire still represent good value for money. Neither has seen much movement in price during the last 10 years.

Other factories used this design and shape of handle, but none exhibits quite the same fine detail you can see here in the way that the sinuous, eel-like lamprey grips the body of the jug with its sucker mouth.

This is just what you'd expect to see on a piece of Worcester of this period – crisp clean, beautifully defined moulding. Look at the detail on the fish and the scallop shell. Shells were popular decorative motifs in Georgian England, and the crossed tridents under the tail reflect the period when Britannia ruled the waves.

Worcester made strong use of yellow at this time. It was a difficult colour to fire, so the skill of the craftsmen shines through here in the vibrant effect they managed to achieve.

Look carefully and you can see how the glaze has pooled slightly in the recesses, giving a slightly greenish tinge, mixed with minute fragments of black pitting which is simply dirt off the floor of the kiln. The inside rims of many Worcester pieces were wiped clean of glaze to avoid this pooling.

# 18th-Century English Pottery

The pottery industry at the beginning of the 18th century operated in much the same way as it had during the 17th century. All pieces were still individually hand-potted, decorated and glazed, with the staple products being lead-glazed earthenwares and tin-glazed delft wares.

Towards the end of the 18th century, the industry was revolutionised by Josiah Wedgwood whose name stands head and shoulders above any others in Staffordshire, although he was not alone in developing Black Basalt, a dense, hardened stoneware, pearlware and creamware. He was working in Staffordshire, which increased in importance as a centre for pottery making, but Nottingham, London, Liverpool, Bristol, Leeds and various other centres in Yorkshire were also producing stonewares, creamware and delftware which are all widely collected today.

Slip-glazed wares with their characteristic naive decoration in white slip (liquid clay) against a brown earthenware body continued to be made as they had been in the 17th century, as did the green-glazed wares generally referred to as Whieldon and Wedgwood types. In the 1740s, a dense red stoneware started to be made by the Elers brothers who set up in Stoke-on-Trent, emulating the Yixing wares being exported from China.

## ▲ TORTOISESHELL GLAZED TEAPOT AND COVER

*c.1750; 10.2cm (4in) high;* **£400**
Tortoiseshell glazed wares are among the most attractive pieces produced at this time. This small teapot has a crab-stock spout and face masks above its three paw feet. Copying the silver shapes of the time, it shows enormous humour and inventiveness in design. Thinly potted, it is curiously applied with a trailing grapevine. The bird's head is missing from the knop, otherwise it would be worth £600–800.

## ▲BLACK GLAZED COFFEE POT

*1750; 25.4cm (10in) high;* **£600–800**
This mirror black colour was used by Staffordshire factories but it is usually associated with the Shropshire pottery of Jackfield. Like the teapot, *left*, it is also copying a silver shape. The decoration and the bird finial are heightened with cold gilding, applied after the piece has been fired and cooled. The theory is that these black glazed wares were popular because against them, the white skin of a lady's hand was admirably accentuated.

## ▲ CAULIFLOWER TEAPOT AND COVER

*c.1775; 15.2cm (6in) high;* **£600–800**
These green glazed pieces are associated with the period when Wedgwood and Whieldon worked together, but are not usually attributable to a particular factory. The glaze was often applied to novelty forms like this cauliflower teapot, as well as cabbage leaf plates and pineapple coffee pots. Note how well-balanced the teapot is and how bright the glazes still look.

## ▼ SALT-GLAZED STONEWARE PLATE

*1745–50; 23cm (9in) diameter;* **£250–350**
A shovelful of salt was thrown into the kiln while red hot, hence the name given to these dense, white, very light stonewares. Most of the pieces cannot be attributed to particular makers. It was a medium which lent itself to well-defined, crisp moulding, seen here in the form of a portrait of Frederick of Prussia and the sentiment, "Success To The King Of Prussia And His Forces" on the rim of the plate. The best salt-glazed stonewares were considered acceptable substitutes for porcelain and decorated with onglaze enamels. Apart from plates, salt-glazed stoneware was used to make tureens and a whole range of novelty teapots, modelled as pectin shells, camels and houses.

### ▶ LEEDS CREAMWARE MUG
*1777; 15.2cm (6in) high; £200–300*

It is worth noting that this piece would be worth double were it not cracked and chipped, but it is still a charming example of Leeds creamware and is desirable because it is dated as well as named. Thinly potted and with a good strap handle, these Leeds creamwares are covered with a glaze which has a pale, greeny yellow hue when it pools in recesses. The mixture used to make up the glaze contained arsenic!

### ▶ STAFFORDSHIRE PEARLWARE MUG
*1780–90; 18cm (7in) high; £100–150*

Pearlware is a white earthenware body covered with a bluish white glaze, developed by Wedgwood and then manufactured extensively in Staffordshire and in Leeds, eventually replacing creamware. The decoration on this mug, which is printed with flower sprays, illustrates how the unstable cobalt dioxide often ran into the glaze to give blue "haloes" around the print. It didn't always happen and sharper definitions are preferred by collectors.

### ▶ JASPERWARE VASE AND COVER
*c.1790–95; 30cm (12in) high; £500–700*

This shade of blue found such favour in the 18th century, that it has been known as "Wedgwood Blue" ever since. Jasperware was the name Wedgwood gave to the hard, fine-grained stoneware he introduced in 1775, after many experiments, and which allowed him to manufacture classical style vases like this one on a grand scale. He also used Jasperware to make a wide variety of reliefs, portrait medallions, cups and saucers, cameos and other ornamental wares. Wedgwood employed some of the top English modellers and sculptors of the day, including John Flaxman and George Stubbs.

### ▶ STAFFORDSHIRE CREAMWARE TRANSFER PRINTED JUG
*1785–90; 30cm (12in) high; £300–400*

Mass-produced and transfer-printed, this jug is a good example of the types of wares being manufactured by the end of the century, when technology had moved forward apace. The scene here shows a spinning machine and the print is signed by the engraver, J. Baddeley. Jugs of the same shape were produced in Liverpool at the Herculaneum factory and decorated with prints supplied by Messrs. Sadler and Green, also of Liverpool, which was one of the pre-eminent names in the field of transfer printing.

## COLLECTORS' NOTES
• Perfect pieces should be regarded with some suspicion. So much of this 18th-century pottery has been damaged that a perfect piece will command a premium, but it may have been invisibly repaired by a good restorer. Honest damage is preferable to over-restoration.
• The vast majority of pieces, apart from creamwares and Wedgwood wares, are unmarked. Pieces which do bear makers' marks are there-fore highly sought after. Look for impressed marks, which are preferred to printed or painted marks.
• If you are prepared to accept chips and cracks, most objects from this period are still relatively affordable so there is plenty of scope to build a nice collection.
• The shapes tried to echo silver shapes of the period, so if a piece looks as if it may have a Georgian silver counterpart, it may well be 18th century.

## AVOID
• Pots which are heavily crazed and stained.
• Those worn through with use or with rubbed glaze.
• Pieces with inferior printing, loss of definition or a run or blurred glaze.

## COLLECTING TIP
Look out for English creamware decorated in Holland. During the 18th century, the Dutch imported blank creamware from England and decorated it, often with portraits of members of the House of Orange as well as related emblems such as orange trees. They also favoured religious scenes with the relevant biblical text inscribed in Dutch. Decoration is relatively naive and colourful and the wares turn up at auction all over the world. Still underrated and not much sought after, they represent good value for money. Price is determined by subject: Jonah and the Whale or Noah's Ark will always be preferred to a crucifixion scene.

# 19th-Century Continental Porcelain

During the early part of the century, the import and export of wares across Europe were adversely affected by the Napoleonic Wars which raged on several fronts. The resulting political instability did little to promote the growth of commerce between the nations. Until around 1830 most porcelain was manufactured for the home markets, but after the capture and eventual death of Napoleon Bonaparte, and the warming of relations between England and France, much Sèvres porcelain was exported to England and the United States. The ornate style was enormously popular in both countries and no wealthy household was complete without its enviable collection of French porcelain. By the end of the 19th century, the most important centre of French porcelain manufacture was Limoges.

In Germany, the Meissen factory continued to hold the premier position in porcelain production, relying upon the reissuing, remodelling and adapting of 18th-century and neo-classical-inspired wares. Nymphenburg and Berlin continued in the same tradition. Meanwhile, the neighbouring Austrian factory at Vienna also went on making richly decorated and often ostentatious pieces which demonstrated the skill of their factory artists, especially the figure painters who worked in the distinctive neo-classical style of the celebrated Swiss painter, Angelica Kauffmann.

The Italian porcelain factories in Naples found a ready market for vases and tablewares finely modelled in low and high relief with classical figure subjects in the manner of the 18th-century Doccia factory.

**▲ SÈVRES-STYLE PORCELAIN BOWL**
*1860; 45.5cm (18in) high;* **£600–800**
A genuine Sèvres piece, made in the 18th century, would have been mounted within an ormolu frame rather than in gilt metal as this has been. This is very much a pastiche of an 18th-century example, and was much cheaper to produce. The quality of the porcelain, the gilding and the mounts fall well below the standard achieved a hundred years earlier. Nevertheless, these objects now have considerable value in their own right.

**◄ SÈVRES-STYLE PAIR OF VASES**
*1870; 35.5cm (14in) high;*
**£800–1,200**
Although these are decorative and pleasing to the eye, they were very much a commercial proposition and hurriedly painted in order to sell to a market hungry for Sèvres-style porcelain. The subjects are in the manner of François Boucher (1703–70), the French painter and designer who greatly influenced the course of design in the decorative arts until about 1770. A pair of vases like this would quite likely have been shipped to the United States or England.

**▲ PAIR OF PARIS COLOURED BISCUIT PORCELAIN FIGURES OF ORIENTALS BY PAUL DUBOY**
*1870; 45.5cm (18in) high;* **£800–1,000**
The French were fascinated with the Orient in the later 19th century, as can be seen by the number of figural subjects they produced which portrayed Orientals, particularly the Chinese. Here, the figures of a Maharajah and his wife represent the highest standard of colour enamelling and gilding found on biscuit porcelain figures of this date. Earlier examples in a high-gloss glaze can often be attributed to the Paris maker Jacob Petit. This pair might well have been intended for the British market.

▶ **PAIR OF
VIENNESE EWERS**
*1860; 35.5cm (14in) high;*
**£1,000–1,500**
Typically ornate, these
ewers display the Viennese
preference for finely detailed
figural subjects. In common
with most of their tablewares,
these were always intended to
be admired rather than used:
they started out in the display
cabinet, rather than gravitating
there from the drawing room or
dining room. The overall reserve
of deep claret and imperial green
is embellished with rich gilding
on an underlying raised enamel
to give it some texture.

▲ **PAIR OF VIENNESE NEO-CLASSICAL
VASES AND COVERS**
*1860; 45.5cm (18in) high;* **£2,000–3,000 the pair**
The Swiss painter Angelica Kauffmann (1741–1807), inspired
much of the type of decoration seen on these vases, which were
produced in both England and on the Continent. These scenes
are set against pale lemon reserves richly gilded with scrolling
and fronded leaves. The domed covers are topped with flower-
bud finials and the vases are raised on squared-shaped plinths.
Late 19th-century Vienna wares have a beehive mark on the base
in underglaze blue, often accompanied by a title. Various other
factories set up in Vienna at this time and used the same mark
in onglaze rather than underglaze blue, but the sheer quality of
the decoration distinguishes the earlier factory from the others.
Berlin produced similar ornamental vases throughout the 19th
century, marked in underglaze blue with a sceptre motif.

◀ **PAINTED BERLIN
PLAQUE**
*1880; 23 x 12.5cm (9 x 5in);* **£800**
These Berlin KPM factory plaques
are examples of the best in late
19th-century portrait and figural
decoration. They became popular
from the 1880s onwards and are
still highly sought after today,
particularly by Japanese collectors. They were fired absolutely
flat, which is a difficult procedure
to achieve, and if you look
closely, it is often possible to see
tiny pinhead bubbles, caused
during the firing process.

◀ **MEISSEN FIGURAL GROUP**
*c.1880; 15cm (6in) high;* **£500–800**
Many of the 18th-century figures continued
to be popular throughout the following
century and were reissued on reworked
bases: this is a late 19th-century copy of
an 18th-century model, known as *The
Gardener and His Wife.* An 18th-century
example of this figure group would
be worth nearer £3,000, and it
might also be marked on the visible
surface of the base, which would be
filled in. 19th-century examples have a
hollow base with a larger, underglaze
blue crossed swords mark under
the base.

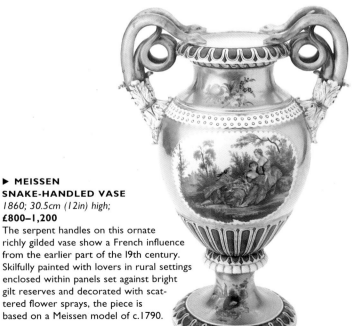

▶ **MEISSEN
SNAKE-HANDLED VASE**
*1860; 30.5cm (12in) high;*
**£800–1,200**
The serpent handles on this ornate
richly gilded vase show a French influence
from the earlier part of the 19th century.
Skilfully painted with lovers in rural settings
enclosed within panels set against bright
gilt reserves and decorated with scattered flower sprays, the piece is
based on a Meissen model of c.1790.

**COLLECTOR'S NOTES**
• The premier factories
continue to be eagerly
sought after and no doubt
will continue to be so for
generations to come.
• The price paid for 19th-
century Meissen figures can
be little more than the
equivalent model produced
by the factory today, and
there is often a waiting list
for a modern example.
• 19th-century Viennese
wares often demonstrated
not only the virtuosity of the
artist but also the immense
skill of the gilder.

# Staffordshire Wares

Small family groups of craft potters worked all over England from medieval times, but from the 17th century onwards the abundance of coal and red clay discovered close to the surface around Burslem in Staffordshire gave its potters the edge, so that by 1710 Burslem was probably the largest pottery centre in Great Britain.

The inventions and clever marketing strategies of Josiah Wedgwood helped to promote the industry still further. His creamware (or Queen's Ware as it came to be known) found great favour with the royal family and attracted many wealthy aristocratic clients. By 1740 china clay and flint were being transported to the Potteries, to provide the ingredients for the fine white bodies which began to rival the imported porcelain from China. After 1777, when the Trent and Mersey Canal was opened, the celebrated wares of Staffordshire could be transported in large quantities to the port of Liverpool, and shipped to new markets opening up all over the world, particularly in the United States.

Nowhere was the advance of the Industrial Revolution more apparent than in the Staffordshire potteries. This small landlocked area in the centre of England was serviced by canals that soon gave way to the rapidly growing railway network, and, later, improvements in the road system. The cottage industry of the mid-18th century was superseded by factory mass production with improved techniques by the early 19th century. Countless brick bottle ovens belched out fumes which polluted the atmosphere to such a degree that, on a still day, the sun was obliterated and day became night.

Further inventions developed during the early 19th century included new bodies, particularly stone and bone china, and transfer printing from copper plates, which meant that one printer could do the work previously handled by several decorators.

**STAFFORDSHIRE BLUE AND WHITE TRANSFER PRINTED EARTHENWARE SERVING DISH**
c.1830; 40.6cm (16in) long;
**£300–400**
Made in a design known to have been manufactured by Bridgewood and Harris, the scene, entitled *North End, Hampstead* (then a rural suburb of London) shows figures walking along an embankment above a lane, observing a passing horse-drawn carriage.

You often find these joins on transfer printed wares where the tissue paper print around the edge of the dish has been placed with no great effort made to conceal where the two ends meet. The borders were often decorated by apprentices while the centres were crafted by the most skilled and experienced workers.

These floral surrounds (in this case large, luscious passion flowers) can help with dating. They became more common after c.1830, before which willow and temple designs were more prevalent.

A fair proportion of blue and white printed wares are not marked, but recent research has enabled many patterns to be attributed to specific factories. This dish is elaborately marked, but not, infuriatingly, with the name of the maker.

**COLLECTORS' NOTES**
The best known transfer-printed Willow pattern did not originate in China, as popular myth suggests. It was probably designed by Thomas Minton for the Caughley factory in Shropshire around 1780 and has since been copied by all the major factories. Although still in production, early examples are highly sought after. The design varies but always includes a willow tree, a temple, figures crossing a bridge and a distant land beneath two birds representing a pair of lovers.

Early shapes were directly copied from the Chinese export wares so popular during the late 18th century, but as the 19th century progressed, shapes became more elaborate. The pieces made during the Rococo Revival period of the 1830s often incorporate shell moulding and "C" and "S" scrolls.

The scene in the centre of this dish was printed by placing a single sheet over the well of the dish, which requires great dexterity to prevent creases from forming. The tonal quality was achieved during a previous stage, by the engraver who cut more deeply into the copper plate in certain areas, allowing the paper to soak up more ink.

# Other 19th-Century Staffordshire

As the 19th century progressed, the Staffordshire potteries consolidated their position as the most important centre of production of domestic and ornamental pottery and porcelain both in Britain and throughout the rest of the world.

The potters from the various Staffordshire factories produced stunning ceramic wares, combining inventive forms with fine painting and gilding. The growing middle class of both Victorian and American society could now afford not only a dinner service but added dessert and tea services to their china cupboards as well. Ornamental wares became equally affordable and the growth of the Staffordshire portrait figure enabled the working classes to own effigies of Queen Victoria or other well known celebrities of the age, together with an almost infinite variety of spill vases, pastille burners and the ubiquitous Staffordshire spaniels.

By the end of the 19th century, Spode, Wedgwood, Royal Doulton, Davenport, Minton, Ridgway, Mason's and other Staffordshire factories had earned a world-wide reputation for excellence. Just this one area in England, comprising five small towns, was able to produce ceramic goods as varied as a humble fire brick or simply-painted serving dish, to the finest parian statuary or hand painted vase that could rival the best that Sèvres had to offer. It provides rich picking for today's collectors, who can choose from a vast range of objects still circulating the world.

▶ **TABLEAU GROUP**
c.1830; 30.5cm (12in); **£10,000–15,000**
Wombwell's Menagerie, *right*, was a travelling circus that doubled up as a zoo between performances, travelling the length and breadth of the country. In 1835 it visited Wolverhampton and it is possible that Stoke potters made the trip south to see the extraordinary assembly of caged, wild beasts and were inspired to model them. Traditionally, these groups depicting the Menagerie are attributed to the factory of Obadiah Sherratt, who is also credited with a number of arbour groups showing subjects such as *The Blacksmith of Gretna Green and the Tithe Pig*, and *The Teetotallers and Dr Syntax*, an 18th century caricature of a cleric. Sherratt's work is rare and keenly sought after both in Europe and America.

◀ **C & J MASON JARDINIÈRE**
c.1820; 45.7cm (18in) high; **£1,000–1,500**
Mason's Patent Ironstone china grew in popularity during the 1820s because of its durable nature. The factory made a range of both useful and decorative wares including dinner services and ornamental vases with covers of oriental inspiration. Wares of the 1820 period tend to be impress-marked "Mason's Patent Ironstone China" whereas the later wares of the 1845 period have a crown and drape mark printed with the same lettering. The factory was bought by the Ashworth brothers in the late 19th century and the name changed. This century, it has reverted to the name Mason's Ironstone.

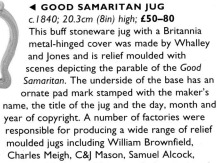

◀ **GOOD SAMARITAN JUG**
c.1840; 20.3cm (8in) high; **£50–80**
This buff stoneware jug with a Britannia metal-hinged cover was made by Whalley and Jones and is relief moulded with scenes depicting the parable of the *Good Samaritan*. The underside of the base has an ornate pad mark stamped with the maker's name, the title of the jug and the day, month and year of copyright. A number of factories were responsible for producing a wide range of relief moulded jugs including William Brownfield, Charles Meigh, C&J Mason, Samuel Alcock, Minton and Ridgway. Their popularity continued well into the last quarter of the century. The Britannia metal lids were an optional extra.

▶ **RIDGWAY DESSERT PLATE**
c.1845; 24cm (9½in) diameter; **£40–60**
The Ridgway factory, founded by Job Ridgway and his sons at Hanley in 1794, produced a variety of ceramic wares throughout the 19th century including the opaque china used to make this plate decorated in colourful onglaze enamels. The outlines are transfer printed with underglaze cobalt blue leaf and stem detail. Opaque china was popular in the mid-19th century. With its white earthenware body and translucent blue tinted glaze, at some factories this opaque china was known as pearlware, but the term should not be confused with the type of pearlware produced during the late 18th and early 19th century.

### ▶ SPODE VASE
*1820; 25.5cm (10in) high;*
**£2,000–3,500**
This two-handled vase is part of an extensive range of ornamental and useful bone china ware produced by the Spode factory in the early 19th century. This pattern (no.1166) is considered among the most desirable by collectors and dealers. Josiah Spode is generally credited with pioneering the development of bone china. His successor Josiah Spode II was appointed Potter and English Porcelain Manufacturer To His Royal Highness The Prince Of Wales after he toured the factory in 1806.

### ▶ MINTON MAJOLICA INKWELL
*c.1870; 22.9cm (9in) long;*
**£2,000–3,000**
The majolica-glazed wares of Minton, George Jones, Wedgwood, William Holdcroft and others, are peculiarly Victorian in both form and application. The term "Majolica" is loosely derived from Maiolica, the term for the colourful tin-glazed wares of Renaissance Italy, but the glazes used by Staffordshire potters were lead-based and could be applied in opaque or semi-translucent form. The range of wares produced varied greatly in scale, from small pin trays through to 9.84 metre (30ft) high ornamental fountains. Majolica jardinières were particularly popular.

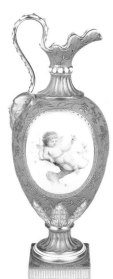

### ◀ MINTON EWER
*c.1875; 25.5cm (10in) high;*
**£300–400**
Minton was the most dynamic of all the 19th-century Staffordshire potteries, and employed many French modellers and decorators. Originally one of a pair, this French-inspired ewer, based on a silver or metalwork shape, has reserves of Bleu Celeste (as this shade of blue is known) which is derived from 18th-century Sèvres porcelain. The hand-painted panel by Antonin Boullemier, who specialized in painting small children, depicts a small winged cupid with a butterfly. The treatment of the subject is distinctly 19th-century, as is the trailed and raised gilding against the blue reserves.

### ▲ COPELAND DESSERT SERVICE
*c.1850; plates 25.5cm (10in) diameter;* **£2,500–3,500**
This selection of plates, taken from an extensive dessert service, illustrates the demand during this period for Sèvres-style table and decorative wares. The combination of white biscuit figures together with well-painted landscapes in the manner of Watteau, Boucher and other popular French artists from the previous century, attracted worldwide acclaim. Similar pieces were exhibited at The Great Exhibition of 1851 and resulted in substantial orders from the British aristocracy and the newly wealthy of North America.

### ▶ WEDGWOOD VASE AND COVER
*1880; 22.9cm (9in) high;*
**£250–350**
This Wedgwood Victoria ware vase and cover is a variation on the firm's Jasperware but uses an overlying glaze and a blue-grey and dark terracotta body. The effect of the glaze on the applied figures came close to simulating the time-consuming and expensive technique of *pâte-sur-pâte* popularised by the Minton factory and, to a lesser extent, by George Jones. Jasperware was greatly popular throughout the 19th century and is still manufactured today, but Victoria ware did not prove commercially successful and was relatively short-lived.

### COLLECTORS' NOTES
Because the field of pottery and porcelain from this period is so extensive, collectors tend to concentrate on specific types of ware – for example, Parian figures, majolica, ironstone or blue and white transfer printed pieces, all of which formed part of many factories' overall output. The alternative approach to collecting in this area is to concentrate on particular objects, so that you might decide, for instance, to seek out pastille burners, inkstands, miniature watering cans or flower baskets.

### COLLECTING TIP
The Minton factory has yet to be given the recognition it deserves as it was, without doubt, the leading innovator in 19th-century design and production. The wares don't command the same level of prices as those of other leading factories of the time.

# Staffordshire Figures

The earliest Staffordshire figures were made in the late 18th century to undersell Derby porcelain and to copy the fine but expensive figures produced by the top Continental factories such as Meissen. Square-based with a pearlware glaze, they graced many an elegant Georgian drawing room.

As the 19th century progressed mass production techniques improved and the increase in industrialization brought a burgeoning middle class with more disposable income and a desire for decorative ornaments. They could not afford the finest porcelain, but Staffordshire earthenware figures with flat, undecorated backs were

an ideal alternative. The real growth in production of the portrait figure kept pace with the illustrious reign of Queen Victoria. Indeed, the innumerable representations of Victoria, Prince Albert and their children were very popular.

By the end of the Victorian age, every cosy, overstuffed parlour in England contained its share of these fascinating figures which reflect the life and times in which they were made. From royalty to politicians, sportsmen to military and theatrical giants and even highwaymen – all were modelled in various guises and today are popular with collectors all over the world.

### ▶ THE GARDENER
*c.1825–30, 12.7cm (5in) high;*
**£200–300**
Based on a figure originally made in porcelain at the Derby factory, earlier versions of this rural character are sometimes found on a square base. He is well modelled with good facial detail, a feature very much designed to compete with porcelain. The bocage (leaf) decoration behind him is a prominent feature on early pieces, but, being hand-made, was expensive and later gave way to much cheaper strands of shredded clay.

### ◀ THE CUSHMAN SISTERS
*c.1850; 30cm (12in) high;*
**£400–600**
A good proportion of the value of this piece is tied up in the size: it is about as large as Staffordshire figures generally get and well-modelled and detailed. The Cushman sisters were American actresses famed for their portrayal of Romeo and Juliet. The high quality of this example and the way that the grass has been painted on the base suggest it may have been made by the firm of Kent and Parr.

### ◀ STANSFIELD HALL
*c.1855; 20cm (8in) high;*
**£200–300**
Serious collectors hanker after examples of the various models of the buildings and characters involved in the famous murder at Stansfield Hall in 1848, where James Rush, a farmer, shot the owner, Isaac Jermy, who was about to foreclose on a mortgage on Pot-Ash Farm where Rush lived with his mistress, Emily Sanford. He was hanged at Norwich Castle.

### ◀ QUEEN VICTORIA
*A young Queen Victoria riding side saddle, 1850; 15cm (6in) high;*
**£100–120**
The Queen was depicted in various guises and was naturally a good commercial subject. This is a relatively simple piece, showing her dressed in a cobalt blue gown. The title is quite naively moulded in low relief and heightened in an attractive, soft gilt. It is likely that originally this was one of a pair. Prince Albert would have had pride of place at the other end of the mantelpiece.

## STAFFORDSHIRE KING CHARLES SPANIEL
*c.1855; 15cm (6in) high;* **£150–250**

Animals were among the most popular subjects of the Staffordshire potters. Rarer species such as elephants, giraffes and zebras, which most people had the opportunity to see only in books, were hugely popular, but so were the more common domestic animals such as this flatback group of a King Charles spaniel and pup. That Queen Victoria herself had a King Charles spaniel earned the breed a special place in the nation's heart.

The face is typical of the date. It has well-detailed blue eyes with black pupils. Later examples have yellow eyes, again with black pupils. The well-modelled snout is heightened with grey enamel and his collar is embellished with a padlock, heightened with gilt. Later dogs often have a chain extending from the collar and trailing down across the body, again heightened with gilt.

This has been decorated in a rich, slightly irregular underglaze of cobalt blue and finished with a single line of flat, mellow gilt. If you find yourself looking at brassy, shiny, mirror-bright decoration, you know the piece was made after 1880.

Look for this exaggerated feathering achieved by painting in enamel over the glaze. This is a feature on the better quality, earlier examples.

The puppy is as well modelled as his mother. Notice how the potter has allowed his front paws to overlap the base, adding a further touch of realism. You would be less likely to find this feature on later pieces.

## COLLECTORS' NOTES

### LOOK FOR
- Finely detailed floral decoration.
- Good facial detail: feathered eyebrows and painted and scratched hair.
- Rouged cheeks, rosebud lips.
- Soft, mellow gilding.
- Where titled, elegant script.
- Finely painted captions.

### AVOID
- 20th-century examples made by the same families of potters

who worked in the 19th century, such as James Kent who potted up to the 1960s. The moulding is poorly defined and the hurried decoration involves strong use of copper lustre against dark green.
- Fakes, which can be recognized by their exaggerated crazing, mirror-bright gilding, poor decoration with no detail, fake dirt made by washing the crevices with a pale grey to give the impression of age and a glaze-free rim round the base.

### COLLECTING TIP
Scottish figures tend to get sold as Staffordshire and are well worth looking out for. The Portobello factory produced dogs, horses and lions. The dogs and lions have glass eyes. The horses have painted eyes, but all have a greyish body with a bluish glaze, and were made between 1860 and 1890.

### CHARACTERISTICS
**c.1820–1830**
- Earthenware body
- Blue/grey glaze

- Thickly potted base
- Decorated in the round

**c.1835–1845**
- Creamy white body prone to staining
- Colourless glaze
- Flat base, gently concaved with small, gas escape holes
- Decorated in the round

**c.1845–1900**
- Coarser earthenware body
- Blue-tinged glaze
- Concave base
- Gas escape hole in the back of the figure
- Decorated in the front only

# 19th-Century British and Irish Ceramics

Because the centre of manufacture during the 19th century pivoted on the five towns which make up the city of Stoke-on-Trent, it is easy to forget how many interesting and important factories were operating in other parts of the British Isles producing pottery and porcelain which is as widely valued and collected as its Staffordshire counterpart.

Yorkshire contained a large number of potteries in the Rotherham and Leeds area. In South Wales, the Swansea Pottery continued producing wares well into the middle of the 19th century and in Northern Ireland, the Belleek factory of County Fermanagh began to emerge as a formidable enterprise during the last quarter of the century.

Successful Scottish enterprises producing mainly tablewares included factories on the banks of the river Clyde and in Portobello in Edinburgh on the east coast. Slightly further north, the Kingdom of Fife was home to the Wemyss pottery of Robert Heron and Sons, today probably the most famous of all Scottish ceramic concerns.

In the northeast of England, particularly in the Sunderland area, there were at least a dozen potters active throughout the 19th century, many of whom were producing commemorative wares showing scenes such as the Sunderland Bridge printed in black. These were usually lustred in pink, a type of decoration known generically as Sunderland lustre. In the same area, the Tyneside-based St. Anthony's Pottery made a variety of animal figures such as cow creamers and horses.

The Coalport, Derby and Worcester factories, producing fine porcelain and bone china, probably offered the most serious competition to Staffordshire. Also, the Shropshire tilemakers Maw and Co. were one of the largest manufacturers in the country, exporting their wares to all corners of the world.

In the capital, brown salt-glazed stoneware was produced in the Doulton factory at Lambeth with similar types of pottery being produced at the Fulham pottery of C.J. Bailey. Collectors in this area tend not to spread their interests, but like to concentrate on the wares of a particular region or even of one factory.

**▲ DERBY GARNITURE**
*1825; vase 30.5cm (12in);* **£1,500–2,000 the set**
The neo-classical forms of this garniture (a set comprising a vase and two ewers) reflect the fashion of the times. The reserves are of gilt with Regency stripes and the handles of the central vase are formed as winged caryatids, a popular motif during the early years of the 19th century. The oval panels enclose rustic figures in pastoral settings, enamelled in colours. In 1815 the Derby factory was leased to Robert Bloor until its closure in 1848, and the wares such as these produced under his management are considered to be of inferior quality to those of the late 18th century. Garnitures are quite unusual and are therefore at a premium. You are far more likely to come across a pair of vases.

**▲ WORCESTER FLIGHT & BARR PART SERVICE**
*c.1807; teapot 15.2cm (6in) high;* **£700–1,000**
The popularity of this period of Worcester porcelain production has remained buoyant over the past 20 years. Each of these pieces is decorated in a "Japan" pattern, a European interpretation of Japanese Imari decoration which was taken up by most of the English porcelain manufacturers, but particularly by Derby and, in later years, the Royal Crown Derby China Works. The teapot is still on its original stand. The tea cup and coffee can (the name given to cylindrical cups) share the same saucer and are collectively referred to as a trio.

**WORCESTER PERIODS**

| | |
|---|---|
| 1751–74 | Dr Wall |
| 1774–83 | William Davies |
| 1783–92 | Flight |
| 1792–1804 | Flight & Barr |
| 1804–13 | Barr, Flight & Barr |
| 1813–40 | Flight, Barr & Barr |
| 1840–51 | Taken over by Chamberlains of Worcester |
| 1851–62 | Kerr and Binns |
| 1862–Present | Worcester Royal Porcelain Co. Ltd |

**▲ COALPORT FLOWER ENCRUSTED BOWL AND COVER**
*c.1825; 4in (10.2cm) high;* **£200–250**
Floral-encrusted porcelain enjoyed great popularity during the Rococo Revival years of the early 19th century. The three factories responsible for producing the best examples were Coalport, Coalbrookdale and the Minton factory in Staffordshire. The modelling of the flowers and the flower spray decoration on this example tell us that it was made at Coalport despite the fact that the piece is unmarked. Minton pieces tend to be more thinly potted and are applied with finer and more densely petalled flowerheads, often of the Chrysanthemum type. These wares are very suscep-tible to damage and should be carefully examined for any restoration work.

**▶ ROCKINGHAM TEAPOT, COVER AND STAND**
*c.1830; teapot 20.3cm (8in) high;* **£500–700**
The Rockingham factory at Swinton, Yorkshire was on the estate of the Marquis of Rockingham and operated under his patronage from 1826, although it was run by the Brameld family from 1778, closing in 1842. It produced some of the finest bone china wares of the early 19th century which sell at a premium today. You might pay £80–100 for a Rockingham teacup and saucer, whereas a Coalport might fetch only £30–40. Commissioned to make several exquisitely decorated royal dinner services, the factory was also noted for its small figures and baskets.

**▲ WEMYSS DECORATED PIG**
*c.1895; 12.7cm (5in) high;* **£500**
The Wemyss factory was started in the early 19th century in Kirkcaldy, Fife, in Scotland, but it was not until around 1870 that proprietor Robert Heron achieved commercial success with a range of brightly painted pottery. The white glazed earthenware, made into toiletwares, plates, jam pots, jugs and the famous pigs, were brightly painted with a range of motifs inclu-ding pink cabbage roses, thistles, irises and more subtly with fruit, geese, cockerels and hens painted in black.

**▼ HORSE FIGURE BY ST. ANTHONY'S POTTERY, NEWCASTLE UPON TYNE**
*c.1825; 17.8cm (7in) high;* **£1,000–1,500**
Wares from this pottery are relatively scarce and therefore command high prices. The thin, shaped rectangular base and cut-away hooves are features associated with the Tyneside pottery, but are not exclusive to them. This example, decorated in underglaze enamels, closely resembles the type of object produced by several potteries in Yorkshire. The naive modelling and decoration add to its appeal as "folk" art, which is very much in favour at the present time.

**◀ BELLEEK TEAPOT AND COVER**
*1880; 12.7cm (5in);* **£200–300**
The Northern Irish factory of Belleek is renowned for its eggshell thin wares often modelled as shells and sea urchins, edged in emerald green or pink. The designers took marine life as their inspiration. This teapot is modelled in the form of a limpet and is part of a range of teawares first made around 1880.

**▶ SUNDERLAND LUSTRE JUG**
*1840; 25.4cm (10in) high;* **£150–250**
Several factories in Sunderland produced white glazed pottery with lustred pink reserves and panels often printed in black showing scenes such as a sailor's farewell or even masonic sym-bols. The purple lustre is given a mottled effect with brushwork and oils. On some examples, like this jug, the black and white prints are em-bellished with colours. Pieces carrying the maker's impressed mark are always at a premium and can add £100 to the value.

**COLLECTORS' NOTES**
As you might expect, these 19th-century wares are far more plentiful than their 18th-century counterparts. The variety is enormous and prices can be surprisingly reasonable, especially when compared to modern equivalents. Collectors have so much to choose from that it is advisable to concentrate on one factory or one type of ware, such as parian.

**COLLECTING TIP**
If you are on a tight budget, you could do a lot worse than start a collection of single, hand painted tea cups and saucers, especially those produced between 1800 and 1860. You can still pick up examples for as little as £10–15. Worn gilding makes a piece look tired, shabby and undesirable so seek out examples which have retained as much of their original gilding as possible.

# British and American Studio Wares

The reaction against the mass-produced pottery and porcelain of the early Victorian age came to a head after the Great Exhibition of 1851. Inspired by the writings of John Ruskin, small groups of artisans formed art union groups and thus paved the way for the Arts and Crafts Movement. Led by William Morris in England, its members sought to return to the values of the medieval guild system where hand-made objects were produced in small numbers by groups of dedicated craftsmen. On the whole, their ideas proved commercially unworkable, but many art potteries that started up at this time proved more successful and continued producing throughout the 19th and into the 20th century. Probably the largest commercial enterprise making hand-decorated stoneware and pottery was the Lambeth studios of Doulton.

Sir Henry Doulton did much to promote the emancipation of women by employing those newly graduated from the Lambeth School of Art to decorate his extensive range of ornamental and useful wares and the popularity of Lambeth stoneware was further enhanced by the work of the Martin brothers of Fulham and later Southall in London.

In the north of England, the arrival of William Burton and his brother Joseph at the Pilkington Pottery in Lancashire resulted in the production of some of the finest hand-decorated lustrewares ever manufactured. In Leeds, in Yorkshire, the Burmantoft factory was responsible for a range of Turkish-inspired hand-decorated wares in the manner of William de Morgan, the most celebrated Victorian art potter, who operated from various studios in the London area.

The most prominent of the Staffordshire art potters was William Moorcroft who worked for James Macintyre & Co. when he was a young designer, before setting up his own pottery in 1913 in Corbridge. To this day it produces superbly hand-decorated, well-designed pottery popular with collectors all over the world.

In the United States, the works produced at the Rookwood Works in Cincinnati achieved international acclaim, as did those of George Ohr and the Newcomb College Pottery.

▲ **DOULTON LAMBETH MUG INCISE-DECORATED BY HANNAH BARLOW**
*c.1880; 10cm (4in);* **£250–350**

▶ **DOULTON LAMBETH BUFF STONEWARE EWER INCISED AND DECORATED BY GEORGE TINWORTH**
*c.1880; 30.5cm (12in);* **£300–350**
These pieces are good examples of the work of two of Doulton's best known modellers and decorators. Tinworth was the only artist to have his signature on the body rather than on the underside of his pieces. This piece is small in comparison with his more usual life-size terracotta sculptures and tableaux. The mug is typical of Hannah Barlow's *sgraffito* work; animal subjects were her particular strength. If pieces incorporate human subjects it adds greatly to their desirability. The most sought after are those that were destined for the Australian market and decorated with kangeroos.

◀ **WILLIAM DE MORGAN TWO HANDLED VASE**
*1900; 36cm (14in) high;*
**£1,000–1,500**
William de Morgan was seen as the guiding light of English Arts and Crafts pottery manufacture. His earliest pieces were decorated on blanks bought at the Staffordshire potteries. His work is divided into three periods named after the location of the Pottery – Chelsea (1872–82), Merton Abbey (1882–87) and Fulham (1888–1907). He is principally recognised for reviving the art of lustre decoration and popularising Persian- and Iznik-type forms on both ornamental wares and tiles. This vase is a good example, but with fish decoration of a type never found on original Iznik pottery.

### ◄ WILLIAM MOORCROFT FLAMBÉ GLAZE VASE
*c.1925; 30.5cm (12in);*
**£1,800–2,200**
Moorcroft started his career with James Macintyre & Co. and was responsible for the highly sought after Florianware series. The technique he used to make these tube-line decorated wares, in which trails of slip are applied to form a raised outline on the body of the piece with colour then filled in, is one he continued and developed after opening his own company in 1913. Early wares are the most desirable, with pomegranate and leaf and berry design also popular. The flambé glazes he often applied, as seen here, are highly sought after.

### COLLECTORS' NOTES
Little of this late 19th- and early 20th-century studio pottery has been faked because it has proved too hard to copy, with the exception of a few spurious Martinware birds which have appeared on the market in recent years.

Despite the fact that most studio pieces were hand-made, there is a wide choice, both in volume and variety, available to collectors who tend to concentrate on a particular factory or on the work of one artist within a factory.

Moorcroft pieces are often restored because some of the shapes were very prone to chipping and cracking. Restorers are able to reproduce the glazes quite accurately and their work is often hard to spot with the naked eye. Any area where the glaze is slightly irregular, with either a high gloss or slightly matt appearance contrasting with the overall glaze, is suspect. Top rims, foot rims, handles and spouts must always be closely examined.

### COLLECTING TIP
Pilkington's monochrome and Lapis glazes are still affordable and you should be able to pick up a small vase for less than £50. The Lapisware from Pilkingtons's Royal Lancastrian period (post-1912) is more expensive. Look for examples that bear the incised initials "ETR" for E. T. Radford, the celebrated thrower.

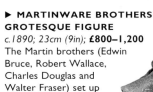

### ► PILKINGTON'S LUSTRE-DECORATED POTTERY VASE
*c.1906; 12.7cm (5in) high;* **£250–350**
Initially a tile manufacturer, the Pilkington factory in Lancashire, England, developed a range of ornamental wares after the arrival of the Burton brothers, William and Joseph, in the late 19th century. Their lustre-decorated pieces received international acclaim when exhibited at various European fairs. They also produced an interesting range of vases decorated with unusual glaze techniques; their Lapisware involved a technique where the pigment is fused with the glaze. This piece was painted by William Salter Mycock, one of several talented artists at the factory.

### ► MARTINWARE BROTHERS GROTESQUE FIGURE
*c.1890; 23cm (9in);* **£800–1,200**
The Martin brothers (Edwin Bruce, Robert Wallace, Charles Douglas and Walter Fraser) set up an art pottery studio in Fulham, London, in 1873. They produced a highly distinctive range of stoneware objects, the most famous of which are their birds with detachable heads modelled as tobacco jars. Early this century, they developed a series of vases and bowls of organic inspiration.

### ▲ GEORGE OHR EARTHENWARE TEAPOT
*1895; 10cm (4in);* **£2,000–3,000**
This teapot has a shape and form as eccentric as its creator, George Ohr, the American art potter who worked in the artist's colony of Biloxi, Mississippi. A Dali-esque figure with an exaggerated moustache, he specialized in thinly walled, lightweight pieces fashioned on a wheel and fired in a wood-burning kiln. This piece has a loop handle and an elongated spout in the form of a snake and is covered in a crystalline glaze in tones of buff and blue/grey.

### ► ROOKWOOD POTTERY EWER
*1885; 25.5cm (10in);* **£500–700**
The Rookwood pottery, founded in 1880 in Cincinnati by Maria Longworth Nichols, became famous internationally for its high-quality pieces, especially those showing native American Indian portraits painted by Matthew Daly in 1897–1903 and decorated in a "standard" glaze. In 1904 a vellum (matt) glaze was introduced, and was often used on wares with floral or landscape motifs.

# Glass

Glass is the most tantalizing and mysterious of substances. As long ago as the Bronze Age, in the region of Mesopotamia, the first glass objects were made by building up a core formed of clay around a metal rod which was then dipped into the molten liquid in a furnace. The core was scraped out once the piece had cooled. Moulds were also used to create vessels, and later, by the first century BC, the technique of blowing glass was invented, enabling quantities of useful wares to be made to satisfy the daily demands of Roman society.

Some wonderful examples of ancient Greek and Roman glass survive and while many exceptional examples are prohibitively expensive and other pieces belong firmly in a museum, glass of this age can still be bought for a reasonable price. The most famous example of Roman cameo glass is the Portland Vase in the British Museum in London. It is beyond price, but many interesting little dishes and perfume bottles do change hands for relatively small amounts of money.

The first glass was made from a mixture of silica (silicon dioxide – one of the principal constituents of sand) and lime with either soda or potash. When heated, this powdery mix became a molten liquid which could be moulded, cast or rolled into an endless variety of forms. The basic recipe remained the same until the 17th century, when lead glass was developed by George Ravenscroft in England.

The addition of lead oxide to the mixture, resulting in glass of greater clarity and resonance, proved a turning point in the industry. The Glass Sellers' Company, a City of London guild, employed Ravenscroft in 1674 to research into new techniques in glass production. Success did not come immediately, as his first attempts produced glass which "crisselled," or became covered in minute crackling after a short time, but once a way had been found to stabilize the mixture, the English glass industry took off (alongside that in Bohemia), and by the end of the century there were over one hundred glass houses operating all over the country. It laid the foundations for an expansion in glass-making all over Europe and, during the 18th century, English and Irish glass makers were lured to the Continent and the United States.

Since glass can be shaped into different forms by different techniques during the various stages of its malleability, and can be treated as a liquid or as a stone which can be cut, etched or engraved, it has always proved the most versatile of materials. Spun like silk or densely walled, brightly coloured or clear as air, its applications are wide enough for its properties to have been exploited by both artists and artisans throughout history for useful and decorative wares alike.

*Left: from left to right* British mixed-twist, bell-bowl wine glass, c.1765; *front* English "lemon squeezer" base rummer glass, c.1800; *back* Triple-ring-neck Georgian decanter, c.1810; Bohemian cobalt overlay on cranberry candlestick, c.1865; *front* British engraved goblet, c.1875; *centre* English Sowerby basket, c.1880; *back* British cut jug, c.1840.

# Where to begin

The striations, imperfections in the metal and evidence of finishing are all tell-tale signs of a piece of hand-made glass. Learning to spot the difference between an 18th-century wine glass and a 20th-century reproduction is just one of the tasks for the beginner on the road to becoming knowledgeable about glass.

## The Metal

This is the substance of glass when it is molten and also when it has cooled and been formed into a shape. The metal varies depending on the ingredients.

Early glass, made from around 3000BC, contained silicon dioxide (sand), soda made from the ash of the barilla plant gathered in salt marshes and used as the alkaline to help the batch melt, and lime to stabilize it and make it less vulnerable to the adverse effects of water. After c.1000, the composition of glass in Europe changed. Northern glass-makers had relied on supplies of soda from Mediterranean countries, but found that the ash from burning local supplies of bracken, beech-wood and other plants worked just as well as a flux to lower the melting temperature of the silica. This type of glass, known as *Waldglas* in Germany and Bohemia and *verre de fougère* in France, went on being made until the 17th century, but as it is prone to weathering, little of it survives. High quality, fragile, soda glass continued to be made in Venice. No significant changes in the industry occurred until 1674 when experiments by George Ravenscroft in England revealed that lead oxide could provide the fluxing element. With this he was able to produce a durable and exceptionally clear glass.

## Main Techniques

CORE-FORMING was used from earliest times in Mesopotamia, Ancient Greece, Western Asia and the Mediterranean. Small glass vessels were built up around a central, removable core made of animal dung and clay, modelled to the shape required for the interior and then dipped in molten glass in a furnace. The rod was turned to ensure even coating until the required amount of glass had built up, when it was removed and allowed to cool. The rod was snapped from the core which was then scraped out. These vessels were used mainly as oil and perfume bottles, with soft glass of a different colour trailed like a thread around the body as decoration.

CASTING WITH MOULDS was a method employed from the Bronze Age until Roman times. Jewellery, tableware, inlays and plaques were made by forcing hot glass into an open mould, or by using two interlocking moulds. Hot glass could be forced into the hollow space between an inner and outer mould, or the space could be filled with powdered glass and then the moulds fired in the kiln. Mosaic vessels were made in this way, by placing small discs of glass of different colours around a mould. An outer mould was then placed on top and the kiln fused the canes together. Sagging or slumping involved forming the vessel in the kiln by placing a disc of glass over a ceramic mould and allowing it to slump over the mould in the kiln to achieve the desired shape.

FREE BLOWING was used from c.75–50BC in the Roman world and later all over the world; it is still used today. A blow pipe inserted into the furnace is rotated to pick up an even coating of molten metal. Once removed from the furnace, the glass is rolled back and forth across a metal or stone surface known as a marver to make it cylindrical before the bubble is blown to form the body of the vessel. Once blown and worked to the required shape and size, a rod known as the pontil rod is attached to the base and the blow pipe removed. Further working while rotating the pontil rod creates the opening. Once complete, the pontil rod is broken from the base with a tap, leaving the characteristic "pontil mark." The mark could be ground and polished away. From c.1830, the spring clip replaced the pontil rod and this left no mark.

BLOW MOULDING was produced in ancient times and again in the 18th and 19th centuries. Molten glass was blown into moulds, taking the shape and pattern of the mould inside and out. After cooling and removing from the moulds, the pieces were hand finished.

PRESS MOULDING was pioneered in America in the 1820s, and taken up in Europe during the following decade. It was an innovative mechanical technique which involved pouring molten glass into a brass or iron mould and pressing it against the sides with a metal plunger. The mould formed the outer surface of the glass, the plunger the inside. In early American pressed glass, the decoration was set against a mass of stippled dots to disguise any blemishes, giving it the name "lacy glass."

## Decoration

Many techniques can be applied to glass objects to produce different types of decoration, both internal and external; the principal types are listed below.

## Internal Decoration

CASED When one layer of glass is applied over another, or when three or more layers are fused together and then the outer layer or layers cut away (*see* CAMEO).

**SIMPLE COLOURED TINT** The glass is mixed with a metallic oxide while still in powder form.

**LATTICINIO** Clear glass embedded with white glass threads giving the appearance of spiral fluting. The threads are woven into the semi-molten metal.

**LITHYALIN** Opaque glass which shows visible striations of various colours and, when polished, gives the appearance of agate.

**MARQUETERIE DE VERRE** Shaped and coloured lumps of glass pressed onto the body of a vessel and carved after the glass had cooled. It is found mostly on Art Nouveau glass by Emile Gallé.

**MILLEFIORI** Meaning literally "a thousand flowers," slices of coloured glass canes are embedded in clear, molten glass to form flower heads or other patterns. Used on paperweights, jugs and other tablewares.

**OPALINE** A translucent, milky white glass which, by adding various metallic oxides, could be coloured pink, mauve, turquoise, green and several other shades.

**ZWISCHENGOLDGLAS** The German term used to describe gilt and coloured enamel decoration literally sandwiched between two layers of glass.

## External Decoration.

**ACID ETCHING** The surface of the vessel is covered with an acid-resistant medium such as varnish or gum and the design scratched through with a sharp tool. The piece is then exposed to hydrofluoric acid, resulting in shiny, matt or frosted decoration of the exposed area.

**APPLIED** Glass trailed across the surface or applied to the sides of vessels in the form of small, circular blobs known as prunts in clear or coloured glass.

**CAMEO** Cased glass in two or more layers, with the outer layer carved on a wheel to create a design in relief.

**CUT** Facets and grooves made by cutting into the surface of glass with a wheel of iron or stone. Done in ancient times and taken up again by the Irish and English industry in the late 18th and 19th centuries.

**ENAMELLING** Fine glass powder mixed with metallic oxides to give colours which are painted onto the surface of the piece then fired to fix them.

**ENGRAVING** Cutting a design into glass with a sharp tool such as a needle or wheel. *Wheel engraving* involves working the piece on a rotating wheel which acts as a form of grindstone to remove areas of the surface and create a pattern or inscription. *Stipple engraving* is achieved by tapping the surface of the glass in varying densities with a sharp needle to create a series of dots which build up into the desired pattern.

**INTAGLIO** The technique of cutting or engraving a design below the surface of the glass to produce a relief image. The opposite of cameo carving.

**FLASHING** Applying a thin layer of contrasting colour to the body of a piece by dipping it into thin, transparent, coloured glass enamel in liquid form.

## Fakes, Copies and Alterations

Glass is as open to the art of the deceiver as any other area of antiques. Fake Roman glass has been known to have found its way into museum collections, and research into materials and techniques is a constant and evolving process which helps to shed more light on the past.

During the late 19th and early 20th centuries, reproductions of English 18th-century drinking glasses, especially with air twists were made, but most are readily identified by the uniformity of the shape and the clarity of the metal. Original 18th-century examples often contain impurities, with evidence of hand-finishing such as the vertical lines faintly visible on bowls.

Defects such as chips to foot rims or top rims of pieces are often ground and polished. Look out for irregularities. The rims should have a uniform outline. If a foot rim is not a true circle, be suspicious. If the foot rim of an 18th-century wine glass is smaller in diameter than the top rim of the bowl, this is evidence that it has been reduced by grinding.

Damaged bowls of wine glasses are sometimes discarded and another bowl of the same period welded onto the stem. Look for an unnatural ridge where the stem joins the bowl which gives the appearance of the two parts having been pushed and screwed together.

Lalique glass is particularly prone to alteration. A piece badly damaged around the base may be reground and the original mark lost in the process. The signature is re-applied using a wheel-cut technique or stencilled acid cutting. The base is often highly polished in appearance and shows little evidence of the expected wear and tear of 50 or more years.

## Care and Maintenance

Glass suffers from extremes in temperature, especially if it has any metallic inclusions. The different stress rates in the constituents can cause fracturing. Moisture can also cause devitrification. Enamel glass, particularly, should never be scrubbed, but washed gently in warm, soapy water and wiped dry with a soft cloth. Decanters should be stored with their stoppers off and contents drained regularly to prevent staining and damage to the surface.

# Drinking Glasses

Eighteenth-century English wine glasses are collected internationally, symbols of one of the most important stages in the development of glass manufacture. The increasing affluence of the middle classes during the 18th century resulted in the manufacture of many of the antiques we enjoy and collect today, and glass is no exception. Fine tablewares were being produced all over Europe and to accompany the silver and porcelain, great numbers of drinking glasses were made, the majority of them, like the examples shown here, in England. Many have survived, despite their relative fragility.

At the end of the 16th century, Venice still led the world in the field of glass making, as it had done for 400 years, producing fragile, elegant drinking glasses. Further north, German glass production expanded rapidly after the end of the Thirty Years War in 1648, when the industry began to enjoy the protection of wealthy patrons, and by the middle of the 18th century the Venetians were beginning to lose their prominent position. German *roemers* (glasses with a large ovoid bowl), and *humpen* (tall, cylindrical beakers) were often large, heavy and colourfully enamelled. Some were decorated with heraldic designs and others to commemorate marriages.

But the discovery of the formula for making lead glass pioneered by Ravenscroft in c.1676 transformed the glass manufacturing industry in Britain. Until this time wine glasses had been imported into the British Isles from Italy, the Low Countries and France, but the new methods, which produced stronger, clearer bodies, encouraged the design of many new styles in drinking glasses and made them available to a wider range of people. Early 18th century English drinking glasses tend to be heavy, solid and plain, but as the century progressed, glass makers experimented with a variety of bowl shapes, and, more interestingly, with decorative stems involving air twists, and opaque white and coloured enamel twists. Happily, these are still widely available and relatively affordable, as can be seen from the selection shown here. There can be few greater pleasures than sipping wine from a simple, handmade glass which bears all the individual signs of the craftsman who made it and which has survived for 200 or more years.

### ◄ PLAIN-STEM DRINKING GLASS WITH BELL-SHAPED BOWL
*1730–40; 15.2cm (6in) high;* **£80–100**
English plain stem glasses probably derived from some made in the Netherlands in the late 17th and early 18th centuries. Those with very fine stems were used to toast a lady and then deliberately broken – consequently not many have survived. Relatively simple and inexpensive at the time it was made, a glass like this is a good starting point for the novice collector. The fold-over foot is quite apparent in this example.

### ► NEWCASTLE LIGHT BALUSTER
*c.1740–50; 19cm (7½in) high;* **£600–800**
With a baluster stem and an ogee-shaped bowl, this glass represents some of the best work being done in England in the mid-18th century. The northeastern town of Newcastle was a celebrated area of glass making, its wares exported all over Europe. The stem is composite, made in separate parts comprising a hollow section forming the knop at the top of the baluster with a secondary knop beneath the ogee-shaped bowl, and a plain conical foot.

### ◄ ALE FLUTE
*1830; 19.7cm (7¾in) high;* **£200–300**
Ale at this time was a strong, dark drink and considered far safer than water, which tended to be heavily contaminated. This piece has petal fluting around part of the bowl, with a short inverted baluster stem, resting on an annular knop. Many ale glasses are engraved with hops and barley, the essential constituents of ale.

### ► PAN-TOP WINE GLASS
*1760; 15.4 cm (6⅛in) high;* **£300–400**
This distinctive bowl with an everted top section is always referred to as a pan top. In this case it has been engraved with trailing flowers. The stem is known as a mercury twist, achieved by using larger openings in the section of glass that eventually forms the stem. The resulting play of light gives the appearance of a solid core of mercury, hence the name.

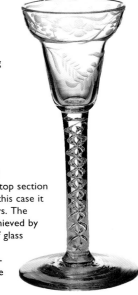

**ENGLISH LEAD WINE GLASS
WITH BELL-SHAPED BOWL
AND AIR TWIST STEM**
*1760; 16cm (6¼in) high;*
**£200–300**
This is a very typical wine glass of
the mid-18th century. The metal (the
substance of the glass made up from
the various ingredients used) has a
greyish hue. By the 19th century the
metal had become brownish, and by
the 20th, almost white, its machine-
made perfection displaying none of
the specks or air holes associated
with glass made in the 18th century.

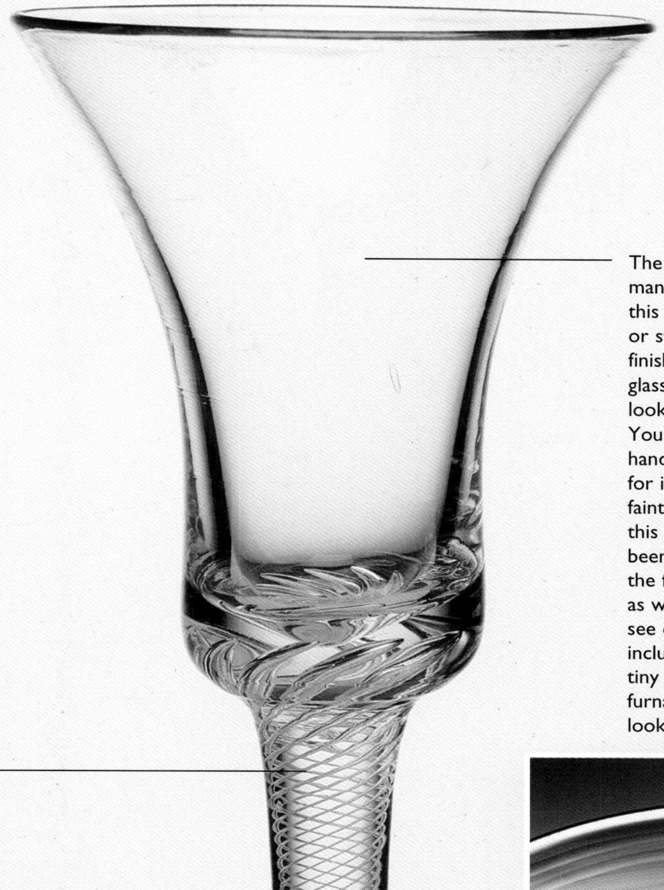

The spiral (or helix) is created by
trapping vertical tubes of air in the
central core which is then heated,
stretched and twisted before being
cut into sections. The appropriate
length is then annealed to the bowl
at one end and the conical foot rim
at the other. You can see quite
clearly that the spiral is slightly
irregular, a nice feature. Some
stems have one or more
decorative bulges or knops.

The bell shape is one of the
many bowl forms favoured at
this time. You can see the lines
or striations caused by the hand
finishing. When you examine a
glass like this, you should not be
looking for absolute perfection.
You want to see clues to its
hand-made origins. You might,
for instance, see four or five
faint vertical lines (not visible on
this glass) where the piece has
been held after removal from
the furnace. On this example,
as well as the banding, you can
see other slight imperfections
including an air bubble and a
tiny speck of black from the
furnace. A worn rim may
look slightly opaque.

The foot rims of these wine glasses
are prone to chipping and some
glass makers resorted to folding the
glass over the rim to give it extra
strength. This example does not
have a fold-over foot, but to identify
one, look for a thick band of glass
around the outer rim (*see also the
glass at the top of p.80*). Another
way to date an early glass is to run
your finger gently from the centre
of the base of the glass to the edge.
As it reaches the outer rim, you
should feel a slight sharpness. This is
a feature of 18th-century examples.
Victorian and later copies have a
rounded, soft edge.

The foot was attached to the
pontil rod while it was worked
into a concave shape. The rod
was then snapped off and the
resulting blemish is referred to
as the pontil mark. The finish
was often sharp which is why
it was necessary to create a
concave foot rim, lifting the
pontil mark from any surface on
which it might sit. 19th-century
glasses often have ground and
polished pontil marks.

# Other Drinking Glasses

### ◄ RARE VENETIAN WINE GLASS

*late 16th century; 17cm (6¾in) high;* **£10,000–15,000**

The beauty and delicacy of Venetian drinking glasses in this period set the standard for glass makers throughout Europe to such an extent that pieces made in France and the Low Countries which resemble them are referred to as "façon de Venise," literally, in the Venetian style. This glass has a conical bowl with a ribbed lower section and a trailed band above. It is set on an incised, twisted openwork stem with blue-tinted c-scroll wings above a wide conical foot with a folded rim. The glass has a yellowish tint.

### ► ENGLISH CHAMPAGNE OR ALE FLUTE

*1760; 17.8cm (7in) high;* **£250–350**

The example shown here is probably a champagne glass as most ale glasses of this period were engraved with hops and barley. The elegant bowl rests on an air twist stem worked with twin knops and raised on a conical foot.

### ◄ IRISH CUT PORT GLASS

*1800; 10.8cm (4¼in) high;* **£40–50**

This type of heavy glass was usually made in Ireland, which was exempt from the glass excise tax imposed on the British until the 19th century. It has a slightly bluish tint. It is also as heavy as it looks, with the emphasis on the hob-nail cutting on the bowl. The base is star-cut on the underside and has a concentric stepped upper surface with a short stem incorporating an annular knop.

### ◄ ENGLISH CORDIAL GLASS

*1760; 16.5cm (6½in) high;* **£300–400**

The small bowl tells us that this glass was made for holding cordial, a strong liqueur type of drink made with fruit which was drunk either with tea or after dinner by the ladies who withdrew from the dining room, leaving the men to their port and brandy. The lower bowl is moulded with petal flutes and the upper section is engraved with a continuous band of flower and leaf decoration. The stem houses an opaque white multiple twist with a central gauze core.

### ◄ ENGLISH RUMMER WITH "LEMON SQUEEZER" TYPE BASE

*1800; 14.6cm (5¾in) high;* **£80–100**

The rummer is derived from the traditional German *roemer*, a drinking vessel with an ovoid bowl made in varying sizes, but usually larger than any English equivalent. The clear bowl on this glass is engraved with a medallion enclosing the initials of the owner. The capstan stem sits on a heavy square base with the underside domed and ribbed in a style known as "lemon squeezer."

### ◄ ENGLISH JELLY GLASS

*1800; 10.8cm (4¼in) high;*
**£20–30**
The shape of this glass gives a clue to its function. Delicately coloured jellies and syllabubs were often displayed in small glasses like this one, placed on circular, tiered footed stands or tazzas, and eaten towards the end of a meal. It is decorated with panel flutes on the lower bowl beneath diagonal and geometric cutting.

### ► SIMPLE ENGLISH FACET STEM WINE GLASS

*1770; 14.7cm (5¾in) high;* **£80–120**
The majority of wine glasses with facet-cut stems were made between 1775 and 1790, most with plain bowls like this example, but some engraved with flowers, or, more unusually, with landscapes. This lead glass was a much easier material to cut than its Continental counterpart which contained potash and was more suitable for engraving.

### ◄ ENGLISH ALE TUMBLER

*1790–1800; 9.5cm (3¾in) high;*
**£70–90**
Made in Roman times and earlier, tumblers were the earliest drinking vessels, taking the form of hollow beakers made from cow horn and used every day by working people across Europe. This utilitarian tumbler with a heavy base, engraved with hops, would have been used in the home of a wealthy farmer rather than a nobleman. As the 19th century progressed, tumblers were made with a carafe, to which, when upturned, they formed the cover.

**COLLECTORS' NOTES**
18th-century drinking glasses, particularly English examples, are one of the few areas where the novice collector can build up an acceptable range of pieces without breaking the bank. In some instances, an 18th-century glass costs little more than some modern hand-made counterparts.

Because the bases of antique drinking glasses are prone to chipping, they are often reground. When this is done to excess the diameter of the foot rim can be less than that of the bowl and the result is an out-of-proportion glass which is top heavy and definitely to be avoided.

**COLLECTING TIP**
"Lemon squeezer" based rummers, like the one shown on p.82 are particularly undervalued and often incorporate beautiful ornamental engraving.

### ▼ GERMAN HUMPEN

*1662; 17.2cm (6¾in) high;* **£5,000–7,000**
A *humpen* is a tall, cylindrical beaker used for drinking beer or wine, made of "forest glass" in Germany, Silesia and Bohemia from the mid-16th until the 18th century. This is a splendid and typical example, elaborately decorated with enamels. *Humpen* were often made as marriage pieces, inscribed with verse and the arms of both families, and dated. The painting follows the stained glass of the period except that the *humpen* were covered with opaque enamels whereas the stained glass panels had translucent colours. This is thickly walled with a short, solid foot rim.

# Decanters

The glass decanter came into its own during the 18th century. Early shapes tend to have long necks, wide shoulders tapering slightly towards the base and spire-shaped facet-cut stoppers. As the century progressed, the straight-sided bottle shape became more prevalent, often engraved with a label identifying the contents it was made to hold, which might have included hop and apple-based drinks as well as wines, spirits and liquers.

Once cut glass decanters became fashionable in England, the engraving of labels became impractical. In Ireland, decanters were mould blown with standard-sized bases and vertical flutes. The necks were often decorated with multiple rings and the stoppers became panel cut in bulls-eye and lozenge shapes, although by the end of the 18th century, the mushroom stopper was the most prevalent. Irish decanters enjoyed enormous commercial success, being exported to America, the West Indies and Portugal.

The British also exported their cut glass decanters to the Continent, and were rivalled only by the Bohemian glass makers. Such was their popularity that by the 19th century, travelling examples were made comprising four square bottles with ball stoppers, all sitting in a fitted mahogany box. The French also made pieces of this kind, often gilded on the shoulders, the only area visible when the decanters were nestling in their travelling box.

### ◀ ENGLISH TAPERING DECANTER
*1780; 23.5cm (9¼in) high;*
**£120–150**
The emphasis on this decanter is on its simple, elegant form and the clarity of the glass; decoration is limited to the applied double rings around the neck. The stopper is balloon-shaped and facet-cut. This type often had an engraved label, which simulated the silver wine and other labels that were hung around the neck of some decanters.

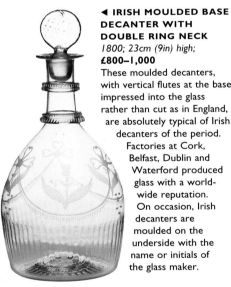

### ◀ IRISH MOULDED BASE DECANTER WITH DOUBLE RING NECK
*1800; 23cm (9in) high;*
**£800–1,000**
These moulded decanters, with vertical flutes at the base impressed into the glass rather than cut as in England, are absolutely typical of Irish decanters of the period. Factories at Cork, Belfast, Dublin and Waterford produced glass with a world-wide reputation. On occasion, Irish decanters are moulded on the underside with the name or initials of the glass maker.

### ▶ ENGLISH LIGHT CUT DECANTER
*1810; 21.6cm (8½in) high;*
**£120–150**
Decanters of this design are described as light cut, in this case with a mushroom stopper, triple-ring neck, cut basal and shoulder flutes interspaced by a band of circular windows and a moulded stopper cut with a starburst. It is heavier and more robust than earlier examples. The basal fluting acted as a means of disguising the unsightly sediment which often collected in the base of the decanter over time.

**COLLECTORS' NOTES**
• Avoid decanters with a cloudy bloom, a form of glass disease not necessarily caused by past contents.
• The top rims of decanters should be inspected to see whether they have been chipped and subsequently ground and repolished. From above, the rim should look perfectly circular.
• Particular care should be paid to whether or not the stopper is original to the decanter, or is a later replacement. Each was ground individually to ensure an airtight seal, so a loose stopper is not the original.

**COLLECTING TIP**
Decanters offer wonderful value for money as can be seen from the examples shown here. They are also widely available and can be used as well as displayed.

### ◀ ENGLISH DECANTER
*1830; 21.6cm (8½in) high;*
**£60–90**
This is a good example of how the decanter had evolved by the early 19th century. Moulded and cut with wide flutes, it has a triple-ring neck and a hollow button-shaped stopper decorated with a starburst. Pieces like this were made in their thousands to meet the demands of the growing middle class and they have survived in great numbers, a fact which is reflected in their price.

### ◀ MID-VICTORIAN DECANTER
*1860; 21.6cm (8½in) high;*
**£40–60**
Pieces of this shape are known as shaft and globe or onion-style decanters and were extremely popular during the mid- to late 19th century. The body is decorated with broad geometric cutting and the slender neck is fluted. These are highly functional decanters: the bottom-heavy design made them extremely difficult to knock over.

# Paperweights

The colourful paperweight is very much a mid-19th century phenomenon. France became the main centre of manufacture during the short period when they flourished, between 1845 and 1860. Important pieces were also made in America, principally because two French glass workers, François Pierre and Nicholas Lutz, joined the New England Glass Company and the Boston and Sandwich Glass Company respectively.

The three main factories in France were St. Louis and Baccarat in the Vosges and Clichy in Paris where *millefiori* ("thousand flower") and lampworking were the two main techniques of decoration. Most of these highly complex, heavy paperweights were made anonymously and were little appreciated at the time. The individually sculpted flowers, reptiles and butterflies of the lamp-worked weights were made in coloured glass over heat and the design then captured in a dome of clear glass. The *millefiori* glass rods or canes were either arranged concentrically or placed in whirling groups before being cut and embedded in clear glass. The passion for collecting weights revived in the 1960s and many factories are once again producing fine quality examples.

**◀ SCRAMBLE MILLEFIORI PAPERWEIGHT BY BACCARAT**
*1850; 8.3cm (3¼in) diameter;* **£250–350**
A scramble weight is often also known as an end-of-day weight, which refers to the time when the setters assembled all the odd canes and misshapes they had discarded during the day to create this happy jumble of colour. Although pretty and decorative, scramble weights are not as desirable as set pieces.

**▶ MILLEFIORI PAPERWEIGHT BY BACCARAT**
*1848; 7cm (2¾in) diameter;* **£500–700**
When it comes to valuing *millefiori* weights, size and the number of canes used to make the silhouettes are all-important – the more the better! The silhouettes were made by placing rods of different coloured glass together, cutting them into sections and placing them on end so they resemble tiny flowers. This one is very desirable as the letter "B" for Baccarat and the date 1848 are visible on one cane. The flowers are set against a carpet of tumbled muslin composed of opaque white *latticinio* canes.

**▶ CLICHY MILLEFIORI GARLAND WEIGHT**
*1850; 5.7cm (2¼in) diameter;* **£300–500**
The large rosette is centred with a typical Clichy closed rose cane which is peculiar to the factory. The surround is composed of a simple garland of pink and green canes. The more elaborate the garland, the more desirable the weight.

**▶ ST. LOUIS FRUIT BASKET WEIGHT**
*1850; 5.7cm (2¼in) diameter;* **£600–800**
The lampworker was responsible for this stunning piece of glass work. Each of the fruits has been individually modelled and then set carefully onto the *latticinio* basket of fine threads of milk white glass before being enclosed in a gather of clear glass. This type of weight is a great favourite with collectors, who also seek out weights encompassing flowers, reptiles, butterflies and dragonflies. Reptile and butterfly weights are particularly rare and command great prices.

**◀ BOSTON & SANDWICH WEIGHT**
*late 19th century; 6cm (2½in) diameter;* **£450–600**
Along with the New England and Mount Washington glass companies, Boston & Sandwich were leading American producers of weights in the 19th century. Many American factories concentrated on flower decoration. Here, their typical rose is set against a *latticinio* background. The most desirable of these weights are those attributed to the factory's top craftsman, Nicholas Lutz.

**COLLECTORS' NOTES**
Unfortunately paperweights are prone to bruising when dropped, and shallow bruising and surface scratches can be expertly polished away. Carefully examine the profile of all weights for any depressions and distortions.

The most desirable French paperweights tend to be the finest *millefiori* weights, followed by those enclosing reptiles, in particular the Baccarat snake weights.

Magnum weights, which have a diameter of 10.2cm (4in) or more, as opposed to the usual 5cm (2in), are rare and very desirable.

**COLLECTING TIP**
The market is awash with Bohemian and Venetian *millefiori* weights which are often of inferior quality. Look instead to the modern day Caithness weights made in Scotland where the tradition of excellence established by the French factories has been taken up (see p.210). Those made in the last 30 years are already being keenly collected.

# Cut Glass

Before the second half of the 18th century, cut glass constituted only a tiny proportion of glass production throughout the world, although it was a technique used to great advantage by the Romans, and later, in the 17th century, by Bohemian glassworkers. Much of this work, however, did not display the cutting of standard geometric patterns onto the metal that we have come to associate with cut glass. It was after 1750 that cut glass came into its own, proving the ideal medium to display many of the neo-classical forms and patterns which were fashionable all over Europe from 1760.

English lead crystal glass provided the ideal material for cutting and polishing, being heavier and easier to work than the Continental equivalent. English and Irish cut glass of the 18th century led the world market, so much so that Irish patterns were copied on a grand scale in France, and factories in Norway and America lured workers from the British Isles to help develop techniques there. In addition, France, Germany, the Low Countries and Bohemia set up their own factories quite independently of any British input and produced commercially successful cut glass.

The type of cutting based on the diamond shape was an English innovation and by the end of the 18th century, cut glass tableware was made in large matching services which were exported to America, Spain and Portugal, as well as being in common use all over England. The English and Irish also monopolised the manufacture of fabulous cut glass lustres and chandeliers during this period, but were challenged during the mid-19th century by the French factory of Baccarat.

By the beginning of the 19th century, the art of cutting glass was also well established in the United States with several factories operating in Pittsburgh alone. So successful was this industry that it adversely affected the export of Irish glass which began to suffer a decline, exacerbated after 1825 by the removal of tax advantages in Ireland and the introduction by Britain of excise duties. By the middle of the 19th century, the Irish glass industry was in ruins.

Both 18th- and 19th-century cut glass is still widely available, and prices often compare very favourably with the modern equivalent. In a short space of time, and with a keen eye, the new collector will be able to tell the difference between antique and modern cut glass. An old piece of cut glass can often be spotted at a boot fair or jumble sale and the sense of achievement that this brings is enormous!

**GEORGIAN CUT GLASS BOWL**
*1800; 30cm (12in) diameter;* **£250–300**
Banded with hob-nail cutting above and vertical fluting below, bowls of this type were sometimes used as the main item in a table centrepiece, fitting into a silver frame with bracket arms leading off to hold smaller bowls of the same design. It was made primarily to hold fruit and is a good example of English Georgian cut glass. It has a bluish-grey tinge to it and is simpler in form than its Victorian counterpart, which would exhibit a slight brown colour and a decorated rim. Hob-nail cutting was popular during this period.

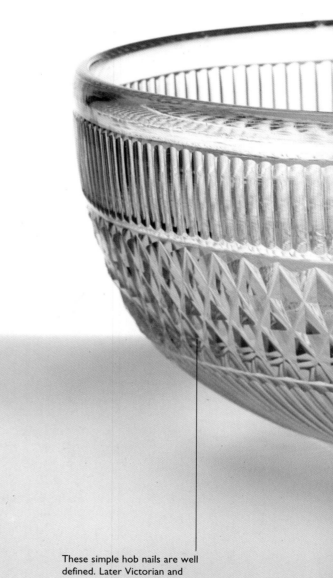

These simple hob nails are well defined. Later Victorian and Edwardian glassworkers often embellished the hob nails with additional decoration by flattening each point in an attempt to make a star-cut form.

Here is an obvious sign of hand-cutting: the craftsman has made a mistake, probably while cutting the final flutes and was unable to make a clean finish.

The scratches are a good sign of wear, but beware of excessive signs of this: it is one of the best indications that a piece has been faked. This is just the right amount of wear for a piece that has survived almost 200 years.

You can see here that the pontil mark has been ground away and polished showing that the bowl was hand-blown rather than machine-moulded – another clue to its age. A later example would be completely flat without the circular area in the centre where the pontil rod was attached to the glass while it was worked in the furnace.

# Other Cut Glass

**▲ CONFITURE JAR AND COVER**
*1820–30; 16.5cm (6½in) high;* **£150–180**
With hob-nail banding, oval prism-cut windows and a heavy star-cut base, this is the sort of piece that would have been placed on the dining table of a well-to-do household and filled with jam or fruit compote at breakfast or tea time. It has a mushroom finial, something that would be missing from earlier pieces of this kind, which were plainer and had more pronounced, domed covers or were goblet-shaped with facet-cut painted covers.

**▲ CZECHOSLOVAKIAN CUT GLASS DISH**
*1925; 35.5cm (14in) diameter;* **£150–250**
The complicated design all over the surface of this dish beautifully illustrates the glass cutter's skill and artistry. Its one fault is the slightly offset central roundel. This piece is unmarked, whereas on a British piece of this quality you would expect to find a stencil mark. Factories in Czechoslovakia were manufacturing this type of glass in competition with Stourbridge in England and exporting large quantities of it to the United States and the rest of Europe.

**◄ IRISH BOAT-SHAPED SALT**
*1800–1810; 8.3cm (3¼in) high;*
**£30–40**
Glass is the perfect medium for storing salt as it resists salt's corrosive properties. For this reason many silver salts have glass liners. This boat-shaped example, a shape favoured by Irish glassmakers, is supported on a heavy base and was probably one of a set placed at intervals along a dining table. It is decorated with a crimped rim and a hob-nail band above swags.

**COLLECTORS' NOTES**
It is important to be able to differentiate between cut and pressed glass. This becomes increasingly difficult when looking at later 19th-century pieces made after the invention of machinery which could produce convincing moulded wares which emulated cut glass and were able to undersell it. Look at the grain of cutting. Usually you can see where the cutter's wheel has left a distinctly sharp edge. Cut glass also tends to sparkle and reflect with far more intensity than pressed glass.
Despite the high level of skill employed by glass cutters, it is often possible to spot tell-tale imperfections in the cutting which reveal the handcrafted element involved in a genuinely old piece of cut glass.
When you see a piece marked "Waterford" with an acid-cut mark, it will have been made after the Second World War when the glass making industry was revived in Ireland.

**COLLECTING TIP**
It is worth examining a piece for the often indistinct acid-cut signature on the base attributing it to one of the top English makers such as Thomas Webb, Richardson, Stuart, Royal Brierley or Tudor.

**▲ HELMET-SHAPED CUT GLASS JUG**
*1920s; 14cm (5½in) high;* **£20–30**
A large quantity of glass was made in England during the 1920s and 30s in the Georgian style. The helmet shape was introduced in the late 18th century and was particularly favoured by the English, who produced jugs of this shape not only in glass, but also in ceramic and silver. The cutting on this piece is a fanciful interpretation of what you might see on its early 19th century counterpart. The combination of this type of cutting with these motifs is of a type seldom found on original pieces.

# *Pressed and Moulded Glass*

Pioneered in the United States, the pressed glass method was developed there in the 1820s and in England and the rest of Europe during the 1830s. A particular quantity of molten glass was poured into a mould and pressed against the sides with a plunger which formed the pattern. When removed from the mould after cooling, the two halves of the object were annealed together and the seam lines polished away. The seams are occasionally visible, but pressed glass often has the appearance of cut glass and employed similar patterns, although the definition of pressed glass is not as sharp as on cut glass. A popular type of American pressed glass was "lacy" glass, which contained intricate, faceted designs.

The mass production techniques of manufacturing this type of glass meant that large quantities of it could be made and sold at affordable prices, making decorative glass available to a whole new range of people. At first only a limited range of solid objects such as door handles were made, but it was not long before the range extended to dishes, tumblers, bowls and all manner of other items. In Europe, the French factories of Val-St. Lambert, Baccarat and St. Louis were making pressed glass by 1830, followed by factories in Scandinavia, Bohemia and England. In the United States, pressed glass was often used to make commemorative wares.

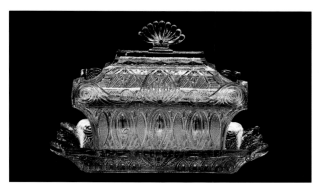

▲ **AMERICAN COVERED CASKET AND TRAY**
*c.1830–40; 12.7cm (5in) high;* **£800–1,200**
Probably intended as a butter dish, this covered casket follows the American Empire style. It demonstrates well how advanced the American glass industry was at this time in comparison with its contemporary European counterparts. Many American makers used pressed glass for commemorative wares, including dishes, jugs and tumblers, which are very popular with collectors today. This type of glass lent itself well to very intricate designs.

▶ **PRESSED GLASS TOP HAT**
*1885; 10cm (4in) high;* **£80–120**
Made in the northeast of England, clear glass examples of these top hats are worth £40–60, but peach ones are rarer and worth more. Top hats are popular with collectors and were a staple part of production for factories who probably made them to be used as toothpick holders. Occasionally, they can be dated accurately because they have either a registration number or a diamond registration mark moulded into the base or integral with the decoration.

▶ **BACCARAT CANDLESTICK**
*1860; 21.5cm (8½in) high;* **£150–200**
The Baccarat factory was the premier French producer of moulded glass during the 19th century and continues to use the same techniques today. This candlestick is in the Gothic Revival style which enjoyed great popularity at this time and was taken up with gusto by Baccarat. The mould line is visible on the base, otherwise it closely resembles cut glass. The signature is moulded in low relief on the base. At the end of the 19th and the beginning of the 20th century, Baccarat pressed glass was sometimes signed only with a butterfly motif.

▶ **SOWERBY ORNAMENTAL BOWL**
*1885; 14cm (5½in) long, 8.3cm (3¼in) high;* **£80–120**
The famous factories of the northeast of England including Greener's, Sowerby's and Davidsons, produced thousands of small, decorative pieces of pressed glass which found their way to all parts of Europe, the United States and the Commonwealth. The design of this bowl is attributed to Walter Crane, a leading light of the Arts and Crafts Movement, and the piece is signed on the inside with a peacock motif. Similar pieces were made in a striated purple glass which simulates agate.

**COLLECTORS' NOTES**
• American lacy glass is mainly early 19th century and is relatively scarce, especially in comparison with the huge quantities of pressed glass made later in the century.
• English designs can often

be attributed to factories by the registration numbers impressed into the bases and sides of pieces.
• Pressed glass probably offers the widest variety and the lowest prices of any area of collectable

glass. Beware of reproductions, which lack the weight and slight imperfections of the original wares.

**COLLECTING TIP**
If you want to start a collection of glass on a very limited budget, seek

out the purple slag glass produced by Sowerby which simulates agate. A fascinating variety of objects was manufactured, from small top hat toothpick holders worth £30–40, to a pair of candlesticks which might cost £80–120.

# Engraved Glass

Engraved glass became highly popular in the 19th century, superseding cut glass. Before this date, glass had sometimes been engraved, but very much as surface decoration. It was the development of thickly walled glass which allowed the engraver free rein.

The classical forms which began to adorn glass showed the type of sophisticated intricacy that the talented engraver was able to achieve by the middle of the 19th century, and it was a completely new medium. The shapes and motifs were familiar, but never before had such superb quality been achieved.

England led the way, and the technique was soon taken up in Bohemia and France. Many skilled craftsmen from Bohemia came to live in England, which is undoubtedly the reason why so many top quality pieces came to be made there. They worked in London for various retailers, decorating blanks supplied by the leading manufacturers such as Thomas Webb of Stourbridge. They also settled in Edinburgh, but, in common with many porcelain decorators, their talents were in great demand and they moved from place to place over a number of years.

The practice of engraving on glass is a delicate one, requiring great steadiness and accuracy. In the 19th century, the piece was held in a treadle powered by a machine fitted with wheels that ranged in size from a pinhead to about 10cm (4in). The size of the copper wheel determined the intricacy of the finished pattern or scene. This method was known as wheel engraving. The other main types are diamond point and stipple engraving (both of which used a diamond needle or "nib" to draw or tap out a pattern), and acid etching, which looks similar to wheel engraving, but produces a more even finish.

◄ **VICTORIAN MOULDED AND STIPPLE-ENGRAVED TUMBLER**
*c.1865; 14cm (5½in) high;* **£200–300**
This tumbler is decorated using a diamond needle in a style made famous by the Dutch stipple engravers of the early 18th century. The work on the piece is relatively naïve in comparison with the almost ethereal quality usually achieved by the Dutch in their work. The subject matter, showing a huntsman with hounds, is appealing to collectors of English folk art. However, dated examples are always more desirable.

► **ENGLISH VICTORIAN LEMONADE JUG**
*1880; 28cm (11in) high;* **£150–250**
This type of engraving whereby the design is all over the piece, rather than being confined within panels, is typically late Victorian. So, too, is the fanciful nature of the piece, where a romantic shape is combined with the naturalistic form of the birds among blossoming branches. The detail is superb. Even the handle has been ribbed on the engraver's wheel, a decorative and practical feature, making the jug easier to grip.

▼ **THOMAS WEBB AND SONS "ROCK CRYSTAL" ENGRAVED GLASS BOWL**
*c.1900; 13.4cm (5¼in) diameter;* **£150–200**
The engraving technique used on this bowl emulates the engraved rock crystal wares of Renaissance Italy and earlier. The process involves engraving the glass and then polishing the engraved area. Two of the chief exponents of this work were William Fritscher and Frederick Kny, craftsmen who worked for the British Stourbridge-based company, Thomas Webb and Sons. The pieces are marked with a small acid-cut stencil mark in a circular form, inscribed "Thomas Webb."

◄ **BOHEMIAN GOBLET**
*1850; 19cm (7½in) high;* **£4,000–6,000**
As can be seen by the texture of the bowl, this goblet shows the very finest quality deep-cut engraving achieved by using several wheels of different sizes. The busy, well-detailed composition features a German boar hunt. The value of such pieces increases with the number of figures and beasts depicted. An almost three-dimensional effect is achieved by deep-cutting the woodland background in a manner similar to low-relief carving. The decoration has been further enhanced by polishing and frosting the detail, and the thick walls of the vessel can be seen by examining the top rim. It would be more valuable still if the base was ruby-flashed. A band of hob-nail cutting runs around the base of the bowl above a waisted panelled stem with a central, multiple annular knop.

## ENGLISH ENGRAVED HOOP-SHAPED DECANTER

*1880; 24.3cm (13½in) high with stopper;*
**£400–500**

This unusual, somewhat novel, shape is peculiarly Victorian, although it does sometimes appear in late 19th-century German Westerwald blue glazed stoneware. The introduction of a range of new machinery enabled the Victorian glassmakers to produce large quantities of highly decorative glassware. The type of decoration followed that on pottery and porcelain, and included such favourites as humming birds, Japanese cranes, lilies-of-the-valley and ferns.

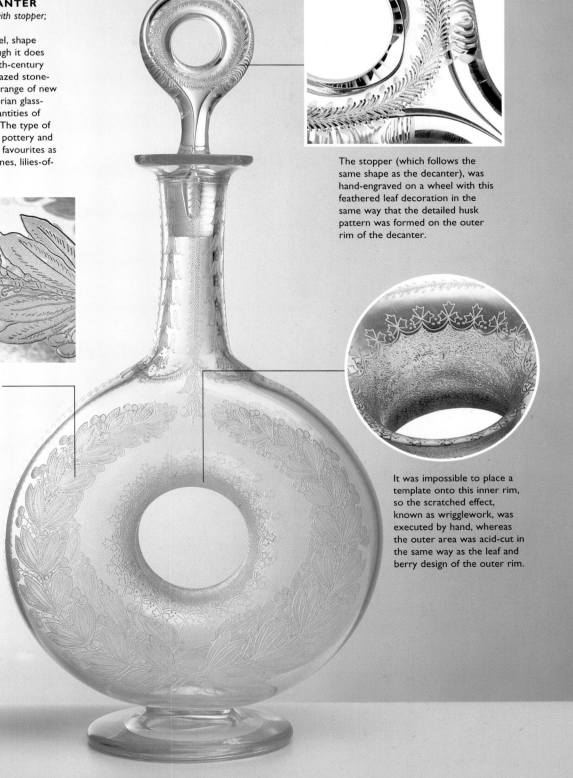

The stopper (which follows the same shape as the decanter), was hand-engraved on a wheel with this feathered leaf decoration in the same way that the detailed husk pattern was formed on the outer rim of the decanter.

The entire surface of the piece was covered with wax before the main leaf and berry outlines were applied using the point of a needle, with a template as a guide. Acid was then applied to create the deep-cut outlines and detail. The frosted effect was added by removing the wax within the main outlines and again applying acid. Before 1870, a fine wire brush was used to give a frosted effect, and the French continued to scratch their glass in this way after the British had abandoned the method.

It was impossible to place a template onto this inner rim, so the scratched effect, known as wrigglework, was executed by hand, whereas the outer area was acid-cut in the same way as the leaf and berry design of the outer rim.

### COLLECTORS' NOTES
• The value of a piece is often dictated by the intricacy of the engraving and the overall balance of the composition.
• Rock crystal wares by Thomas Webb are sought after but many are still very affordable.
• In the case of Bohemian pieces, size is important. Large pieces, often featuring stags in woodland settings can fetch several thousand pounds when in perfect condition.

• Ruby flashing is generally more desirable than either blue or amber flashing.

### COLLECTING TIP
You can build up a respectable collection of spa glasses, flashed in only one colour, for a reasonable sum. They can still be bought for around £150. Also, Victorian acid-cut tableware is relatively plentiful and often cheaper than modern-day equivalents.

# Coloured and Decorative Glass

The secret of making coloured glass was discovered by accident during ancient times, when iron oxides and various impurities added colour to glass intended to be clear. Ensuing experiments led to the discovery that the addition of copper produced blue and green glass, manganese purple, and cobalt dark blue.

By the 12th century, the windows of churches and cathedrals across Europe were filled with stained glass panels. Venice had long been an important centre of glass making, and by the 16th century it had emerged as the dominant European glass producer, with the factories removed to the islands of Murano just north of the city. Their coloured glass, richly enamelled or delicately translucent, was fashioned into pieces sought after all over Europe.

Such was the demand for the type of glass made in Venice that their workers were lured to other parts of Europe to hand on their skills in the fashioning and decorating of a stunning range of goods. Spain, too, produced distinctive ranges of coloured glass during the 16th century.

A much more robust type of glass became fashionable during the 17th century when Northern Europe began to usurp the Venetian domination. In 1679, Johann Kunckel developed the process of making ruby glass by adding tiny amounts of gold chloride. Pieces also began to be decorated in transparent coloured enamels with mythological subjects, hunting and harbour scenes and landscapes in black, iron red and gilding.

Glass making techniques, including enamelling, gilding and the production of *milchglas*, an opaque glass which imitated porcelain, continued to be used throughout the 18th century. During the 19th century, factories in Bohemia introduced a new range of colours admired and imitated by all of Europe. Friedrich Egermann developed yellow and ruby staining to cover clear glass, and this was used to great effect on a vast range of pieces made in Bohemia. In France and England, new mechanization resulted in the mass production of colourful, decorative glass that now provides one of the most varied and entertaining areas for the collector.

Coloured glass has a great advantage over clear glass for display purposes. Light does not have to pass through the objects to show them to good effect and because of the vast range of pieces available, it is an easy area in which to specialize. You might concentrate, for instance, on perfume bottles or liqueur glasses or even little nightlights, which were made by the million.

### ▶ VICTORIAN GLASS ÉPERGNE
*1895; 46cm (18in) high;* **£400–500**
Decorative table glass épergnes were produced in most glass making centres in England during the second half of the 19th century for serving fruit or displaying flowers, and continued to find a market until c.1920. In this case a central vase stands proud of triple trumpet vases and triple barley twist brackets from which pendant baskets are suspended. The pale green vaseline glass has been toned to semi-translucent and opaque white, edged with turquoise.

### ◀ FRENCH WHITE OPALINE GLASS VASE
*c.1865; 35.5cm (14in) high;* **£250–350**
It was this type of glass, produced during the middle of the 19th century, that prompted many small glass houses in France to mass-produce opaque coloured glass ware. This is a nice piece and well-painted, but many examples of this type of ware display hurriedly enamelled floral decoration and are of much poorer quality. Much of it has survived because such huge quantities were produced and exported to other parts of Europe and the United States during the late 19th century. Some is of such dubious quality that is is hardly worth collecting.

### ▶ SOWERBY BLUE GLASS JUG
*1885; 14.6cm (5¾in) high;* **£80–120**
Cobalt oxide is needed to create this deep blue colouring in glass popularly known as Bristol blue. In fact, this type of coloured glass was made all over Europe and was popular from the late 18th until the early 20th century. The point of import in Britain was Bristol, hence the name. This simple jug is mould-blown with applied white piping.

### ◀ FRENCH PINK AND WHITE CASED PRESERVE JAR COVER
*1870; 19cm (7½in) high;* **£40–60**
Two layers of glass have been annealed to create this piece of cased glass, which is rose pink on the exterior and white on the interior. The flat, thin gilding (prone to wear) outlined in black is an indication that it was made in France. Covers like this were made in large numbers to keep flies and wasps off the jam pot while it sat on the dining room or garden table in the summer.

## BOHEMIAN SPA GLASS
*1850; 12.7cm (5in) high;* **£250–350**
Spa glasses were made in large quantities
for the numerous spa towns in Germany,
and were bought by visitors as souvenirs of
their stay while taking the waters. They vary
greatly in form and style but all are thickly
walled and have a heavy base. This example
is flashed and engraved in amber and puce.

The two amber panels
have been left undecorated
intentionally so that each
acts as a prismatic view-
finder, capturing the scenes
engraved in the other
roundels on the glass.

The puce and amber
coloration is known
as flashed decoration,
achieved by applying a
translucent pigment which
then anneals to the body
when fired. The engraving
takes place after this
process is completed.

The flashing has worn
through exposing the clear
glass beneath and the base.
This shows the wear and
tear you'd expect to see on
a glass almost 150 years old.
The star cut on the base is
typical of these glasses.

It is pleasing to see the type
of good quality, finely detailed
engraving accompanied by well
executed lettering shown here.
This is not absolutely top of
the range, but a poorer quality
piece might feature only very
basic, naïve buildings, simple
lettering and acid- rather than
wheel-cut decoration.

### COLLECTORS' NOTES
Cased glass pieces, where two
layers have been fused together,
with one colour on the outside
and another on the inside, are
generally more desirable than
opaque or semi-translucent single
colour glass wares.

Be wary of pink and yellow
glass purporting to be Webb's
Burmese glass. This type of glass,
first developed at the end of the
19th century, took its body colour
from a metal containing gold and
uranium oxides. Genuine pieces
should carry a circular stencilled

and etched factory mark but
reproductions (without the mark)
have been finding their way onto
the market in recent years.

### COLLECTING TIP
Look out for the pieces that
the English glassworkers made to

carry in civic processions to
advertise their skill as craftsmen.
Objects made include walking
sticks, large, ornamental pipes and,
on occasion, decorative swords.
A pipe might cost £200–300 but
a fairly plain walking stick can still
be bought for £30

# Silver

The gleaming brilliance of silver, a metal prized by even the earliest civilizations, ensured that it was reserved for making some of society's most valued objects owned by its wealthiest members. But highly regarded though it has always been, silver is less precious than gold, and for that reason has also been fashioned into some of the more basic domestic items. Hence, it offers the type of variety in value and form which makes it almost as accessible to collectors as glass or ceramics. The finest engraved wine cisterns, salvers or candelabra by the leading silversmiths of the 18th century may be beyond the pocket of most collectors, but wine labels, trinket boxes, babies' rattles, tea strainers, tablespoons and a host of other smaller items can often still be bought for little more than the price of a good meal.

A study of the world's silver yields some fascinating details on the rise and fall in the fortunes of people during specific periods and the major events which shaped their lives. During the 16th century, for instance, when some of the first voyages of discovery took place, objects of curiosity and interest were brought back and mounted in silver. Coconuts carved into cups and Chinese porcelain were given this treatment and surviving examples reflect the adventurousness and originality of the age.

Early silver also fell victim to economic and political vicissitudes. For example, the English Civil War during the 17th century was a disastrous period in the history of English silver as large quantities of it were melted down to provide metal for coinage to pay the soldiers of both King and Commonwealth. Similarly, many beautiful pieces were lost (including the silver furnishings at Versailles) during the economic crises in France that occurred during the reigns of Louis XIV and XV, and even more during the French Revolution, when Napoleon's armies looted and hammered pieces flat for ease of transport. The reverse of this was the case on the other side of the Atlantic, where some of the earliest American silversmiths made objects of great beauty from coins brought to them by their customers.

Silver is too soft to be used in its pure state and is alloyed with other metals, usually copper, in varying proportions according to its country of manufacture. Many countries operate a hallmarking system, but none so vigorous as has existed in Great Britain since the beginning of the 14th century. The thrill of examining a good, clear set of full hallmarks which gives precise details of the maker, the town where he or she worked, the date of manufacture and which assay office the piece was sent to for testing, opens up an avenue of exploration which is not often accessible in other fields, and enthrals collectors from all over the world.

*Left: far left* American tea caddy by James Ball and Poor, c.1845; *centre back* American hot water jug by Louis Comfort Tiffany, c.1880; *centre front* Swiss teapot by Andreas Braun, c.1745; *right* English hot water jug by Thomas Oliphant, 1777.

# Where to begin

Experienced experts will look first at the overall design of a piece of silver and the colour of the metal before picking it up to feel the weight. Not until they have judged its general merits will the hallmark be examined. For the novice, however, looking at the hallmark is instinctively the first move, and quite natural. Once you have gained confidence and experience, you will start to recognize the work of particular makers, but, until then, an understanding of hallmarking is essential.

A hallmark consists of a series of stamps in the form of punched marks which indicate the quality of the precious metals used to make the piece as well as information on when, where and by whom the piece was made. In both ancient Greece and Rome, makers' marks and stamps indicating purity of metal were used. In Western Europe the practice began around the end of the 13th century when steps had to be taken to prevent unscrupulous silversmiths from adding large amounts of alloy to silver and gold. The method was so successful that by the middle of the 14th century, most European countries had some method of hallmarking system in place, although it varied from country to country.

## British Hallmarks

Great Britain operates the most rigorous system of hall-marking anywhere in the world. The first statute governing standards was passed in 1238, but the proper system came into operation with the introduction of the leopard's head mark in 1300, to be struck on both silver and gold throughout the realm. The standard set for coinage (92.5%) was also used for silver objects. In 1363 a further statute was passed by which every gold and silversmith added his maker's mark to pieces (at this time in the form of symbols as few could read or write) to counteract the widespread practice of forging the leopard's head mark on substandard wares. In 1478, the third mark was added in the form of a letter. From this date all work had to be taken to Goldsmiths' Hall for testing and marking by touchwardens (hence, Hall Marks). This was to stop gold and silversmiths from bribing the touchwardens who had previously come to their workshops to do the testing and marking. Sub-standard wares had been marked, accepted by the Mint and converted directly into coinage which led to a loss of confidence in the currency. But with this third mark, originally called the Assay Master's mark, the Assay Master or touchwarden could be identified if a marked piece was found to be substandard. As this letter mark changed each year, usually running in alphabetical order and varying a little between assay offices, it soon came to be regarded as the date letter. In 1544, the fourth symbol, the sterling lion (also known as the lion passant) came into being, to symbolize the royal control over the assay office, effectively replacing the leopard's head as the mark of the silver's standard. The leopard's head then became the town mark for London. When other assay offices began to be established in the 18th century, they used their own town mark (*see* p.99), but sometimes retained the leopard's head as well. Provincial Assay offices were established in many centres all over the British Isles. Among the earliest were Chester, Bristol, Norwich and York. Sheffield and Birmingham were established in 1773. Today, all sterling silver is sent to one of four centres – London, Birmingham, Sheffield or Edinburgh.

In Scotland and Ireland a thistle and a crowned harp were the respective marks used instead of, or sometimes as well as, the sterling lion to indicate the silver standard.

**BRITANNIA STANDARD** A radical change in British hallmarking took place between 1697 and 1720 when the Britannia Standard was introduced to protect the coinage from being melted down to make objects, at a time when silver supplies were limited. With the passing of the Wrought Plate Act, the standard for silver was raised from 92.5% to 95.84%, so that silver coins could not be used by silversmiths. The marks were changed. The sterling lion was replaced by the figure of Britannia, the crowned leopard's head by the lion's head in profile and the first two letters of the maker's surname replaced his initials. In 1720, the original marks were revived but some Britannia Standard silver continued to be made because certain silversmiths preferred working with the softer, purer metal. The option to use it continues today.

**THE DUTY MARK** Silver made between 1784 and 1890 had a fifth mark added in the form of the reigning monarch's head, struck to show that the duty had been paid. After 1890, the standard set again comprised four marks: the sterling mark; the town mark; the maker's mark and the date letter. This has been the same until the present day apart from three exceptions. In 1934–5 pieces were stamped with a Jubilee mark showing the heads of George V and Queen Mary to commemorate their Silver Jubilee; in 1953 a Coronation mark of Elizabeth II's head facing right was used in honour of her coronation; and in 1977 an optional Silver Jubilee mark appeared on some pieces over 15 grams in weight which showed the head of Queen Elizabeth II facing left and commemorated the Silver Jubilee of her accession.

## Continental Hallmarks

In most continental countries the systems of hallmarking were not as strictly applied as in Britain, although many European towns did have their own distinct and recognisable marks. In France a mark for Paris existed as early as 1300, but hallmarking as a legal requirement started in 1313. At first all wares were stamped in Paris, but by the end of the 14th century, 186 cities had the responsibility of testing and marking gold and silver. The testing was undertaken by wardens elected by local guild members, who, in turn, were supervised by the local department of the mint. A maker's mark was introduced in 1378. In 1672 two new marks were added in connection with tax on the metal. A maker brought his unfinished object to the *fermier* (a man who bought the right to levy duty on plate) after it had been assayed by the guild, and he stamped it with the "*poinçon de charge*" (before the tax was paid) and then again with the "*poinçon de décharge*," the discharge mark, after the tax had been paid. Each *fermier* had his own distinctive mark and many are recorded, which is helpful in dating objects from this period until the Revolution, after which the guilds lost their powers and the *fermiers* were disbanded. In 1797 a new hallmarking law was passed which formed the basis of the modern system.

In Germany, silver was marked from the 15th century with the mark of the maker and of the town of origin. Town marks evolved slightly over time and small changes can be observed in the design of the image on the mark of a particular town through the centuries. The Berlin town mark between the 17th and 19th centuries was a bear standing on his hind legs facing left, added to which is a date letter after c.1750. In Frankfurt the mark of a spread eagle was used with very minor alteration between the 16th and late 18th centuries. The town of Hamburg had a three-turreted castle on a shield as its mark between the 16th and 19th centuries.

A uniform system of hallmarking was not adopted in Italy until 1873. This had its origins in a Napoleonic decree of 1810 when the Emperor had established several official assay offices in regional centres. Before this, however, many towns and states had their own marks stamped by the guilds. In Florence, from the 17th to the early 18th century a seated left-facing lion above the letter "F" was used. This gave way in the later 18th century to a crowned letter "F." The town stamp for the city of Rome which was used between the 17th and late 18th century consisted of the crossed keys of St. Peter under a bishop's mitre.

From the mid-17th century onwards silver in the Netherlands was marked with a maker's mark, town mark, date letter, assayer's mark and crowned lion to indicate the silver standard. In the 17th and early 18th century the town mark of Amsterdam varied from a vertical line of three crosses in a shield topped by a crown, to a left-facing lion in a crowned shield.

Spanish hallmarks, in use from the 16th century, consisted of a maker's and a town mark. Certain towns began to use a date mark from the end of the 18th century. In Barcelona, the letters "BA" or "BAR" in a horizontal line were used between the 17th and 18th centuries and in Madrid at the end of the 18th century, a small castle turret was used with the last two digits of the date underneath.

## Hallmarking in the United States

During the late 18th and early 19th centuries an attempt was made to imitate English hallmarking, and items were stamped with a date letter, a duty mark and a lion. The strongest efforts were made in Philadelphia and Baltimore, but the practice was abandoned and most examples of American silver are stamped with the maker's signature alone. Many objects were stamped with the silversmith's name in full. By the late 1860s, the sterling standard was often used by Baltimore silversmiths, expressed as 925/1000 below the signature.

## Duty Dodgers

It should be remembered that hallmarks are not always infallible and should not be your only criterion when judging or buying a piece of silver. It is possible that alterations have been made, for various unscrupulous reasons. For example, in Britain, when the sterling standard of silver was restored in 1720, a duty of 6d an ounce on wrought silver was also introduced. To avoid paying, silversmiths would make a small piece, send it for assay and then cut out the marks and apply them to much larger, more expensive objects. Although these items don't conform to the regulations, they were made by the craftsmen who carried out the fraud, and done at the time the pieces were made. Another type of dodging occurred when the silversmith took the marks from a small, older piece and set them into his newly made heavier item, adding his own maker's mark and striking over the date letter to obscure it. By not sending it for assay, he avoided the duty. Neither forms of duty dodging are to be confused with the type of illegal alterations dealt with later in this section.

## Decoration

The type of decoration on a piece of silver can provide a good indication of its date, as styles varied in different periods. Pay special attention to the condition of the decoration as well as the overall condition of the piece as both have a bearing on value. The main types of decoration are listed below.

**ENGRAVING** This is a technique of decorating the surface of the silver from the front, removing the metal by incising lines, patterns and portraits. As far back as the 3rd millennium BC it was done with flint, bronze and copper tools. Today, it is achieved by hand with a sharply pointed steel tool held on an engraver's block, or by machine.

**BRIGHT CUTTING** Another form of engraving where the metal is cut in small gouges at an angle and removed by a tool with two cutting points so that the work is accomplished in narrow channels with slanting sides to give a faceted, bright appearance. The best bright cutting in England was done between 1770–90.

**CHASING** A way of decorating the front surface by indenting it and raising the design without cutting into the metal or removing part of it. The work is done with tools known as tracers and a chasing hammer. When the same technique is used to create a pattern but without raising the surface of the metal, the method is referred to as flat chasing.

**CUT-CARD WORK** Introduced in Europe in the second half of the 17th century, thin sheets of silver were cut into decorative patterns, often based on leaf shapes, and soldered onto the main body of the piece, as an integral part of its decoration. It was often used to embellish the bases of bowls or cups or around the handle sockets of tea or coffee pots.

**PIERCING** A method of openwork made by piercing the metal to make a pattern of small holes, it was used for purely decorative effect. Until the second half of the 18th century, it was done by hammers and a selection of small chisels, but after this date, the piercing saw frame was developed which enabled the silversmith to make a series of tiny, vertical and precise cuts. This type of work if most often seen on strainers, covers of casters, mustard pots, fish slices, wine coasters and baskets.

## Types of Metals

As well as sterling silver there are two other types of silver metal in which pieces are fashioned, Sheffield Plate and Electroplate. Items in both types are collected and have their own distinguishing features and marks.

**SHEFFIELD PLATE** The method by which a thin sheet of silver was fused to a much thicker sheet of copper and then passed through a rolling mill to create a sheet from which objects could be made. Thomas Bolsover of Sheffield made the discovery in 1743, but it was not until 1765 that the new method spread to other cities in Great Britain. Similar techniques were used on the Continent. Although less expensive than solid silver, Sheffield Plate in good condition is highly sought after and collected in its own right. It can be detected at any sheared edge where the copper can be seen lying between the sheets of silver. It is always decorated by flat chasing rather than engraving as any incising of the metal would reveal the copper beneath. Much is unmarked although some makers used their own marks, often in the form of their names or initials. In the late 18th century some pieces of Sheffield Plate were marked with a set of marks very close to those used for sterling.

**ELECTROPLATE** The process of depositing a thin layer of silver onto the surface of a base metal by means of an electric current. The technique was discovered by John Wright of Birmingham in 1840 and patented by the Birmingham company of G. R. and H. Elkington. Objects to be electroplated are fully formed before being immersed in the plating bath, whereas Sheffield Plated objects were formed from plated sheets. Items made by the two processes can be distinguished by looking at seams. Seams or joins cannot be seen on electroplated wares because they are concealed by the film of electrically deposited silver, whereas Sheffield Plate hollow wares such as candlesticks and coffeepots have a visible seam unless the piece has been replated. Electroplate is a whiter colour than Sheffield Plate, which has a bluish tone. It is not hallmarked but carries various marks such as "EP" (electroplated), "EPNS" (electroplated nickel silver) or the words "hard soldered."

## Patina

The colour which builds up on a piece of silver is as important as that on antique furniture, and looking at enough of it in good daylight will help you recognize the deep greyish blue glow which is built up over years of buffing and handling.

## Fakes and Alterations

The system of hallmarking was designed specifically to provide a revenue for the crown and government and to protect the silver standard. However, there has always been the odd deceitful silversmith and silver is a malleable metal that can be reshaped with skilful hammering. Despite this, even the most skilful craftsman will make the metal thinner by tampering with it, so thin, worn areas should be closely examined. Thin areas can also be caused by erasing crests and unwanted engraved inscriptions. The marks are sometimes taken from badly damaged pieces which are only good for scrap and put onto newly made pieces. These transposed marks can sometimes be detected by breathing on the suspect area. You may be able to see a faint outline around the marks where they have been soldered onto the piece. Genuine marks were put on one at a time and are not usually evenly spaced or in a completely straight line. Beware of those which are, as forgers have been known to make a single stamp carrying all the marks. A genuine set usually has some wear from cleaning, and although this look can be faked, it is difficult to fool the expert, so always seek advice if you are suspicious.

The most common alteration is to turn one type of object, which may be out of fashion and of little value commercially, into a much more saleable one.

Christening mugs made by the thousand have been converted into much rarer jugs by adding a pouring lip; tankards have been hammered up into coffeepots; oval teapots with their handles and spouts removed become tea caddies; spoons become forks and a caster missing its top can become a cream jug. Much plain 18th-century silver was heavily embossed in the 19th century. In Britain it is illegal to sell silver which has been altered without the addition being returned to Goldsmith's Hall for new marks to be added. Many alterations still bear the genuine marks but they may not be where they should be. Hallmarks on detachable lids, handles and stands should match those on the body. If the date mark is different, the piece has probably been altered.

## Repair and Restoration

Condition is a very important consideration and repairs will affect value unless a piece is particularly rare. Breathing on something can show up pale, frosted areas which may indicate repairs, although silver solder can be hard to spot. If you come across brown stains which don't disappear when you clean the piece, it can be an indication of repair because soldering often causes staining. Look for it around joins and hinges. Check any pierced decoration carefully because it is very prone to damage and look on the inside of hollow wares. If you see a bright area different from the rest of the interior, you are probably looking at a repair.

## Care and Maintenance

Silver is not as fragile as porcelain or glass but still deserves to be treated with care. If you don't have it on display, or if you need to store part of your collection, wrap it in either pure cotton fabric, acid-free tissue paper or felt tarnish-proof bags. Wool, plastic bags, chamois leather and newspaper can all damage silver. Use a good long term silver polish when it needs to be cleaned and work with small, circular movements, keeping the pieces in your hand while you clean rather than leaning them on a table. Don't overclean the area around the hallmark. Wear cotton, not rubber, gloves because rubber leaves permanent black marks on silver. After you have finished cleaning, use a very soft, old toothbrush to remove any residue of polish from ornate areas. Don't keep salt in silver salt cellars because it corrodes the metal; as soon as you have finished eating, wash your silver forks, wipe them dry and put them away.

## Standard British Hallmarks

| | | |
|---|---|---|
| Leopard's head | Maker's mark | Date letter |
| Lion passant | Britannia Standard | Lion's head |

### Duty marks

| George III 1784-85 | George III 1785-1820 | Victoria 1837-90 | Jubilee 1934-5 | Coronation 1952-3 | Silver Jubilee 1977 |

### Town marks

| Birmingham | Bristol | Chester | Exeter | Norwich |
| Sheffield | York | Dublin | Edinburgh | Glasgow |

### Date letters

A B C D E F G H I K
L M N O P Q R S T U

London 1796–1815

# Teapots, Coffee Pots and Chocolate Pots

Tea was so rare and expensive when it first appeared in Europe that it was recommended as a cure for various ailments. A 16th-century Italian traveller, Giambattista Ramusio, was told of its virtues by a Persian merchant he met in Venice. In England, Samuel Pepys recorded in his diary in 1660, that he "did send for a cup of tee (a China drink) of which I never drank before." The Chinese have enjoyed its delicate flavour for over 4,000 years, and at the time of the Ming Emperors (1368–1644) either boiled tea dust in a kettle, or mixed a selection of leaves in an open bowl of boiling water. As the popularity of tea increased in Europe (nowhere more so than in England), greater quantities were imported from China by the English and Dutch East India Companies.

There was more fluctuation in the value of tea than in any other type of food or drink – those with money were prepared to pay any price for it – and a bewildering number of rituals grew up around its preparation and consumption. The drinking of coffee and chocolate remained more popular on the Continent and in America, where it had become an established part of the daily routine at an earlier date. In England, the first coffee house opened in 1652 and in America, in Boston, in 1670.

All three were expensive beverages, drunk only by the nobility and the rapidly growing wealthy middle class. Their popularity offered great scope for silversmiths, who began to make not only pots for coffee and chocolate, and then for tea, but the caddies, spoons, jugs, trays and a great many other accessories that went with them. Many so-called coffee pots were probably also used to serve chocolate, but if you are looking through auction catalogues, only those with a removable finial in the centre of the cover through which a stick could be inserted to stir the contents, should be described as chocolate pots.

Those collectors whose budgets cannot run to a solid silver tea, coffee or chocolate pot, can start by buying spoons, strainers, milk jugs or sugar boxes. A small 19th-century milk jug can still be bought for £200–300 and a plain teaset with loop handles for £600–900. You may still be able to find an early 20th-century silver teapot for as little as £200.

## SILVER GEORGE III TEAPOT
*1791; 17.9cm (7in) high; 29cm (11½in) wide;* **£600–800**
Made in England by Peter and Anne Bateman, two members of a very well known family of silversmiths working in Georgian London, this teapot is of shaped oval form decorated with bright cut engraving. The pineapple finial (a symbol of hospitality) is made from solid silver, but it is more common to see them in ivory which has been stained green.

An engraved piece of silver is cut into in straight lines, whereas a "bright cut" engraved piece, like this one, is fashioned by cutting into the metal at an angle with a scalpel so that the resulting pattern reflects the light – hence the name. Over the years, bright cut engraving tends to become flattened by cleaning, and loses its sharpness. Most of this decoration has retained its original brilliance, which helps its value.

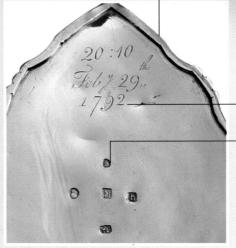

Where the spout joins the base there is a tendency over time for the soldering to wear and eventually split. Here, the silversmith has continued the straight sides of the main body of the teapot, and turned them under the base, rather like a hem, before soldering. This gives the piece extra protection and is a recognized sign of high-quality craftsmanship.

The inscription on the base here is contemporary – that is, it was put on when the teapot was made rather than added at a later date – which is nice to see. The top figures "20:10" may be the weight of the silver and the date may signify that it was made for a special occasion, possibly as a wedding present.

The full set of hallmarks are peculiar to the rigorous British system of hallmarking. They include the lion passant for sterling silver, the leopard's head which is the town mark for London, the maker's mark in the centre, the date letter, and, in this case, a duty mark, which was put on between 1784–90. This showed the head of the reigning monarch to indicate that the correct amount of silver duty for the weight of the teapot had been paid to the Government.

You often find a hinge standing proud of the cover. Here it lies flush, giving a smooth, continuous line and showing that the silversmith took a great deal of time and trouble over this section. This method is more expensive and time-consuming but well worth the effort. When the hinge sits on the outside of a teapot, it is more susceptible to wear.

When the pot is full, the solid silver handle would be impossible to touch with bare hands were it not for the ivory insulators (this has one at the top and another at the base of the handle). Carved fruitwood handles do not need insulators. The handle is detachable from the body and is therefore hallmarked as well. On a genuine piece such as this, the marks on the base will indicate the same date and maker as those on the handle.

101

# Other Teapots, Coffee Pots and Chocolate Pots

**▲ QUEEN ANNE IRISH TEAPOT**
*1706; 18cm (7in) high;* **£6,000–8,000**
Early teapots were small because of the high cost of tea. This squat, circular pear shape was the most common type made in the early 18th century, in this case by Thomas Bolton of Dublin and engraved with the arms of the Earl and Viscount of Lanesborough, Baron of Newton-Butler, County Fermanagh. The faceted spout is modelled as an animal's beak, the high, domed cover finished with a ball finial, and the wooden handle carved and embellished with a scroll. Often, the hinge on these early teapots has been repaired where it meets the upper handle socket and should be carefully examined.

**▶ QUEEN ANNE CHOCOLATE POT**
*1711; 26.3cm (10³⁄₈in) high;*
**£7,000–10,000**
Made in London by Richard Green, the tapering cylindrical shape of this fine chocolate pot ends in a moulded foot. The centre section of the hinged cover lifts up so that a stick can be inserted in order to stir up the contents – which were best left alone in the case of coffee. This is often the feature which separates a coffee from a chocolate pot. In common with many early pieces, the handle is at right angles to the spout. Silversmith Richard Green was a xenophobe who put his name to a petition circulating at this time to prevent French Huguenots and Dutch silversmiths working in England after they fled persecution in their own countries.

**▲ VICTORIAN TEAPOT**
*1885; 12.7cm (5in) high;* **£400–600**
The flared lip around the top of this teapot leads this shape to be described as a cape design. It was made by R. Martin and E. Hall of London and is of a type peculiar to England. A band of engraved acanthus leaves surrounds the upper body, the handle is fitted with insulators and is separately hallmarked, and the cover is topped with a beaded, tiered finial. The inscription slightly detracts from its value, but is pleasing and interesting because the teapot was presented to one Charles Garrett in 1886 after 28 years of service to Hennell of Bond Street, one of London's leading retailers and still thriving today.

**▲ ENGLISH ART DECO TEAPOT**
*1936; 11cm (4½in) high;* **£200–300**
Silver lent itself well to the brave, clean, stepped lines of the Art Deco style, and in England the custom of taking afternoon tea reached new heights during this period. The plantations in India supplied leaves which sold for a price everyone could afford; the Lyons Corner Houses served it in an atmosphere of comfort and elegance, and both silver and ceramic tea services were made in huge numbers. This example lacks the more extreme geometric shapes of the period and is plain and circular with reeded borders and a bakelite finial and handle embellished with a stepped scroll.

## ▲ GEORGE III COFFEE POT

*1777; 25.6cm (10⅛in) high;* **£1,000–1,500**

This baluster shape, as opposed to a straight or tapering cylindrical form, had begun to appear around 1750, and by the end of the century was quite common. This has a scroll handle and leaf-capped spout, a domed hinged cover with a cone finial, chased foliate decoration and fish scalework. The maker's mark is indistinct, but is probably that of John King of London.

## ▶ RUSSIAN COFFEE BIGGIN

*1851; 22cm (8¾in);* **£400–600**

This unusual and ingenious piece of equipment was made by Nicholls and Plincke of St. Petersburg. A biggin is a container which could be heated over a camp fire, although it is likely this one was used in a more salubrious setting. Inside the upper section is a pull-out strainer into which the coffee grounds are placed. The water is poured on and drips through into the lower section. A lift-up opening on the top of the lower handle takes hot water into a lining around the lower section so that the contents can be kept warm for a period.

## ▼ FRENCH CHOCOLATE POT

*c.1830; 21cm (8¼in);* **£800–1,200**

The habit of drinking hot chocolate was well established on the Continent before it was taken up in Britain, and has continued to be popular there. This example, made in Paris, has a plain, tapering cylindrical body with a carved ebony baluster-shaped handle at right angles to the spout, which is capped with a mythical bird's head.

## ▲ 19TH-CENTURY AMERICAN TEAPOT

*1845; 21cm (8¼in);* **£500–800**

Stylistically, this fluted, pear-shaped teapot has all the hallmarks of a piece made in the late 19th century because the decoration is so elaborate and mixed. The acanthus leaves scrolling up from the base and lapping the lid follow the classical theme, whereas the handle formed as a branch and the tendrils around the spout are in the rococo revival style. Yet from the date mark underneath we know this was made in 1845 by James Ball and Poor of Boston, silversmiths who went on to become one of America's leading manufacturers, Shreve, Crump and Lowe Co. Inc.

### COLLECTORS' NOTES

English chocolate pots were made only in the early 18th century and are therefore scarce and expensive. The habit of drinking hot chocolate continued on the Continent, however, and pots went on being made into the 19th century. Thus, Continental chocolate pots are more available and affordable.

The most common area of faking with coffee pots concerns those made from silver tankards. Check the proportions and if they are dumpy, beware. True coffee pots have a long, elegant appearance. Check the marks on the lid, where there should be only three or less. Four or more hallmarks indicate that the piece has been converted.

Check handle sockets, hinges on lids and finials for damage and repair on teapots, coffee and chocolate pots.

Look for any signs of where initials or armorial engraving may have been erased if the piece is plain, and look for later engraving on an early pot. Both areas of tampering may have created thin patches.

If you can, fill pots with water before buying to check for leaks, especially around the handle, spout and base. Many of these objects have been put to a good deal of use.

When starting a collection it is a good idea to collect pieces in chronological order, by the history of the habit.

### COLLECTING TIP

1930s engine-turned teapots and coffee pots have yet to acquire their full potential in the market place.

# Flatware

The matching set of cutlery precisely placed around a dining table is a comparatively recent concept. In medieval Europe, most people carried a wooden or pewter spoon, with the wealthy few having silver examples. Slightly later, a knife was added, but silver spoons, hammered from a single, small ingot, have survived in greater numbers than knives of the period, which had steel blades and were more vulnerable to wear.

The French had developed more sophisticated dining habits by the middle of the 17th century, beginning to use two-pronged forks, while the English still used their fingers or a knife-point to transfer food from plate to mouth. Charles ll returned from exile in France in 1660 and brought with him the idea of setting a table for eating. Sets of cutlery were still made only in very small numbers before the first decades of the 18th century and it is highly unusual to find complete sets which date from before the late 18th century.

Individual designs each had their own name. In England, the Trefid pattern gave way to the Dog Nose pattern around 1702. By 1710, the Hanoverian or Rat Tail was in common use, followed by Old English by 1760, Fiddle by 1770 and King's by 1810. These patterns had their own variants and have been reproduced ever since so it is important to check hallmarks rather than using patterns as a way of dating. Antique silver services are expensive so collectors often build a service slowly. It is acceptable to buy single pieces of the same pattern. Even more challenging is to buy pieces by the same maker from the same period.

**◀ ELIZABETH I PROVINCIAL SEAL-TOP SPOON**
*1565; 15.2cm (6in) long;* **£600–900**
**COMMONWEALTH PURITAN SPOON**
*1655; 16.9cm (6⅛in) long;* **£700–900**
**WILLIAM AND MARY SILVER-GILT TREFID SPOON**
*1689; 16.2 cm (6⅜in) long;* **£700–1,000**
Silver spoons were not only useful and valued personal possessions, they were often given as presents on special family occasions and handed down through the generations, which is why so many have survived and why they provide such fertile ground for collectors. In England the seal top spoon, *far left*, gave way to the plainer slip top seen next to it, and known as a Puritan spoon because it was made during the English Commonwealth period. It was superseded by the Trefid spoon on the *right* with its flattened end with two small notches cut into it.

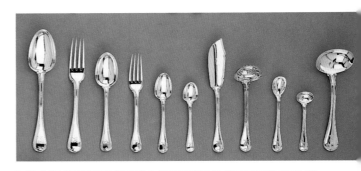

**▲ PLACE SETTING FROM A VICTORIAN CANTEEN FOR 12**
*1844; pieces 8–18cm (3–7in) high;* **£3,000–4,000**
Made in the Old English Military Thread Pattern (the Military Thread refers to the reeded, decorative lines around the outside edge of the pieces) by William Eaton of London, this large canteen comprises every conceivable type of utensil required by a dozen people dining in the nineteenth century. Only the knives are not included as these have suffered the ravages of time and fallen apart.

**▶ TWO FROM A SET OF 11 HANOVARIAN PATTERN DESSERT FORKS**
*1708; 15cm (6in) high;*
**£1,500–2,000 the set**
**TWO FROM A SET OF 12 HANOVARIAN PATTERN DESSERT FORKS**
*1767; 15cm (6in) high;*
**£600–800 the set**
In the early 18th century, when the first sets of forks were made, diners kept the same knife and fork throughout the meal, and few dessert forks were made. After the middle of the century, the complete canteen of cutlery, with implements for various courses, was more common, hence the lower price of the second pair of forks *(bottom)*.

**◀ DUTCH FAÏENCE-HANDLED KNIFE AND FORK**
*c.1720; each approx. 25.5cm (10in) long;* **£300**
This pistol-handled blue and white decorated knife and fork would once have belonged to a set of 12, 18 or perhaps even 36 knives and forks which regularly adorned the table of a wealthy household. Porcelain was quite a common alternative to silver for the handles of knives and forks, as were bone, horn and ivory. The Meissen factory made particularly fine porcelain handles for cutlery.

## TABLE FORK, FIDDLE THREAD AND SHELL DESIGN
*1840; 23cm (9in); £25*
## TABLE KNIFE WITH REPLACEMENT STAINLESS STEEL BLADE AND TRAILING GRAPE VINE DECORATED SILVER HANDLE
*1850s; 26.7cm (10½in); £25*

All the tines of a fork should be of equal length and not obviously worn as they are here. In addition, they should not appear too short in relation to the handle: they are sometimes cut down to eradicate worn ends and disguise damage. Tines normally wear on the left side where they are more forcibly in contact with food and plates.

Steel blades suffer over time. The servants polished the blade separately in a grinder and, inevitably, they became worn, which is why this one has been replaced.

If you're buying a knife to use, check carefully for a weak or split joint. The point at which the steel blade and silver handle meet is particularly prone to wear and not many antique examples survive in original condition. For each different handle design an ingot was rolled and the design embossed on it before being cast. The hollow silver shells were then filled with pitch and the rod protruding from the steel blade inserted into the pitch before the two parts were soldered together. Over time, water is able to seep in, causing the pitch to swell and split the joint.

Check that the handle of the fork is smooth and slightly upturned and that there is no dip where a coat of arms or initials have been erased in order to disguise the identity of a seller who, during hard times, may have decided to dispose of the family silver.

SHEFFIELD
MADE
FIRTH
STAINLESS

### COLLECTORS' NOTES
• As well as checking for worn tines on forks, check the bowls of spoons for signs of wear. A worn bowl will have an angled, almost cut-off appearance.
• The rounded-bowl soup spoon didn't come into being until c.1900, so what we call a table-spoon actually started life as a soup spoon.

### AVOID
•Tablespoons that have been cobbled to create desirable "apostle" and seal-top spoons by hammering the bowl into a fig shape and the stem into a thin shaft before adding the seal of one of the 12 apostles. A genuine early spoon should have the town mark in the bowl and the other three hallmarks (date, maker and quality) on the stem, whereas fakes tend to have all the marks together on the stem.
• The 19th century was the great age of over-ornamentation and some plain 18th-century table-spoons were later stamped with fruit in the bowl and elaborate chasing on the handles. Buying a later-decorated piece is fine providing you know what you are looking at and the alterations are reflected in the price.

### COLLECTING TIPS
• Few collectors are fortunate enough to be able to buy a full set of solid silver cutlery, but the choice of individual items such as caddy spoons and fish slices is endless and prices can be as low as £25 for a single piece. In the case of English silver, which is metic-ulously hallmarked, many collectors buy by maker, pattern or town.
• So many knives have disintegrated over the years that it is now quite acceptable to buy antique forks and spoons and a set of modern, perhaps bone-handled knives to accompany them.

# Candlesticks

We take the convenience of electric light so much for granted that it is easy to forget just how dependent our ancestors were on candlelight. The earliest surviving silver candlesticks were made solely for ecclesiastical use, as it was only the church who could afford such luxuries. Early candles were both smoky and smelly, made from beeswax or tallow, with those made in France considered far superior to the English variety.

Although silver candlesticks have been made in great quantity from the late 17th century, they have always been expensive items, intended for the wealthiest members of the population. The majority lit their way through the dark with far cheaper rush lights or candles burning in brass or pewter candlesticks. This exclusivity is reflected in prices today, so that it is possible to pay over £10,000 for a fine pair of English silver candlesticks by a well known silversmith. Single sticks are a lot more difficult to sell and therefore much more affordable, and will usually be well below half the value of a pair.

Candlesticks fall into two main categories, cast and loaded; the former (shown on the facing page) cast in moulds and soldered together, the latter stamped or hammered out from sheet silver, soldered together and then filled with pitch or plaster of Paris to give them weight and stability. Cast candlesticks have hollow bases, and loaded examples filled-in bases covered with green baize to protect the surface on which they sit. Cast candlesticks are made from a much heavier gauge of silver than the loaded variety and were made in England and Continental Europe in significant quantities from the early 18th century and in the United States from the mid-19th century. They are less prone to wear than the lighter gauge-loaded variety introduced c.1765. The rules on dating are not hard and fast, however, because some earlier examples were made from sheet, and cast candlesticks went on being made, particularly during the English Regency period when earlier styles were copied.

**▲ ONE OF A PAIR OF OLD SHEFFIELD PLATE CANDLESTICKS**
c.1785; 30.2cm (12in) high;
**£300–500 the pair**
This Sheffield plate candlestick has a square-domed and sloping base decorated with fluted batwing section. The octagonal knops are topped with urn-shaped capitals. Prices for Sheffield plate rose during the late 1970s but have now dipped to very affordable levels.

**▲ EARLY VICTORIAN SINGLE SILVER CANDLESTICK**
1843; 34.2cm (13½in) high;
**£600–800**
Tall and beautifully made by Richard Sibley of London, this candlestick has considerable value despite being a single and having been drilled for elecricity at some time. Modelled as a serpent wrapped around a tree with an upper and lower acanthus border, the stick in its original condition would be worth £800–1,200.

**▲ PAIR OF AUSTRO-HUNGARIAN SILVER GILT CANDLESTICKS**
1821; 24.1cm (9½in) high;
**£400–600**
Borders were constantly changing in this area of Europe during the early 19th century and the shifting population created a climate of great creativity. Much of the silver produced in Austria-Hungary at this time was highly innovative in design. The lines and shapes were clean and simple, as can be seen in these elegant candlesticks with their stepped oval bases, plain tapering columns and urn-shaped capitals. They foretell of the leading part Austria was to play in design in the early 20th century.

**▲ PAIR OF GEORGE III SILVER CANDLESTICKS**
1766; 26.2cm (10½in) high;
**£1,500–2,000**
By 1760, the English had more or less forsaken their rather half-hearted dalliance with the Rococo style and embraced the neo-classical movement. These candlesticks are very typical of the period when designers recreated the Five Orders (which comprise the various classical columns, their capitals and the super-imposed entablature) in both architecture and the decorative arts. Here, the silversmith William Gould of London, has recreated a pair of Corinthian columns with the appropriate pierced capitals.

**◀ PAIR OF ITALIAN CANDLESTICKS**
late 18th century; 26cm (10¼in) high; **£2,000–2,500**
Rome, Turin, Venice and Genoa were all leading Italian centres of silversmithing when this pair of candlesticks was made. Italian silver is light compared to English silver and these examples have high bases, with no loading and short stems. The acanthus leaf motif, used to great effect here, was a favourite of the neo-classical period and was used by designers in all media of the decorative arts.

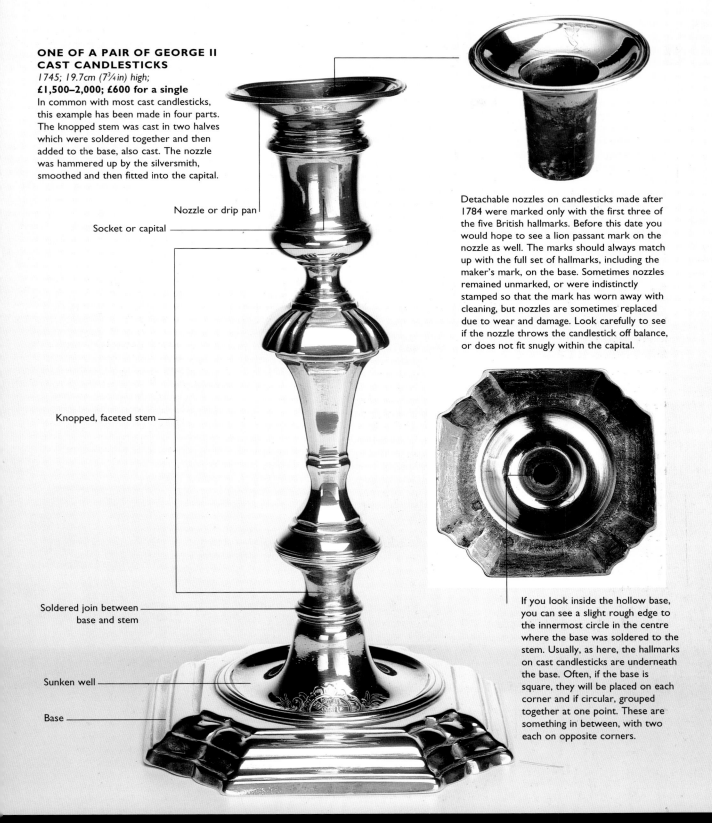

## ONE OF A PAIR OF GEORGE II CAST CANDLESTICKS

*1745; 19.7cm (7¾in) high;*
**£1,500–2,000; £600 for a single**

In common with most cast candlesticks, this example has been made in four parts. The knopped stem was cast in two halves which were soldered together and then added to the base, also cast. The nozzle was hammered up by the silversmith, smoothed and then fitted into the capital.

Nozzle or drip pan

Socket or capital

Knopped, faceted stem

Soldered join between base and stem

Sunken well

Base

Detachable nozzles on candlesticks made after 1784 were marked only with the first three of the five British hallmarks. Before this date you would hope to see a lion passant mark on the nozzle as well. The marks should always match up with the full set of hallmarks, including the maker's mark, on the base. Sometimes nozzles remained unmarked, or were indistinctly stamped so that the mark has worn away with cleaning, but nozzles are sometimes replaced due to wear and damage. Look carefully to see if the nozzle throws the candlestick off balance, or does not fit snugly within the capital.

If you look inside the hollow base, you can see a slight rough edge to the innermost circle in the centre where the base was soldered to the stem. Usually, as here, the hallmarks on cast candlesticks are underneath the base. Often, if the base is square, they will be placed on each corner and if circular, grouped together at one point. These are something in between, with two each on opposite corners.

### COLLECTORS' NOTES

Although cast candlesticks are less prone to wear because the silver is of a heavier gauge, they do suffer from years of enthusiastic polishing. The corners should be sharp, as should any knopped stems, and if they are worn, the price should reflect this.

In the case of loaded candlesticks, again because of cleaning, the corners have a tendency to wear, so much so that it may be possible to see the black pitch which fills them. If you spot this, avoid buying them because it is almost impossible to repair them successfully. The loading has to be completely removed

a lengthy and tedious process, otherwise when the silver is heated to apply solder, the loading explodes and oozes out.

Sometimes two single candlesticks are carefully matched and sold as a pair. Check the hallmarks on each stick and satisfy yourself that they really do belong together

or, if not, that the price reflects this. Two singles will only very rarely equal the value of a pair.

### COLLECTING TIP

Antique cast candlesticks can be very good value. You can buy a pair for £1,500, whereas a modern equivalent could cost three times as much

# Small Silver and Objects of Vertu

If a full tea or coffee service, or a handsome tray or bowl is beyond your budget, the thimble, trinket box or vesta case need not be. The novice collector can build up a respectable collection by concentrating on small objects. Many of them, particularly when combined with gold, tortoiseshell, porcelain or enamel, come under the heading of "objects of vertu." A plain example of any of these objects may sell for less than £100, but those by a particularly well known maker, or something encrusted with jewels or very finely enamelled, can be worth several thousand.

If you attend views at auction houses, you are quite likely to come across several lesser items being sold in one lot at a surprisingly low estimate. This can prove a good method of starting a collection. Weed out the unwanted pieces and resell them to fund your next purchase. No matter how small or simple the item, buy the best example you can within your budget and, just as with larger more costly pieces, check for damage, wear and alteration.

**▶ CONTINENTAL CUT GLASS SCENT BOTTLE**
*c.1790s; 12.7cm (5in) long;* **£400–600**
Pretty scent bottles can still be bought for just a few pounds, but this is a very fine example, inlaid with a silver-mounted toothpick box. The cover of the box is inlaid with blue glass and decorated with a scene depicting two doves perched on an urn below a crown, inscribed "Amitié."

**◀ STAFFORDSHIRE ENAMEL PUG'S HEAD BONBONNIÈRE**
*c.1800; 4.5cm (1¾in) long;* **£500–800**
A bonbonnière is a small, highly decorative box in which tiny sweets or cachous for breath-freshening were kept and carried about by ladies. Often silver-mounted and enamel-decorated, they are now valued for their elaborate workmanship. Novelty, animal-shaped examples are very popular with collectors. This piece was probably made in south Staffordshire, in England, where a group of French enamellers began working from c.1750.

**▶ SILVER CYLINDRICAL NUTMEG GRATER**
*Late 17th century; 6.4cm (2½in) long;* **£150–200**
Spices such as cloves, peppercorns and the aromatic nutmeg were highly prized when they were first imported into Europe in quantity after the Portuguese captured the spice trade in the 16th century. An elegant little grater like this would have been carried in the pocket so that food and drink could be seasoned with a few scrapes of fresh nutmeg – considered good for the health. This example, typical of the date, is engraved with a band of geometric design.

**▶ GEORGE III PURSE VINAIGRETTE**
*1818; 2.5 x 3.8cm (1 x 1½in);*
**£250–350**
**VICTORIAN "CASTLE-TOP" VINAIGRETTE**
*1840; 6.4 x 3.8cm (2½ x 1½in);*
**£500–800**
Standards of hygiene left plenty to be desired before the advent of modern drainage systems. The vinaigrette was developed as a way of carrying about some instant relief from the terrible smells encountered. Inside the outer lid a perforated one covered a sponge soaked in vinegar which released oils of lavender, cloves or camphor.

**◀ TORTOISESHELL AND GOLD PIQUE** *ETUI*
*c.1750; 15cm (6in) long;* **£800–1,200**
**GILT-METAL** *ETUI*
*c.1760; 12.7cm (5in) long;* **£350–450**
The *etui* was a practical, portable storage box with a hinged cover and a fitted interior. It was used to store useful small implements such as scissors, tweezers, fruit knives and bodkin cases. They were carried mainly by women, but versions for men do survive, often fitted with perfectly scaled-down architectural tools. *Etuis* were made in a variety of materials, and the condition and number of original implements still surviving are crucial to value.

**◀ GEORGE III SILVER SNUFF BOX IN THE FORM OF A BOOK**
*1802; 3.8 x 5cm (1½ x 2in);* **£80–120**
Snuff is powdered tobacco. When the leaves were first introduced into Europe in the mid-16th century, they excited the same measure of fascination as tea and were used for medicinal purposes. Smoking them and powdering them to form snuff occurred around the same time and the snuff box (as opposed to the tightly stoppered bottle used in China) was designed to hold the powder. In common with so many other small silver items, novelty shapes proliferated. This was made by Matthew Linwood in Birmingham in the form of a book.

**▲ DUTCH MINIATURE TEA AND COFFEE SET**
*19th century; pieces from 2.5 to 5 cm (1–2in);* **£500–800**
The Dutch were famous for making "toys," the name given in the 18th century to miniatures or small, decorative precious objects. Stamped only with the maker's mark, this miniature tea and coffee set, complete with hot water jug, is highly desirable because sets like this were often made for dolls' houses and few survive in such good condition. They were loved and played with and when the inevitable damage occurred, disposed of.

**▲ CONTINENTAL PARCEL-GILT HAND SEAL**
*19th century; 11.5cm (4½in) long;* **£300–500**
Until the envelope was designed, letters were folded and sealed with a special wax, which was either black or red. Many inkstands incorporated tapersticks and small candles with which to melt the wax. The matrix of a seal often left the imprint of a motto, monogram or initials on the melted blob, which soon dried to leave the contents secure. This unmarked parcel-gilt example is modelled as a tree trunk and depicts a scene after the hunt. The bloodstone matrix is carved with a coat of arms.

**◄ BI-COLOURED GOLD THIMBLE**
*19th century; 2.5cm (1in) high;* **£150–200**
Thimbles are a delight to collect, as they take up little space and are easy to display. Most are worth very little but this example is in two-coloured gold, with engraved overlapping sections, and still rests in its original fitted case (not shown). Some of the most valuable thimbles are in porcelain, made at top factories such as Meissen, and meticulously painted.

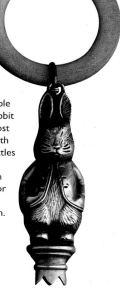

**► SILVER BABY'S RATTLE MODELLED AS PETER RABBIT**
*1938; 14cm (5½in) long;* **£50**
Few collectors of babies' rattles would be able to resist this example modelled as Peter Rabbit with an ivory teething ring attached. The most sought after are the silver examples fitted with bells, a whistle and a coral teething stick. Rattles began to be made when a more caring and liberal attitude to small children developed in the 18th century; tight swaddling bandages for babies were abandoned and they had more freedom to move around and be played with.

**◄ ELECTROPLATED RECTANGULAR CARD CASE**
*19th century; 10.8 x 9cm (4½ x 3½in);* **£150–200**
The calling card was an essential accessory in the last century before the telephone had been invented. Cases in a wide range of materials were designed specifically to hold them, some extremely ornate, others quite simple. This example was made by Elkington & Co., an English company based in Birmingham who pioneered the process of electroplating.

**◄ TIFFANY SILVER AND MIXED METAL CIGARETTE CASE**
*c.1920; 7.5 x 5.7cm (3 x 2⅛in);* **£400–600**
Smoking was thought a most desirable and elegant pastime when this delightful mixed metal cigarette case was made, with the design of dancing turtles on the lid inspired by Lewis Carroll's *Alice's Adventures In Wonderland*. The maker of this case, American designer Louis Comfort Tiffany, was one of the most innovative on the international scene at this time, and a wide range of fascinating objects in a variety of materials emerged from his workshops, particularly during the Art Nouveau period.

---

**COLLECTORS' NOTES**
• Carefully examine anything decorated in enamel for chips and cracks as any damage seriously affects value.
• Look carefully at card and vesta cases to see if crests or initials have been erased, in

which case the surface may be very thin.
• Vinaigrettes are susceptible to worn hinges and worn detail in the fragile decoration caused by over-cleaning.
• Unsurprisingly, babies' rattles often survive in very poor

condition. The bells should be intact on those fitted with them, and the coral should not be chewed. Look too, at the point where the coral joins the silver as this has often worn loose and been stuck back on with ordinary glue.

**COLLECTING TIP**
Card cases have recently gone up enormously in value, especially those with ornate decoration, but vesta (match) cases are still good value and were made in a huge variety of desirable novelty shapes

# Clocks & Watches

It is generally accepted that the oldest existing working clock in the world is in England, housed in the turret of Salisbury Cathedral. Made in 1386, it is still keeping good time. It had neither face nor hands, but was designed to mark the hours by its strike, calling the monks to prayer. Ever since man began to measure time, not only by dividing its passage into years (the time-lapse necessary for the earth to complete its journey round the sun), but by further dividing it into units of months, weeks, days, hours, minutes and seconds, he has sought to increase the accuracy of clock mechanisms.

Clocks were being made in the 14th century in Italy, and the earliest portable timepieces in Nuremberg, South Germany, by the early 16th century, when the advent of spring-driven mechanisms allowed clocks to come down off the wall and be carried about or placed on a table. The invention of the long pendulum in the mid-17th century was revolutionary, leading to the development of the longcase clock. Later came carriage clocks, pocket watches and ultimately, wristwatches.

The earliest clocks were made of iron by the local locksmith or blacksmith, until brass began to replace iron for part of the mechanism in c.1550. By the 17th century, clock makers were highly skilled and respected craftsmen who formed powerful guilds. English clockmakers such as George Graham and Thomas Tompion were so widely respected that, on their death, they were buried in Westminster Cathedral.

It is a fascinating area for the collector because clocks and watches are not only attractive decorative objects made in a variety of shapes, sizes and materials, but are also complicated precision instruments. What is going on inside a handsome walnut or mahogany case is often of more interest to the enthusiast than the outward appearance of the clock.

If you are new to the subject, it is helpful to try to understand the evolution of clock-making. The mechanisms are the same in principle. The motive-power is provided by weights or springs which drive a series (or train) of meshing toothed wheels and pinions which send the hands around a dial marked with the hours. The escapement mechanism of the clock allows the power to be released in a controlled sequence, thus regulating its timekeeping.

*Left: left back* Black Forest cuckoo clock, c.1850; *left front* French carriage clock, c.1870; *right back* English bracket clock by John Rycutt of London, c.1780; *centre and right front* French marble and ormolu garniture set, c.1890.

# Where to begin

The most satisfying thing about buying an antique clock is that, with careful repair and maintenance, it will give you as much pleasure as it did the original owner.

In auction catalogues, and when you talk to experts, you will read and hear descriptions of both clocks and timepieces. Clocks strike and timepieces do not.

## Mechanisms

The *motive-power* of a clock is a either a weight, or fusee and spring which drives a train of wheels.

The *fusee* is a conical-shaped brass drum, with the gut line from the spring wound round it like a spindle filled with thread, which controls, by different ratios, the power output of the spring to enable the clock to keep a regular time. Fusees were used on clocks and watches until the late 19th century, not given up until slimmer Swiss watches became fashionable in the early 20th century. The *escapement* is the part of the clock, watch or timepiece which allows the power driving the mechanism to escape, and controls the speed at which a clock runs down. The various forms of escapement release the escape wheel at regular short intervals (giving the "tick tock" sound), allowing the driving force to operate, lock and release again, in a regulated sequence.

The earliest types of clock mechanism had *verge escapements*, with a *balance wheel* on a short pendulum. These were used from the second half of the 17th century in bracket or table clocks, lantern clocks and, more rarely, longcase clocks. The verge and pendulum continued to be used until 1800, but it was an inaccurate method of timekeeping.

The *anchor escapement* was developed around 1670. Shaped like an anchor, it allowed either a short or long pendulum to be used and gave greater accuracy than was possible with the verge escapement. It was used in longcase clocks and in bracket and wall clocks. The arc of the swing was much smaller than that required by the verge and so it was seen as an enormous advance. Clocks with a verge escapement generally use a small, pear-shaped bob on the end of the pendulum as a large weight is not needed. Anchor escapements require a larger disc-shaped bob which is lead-filled to give it weight.

Cylinder, lever and balance wheel escapements (see Carriage Clocks, p.120, for balance wheel escapements) were mounted onto platforms on the top of carriage clocks or mantel clocks from c.1840 and continue to be used today. The platform on which these escapements are carried is detachable as a unit, as opposed to being an integral part of the clock.

The earliest *striking mechanisms* determined the hours with a *locking plate* incorporated into the mechanism, with notches cut out of it to determine the number of hours a clock needed to strike, the maximum being 12. The locking plate, developed by the 1670s, was used on French clocks up until the late 19th century.

The *"rack and snail"* is another form of striking mechanism. The number of hours are controlled by a snail-shaped disc fixed to the hour hand, with steps cut away equalling the number of hours to be struck. This is a more reliable type of mechanism and ensures that the wrong number of hours cannot be struck, as can happen with a locking plate strike. The "rack and snail" is still used on clocks today. The majority of clocks strike on the hour only. Chiming clocks were developed in the early 18th century and could sound on a number of bells at the hours and quarter hours, playing popular tunes. Wire gongs became popular in the 1840s and developed in the latter half of the 19th century into large gong rods, like pipes, found in high quality longcase clocks made in England and Germany in c.1900. In the 20th century, German clocks often had two wire gongs to provide a "ting tang" strike at the quarters.

## Dials

By 1730, *enamel dials* were common on English pocket watches. They were sometimes produced in the 1780s for longcase clocks, but are very rare. More common are painted enamel dials on longcase and bracket clocks, fitted to high quality pieces. Enamel sections are most frequently found on French clocks. Often the dials are gilt, with the numerals set against enamel reserves. Enamel dials are extremely prone to cracking and chipping, so examine examples very carefully. Hairline cracks are often camouflaged by bleaching but you should be able to spot the differences in colour. Cracking creates a cobweb effect over the dial and if you come across this, the price should reflect the damage that has occurred.

*Wooden painted dials* were used for tavern clocks in England from the mid-18th century and on Black Forest clocks in the early 19th century. The latter are usually 30cm (12in) square, with an arch above, painted white and then decorated with flowers, before being varnished. Wooden dials are susceptible to woodworm and are often in split condition. They can be properly restored by specialists.

The *brass dials* you see on bracket, wall and longcase clocks were probably once silvered, but the silvering has been polished away over the years. The effect is achieved by using silvering salts which change the colour of the brass. Resilvering is not expensive, but should be done by a specialist. Like re-gilding, this kind of restoration is regarded as sympathetic.

## Hands

Early clocks had very simple, finely sculpted blued-steel hands (whereby the steel was polished and blued with a flame, preventing the metal from rusting and giving a distinctly burnished blue appearance) in straightforward designs. Along with the style of dials, the hands became more elaborate. Blued steel gave way to gilt metal in the latter half of the 18th century on country longcase clocks. Hands get damaged and are often repaired, but it only affects value greatly if the clock is an absolutely top quality one and the replacements are very obvious.

## Fakes and Alterations

You will come across few outright fakes in this area because there is so much work involved in making a clock. Most of the changes are in the form of alterations, done to make a piece more fashionable or desirable. The movements and dials of longcase clocks are sometimes moved from one case and married to another to create a more fashionable-looking clock, in which case you will see blocks of wood on the case cheeks (*see* p. 115 ).

When a later dial is fitted to an earlier movement, new holes have to be drilled to accommodate the new dial and you will then see a spare set of holes. Sometimes, on brass dial clocks, when a striking dial has been fitted onto a chiming mechanism the old holes are blocked and filled, and a new set is drilled, so look for discoloured areas on the dial which have been camouflaged with engraving.

Pretty provincial longcase clocks, with a decorative brass or painted dial, which only run for one day before having to be wound, are not as desirable as those with an eight-day movement. An eight-day movement is often fitted to the existing dial, and holes drilled, as 30-hour clocks often have no winding apertures.

Unsympathetic restoration can seriously devalue a clock. Common misdemeanours include refinishing a clock case by taking off the surface and revarnishing it; over-polishing the movement by using an electric buff; reveneering in walnut bracket clocks which were originally black-lacquered or ebonized, and stripping down painted pine cases, destroying the original surface and creating a stripped pine effect.

## Care and Maintenance

Clocks are mechanical objects and therefore need servicing on a regular basis. This is well worth bearing in mind when you decide to buy one, because unless you intend learning about the intricacies of clock mechanisms in minute detail, you will have to enlist the help of a reputable, professional clockmaker to make sure that the piece is cleaned and serviced every four to six years.

The wheels are mounted on arbors which have pivots turned at each end which in turn run into brass plates. These have oil sinks which provide the essential lubrication for the mechanism, and if conditions are warm and dry, these are likely to dry up and cause problems. Wear will occur and the timekeeping will suffer, causing the clock to stop eventually. Thorough checking and oiling of a clock is a very specialized skill which you should not attempt yourself.

Both dust and heat are the enemies of clocks. Dust gets into the oil and acts like a grinding compound which wears out the mechanism. Some French clocks were made without backs, but were supplied with glass shades or domes which have broken over the years. These pieces are often displayed on open shelves and the dust floats in, so keep them in glazed cabinets. Heat can cause warping and splitting of wooden clock cases in the same way as it affects all antique furniture.

## Moving Longcase Clocks

Major problems can occur when it becomes necessary to move a longcase clock, an operation which should be done very carefully in various stages, involving completely disassembling the clock. First of all, slide off the hood. Finials may be loose so remove those if a long journey is involved and wrap them separately. Mark the weights, left and right, and then unhook the pendulum, possibly fixing it to a wooden rod to keep it straight and protect the delicate suspension spring. The mechanism may fall out once the weights are removed, so be prepared. Otherwise, lift it down carefully. Protect the dial from getting scratched, and the crutch piece on the back of the movement from being bent. Wrap all the pieces separately and make sure you keep all the keys in a safe place. The case itself can be moved in the same way as a piece of furniture, but take care as you are disassembling the clock that it does not fall over. You may want to secure the case to the wall once it reaches its new destination, something which is considered a sensible safety precaution since longcases can topple over. You won't spoil it if you do it carefully.

# Longcase Clocks

The development of the long pendulum in 1657 was probably the most significant invention in the history of timekeeping. Most authorities agree it can be attributed to the Dutch physicist and mathematician Christiaan Huygens van Zulichen. His work was introduced into England by Ahasueras Fromanteel the following year. Shortly afterwards, he began to manufacture and sell long-pendulum clocks. Their great advantage was their accuracy. Early clocks were weight-driven with a verge escapement and a short pendulum with a wide swing, prone to inaccuracy. The long pendulum with an anchor escapement had a swing which took one second exactly and was maintained by its own momentum. It was not long before the pendulum was encased, a logical step which protected it from accidental knocks, kept the dust out of the movement and concealed the workings.

**▲ THREE PAINTED LONGCASE CLOCK DIALS**
*c.1800; 30cm (12in) wide;* **£50–100 each**
Painted dials are a particularly British feature. Once considered much less desirable than solid brass dials, they are now sought after. They were often made by specialist firms in Birmingham, commissioned by clockmakers in the various regions who then had their names put on them. Scenes showing the seasons and Masonic symbols were common, as were various country scenes, rolling ships and moons.

**◄ WALNUT MARQUETRY LONGCASE CLOCK WITH ANCHOR ESCAPEMENT BY CATTEL**
*c.1690; 2m (6ft 6in) high:* **£6,000**
The barley twist columns on this beautifully inlaid clock indicate its early date. It has another unusual feature: a pull-quarter-repeat enabling the owner to tell the time to the nearest quarter of an hour by pulling a string. The clock then struck the hour and the quarters. It proved useful to the restless sleeper in the dead of night and saved having to light a candle to tell the time.

**► MAHOGANY QUARTER-CHIMING LONGCASE CLOCK WITH PAINTED DIAL BY WILLIAM JACKSON OF FRODSHAM**
*c.1790; 2.24m (7ft 4in) high;* **£2,500–3,000**
A big handsome clock, this is less commercial than many because its size means it requires a large, tall-ceilinged room to stand in. Fitted with a triple-train movement (one for the timekeeping side, one for the hourly strike and one for the quarter chime) it is in a case with a flame mahogany door and detailed inlay.

**◄ AMERICAN TALLCASE CLOCK**
*c.1780; 2.41m (7ft 11in);* **£10,000**
It is rare to find American tallcase clocks outside their country of origin, where they are highly sought after and sell for large sums. This example, made in Elizabeth, New Jersey, has a case constructed by cabinetmaker Ichabod Williams. In common with most American clocks, the dial is of painted metal rather than brass, with decorative pierced steel hands. The arch top is typically embellished with three matching brass finials.

## OAK-CASED EIGHT-DAY LONGCASE CLOCK BY THOMAS SHINDLER OF CANTERBURY

*c.1720s; 2.09m (6ft 9in) high;*
**£800–1,200**

Shindler, active between 1720 and 1797, may have made the later alterations to this clock himself, having been requested by the owners to adapt it according to the latest designs.

Look out for these gaps between the brass arch and the casing – an obvious space like this one is a good indication that the clock has suffered from alterations. On an unaltered clock, the case would fit snugly around the arch.

It is quite nice to see the way the brass here has been hammered with a punch to give this frosted effect known as matting. It makes the piece more desirable than one with a plain brass centre.

At alteration, extra cheeks have been inserted to increase the height of the movement so that it fits into the increased size of the case. About 80 percent of longcase clocks have had this treatment and the variation in colour of the wood makes it easy to spot.

A circular piece of silvered steel has been put in, bearing the inscription "Tempus Fugit" (time flies) for no other reason than to fill a gap. It is part of the later addition and not considered very desirable by collectors.

As styles developed, clocks were very often altered to fit in with the latest fashions. This clock started life with a square dial, the arch was added c.1760–70, when this style of case became fashionable. An original break-arch dial would be made from one piece of brass, but here you can see the line where the arched section has been placed over the original square.

Subsidiary seconds dial

The spandrels

Chapter ring

Dial centre

Ringed winding hole

Calendar aperture

Bell    Back cock

Crutch piece

Movement plates
Seat board
Added cheeks to raise height of movement

Winding barrel with gut line which suspends the weights and winds down slowly through the 8 days.

### MOST COMMON ALTERATIONS
• Adding an arch.
• Removing a caddy-shaped top to make the clock smaller and possibly more desirable.
• Cutting the plinth to shorten the clock.
• Converting the rising hood on pre-1700 examples to a hinged opening door so that the clock can be wound more easily in a low ceilinged room.
• Adding cheeks to increase the height of the movement (see annotated example).

### COLLECTING TIP
Large numbers of English longcase clocks were made and, considering the work which went into them, they are still good value.

# Bracket and Mantel Clocks

Before the second half of the 17th century, most clocks were made to be hung on the wall and were weight-driven, but after the development of the spring-driven mechanism it became possible to take a clock down and carry it around. Large though they may seem today, the bracket or table clock was designed to be portable. Clocks were luxury items and a single household often contained only one or possibly two, moved from room to room as required. Whereas longcase clocks are often signed on the dial, a bracket clock is more likely to be signed on the backplate, which is also engraved because it is more visible when placed on a mantelpiece with a mirror. Very few bracket clocks retain their original bracket, by which it was attached to the wall. It is quite likely that this was dispensed with early in the life of the clock so that it could be carried about and placed on a table or mantelpiece.

### ◄ EBONIZED CHIMING BRACKET CLOCK
*c.1765; 53cm (21in) high;*
**£4,000–6,000**
The average bracket clock is not worth this kind of money, but this example, made by Henry Jenkins of London, plays a musical tune on eight bells every quarter hour. It also has a calendar and the unusual feature of a moon face in the arch, more commonly seen on longcase clocks. The brass bracket-style feet are typically late 18th century, as are the double scroll foliate spandrels at each corner of the face. The pine cone finials are a simpler forerunner of the more exotic pineapple motif seen on the clock below.

### ◄ ORMOLU AND PORCELAIN MOUNTED MANTEL CLOCK
*1870; 33cm (13in) high;* **£500–700**
This is very typical of the ornate style popular in France (where it was made), England and the United States at the end of the 19th century. Many such pieces were exported and displayed in houses alongside similarly richly decorated porcelain. The eight-day bell striking movement is in a case decorated with oak leaves and an urn finial. The central lion mask supports garlands of foliage.

### ▼ ORMOLU URN-SHAPED MANTEL CLOCK
*early 19th century; 23cm (9in) high;* **£1,000–1,500**
A clock like this – small, elegant and classical in style – would normally be worth £1,500–2,000 but this French example needs total restoration. It has a white enamel chapter ring, onto which the numerals have been painted, an engine-turned centre and a bell-striking movement with a silk suspension.

### ► REGENCY MAHOGANY BRACKET CLOCK
*c.1820; 50cm (9¾in) high;*
**£700–900**
Signed "Stratford of Cheltenham" on the backplate, this handsome mahogany-cased clock displays several typically Regency features including a pineapple finial, side brass frets and ring handles, as well as inlaid brass stringing and ball feet. It is fitted with a twin fusee movement striking hourly on a single bell, and has a painted dial and roman numerals.

## BRACKET CLOCK
*c.1680; 32cm (13in) high;*
**£3,000–4,000**
This is an ebonized bracket clock with pull-quarter repeating, signed Robert Seignor, London. It is typical of the period, with a finely matted centre and winged cherub-head spandrels. It has a domed top with a gilt carrying handle, glazed side panels and bun feet.

Fusee
Mainspring barrel
Gut line

### Detail through side glass of workings
*The fusee* – The conical spool, or fusee, controls the power of the spring. It allows the mainspring to give the same output of power when it is almost wound down as when it is fully wound, thus enabling the clock to always keep even time.
*Gut line* – As the clock winds down, the power transfers from the fusee through this gut line to the mainspring barrel. When the clock is fully wound, most of the line is wrapped around the fusee, gradually transferring to the barrel as the clock winds down.

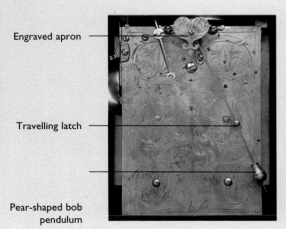

Engraved apron

Travelling latch

Pear-shaped bob pendulum

### Detail through open back door of engraved backplate
*Engraved backplate* – A signed backplate makes the piece more interesting. It doesn't directly affect value, but it is most desirable to some collectors.
*Apron* – A nicely engraved or pierced apron is always a sign of a good quality clock. When the clock stood on the mantelpiece with a mirror at the back, the beauty of the mechanism was clearly visible and a good advertisement for the skill of the craftsman who made it.
*Travelling latch* – This latch kept the pendulum locked while the clock was in transit. They are often broken off, and a missing one does not affect value.
*Pear-shaped bob pendulum* – This is the right sort of pendulum for use on a clock with a verge escapement. If you see a much larger, circular pendulum on a bracket clock of this age, it means the escapement was changed to a more modern type during the 19th century to ensure better timekeeping. Often the bottom of the case was cut out on the inside for the bob to be lowered to achieve correct timekeeping. If this has happened, you will see a hole in the floor of the case.

# Novelty Clocks

The earliest surviving working novelty clocks were German automata made in Augsburg in the 1650s involving mechanical figures, either of human or animal form, which performed as the hour struck. They include dogs, and, most extraordinarily for the early date, cockerels which flapped their wings and opened and closed their mouth, often making a crowing sound. The earliest novelty clock in history is the celebrated crowing cock of the Strasbourg Cathedral clock, made in 1354 and now preserved in the Strasbourg Museum.

These astonishing pieces continued to be made until the 18th century, when they fell out of favour, but the novelty clock enjoyed a revival in the Black Forest area of Germany in the 19th century and included the pie-eating man who lifts a fork to his mouth on the hour. The French also manufactured novelty clocks to a high standard. There are mantel clocks in the form of a rolling ship on a seascape and clocks incorporating model waterfalls, the effect created by spinning glass spirals, each with an automaton separate from the clock which could run for a few hours at a time.

During the 19th century automaton clocks were made, mainly in France, in forms which reflected the new industrial age and included steam locomotives, water wheels and large steam hammers. Produced in quite large numbers, they form part of a growing collectors' market today.

### ▶ AUGSBURG TABLE CLOCK
*1620; 22 x 60cm (8¾ x 23½in);*
**£6,000–8,000**
The clock dial is set onto an engraved plate on the surface of the base of this rare piece, which was made to a high standard. A gilt dog sits atop the base through which the movement can be seen. As the clock ticks, his eyes move from side to side and his jaw opens as the hours strike. Not many of these come on the open market: most have to be admired in museums.

### ▶ BLACK FOREST PEDLAR CLOCK
*c.1840; 15in (38cm) high;* **£1,400–1,800**
This is very typical of the sort of novelty clocks manufactured in the Black Forest area of Germany during the 19th century. They have enormous charm and are very popular with Dutch and German collectors. Made of painted tin and wood, the pedlar cradles the clock in his right arm. A further empty clock case is strapped on his back, to be used for storing the key. The paintwork on his tin clothes is original.

### COLLECTORS' NOTES
The early Augsburg clocks are scarce and most of them have undergone some restoration.

The clocks comprising tin figures holding dials are reproduced in cast alloy and many are being passed off as originals. The original figures have painted tin clothes over a wooden carcass whereas the reproductions are painted directly onto a cast body with casting marks and serial numbers on the base.

Prices of novelty clocks have risen steeply in the last five years whereas the value of other types of clocks has, in many cases, gone down.

### COLLECTING TIP
If you are really lucky you may come across one of the French industrial model type timepieces which can sometimes be found for a few hundred pounds although they can be worth several thousand.

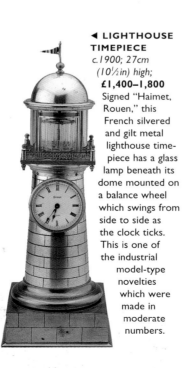

### ◀ LIGHTHOUSE TIMEPIECE
*c.1900; 27cm (10½in) high;* **£1,400–1,800**
Signed "Haimet, Rouen," this French silvered and gilt metal lighthouse timepiece has a glass lamp beneath its dome mounted on a balance wheel which swings from side to side as the clock ticks. This is one of the industrial model-type novelties which were made in moderate numbers.

### ▶ VITASCOPE AUTOMATON TIMEPIECE
*c.1941; 32cm (12½in) high;* **£300–400**
There is growing interest in these eccentric timepieces manufactured by Vitascope Industries on the Isle of Man. The 13.5cm (5½in) dial is in the form of raised dot numerals beneath a window in which the automaton, a ship rolling in a changing sky, operates. To start the motor, a knob is spun on the back of the timepiece which then continues to run in a synchronous movement. The motor drives both the hands and the oval drum operating the automaton. A further drum containing a lamp and a sheet of dyed gelatine rotates, simulating a backdrop of a sunrise, noon and sunset. The first patent on the design was taken out in 1941. The bakelite cases were manufactured in green, cream, dark brown and this pink.

# American Mantel Clocks

In the early years of the 19th century, American clocks made for the home market had wooden movements, but with the introduction of inexpensive rolled brass, by the mills in the Waterbury area of Connecticut, the cost of brass clock movements came down to a level where almost everyone could afford a clock.

Production rose rapidly from 6,000 a year in Eli Terry's factory in Connecticut c.1840, to 8,000 a day in the numerous Connecticut factories by the early 1900s. The clocks sold for as little as $1 each and had paper labels fitted to the back panel of the interior naming the maker and giving instructions on how to set up, operate and maintain them.

The movements in these mass-produced clocks are cheaply made, with brass plates and open mainsprings. The dials were of painted tin or even paper. They were exported worldwide and are therefore widely available in Europe as well as in their homeland.

Prices have remained fairly low for all but those fitted with a very rare mechanism, known as a wagon spring, which are becoming more collectable and can fetch up to £1,000, and are largely collected for their naïve decorative value.

### ▶ WALL CLOCK BY JEROME & CO.
*c.1840s; 66cm (26in) high;*
**£40–50**
This striking wall clock has a 30-hour movement and needs to be wound every day, something unpopular with collectors today, who prefer eight-day clocks. In the 19th century, however, the daily winding of the clock was a comforting ritual. The clock industry slumped in the 1830s and it was Chauncey Jerome who developed the cheap, 30-hour movement. A great success, this lead to a revival in production and the clocks were exported in great numbers.

### ◀ STEEPLE-SHAPED MANTEL CLOCK BY W.L. GILBERT
*c.1870; 50cm (19¾in); high;* **£40–60**
W.L. Gilbert moved his factory to Winchester, Connecticut, in 1841 and ran a thriving business until fire destroyed the building in 1871. In new premises he continued to prosper until a recession in the early 1900s created financial problems and the receivers were called in during 1932. The steeple shape is very common among his clocks. This one is veneered with stained beech, the lower glazed panel showing a view of Rome.

### ◀ MAHOGANY WALL CLOCK BY SETH THOMAS
*1880; 83cm (32½in); high*
**£60–100**
Superior to many of its kind, this mahogany wall clock has painted half-columns with gilt capitals either side of the case and the unusual feature of two gold-painted doors to the front. The painted tin dial has been embellished with some hasty floral decoration and the paper label on the inside is still in good condition. Seth Thomas's Connecticut factory was one of the largest producers of clocks in America. They ranged from inexpensive pieces like this one to regulators of high quality. His goods were a little more expensive than many but with their excellent performance and easy maintenance they were a great favourite both at home and abroad.

### ▶ ROSEWOOD SLOPING-TOPPED MANTEL CLOCK
*1880; 46cm (18in) high;* **£50–70**
This clock may well have been made to a customer's specification, as the glazed panel is painted with a pseudo-crest and the case incorporates a few more refinements than usual, including a platform with turned scroll ends beneath a circular dial. It was manufactured by the Welch Clock Co., of Connecticut, whose paper label claims that its springs are warranted not to fail.

## COLLECTORS' NOTES
• A 30-hour clock is not as desirable as an eight-day piece.
• It is nice to see the paper labels on the inside of these clocks in good condition.
• There are so many American mantel clocks on the market, that it is worth avoiding any that have worn or chipped decoration, and to concentrate on examples which have survived in good condition, building up a collection showing a variety of scenes on the glazed panels.

## COLLECTING TIP
Mantel clocks represent a good social record of a particular period in American industrial history. Now is a good time to buy because supply is eventually bound to diminish and many are now being eagerly shipped back to the United States. Look for those veneered in rosewood with two painted panels

# Wall Clocks

# Carriage Clocks

Wall clocks come in a large variety of shapes and sizes, and are either weight- or spring-driven. They range from the often imaginative Black Forest clocks, first made in the 17th century, to the simple English round-dial clocks introduced in the late 18th century and the expensive, high quality early 19th-century Vienna regulators with their severe, architectural lines and ebony or boxwood cases. American wall clocks, made from the 1780s onwards, began to be exported to England in great numbers during the middle of the 19th century and proved so popular that they had an adverse effect on the English clock-making industry.

The carriage clock is a French innovation, developed from larger portable clocks, and made in great numbers there from the 1840s until the First World War. The demand was created during the Napoleonic Wars when it became necessary to supply armies on the move with a portable method of telling the time. Abraham-Louis Breguet was the earliest carriage clockmaker, but the style was soon taken up by clockmakers all over France.

They were made in varying sizes, with a carrying case (often lost over the years). They range from quarter to hourly striking, some with alarms and calendars set into the dial. The fully glazed case and carrying handle distinguishes them from other types of portable clocks.

A standard late 19th/early 20th century timepiece can be bought for £60 upwards, but a better-quality example from the same period might cost from £200. A gong-striking version is likely to be £300 or more.

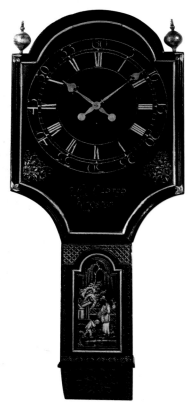

▲ BLACK LACQUER
AND GILT CHINOISERIE
TAVERN WALL TIMEPIECE
*late 18th century; 153cm (60in)*
*long;* **£1,800–2,200**
These large, early wall clocks were designed for use in public places. They are peculiar to England, their development the direct result of a 1797 act of parliament taxing all privately owned timepieces. It became desirable to consult a clock in a public place and avoid owning one personally. Striking pieces were also made but are rare.

▲ VIENNESE ROSEWOOD
WALL TIMEPIECE
*c.1850; 88cm (34½in) long;*
**£1,800–2,200**
The enamel dial on this clock has a decorative gilt surround, a sign of an early example. Between 1800 and 1850 Vienna wall clocks were made with these architectural-style cases, becoming more elaborate later in the century as many German manufacturers copied the Vienna style. The weight-driven movements in these earlier clocks are finely made, but later ones with spring-driven movements are less desirable and not as accurate. Striking and quarter-striking examples were also made.

▲ REPEATING AND ALARM
CARRIAGE CLOCK
*c.1860; 14cm (5½in) high;*
**£600–800**
This is an example of one of the earlier styles of carriage clocks with a one piece case. The lines of the case are clean and simple, giving the appearance of being made in one piece, compared to later examples which have more moulding. The glass on the top surface covers the entire area rather than being a circular or oval-glazed section set into the brass case. These early clocks strike on a bell rather than a gong, so inside the back you would see a polished brass bell rather than the coiled wire gong of the annotated example.

▲ DENT STRIKING
CARRIAGE CLOCK
*1870; 19.5cm (7¾in) high;*
**£2,000–3,000**
Carriage clocks were made in England, but in far smaller numbers than in France and they are usually much larger and have a twin fusee movement. Uncharacteristically, this has a Continental movement finished in the English style. The white enamel dial is surrounded by an engraved foliate dial mask. Dent were one of the top firms of English clockmakers during the 19th century, most famous for making the movement for Big Ben, the clock in the tower of the Houses of Parliament in London.

## FRENCH REPEATING CARRIAGE CLOCK
*c.1890; 15.2cm (6in) high;* **£300–400**
This is a typical, reasonably inexpensive carriage clock of the late 19th century, made in France and exported to England to be sold. It has a white enamel dial with blue stylized Arabic numerals, gilt fleur-de-lys hands and a matt gilt dial mask.

Here you can see the small balance wheel escapement mounted on a platform above the mechanism. The escapement is similar to the device found in a wristwatch.

gong

hammer

The single hammer and the single gong tell us that this is purely an hourly striking clock. Two gongs and two hammers would indicate that it strikes the quarters as well.

This button on the top surface of the clock shows that it is both a striking and repeating example. By pressing the button, the last hour will be struck again, useful, for example, if the owner woke at night unsure of the time. It's a common feature but nevertheless adds interest and some value.

The name of a good well-known local retailer on the dial (in this case the top English firm once known as The Goldsmith's Company but now Garrard's, the Queen's jewellers) is very desirable. Most dials are unsigned or have names that were put on with ink which fades, or a signature that has been changed after restoration or repair.

Many carriage clocks have fully glazed white dials. This example has a gilt dial mask with a matt finish, which is unusual and popular with collectors. As with the repeating button, it gives the clock an edge over those with more common features. The most desirable clocks are those with pierced and engraved masks or with colourful enamelling or porcelain panels covering the glazed area.

### COLLECTORS' NOTES
• The ideal situation for the collector is when the clock has retained its key and original outer leather travelling case. If this applies, all three parts should have identical numbers (the clock numbers can be found on the backplate).
• Often the word "Hands" appears above the setting square on the backplate. In the past, this was misinterpreted as the name of the clock maker, but it actually simply tells the owner where to alter the time!
• Highly elaborate porcelain or enamel cases are widely sought after, as are decorative miniature examples.

• *Grande Sonnerie* (quarter-striking) carriage clocks are more desirable than the hourly striking examples.

### COLLECTING TIP
Look for a factory or maker's mark on the backplate of the clock. These marks are notoriously difficult to find

being small and often camouflaged by part of the mechanism. You may own a clock without being aware that it has the mark of a well-known maker on it, something that could increase its value by 50%. An engraved backplate and case are more desirable than plain examples.

# Pocket watches

The Romans travelled with portable sun dials, some of which included a compass, but the earliest watches made in a form we can recognize date from c.1550, and were made in France and Germany. By the end of the 16th century, most watches were circular, about 5cm (2in) in diameter and around half an inch thick.

The invention of the spring mechanism triggered the evolution of the watch, although early examples were very inaccurate until c.1675 when the balance spring was developed. At this time they were also rare and expensive symbols of wealth and success and were often worn around the neck where they could be easily admired.

Watches have always been collected as much for their cases as for the complexities of their movements and some cases are works of art in their own right, made from silver or gold, often elaborately engraved or enamelled. The earliest cases protected the dials – glass faces weren't introduced until the 17th century. Repeater watches also made their appearance at this time, striking the preceding hour when a lever was depressed.

Early watches were wound by a key, and often had beautifully engraved dials and backplates. Even the balance cocks were finely crafted, and these are collected separately today by some specialist enthusiasts. The first keyless watch was made c.1790, wound by turning the knob at the top of the case.

Most clockmakers made watches at this time, although American examples are rare. The first recorded manufacture of American watches was by Luther Goddard of Shrewsbury, Massachusetts c.1809. Later, around 1850, Edward Howard and Aaron Dennison began the Waltham Watch Company, makers of the example on p.123. Thousands of American pocket watches were being mass-produced and exported to Europe by the end of the 19th century.

These masonic watches, their dials decorated with the appropriate symbols, are very popular with collectors. Both were made in Switzerland at the beginning of the 1930s.

### ▼ SWISS GILT METAL MASONIC WATCH
*c.1930; 55mm (2⅛in) wide;*
**£800–1,000**
The triangular mother-of-pearl dial has masonic symbols in place of numerals and is inscribed "Love your fellow man, lend him a helping hand."

### ▼ SILVER MASONIC WATCH
*c.1930; 55mm (2⅛in) wide;* **£1,000–1,500**
This Solvil Watch Company masonic watch has decoration raised around the dial with a blue stone inset at 12 o'clock.

### ▲ PRECIOUS METAL MINUTE-REPEATING FULL HUNTER WATCH WITH TRIPLE CALENDAR AND CHRONOGRAPH
*c.1900; 55mm (2⅛in) diameter;*
**£2,000–3,000**
The complicated components of this watch ensure that the owner has all the information concerning time that he could possibly require. The enamel dial with Roman numerals has subsidiaries for day, date, month and running seconds, with moonphase and a sweep flyback seconds hand. It incorporates a chronograph, a precision stopwatch that has the facility to zero the seconds hand before restarting it.

### ▲ EROTIC WATCH
*c.1820; 55mm (2⅛in) diameter;*
**£1,200–1,800**
This is a silver open-faced quarter-repeating French watch with an enamel dial and Roman numerals repeating on two gongs, which operate the secret cover that flies up to reveal the concealed erotic scene. Makers of these watches preferred to remain anonymous because erotica was classified as contraband and, if seized, watches like this one were broken up. Nowadays they are highly sought after.

Ladies' fob watches are small watches incorporating a pin or brooch designed to hang from a garment. They have survived in great numbers. They are usually decorative and can be worn today as pendant watches.

### ▶ SWISS GOLD AND ENAMEL FOB WATCH
*c.1900; 28mm (1⅛in) diameter; £350–450*
Pansies have long been a popular motif with jewellers and they are used to stunning effect in enamel here on the back of a small ladies' fob watch. The watch has a white enamel dial, Arabic numerals and a gilt, keyless cylinder movement. The small attached fob, which allows the watch to be worn as a brooch, is decorated in the same way.

### ▶ SWISS GOLD AND ENAMEL LEAF FORM PENDANT WATCH
*c.1860; 33mm (1⅛in) diameter; £500–700*
Signed "H. Grandjean Loche," the gold case of this watch is designed in a leaf form with enamel decoration embellished with rose-cut diamonds. The cylinder movement is key-wound.

### ▶ SWISS 18 CARAT GOLD AND ENAMEL FOB WATCH
*c.1840; 33mm (1⅛in) diameter; £300–400*
This pretty watch is signed "Bovet Fleurier" and has an engraved gilt dial with Roman numerals and a gilt cylinder movement. The case back is decorated in enamels with *putti* and set with diamonds.

## 18 CARAT GOLD FULL HUNTER KEYLESS WIND POCKET WATCH BY WALTHAM OF MASSACHUSETTS

*1915; 50mm (2in) diameter;*
*£250–350*

The Waltham Watch Company pioneered machine-made watch production in the United States and were in business from the middle of the 19th century until 1957. Their products varied widely in quality and were exported worldwide, the gold cases being fitted locally by the retailers. This is a good example of one of their middle-quality pieces, with a white enamel dial, a subsidiary seconds hand, roman numerals and blued steel hands. The fully engraved case was manufactured in England.

*Balance wheel*: the time-keeping element of the watch which works with the escapement, allowing the train to run down at a controlled speed.

*Index*: by moving this very slightly, small adjustments can be made to the time-keeping of the watch. High quality watches have a precision micrometer regulator with a separate adjustment screw to move it.

*Balance cock*: this supports the balance wheel.

*Bridge plate*: to hold the train wheels (not visible) in place.

*Centre wheel*: part of the movement train which runs down to the escape wheel.

*Winding wheels*: these turn as the watch is wound and operate the ratchet click to wind up the spring.

The 18 carat gold case, made in England, had hallmarks put on at the Birmingham assay office.

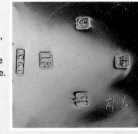

The back cover is attractively engraved and has a central shield onto which initials could be engraved. Unless the initials denote somebody famous, the watch's value is helped by having a vacant cartouche.

### COLLECTORS' NOTES

Millions of pocket watches of varying qualities have been manufactured since the mid-19th century. The lesser ones do not have jewels (or synthetic sapphires) set into the watch plate. A fully jewelled watch normally has 17 jewels (a fact which is often stated on the plate); this is the minimum number of jewel bearings in the workings of a good quality watch.

Check that the dial has no cracks and that the case is free of dents and bruises.

Clock cases of gold plate as opposed to solid gold were made in large numbers. Look carefully in the back: many gold plate cases bear the inscription, "This case guaranteed to wear 10 years."

Any solid gold case manufactured in Great Britain will bear English hallmarks.

### COLLECTING TIP

Small ladies' fob watches are good value because they were made in large numbers and are less sought after than the larger examples. You can still buy a gold cased example for £100.

### WATCH TERMS

*Open-faced watch* – has no covers protecting the glass.
*Half hunter* – has a cover with a hole in the centre through which the hands are visible; the cover is usually engraved with a set of roman numerals.
*Full hunter* – has a cover which protects the entire front of the pocket watch.

# Wristwatches

The very first wristwatches were developed during the First World War as a more convenient method for soldiers to tell the time than by trying to consult a pocket watch on a chain while out in the field. Just after the war, small fob watches were converted to wristwatches by having strap fittings attached to them. It was during the 1920s, after the pocket watch became redundant, that the manufacture of wristwatches really got underway. It was also during this period that the British watch-making industry, reluctant to modernize its outdated working practises, went into a steep decline, leaving the Swiss companies to lead the way in Europe. They were able to produce wristwatches of every quality in numbers large enough to satisfy the public clamouring for this latest method of timekeeping.

Many new Swiss firms started up during this period but older organizations such as Movado and Patek Philippe adapted readily to the new methods. In the 1930s, Rolex led the way by producing one of the first fully automatic and waterproof wristwatches. Many names have since gone out of business, but have recently been revived under new ownership as the interest in mechanical (as opposed to quartz) wristwatches has blossomed over the last couple of decades.

Swiss companies produce high-quality wristwatches to satisfy the demand of collectors, who very often buy brand new examples. At the top end of the market, these can cost up to £400,000. It is one area of collecting where old does not necessarily mean more valuable and where collectors like to wear and enjoy their pieces. It also tends to be an area dominated by men for whom the wristwatch is an acceptable form of jewellery. Women's watches do not excite the same degree of interest. A woman's 9 carat gold Rolex of 1920 might fetch £100–200 whereas the male equivalent is worth £600–800.

### ▼ ROLEX FULL HUNTER WRISTWATCH
*c.1914; 33mm (1¼in) diameter;*
**£200–300**
Similar in style to a pocket watch, with a hinged front cover to protect the face, this is a transition piece, made during the early history of the wristwatch. Nickel-cased, the cover is released by pressing a spring button in the 6 o'clock position.

### ▼ 9 CARAT GOLD ROLEX WATER-RESISTANT OYSTER WRISTWATCH
*c.1930; 32mm (1¼in) diameter;* **£800–1,200**
The Rolex oyster water-resistant wristwatch was the most successful design patented at this time and, with modifications, goes on being made today. On this example the front bezel and back are screwed to the case and, together with the patented screw-down button, form the water-resistant seal.

### ▲ 14 CARAT GOLD OMEGA CURVED CASE WRISTWATCH
*c.1914; 34 x 24mm (1⅜ x 1in);*
**£250–350**
The gilt, oval dial with Roman numerals is contained within a six-sided curved case with a single-hinge loop-strap fitting. Curved watches were made in quite large numbers during this early period and were popular, fitting nicely on the wrist. This was designed as either a small man's or a large lady's watch. The market for some of these early watches is quite restricted, meaning that they can still be bought for a good price.

### ▲ OMEGA STAINLESS STEEL WATER-RESISTANT WRISTWATCH
*c.1935; 24 x 38mm (1 x 1½in);*
**£800–1,200**
This is an example of one of the earliest water-resistant watches. The watch is held in its own sealed compartment, so that the back has to be unclipped and the watch removed for winding.

### ▲ ROSE-GOLD JAEGER LE COULTRE AUTOMATIC WRISTWATCH
*c.1945; 36mm (1⅜in) diam;*
**£1,000–1,500**
This unusual watch has the button mounted on the case back rather than the side, to give a cleaner, uncluttered look, a device which is the hallmark of Jaeger Le Coultre.

| 1ST LEAGUE | 2ND LEAGUE | 3RD LEAGUE |
| --- | --- | --- |
| Patek Phlippe | Jaeger Le Coultre | Omega |
| Audemar Piguet | Rolex | Longines |
| Piaget | International Watch | Baume & Mercier |
| Vacheron & | Company | Ebel |
| Constantin | Cartier | Movado |
|  |  | Breightling |

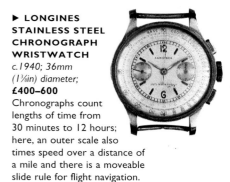

▶ **LONGINES STAINLESS STEEL CHRONOGRAPH WRISTWATCH**
*c.1940; 36mm (1⅜in) diameter;*
**£400–600**
Chronographs count lengths of time from 30 minutes to 12 hours; here, an outer scale also times speed over a distance of a mile and there is a moveable slide rule for flight navigation.

▲ **TWO-COLOUR GOLD LONGINE WRISTWATCH**
*1947; 24 x 35mm (1 x 1⅜in);*
**£400–600**
An attractive design which has great appeal to collectors, this wristwatch is in a polished rectangular case of white gold with a yellow gold surround. Although popular, Longines does not enjoy the same sort of following as Rolex, for instance, with whom they are on a par in terms of production standards.

▲ **18 CARAT GOLD OMEGA CONSTELLATION CENTRE SECONDS WRISTWATCH**
*1965; 36mm (1⅜in) diameter;*
**£400–600**
The dial is inscribed "Officially Certified Chronometer," which means that the movement has been tested for accuracy in different temperatures and positions. Prices for these Omega Constellations with their superior movements have risen steadily in recent years.

▲ **18 CARAT GOLD JAEGER LE COULTRE SECONDS ALARM WRISTWATCH**
*c.1960; 36mm (1⅜in) diameter;*
**£1,200–1,500**
The sound given off by this smart alarm watch is quite loud and very effective. Alarm watches were much in demand during the Fifties and Sixties as fashionable, novelty items but they then fell out of favour. However, they are currently being sought after once again by collectors.

▶ **18 CARAT GOLD VACHERIN & CONSTANTIN AUTOMATIC WRISTWATCH**
*1955; 35mm (1⅜in) diam;* **£800–1,200**
Vacherin & Constantin, a top Swiss watch company, celebrated their bicentennial in 1955 by making this classic, conservatively designed watch in a heavy gold case.

▲ **CARTIER LADIES' TANK WATCH**
*c.1975; 20mm (¾in) wide;*
**£800–1,200**
Louis Cartier brought out this design during the First World War and it became known as the tank watch because it resembled a military tank from the side. In production for the last 70 years, this design has more recently been made with a quartz movement, but the mechanical models are more sought after.

▲ **18 CARAT GOLD PATEK PHILIPPE WRISTWATCH**
*c.1970; 33mm (1¼in) diameter;*
**£1,000–1,500**
Patek Philippe manufactures the nearest thing you can get today to a hand-made watch. They have maintained their standards and produce only between 10,000 and 15,000 pieces a year. Collectors are prepared to wait for up to two years for special pieces which can cost up to £400,000. This one is in a classic plain, polished case.

▲ **18 CARAT GOLD PIAGET AUTOMATIC WRISTWATCH**
*c.1975; 34mm (1½in) diameter;*
**£700–900**
This has a particularly slim, self-winding movement, a hallmark of Piaget design, with a plain, elegant milled, hob-nail finished bezel and baton numerals. The firm also make ladies' watches encrusted with diamonds in designs that follow the latest fashion. Piaget produce only a small number of pieces annually.

▲ **18 CARAT ROSE-GOLD AUDEMAR PIGUET AUTOMATIC CHRONO-GRAPH WRISTWATCH**
*1990; 40mm (1⅝in) diameter;*
**£3,000–4,000**
Modern watches, although collected, have low second-hand value and can therefore be snapped up at bargain prices at auction. This example currently retails brand-new for around £12,000 in its heavy, rose gold case and fitted on a strap with a matching gold clasp.

---

**COLLECTORS' NOTES**
• Look for pieces by the well-known names rather than the more obscure companies.
• Buy solid gold, 18 carat gold-cased examples if you are serious about collecting wristwatches. Gold-plated and silver examples are not

enough, steel is as it is a durable metal which does not tarnish, is more discreet than gold and can be repolished to look like new.
• Rectangular cases are more popular than circular ones as they are more unusual, as are those with curved backs to fit snugly

• It is almost always the case that an old wristwatch will have to be refurbished, as the dials, glass and case become tired and marked with age. This is quite acceptable but must be carried out to the highest standards.
• Buy a good watch strap to bring

wristwatch. Serious collectors are always prepared to spend £200–300 on a really good leather strap.

**COLLECTING TIP**
Steel Omega Constellations dating from the mid-1960s are a good buy at the moment, but avoid the other

# Teddy Bears, Dolls & Toys

Children have always valued their toys, but as playthings and companions to be loved, abused and discarded, according to mood and whim. It is adults who have elevated them to the display cabinet. Who would have dreamt 15 years ago that the major auction houses would devote sales entirely to teddy bears, attracting buyers from all over the world prepared to part with thousands of pounds for a coveted Steiff. In 1994, "Teddy Girl" sold at Christie's in London for a staggering £110,000 and a rare black Steiff, dating from 1912, for £22,000.

The best bisque dolls also make heart-stopping sums these days, on a level with the best porcelain, silver and furniture. Little girls in the ancient world played with dolls made from wood, terracotta, fabric or ivory, and in 17th-century Europe, doll sellers plied their wares from markets or put them on trays and sold them on the street and from door to door. In the 18th century, the now highly prized carved wooden dolls began to be produced, often used as models for ladies' fashions, sent from Europe to America to keep women there informed about the latest styles. Wood, papier-mâché and bisque dolls have been an established part of the marketplace for many years and collectors have now turned their attention to Barbie, Sasha and other thoroughly modern misses.

The interest in old toys began almost 50 years ago, but collectors were few and highly dedicated, motivated by a love of the craftmanship, enjoying the best of German tinplate toy production, or the detail of trains scaled down from the noisy, hissing monsters which had enthralled them as children. They met to swap and share their pieces with little thought for commercial gain. It was in the 1970s that a more general fascination with the past and a passion for collecting began. Toy departments became established in the major auction houses and top examples began to escalate in price.

It may have become a serious business, but collecting toys is still a lot of fun. Some of the most established areas are difficult for the novice collector to crack because prices are high, but there is plenty of scope even among pieces which are well over 100 years old. Always buy the best example you can afford and buy only what you like. You may choose to concentrate on more modern toys, perhaps things which remind you of magic moments during your own childhood, or things which are currently being produced and are not yet appreciated. Sit in on one or two general toy sales before you begin to buy and watch the fun and games unfold. It's one of the best ways to get a feel for this volatile and constantly changing field.

*Left:* Plastic robot from Hong Kong, 1960s; German bear by Steiff, 1907; French Jumeau bébé bisque doll, 1900; Japanese tinplate racing car by Masudaya, 1950s; English diecast Coronation coach and horses, c.1953.

# Bears: where to begin

A bear is more than the sum of his parts, but scrutinizing the parts is as good a way as any to ascertain date, country of origin, authenticity, condition and even maker.

## Identification and Authenticity

First, look at the *fabric*: original old bears (pre-1930) are usually of wool mohair. After that date, new materials were introduced, such as cotton and silk plush and later, in the 1950s, nylon and other synthetic fabrics.

Next, try to determine what *stuffing* has been used. You can do this by assessing the bear's weight: if he is light, he is probably stuffed with kapok (possibly mixed with wood wool); heavier bears that are crunchy to the touch are probably stuffed with wood wool. After about 1940 new, lighter materials were used, of sub stuffing, and later on, lightweight foam.

Then, look at the ears, eyes and nose. The *ears* should be correctly positioned; you'll only be able to know for certain by looking at similar bears or pictures of similar bears that you know to be genuine. Check the bear's head for signs of where different ears might once have been stitched, in which case, the present ones are almost certainly replacements. The *eyes* should also be scrutinized: if the bear was made before 1914, he should have boot-button eyes. During the 1920s, though, glass eyes became the norm. Plastic was sometimes used from the 1950s. Then look closely at the *nose* stitching, as this is a good way to identify a bear's maker, each company tending to have its own distinctive type of stitching. Most noses were made of silk thread; black wool noses are probably replacements. Keep in mind, though, that replacement ears, eyes or nose do not make a bear unbuyable – or unsaleable – but any alterations should be reflected in the price.

The next area requiring attention is the *paw pads*: if these are original on earlier bears they will be of felt, or perhaps cotton; bears made in the 40s and later may have plush or leather pads; ultrasuede has been used from the 70s. Again, though, pads are often replaced and as long as they are sympathetic to the originals, should not detract too much from the value.

An assessment of the above details will help you date and confirm the authenticity of your bear. You may also find more concrete evidence of the maker, and possibly even the date, in a *label*. These may be in the form of embroidered tags attached to the fur, or metal tags, usually on the ear or arm. However, some bears, especially early ones, had no tags at all or only flimsy paper ones which have long parted from the bear. You should always check that the bear itself seems consistent with the maker whose name appears on any label, just in case the label has been added to the bear at a later date.

## Care and Maintenance

Condition is important to price. If the bear is dressed, always look under the clothes to make sure they are not concealing any defects. Never attempt any restoration yourself, but instead seek specialist advice to ensure that the bear is restored in materials and details sympathetic to the original. If you do decide to have a bear restored, remember that the work may change his character.

The simplest, most effective areas of restoration include restuffing, and replacement pads, eyes or nose stitching. You can, though, clean your bear yourself. Start by brushing or hoovering him (with the nozzle covered) in order to remove any bugs and dust. Then, using a small brush apply a solution of very mild wool wash and cool water to the fur. Use as little solution as possible, being careful not to overwet the fur. Remove the foam with a dry cloth; you may also need to use a damp cloth at the end. Rinse the cloth in water and keep dabbing the fur until you have removed all the soap. Then, leave him to dry naturally before combing the fur using a fine metal comb. You may need to carry out this procedure again. Once he is really clean you'll be able to maintain him with just an annual wash and the occasional brush to keep away dirt and insect-attracting dust.

## Storage and Display

Bears should be stored away from sources of heat, whether central heating or a fire. They should also be kept away from direct sunlight, as this will cause the fur to fade. If your bear is going to be stored rather than displayed, keep him in a cool, dry place, perhaps in a cardboard box lined with acid-free tissue paper. Don't forget to put in some moth balls, to keep insects away. When it comes to display, bears are very versatile and look good just about anywhere, whether nestled comfortably in the family armchair or sitting proudly on a display or other table. Some collectors display them in a "family" set up with other bears, dolls or soft animals. You can also utilize old toys and other furniture as props, for example, bears can look very appealing on an old rocking horse or in a pram. Similarly, you can use clothes your children have outgrown to make an attractive costume for your bear, and, as with props, don't forget that a simple pair of glasses, necktie or scarf, are simple ways to help your bear change his image.

# American Bears

Teddy bear fever hit the United States in the early 20th century, reputedly after a bear was made by Morris Michtom to commemorate an incident in 1902 when US president Theodore Roosevelt declined to shoot a bear that had been tied up for him while on a hunting trip. Michtom founded the Ideal Novelty and Toy Company which was making bears in large numbers by 1907. Other important makers included Knickerbocker, Bruin, Aetna, Gund and the Character Toy Company. Novelty bears, which could growl, squeak, laugh, whistle and even tumble, were made from c.1901. You can usually tell an American bear, if it is unmarked, by its long, firm body and short, straight limbs. Bears made by Ideal command a premium, but all American bears are collectable, their desirability usually increasing according to their age.

**▶ IDEAL BEAR**
*c.1905; 33cm (13in) high;*
**£600–700**
This battered but appealing bear is typical of early Ideal designs. He has a wide triangular head, short mohair, large round ears on the sides of the head, tapering foot pads, slender body and long muzzle. Ideal bears made after 1938 have a stitched label and paper tag. Earlier bears are usually identified by their similarity to others positively identified through surviving documentary evidence. With professional restoration the bear would be worth £800–900.

**▼ KNICKERBOCKER CINNAMON BEAR**
*1935; 51cm (20in) high;* **£450**
The toy firm of Knickerbocker was founded in 1869 but started to make bears around 1920. Because they were labelled, and were also well-documented and made in large numbers, Knickerbockers are easier to find than many American bears and are popular with collectors. This one has the typical wide head, short snout and velveteen paw pads and is in pristine condition.

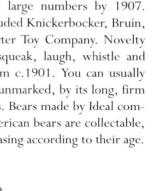

**◀ "ELECTRIC EYE" TEDDY BEAR**
*c.1917; 55cm (22in) high;*
**£550**
"Electric Eye" bears – so called because their eyes light up – were made by several American companies during the early 20th century. Because the mechanisms broke quickly, few of these bears survive today and those that do are rarely in working order. This patriotically red, white and blue mohair bear, still in working order, was made by The American-Made Stuffed Toy Company of New York. They made others in white, and in red, and also in two other, smaller sizes.

**▶ "TRUFFLES" FOR F.A.O. SCHWARZ**
*1993; 73.5cm (29in) high;* **£100**
Although bears made after c.1970 tend to be mass-produced and therefore of lesser quality, some good quality bears are still being made; the best of these capture the quality and character of vintage bears. Most collectable are those based on fictional bears or made to commemorate a special event. The New York-based toy and bear retailer F.A.O. Schwarz occasionally commissions designs from top manufacturers. "Truffles" (accompanied by a tiny English friend) has been made with synthetic fur that resembles old mohair.

**COLLECTORS' NOTES**
• Among early manufacturers look for bears by Ideal, Bruin, Aetna and Hecla.
• Ideal bears have sometimes been faked: you may be able to identify these by their lack of wear, especially on the fur or nose, and by their uneven seams.

**COLLECTING TIP**
Novelty bears are very collectable, especially those made by the Albert Bruckner Company.

# German Bears

German bears are famous for their very high quality and are in great demand throughout the world. The most famous of all bear makers, Steiff, located about 320 km (200 miles) south of Sonneberg, started making bears at the beginning of the 20th century and are still making them today. Other leading manufacturers include Bing, famous for their mechanical bears; Schuco, which specialized in miniatures and novelties; Gebrüder Sussengüth and Hermann. The Sonneberg region was home to hundreds of cottage industries working in the early years of the century right up until the Second World War to fill the huge and ever growing demand for bears of all types. Many of these are unmarked.

# British Bears

When the teddy bear craze hit Britain, existing toy manufacturers were easily able to adapt to making bears instead, and when German imports were banned during the First World War many new manufacturers set up bear factories, including Chad Valley, Chiltern, Farnell and Dean's. Early British bears are of particularly high quality. After the Second World War styles changed and bears became plumper with short limbs and a flat face – features particularly characteristic of British bears. Synthetic fibres tended to replace the softer and more desirable Yorkshire mohair plush used on earlier bears.

▶ **STEIFF BEAR**
*c.1909; 40.5cm (16in) high;* **£1,500**
**CHAD VALLEY BEAR**
*before c.1953; 51cm (20in) high;* **£450**
The best way to learn about bears is through comparison and observation – a short study of the German Steiff *(right)* and the British Chad Valley bear *(left)* shown here will soon reveal some interesting distinctions.

Bulbous bound "coal-shaped" nose; some earlier examples had vertically stitched triangular noses.

This identification label was used between 1938, when the firm was granted a royal warrant, and 1953, when Queen Elizabeth became the Queen Mother and the wording on the label was changed accordingly.

Chubby body with fairly short arms – although arms on Chad bears became even shorter in later years. (Many Chad bodies contain a growler, activated by squeezing the tummy.)

The fur is well-coloured, fluffy mohair stuffed with kapok, making it softer than many German bears, which were usually stuffed with excelsior; after the Second World War some bears were made from the new, less expensive synthetic fibres.

Typical Chad eyes, of amber and black glass, knotted through to the back of the head.

Black boot-button eyes; glass eyes were made from c.1912 and soon replaced boot buttons altogether.

The button-in-the-ear trademark was patented by Steiff in 1904–5 in an attempt to prevent other manufacturers from copying their designs. This metal button was attached to the ear with two prongs after it was found that the loose label originally used tended to get lost. A variety of different buttons was used, but this one, with its underscored "F," was common between 1905 and 1950.

Large flat ears set wide apart on a wide head – features very characteristic of Chad bears.

Typical horizontal nose stitching (used for bears under 40.5cm/ 16in). The very first Steiffs, from c.1904–5 had sealing wax noses.

Luxurious long mohair, which has survived in excellent condition. The most desirable and rare colours of mohair for Steiff bears are cinnamon and white; black was also used.

Characteristically long arms; these were used for a long period, until the 50s, when bodies became fatter and limbs shorter – more like those of a British bear.

Four stitched claws (earlier Steiffs, c.1905 had 5 claws). Often, the feet have stitched claws as well.

This design was made in large numbers so it is worth looking out for one in good condition and with original pads. Apart from this small patch of wear under the leg, this bear is in good condition and retains his original felt pads.

131

Long narrow feet; unusually, the pads are original – many fell victim to moths and had to be replaced.

# Other Bears

### ▶ BING MECHANICAL BEAR
*1908; 38cm (15in) high;*
**£2,000**
The German firm of Gebrüder Bing is particularly famous for its mechanical bears, which are rare today and much sought after. When the key is wound, this bear moves his head from side to side. Early Bings, like this one, are similar to Steiff bears: until 1920 they shared a wide head, short snout and long arms and body. Later faces acquired a wide smile!

### ▲ PAIR OF SCHUCO MINIATURE BEARS
*1930s; 8cm (3¼in) high;* **£600 each**
Miniature bears form a large collecting area in their own right and provide plenty of scope for collectors on a limited budget. This pair, though, command a fair price, as they were made by the German firm of Schuco and are each sitting behind the wheels of a metal car. Rare colours command the highest prices. Many Schuco miniatures open to reveal a powder compact or perfume bottle or have some other novelty feature such as a clockwork mechanism.

### ▼ LARGE CHILTERN BEAR
*1958; 69cm (27in) high;* **£500**
Bears made by the English firm of Chiltern were of consistently high quality and hence have survived in large numbers and usually in good condition, making them very popular with collectors. This one still has his original label, price tag and ribbon. His floppy ears and glass eyes are typical of Chiltern bears made after the Second World War, although the glass eyes were soon to be replaced by plastic.

### ▼ FARNELL BEAR
*c.1920; 33cm (13in) high;* **£750–950**
The British London-based firm of Farnell was one of the first to make bears. Under their Alpha trademark, they are said to have designed the original Winnie the Pooh bear bought for Christopher Robin, the inspiration for A. A. Milne's famous stories. The firm is also known for its use of long, silky, high-quality mohair. This bear also has typical shiny black button eyes. Although he has replacement paw pads, he is otherwise in good condition.

## COLLECTORS NOTES
• Look out for artists' bears: bears made by individuals around the world in limited editions. Most artists are independent, but some have been commissioned by top firms which then mass-produce the bears. Some repre-

sent well-known personalities; others are "characters" dressed in elaborate costumes and with individualistic expressions.
• A record of its family history adds charm and value to a bear.
• Many people augment their collection of cuddly bears with

bears in other media, such as those illustrated on ceramics, or fashioned in glass or silver, or in paper, in the form of postcards and greeting cards. These are all good ways to build up a varied and interesting bear collection at a modest price.

## COLLECTING TIP
If you buy a modern bear, especially one of the limited editions made since the 70s, make sure you keep any box or packaging and, if you were given one, a certificate, as this will all add value in the future.

**▲ CINNAMON PINTEL BEAR**
*late 1920s; 48.5cm (19in) high;* **£1,500**
M. Pintel Fils was the first French company to manufacture plush
teddy bears, producing their first bear in 1911. Bears made before
the 1930s can be identified by the metal button on their chest.
Like many made before 1930, this bear has long, large limbs and
feet and a long muzzle. He has amber and black glass eyes, a nice
feature as sometimes these wear and have become clear.

**▲ STEIFF BEAR BEFORE AND AFTER RESTORATION**
*c.1908; 51cm (20in) high;* **£500** *before restoration,* **£950** *restored*
Old bears often need some attention – stitching comes away, stuffing
can fall out and limbs and parts of faces can drop off – but they can
often be restored to nearly original condition. It is best to consult a
professional restorer, and preferable to let them carry out the work.
Also, when buying a bear, have some idea of the kind of damage that
can be repaired without destroying his original character. Bears that
are worn all over and have dry brittle fabric are best avoided. The
Steiff *above, left* looks in a bad state, with scant stuffing and a worn
nose and pads. He is transformed, *right*, by new stuffing, replacement nose and mouth stitching and paw pads, and a good clean.

**◄ RUPERT BEAR**
*1960s; 51cm (20in) high;* **£75**
The comic strip character,
Rupert, made its first appearance in the British newspaper,
the *Daily Express*. He was an
instant success and spawned
books, postcards and, of
course, bears. This example
is one of several versions
made by Burbank Toys.
Other famous bears include
Paddington, based on the
hugely successful stories by
British writer Michael Bond.

**▲ MERRYTHOUGHT "CHEEKY" AND REPLICA;**
*1960s; 63.5cm (25in);* **£450**; *Replica: 1995; 35.5cm (14in);* **£35**
Since the 1980s some firms have started to produce limited editions,
replicas and modern versions of their earlier designs. They offer a
good way to start a collection of well-made traditional-style bears at
a more affordable price – although some, especially those by Steiff,
are already fetching high prices. The "Cheeky" bear shown *above, left*
was made by the British firm of Merrythought and is almost identical
(except in size!) to the 1960s version *above, right*. Both have golden
mohair, glass eyes and felt paw pads, and both sport a printed label
on one foot.

**► STRUNZ DRESSED BEAR**
*1910; 63.5cm (25in) high;* **£85**
Many collectors dress their
bears or give them accessories
to add to their character and
protect their fur. This one has an
appealing lace-edged pinafore dress
and glasses. If you are going to do
this, it's best to use original old
fabric wherever possible.

# Dolls: where to begin

Dolls are invariably classified according to the medium from which their head is made and the type of head they have, so the head is the first place to start any assessment of a doll you are thinking of buying.

## Media

**WOOD** This was the medium of the earliest dolls, made from the 16th century and possibly earlier. Although it was largely superseded by wax, porcelain and other media, wood continued to be used, to a lesser extent, through until the 19th century.

**WAX** Like wood, wax was used over a long period, from the 17th century until the 20th. Some collectors find wax the least appealing medium for dolls.

**CHINA/PORCELAIN** and **PARIAN** Glazed porcelain dolls were introduced in the 19th century, and were particularly popular in Germany. Parian, which is unglazed, untinted porcelain, was introduced at around the same time, also probably in Germany.

**BISQUE** This unglazed tinted porcelain was introduced in the mid-19th century. Bisque dolls soon became the most popular dolls ever because a high degree of realism could be achieved and also partly due to the fact that people had more disposable income and spent more money on children's "luxuries."

**FABRIC AND CLOTH** This broad category includes rag dolls made at the end of the 19th and beginning of the 20th century, as well as more primitive dolls made from scraps of material. The nature of the medium is such that not many early fabric dolls have survived.

**CELLULOID** This was used for dolls made in the last quarter of the 19th century. Developed as a cheaper alternative to bisque, it proved less durable.

**COMPOSITION** This was introduced at the turn of the century and looks similar to papier-mâché. America and Germany dominated production.

**HARD PLASTIC/VINYL** These were developed after the Second World War, hard plastic winning out over vinyl. Some dolls are made using a combination of both.

## Head Types

If a doll is marked, the mark will often appear at the back of the head, low down towards the neck or high under the wig. However, even if a doll is unmarked, the head will provide the strongest clue as to country of origin and maker. Sometimes the doll is referred to according to its head type. Factories gave their various heads mould numbers, which are often used to classify the doll. You will soon get to know which are the rare

and which the common numbers. The principal head types are listed below:

**SHOULDER HEAD** Often used on early dolls, this type has a neck, shoulder and head moulded in one piece, which fits onto the torso, which might be of cloth or kid.

**SWIVEL HEAD** Here, the head and shoulders fit into a cup on the top of the torso, enabling the head to turn.

**SOCKET HEAD** Like the swivel head, this hollow head slots into a cup at the top of the neck. It is very common among bisque dolls.

**OPEN HEAD** These are hollow, with a pate which could hold a wig. They are usually found on bisque dolls.

**SOLID** This less common alternative head for bisque dolls, is fully rounded and sometimes made in one piece with a shoulderplate.

Get to know the different types of eyes, ears, hair and mouth, the period when each type was used and the preferences of individual factories. Eyes can be painted, carved or, most popularly, made of glass. Hair may be painted on or applied as a mohair or human hair wig inserted in clumps, or in the case of the most expensive dolls, strand by strand. Mouths may be closed, or more commonly open, possibly to reveal a neat row of moulded or inserted teeth and perhaps even a tongue.

Finally, inspect the body, which is usually of fabric such as kid or cloth, or, on bisque dolls, of wood and composition. Until the 19th century, most were modelled on adult women but child and baby bodies became increasingly common from the end of the 19th century.

## Fakes and Alterations

The most common alteration is a "marriage" between a head and a body not intended for it. This is not always done to deceive, but often occurs in the course of repairs. The best way to guard against this is to familiarize yourself with the various head-and-body combinations used by different factories. To safeguard against fakes, always buy from a reputable dealer. Keep any documentation you are given and make a separate note of your doll's features, for example, mould number, eye type and so on.

## Care and Maintenance

As with all areas of antiques, repairs are best left to a professional who can repair eyes, restore fingers and restring joints. However, you can clean bisque and china dolls yourself, using cotton wool soaked in soap and water. Always keep any packaging or spare clothing that comes with your dolls; if you want to give it fresh clothing, store the original garments in acid-free tissue.

# Early Dolls

Many wooden and partly wooden dolls were made by peasants and are unmarked, although large numbers are known to have come from the Grodnertal region in Germany and hence are referred to as Grodnertals. These are usually painted and intricately carved. However, quality deteriorated and dolls made after the early 19th century tend to be more crudely carved.

There are several varieties of wax doll: in the 17th and 18th centuries the most common type was solid wax, with carved details. In the 19th century poured wax became more prevalent; dolls in this medium are more appealing

as they have glass eyes, painted faces and real hair. Wax-over-composition was a less expensive medium, developed in the early 19th century, and was particularly common in England and Germany.

The best way to date china and parian dolls is to become familiar with the hairstyles of the period, which dollmakers faithfully represented. Fashion dolls, which had bisque heads, were made mostly in France between c.1860 and 1890, with an entire wardrobe of elaborate and accurately detailed costumes and a body that could be arranged in different poses.

**◀ GRODNERTAL-TYPE PAPIER-MÂCHÉ DOLL WITH WOODEN ARMS**
*c.1820–30; 23cm (9in) high;* **£500**
This doll is unmarked but is of the type produced in the Grodnertal region of Germany. She has the typical painted features, "spade"-shaped hands, carved and turned limbs and shiny black hair of dolls made in this area. Some of these dolls were dressed as pedlars, with baskets displaying a variety of miniature wooden wares. The best of them have elaborately painted details.

**▶ WAX-OVER-COMPOSITION**
*c.1840; 51cm (20in) high;* **£350**
This anonymous doll has the naive expression and closed mouth typical of wax-over-composition dolls. She has kid arms and a fabric body. The cracks on her face will not detract from the value, as most of these dolls suffer from cracking. This type of doll is also known as a "crazy Alice" or slit-head, because the hair was inserted into a slit in the crown.

**▶ POURED WAX MONTANARI**
*c.1851; 61cm (24in) high;* **£1,200**
Montanari, who made this doll for the Great Exhibition, was one of the finest 19th-century English doll firms specializing in poured wax. Many of the dolls were modelled on royal family members. They had chubby limbs and were beautifully dressed.

**◀ FRENCH FASHION DOLL BY JUMEAU**
*c.1880; 30.5cm (12in) high;* **£1,800**
This unmarked Jumeau can be identified by its prominent, almond-shaped glass eyes and plaintive expression. It has the typical Jumeau leather body and swivel neck. It is worth looking out for Jumeaus in their original costume, even if not in good condition, as the factory is known for its elegant designs.

**◀ CHINA DOLL**
*c.1870; 38cm (15in) high;* **£650**
China dolls offer a vast area to potential collectors, although those made between 1840 and c.1880 are more collectable than ones made later, when quality deteriorated. Price is determined by the standard of facial painting and modelling; this example is of good quality and has typical rouged cheeks and swept-back hair. Most have a fabric or leather body. This doll is in the style of those known to be German.

**COLLECTORS NOTES**
• When buying a dressed doll, check under the clothes for signs of damage.
• Most wax dolls are unmarked, although some bear the name of the firm which carried out any repairs.

**COLLECTING TIP**
Wax-over-composition dolls are among the most affordable dolls today, but must be in good condition and, if possible, still in their original clothes.

# Bisque Dolls

Bisque is unglazed porcelain that has been fired once, then tinted and fired again. It was first used to make dolls' heads in the late 19th and early 20th century, quickly replacing porcelain and china, as it proved to be more durable, more realistic and more versatile than its predecessors. The French led the way, producing huge quantities of high-quality dolls of all types, often depicting young girls, known as bébés, with idealized expressions. The most important French makers included Jumeau, Bru, Gaultier and Steiner. They reigned supreme until competition was provided by the Germans, especially with their "character" dolls and babies, which had lifelike expressions. Leading makers included Heubach, Armand Marseille, Simon & Halbig and Kämmer & Reinhardt.

Many dolls carry mould numbers, the rarer the number, the more sought-after the doll. The quality and degree of facial detail also affect the price, as does the colour of the bisque – generally the paler the better.

Bisque dolls represent the largest collecting area, the best fetching prices as high as £100,000, although many lovely dolls can still be bought for as little as £100, especially the all-bisque miniatures which form a separate collecting area in their own right. Avoid buying dolls with cracked heads, even if the cracks are fine, unless the damage is reflected in the price.

**▶ HEUBACH CHARACTER DOLLS**
*both dolls c.1911; 30.5cm (12in);* **£450 each**
The German firm of Gebrüder Heubach was established in 1820 and continued in business until the end of the Second World War. Their character dolls, which had a variety of expressive faces, often whistling, pouting or winking, are particularly collectable, These two also have the characteristic painted intaglio eyes. Typically, the bodies are not of as high quality as the heads.

**◀ DEP CHILD DOLL**
*c.1900; 40.5cm (16in) high;* **£550**
If you come across the initials DEP incised into the back of a doll's head, these do not represent a particular maker, but simply indicate that the design of the doll has been patented. This one is otherwise unmarked, but has a German head on a French body and was made for the French market.

**◀ SIMON & HALBIG CHARACTER DOLL**
*c.1910; 51cm (20in) high;* **£650**
This "flirty-eyed" German character doll, mould number 126, was made by one of the leading German dolls' head makers of the period, active between c.1869 and c.1930. It has a composition five-piece curved baby body. The head is stamped S&H 126. Simon & Halbig also made heads for other companies, and these will carry the marks of both firms. The firm also made china-headed dolls but the bisques are more popular with collectors.

**▶ SCHOENAU & HOFFMEISTER BABY**
*c.1920; 38cm (15in) high;* **£500**
This character baby has a soft stuffed body and a rather stern but realistic expression. Its head is marked with the firm's initials – the same as those of Simon & Halbig – but Schoenau & Hoffmeister usually added a star with the initials PB for Porzellanfabrik Burggrub, where the factory was based. The firm also made girl dolls, which are less collectable than the character babies.

## FRENCH S.F.B.J. BÉBÉ
*c.1900; 40.5cm (16in) high;*
**£550**
S.F.B.J. is the abbreviation of the Societé Française de Fabrication des Bébés et Jouets, the name given to a consortium of French doll makers formed in 1899 to combat the fierce competition from Germany. There is considerable variation in the quality of S.F.B.J.s although the example shown here is a fine one.

She has "sleep" glass eyes, which are usually open but close when she is lying down. The moulded teeth showing through parted lips is a typical feature.

Typically the doll is marked on the back of the head with the initials "S.F.B.J." and a mould number, of which 60 is one of the most common.

The body is made of wood and composition with French jointed limbs that differ to those on a German body, which uses ball-shaped joints to connect the limbs. S.F.B.J. bodies are slimmer than earlier French models.

The hand has five well-defined fingers, and is slimmer than its German and later French counterparts; sometimes the nails are painted.

Clothes are seldom original; these have been made using antique fabric and copying a French design of the period. However, the shoes and wig are original.

### COLLECTORS' NOTES
• Never repaint or alter a doll; if you change the clothes, store the originals carefully, protected from moths.
• Always look first at the back of the head or shoulder plate for an identification mark.
• Closed or slightly open mouths (known as open-closed mouths) are more desirable than open mouths.

### COLLECTING TIPS
• Unusual characters, Oriental, black and brown dolls all command a premium.
• Popular mould numbers include Kestner's 211 baby and Kammer & Reinhardt's 109, modelled as a boy or girl with appropriate wig and clothes.

# Later Dolls

At the beginning of the 20th century dolls began to be made in a variety of new materials, especially celluloid, composition and plastic, but also in fabrics such as stockinet and felt. French and German manufacturers continued to produce dolls and adapted to the new media, especially celluloid. Some manufacturers even brought out new versions of dolls in celluloid made in moulds previously used for bisque dolls.

American manufacturers steadily increased in prominence, making dolls in all media. New York was the most important production area, with companies such as E.I. Horsman, the Ideal Novelty & Toy Co. (which made the first ever Shirley Temple doll) and the Acme Toy Company. However, the biggest impact was made with Barbie, probably the most successful selling doll ever, introduced in 1959 by the American firm Mattel. Look out also for advertising dolls, such as those made by the American Character Doll Co. to promote Lee Jeans and the English-made Bisto Kids, inspiring customers to buy the famous gravy.

As this is the period of mass-production, collectors should scrutinize 20th-century dolls for quality and also condition – not all these materials were robust: composition can craze and flake and soft fabrics perish easily. Nevertheless, there is a huge range of affordable and attractive dolls available to choose from, and with such a choice, every collector is bound to find something to suit their tastes and their pocket.

**▶ DUTCH MUSICAL GIRL BY ALPHA FARNELL**
*1930s; 46cm (18in) high;* **£100**
This charming Dutch girl has a musical mechanism hidden underneath her skirt which plays when a key under her skirt is wound. She is in good condition – which is essential with cloth dolls. Like Dean's, Alpha Farnell were well known for their teddy bears. Other prominent fabric doll-makers were Norah Wellings in England, Lenci in Italy and Izannah Walker, Martha Chase and the Georgene Novelty Company in the United States.

**◀ BETTY OXO BY DEAN'S RAG BOOK CO. LTD**
*c.1920–30; 51cm (20in) high;* **£650**
This promotional doll, intended to inspire customers to buy gravy, was made by the English firm of Dean's. Although she has a fabric face and body, she has survived in remarkably good condition. Sometimes, these dolls are still found in their original box, and this greatly enhances their desirability and their value. As well as entire dolls, the firm also made and sold cloth doll kits for making up at home, and a wide range of teddy bears. Most of the dolls are stamped with the Dean's logo showing a terrier and a bulldog fighting over a ragbook, sometimes accompanied by the company name. Betty Oxo has a particularly appealing expression, with "googly"-type eyes.

**▲ DOLLS' HOUSE DOLLS**
*1920s; smallest 6cm (2½in), largest 10cm (4in) high;* **£80 each**
Dolls' house dolls were made from the end of the 19th century until the 1920s. As well as being used to furnish dolls' houses, they are popular for those with limited display space. Although made in a variety of media, many, like these three, have bisque heads and bodies. They are particularly appealing because they come in many types, often in sets with all the generations and characters that might have inhabited a grand house. They are often unmarked but many are German-made.

**▶ CHAD VALLEY FELT DOLL**
*1930s; 35.5cm (14in) high;* **£450**
The realistic moulded felt face of this little girl is typical of Chad's soft dolls – although they also worked in velvet and stockinet. The out-stretched right arm and buckled shoes are also characteristic. She has glass eyes and a mohair wig. Chad Valley are best known for their dolls modelled on the English princesses, Elizabeth and Margaret. Like their bears (see p.130), most of the dolls are marked.

**◀ BARBIE AND STACEY**
*1970s/80s; dolls 29cm (11½in) high;* **£30**
The Barbie doll has been a huge success story, since she was first made in 1959 right up until the present day, when if anything, she is becoming even more popular and something of a cult figure. One of the most appealing things about her, apart from her good looks and long legs, is her extensive wardrobe – literally thousands of different outfits have been made to cater for every eventuality, including a ski-ing outfit, a bridal dress and an air hostess costume! Hair is usually rooted to the head, although, as demonstrated by the wigs in the case, nothing about Barbie can be taken for granted. Original boxes, packaging or clothing add considerably to value. The case full of clothes shown here is a collector's dream – and the presence of Barbie's friend Stacey is an added bonus.

**▲ BARBIE**
*c.1970s/80s; 29cm (11½in); high* **£15–20**
Barbie has undergone surprisingly few changes since she was first made: the limbs are invariably jointed, and the eyes either painted or inserted. Most have blonde, usually long, tresses.

**◀ SINDY**
*c.1960s; 29cm (11½in) high;* **£15–20**
Barbie's main rival from the 1960s was Sindy, first produced by the British firm of Pedigree Toys and Dolls. Sindy is younger, cuter and less sophisticated than Barbie, although she also comes with full sets of clothes and accessories. The Sindy shown here dates from the 1960s; more grown-up versions were introduced in the 1970s, although even these were never as popular as Barbie. Other versions include a rare black Sindy, which is worth one and a half times more than the white ones. The presence of a box can double the price; condition is also important because the dolls were made in such huge numbers.

**COLLECTORS NOTES**
• Look out for felt dolls made by Steiff; these usually have a face-seam, button eyes, large feet and occasionally a Steiff button in one ear.
• A distinctive feature of Lenci felt dolls are the separately stitched outer fingers and joined inner fingers.
• American composition dolls from the mid-20th century and later tend to be slightly more expensive than their German counterparts, but are worth the extra as they are usually better made and less prone to cracking and other types of material disintegration.

**COLLECTING TIPS**
• The most collectable Barbies are the brunettes and those with titian hair, as these were made in smaller numbers than the blonde models.
• Among hard plastic dolls, look for Betty Boop and film star dolls, such as Deanna Durbin.
• Shirley Temple dolls were made by the Ideal Toy & Novelty Company in huge numbers during the 1930s and later; the earlier examples are the most desirable and authentic – and therefore command the highest prices. Officially registered ones should be marked on the head or shoulderplate.

# Toys: where to begin

Whether you feel drawn to a particular period in toy manufacture, such as German tinplate toys of the early 20th century or moulded plastic toys from the last 20 years, choose your area carefully and begin to learn about it before making a start on a focused collection.

## Condition

Because many toys were made comparatively recently and in large numbers, condition is the most important aspect for collectors and a list of abbreviations (*below*) exists to describe the various states in which toys can be found. Serious collectors of toys aspire to own pieces in mint condition, but very often have to settle for less, because of scarcity or price. Descriptions of condition apply to the surface of the toy – usually the state of the paintwork and any transfers or lettering on the surface. Similar classifications apply to the boxes that contained them. Any other defects should be listed separately.

M = Mint. As if it had just left the factory.
E = Excellent. Almost as good as mint but with a very few minor scratches or tiny chips to paintwork.
E–G = Excellent to Good. Better than good but not quite good enough to be called excellent.
G = Good. Has been played with but well looked after and in good condition.
F = Fair. Rather worn but still attractive to collectors.
P = Poor. Ranges from still slightly collectable to something in bits.

## Care and Maintenance

Toys were made in a variety of materials, each one prone to a different type of damage. They should be kept in dry, well-ventilated conditions whether they are out on display or stored in boxes. Damp and direct sunlight are the main enemies. It is also inadvisable to allow dust to build up, so dust and move displayed pieces at regular intervals using a soft brush. If you wash something, use a small amount of washing up liquid and steer clear of scouring agents. It goes without saying that, despite these toys being made for children to play with, a treasured collection should not be within reach of small, inquisitive hands except under strict supervision.

The main perils to which each medium is prone are:
Wood: woodworm and rot.
Composition: flaking on the surface.
Tinplate: rust.
Lithographed tinplate or wood: scratching.
Lead: chipping and scratching, oxidizing to produce a powdery surface and breaking of extremities on figures.
Diecast: metal fatigue caused by impurities in the mazac (the magnesium and zinc-based alloy used from 1934), creating a crazed surface on the toy.
Enamel paint: chipping.
Transfers: peeling.
Boxes: silverfish and mice eat the paper and glue.
Plastic: can scratch and scuff. Harder varieties snap, especially those mixed with chalk to which paint adhered more easily.

## Restoration

Generally speaking, a serious collector will always want a piece to be in as original condition as possible, therefore the less restoration a toy has undergone, the better. Original paintwork is particularly desirable, but it may not always be possible to find the most ideal examples within a reasonable price range. It is therefore quite acceptable to buy restored examples providing the seller is not trying to pass them off as original, and the work has been done well. Scrupulous restorers and collectors mark the underside of an object so that as the piece is passed on, the restoration is recognised and the potential for deception greatly reduced. An enthusiast whose main interest is in the development of particular toy manufacturers or types of toy can use a collection of restored toys to tell a story, but in the market place, these toys will always be brought under the same classification as those in poor condition.

## Boxes

If a toy was boxed when it left the factory, then the survival of that box is of enormous importance to the collector. The pinnacle is to find a toy "mint in mint box" – a rarity in today's market and beyond the reach of the average buyer. Nevertheless, boxes are worth mentioning separately because they are of such interest and can represent the greater part of the value of an item. Some toys, particularly Dinky vehicles, were not sold invidually in boxes, but arrived from the wholesaler in large trade boxes. Surviving wholesale boxes complete with their contents are enormously valuable. Collectors who enjoy researching their subject use boxes to tell them which companies were buying from the manufacturers, repacking the goods and selling them on to retailers at a particular point in the history of a toy. If buying modern toys as a long term investment, never remove them from the box. If you are desperate to handle the toy inside, buy two!

# Wooden Toys

Some of the earliest playthings made for children were carved from wood, the most abundantly available natural material in pre-industrial times apart from cloth and wool. Simple dolls, spinning tops, push-along animals, and the bigger rocking horses, wheelbarrows and toboggans were produced by fathers for their children and by professional toymakers. Few pre-18th century examples have survived the ravages of time and woodworm, but wooden toys continued to be made into the 19th century, and examples from this period are now valued as much for their folk art appeal as for their ability to amuse and entertain. The development of the lithographic process of printing was also enormously helpful to toymakers, who combined wood and paper to produce colourfully decorated ships, forts, nests of boxes, building blocks and theatres.

▶ **MONEY BOX IN THE FORM OF A HOUSE**
*c.1820; 25.5cm (10in) high;* **£400–600**
At the time this delightful carved and painted wooden house was made, only very privileged children enjoyed the luxury of being handed a few pennies on a regular basis. Money boxes were made in a great variety of materials including tinplate and pottery, and many were not fitted with any means of recovering their contents and had to be deliberately broken to empty them when full.

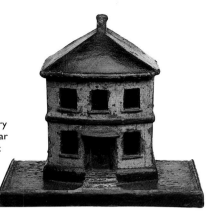

▶ **MODEL OF A ZEBRA**
*c.1850–70; 30.5cm (12in) high;* **£400–500**
Mounted on a platform base with wheels, this zebra would once have been sped around the nursery by means of a chubby hand clamped firmly across its back. The zebra, along with the lion, the elephant and the tiger, had great exotic appeal during the 19th century, long before children were able to watch film footage of these animals in their natural surroundings. This creature was obviously not intended to roam freely as he has been fitted with a saddle and bridle.

▼ **MODEL OF A ROLLER COASTER**
*c.1900; 36cm (14in) long;* **£150–250**
The best toys reflect the world that children see around them, and there was no greater thrill at the turn of the century than a visit to the travelling fun fair culminating in a ride on the roller coaster. This hand-carved and painted roller coaster, complete with enthralled passengers, coud be pushed around the room or sent flying across a polished wooden surface.

▲ **GERMAN NOAH'S ARK**
*1860; 14in (36cm) long;* **£400–600**
Noah's Arks have proved popular toys with generations of children. During the 19th century, playing with toys on a Sunday was frowned upon, but the Noah's Ark, because of its religious connotations, was considered an exception and offered hours of quiet play. These earlier examples were hand-painted, but later ones were paper-lithographed. The side panel on this one slides out so that the Ark acts as a box in which to store the animals. Arks with hulls, rather than these flat-bottomed versions, tend to be more sought after.

**COLLECTORS' NOTES**
Beware the reproduction. Wooden toys are easy to fake and many modern Far Eastern imports have caused disappointment over recent years. There are several ways to identify fake wooden toys. If you get the

feeling that a piece looks both "antique" and in too good condition, it is worth investigating further. If the toy is painted with regular brush strokes sparsely applied, and has no gloss left on it anywhere it may well be a fake. When a toy has been played with

the knocks and scratches will be irregular and more prominent in areas where the toy would have received most handling.

Try to buy the most decorative and well-carved pieces you can, as they would have been the best of their kind when new.

**COLLECTING TIP**
Attractive 19th-century Jumping Jack Flashes (usually in the form of a man whose arms and legs move up and down when a string is pulled) can still be bought for £100–150 and are considered undervalued at the moment.

# Automata

# Tinplate Toys

In the late 18th and 19th centuries, automata were a great source of entertainment and amusement. A number of small workshops in Paris produced the majority of the examples still on the market today. They were made mainly for adults and had mechanical movements (sometimes incorporating music) which, when wound, caused rabbits to rise up out of cabbages or dolls to dance. Dancing sailors and rolling waves, fiddling monkeys and walking, grunting pigs make this a fascinating and varied area for collectors, crossing the world of dolls and toys with that of mechanical music.

The earliest tinplate toys were produced during the first half of the 19th century, as expensive, high quality pieces. Germany was the major centre of manufacture and held the monopoly well into the 20th century until mass-production ensured that tinplate toys, often with a clockwork mechanism, became the favourite playthings of children all over Europe and the United States.

Tinplate toys of every description were made in vast quantities by companies such as Lehmann, Schuco and Marklin in Germany. Production suffered during the First World War and after 1918, British companies such as Meccano, Hornby and Lines Brothers prospered, as well as Marx in the United States. After World War II, Japan dominated the market and by the mid-1960s, most German manufacturers had gone out of business. In the last 25 years, tinplate toys have become very collectable.

◀ **RENOU LITTLE GIRL MAGICIAN AUTOMATON**
*c.1900; 44.5cm (17½in);*
**£1,500–2,000**
When the key is wound in the red velvet covered base, the doll raises her head and both her arms to lift a box revealing moving balls and dice. This is very typical of what would have been a middle-of-the-range French toy of its time. The bisque head is by Ferdinand Gaultier (indeed many leading doll manufacturers supplied heads and limbs to automata workshops), with blue glass "paperweight" eyes, closed mouth and pierced ears. The back of the head is impressed "F.G." Her costume is a more modern replacement.

▲ **TIN TRI-ANG TRAIN**
*1930s; 53.5cm (21in) long;* **£60–80**
Designed with a very small child in mind, this example of the red Tri-ang Express is in good condition. Most surviving Tri-ang trains are rusty from being played with outside and left in the rain, and are worth around £10–20. The Tri-ang range of toys was a trademark of Lines Brothers who began manufacturing in the 1920s in south London.

▶ **RARE GUSTAVE VICHY MUSICAL AUTOMATON**
*c.1880; 20½in (52cm);* **£12,000–18,000**
This musical automaton of a pumpkin eater is by Gustave Vichy, one of the best makers of the late 19th century. The turned circular base contains the keywind stop/start musical mechanism. Above, the cheeky pumpkin eater is of papier-mâché, with brown paperweight eyes. He stands beside a wooden cupboard, his pumpkin on a stool. When wound, he moves his head from side to side and nods; his right arm, which holds a knife, moves in a cutting motion towards the pumpkin, which opens to reveal a white mouse.

▲ **SELECTION OF TINPLATE PENNY TOYS**
*all 1890–1900: Two French whistles; 10.5cm (4in) long each;*
**£100–120 each;** *German ferris wheel; 6cm (2½in) high;* **£80–100;**
*French penny house bank; 5cm (2in) high;* **£60–80;** *Meier bird in cage; 5cm (2in) high;* **£80–100;** *Meier bird in coop; 5cm (2in) high;*
**£80–100**
Small tinplate, lithographed toys like these were made in great variety and profusion in both France and Germany at the end of the 19th and beginning of the 20th century. They were a great favourite with children, who could buy them from street vendors for just one penny. Meier of Germany was the best known maker.

### "LI LA" HANSOM CAB BY LEHMANN
*1903; 15cm (6in) high; £500–800*

The firm of Ernst Paul Lehmann operated in Berlin, producing great quantities of amusing, lightweight, novelty tinplate toys, colourfully lithographed. The sections are always joined by tabs rather than soldering. The action of the figures is the most important aspect of most Lehmann toys. This typical example is of painted and lithographed tinplate, lettered and edged in gilt. When wound, the vehicle is propelled forward while the two angry, seated ladies (wearing cloth skirts and painted blouses) repeatedly hit the dog seated on the outer platform.

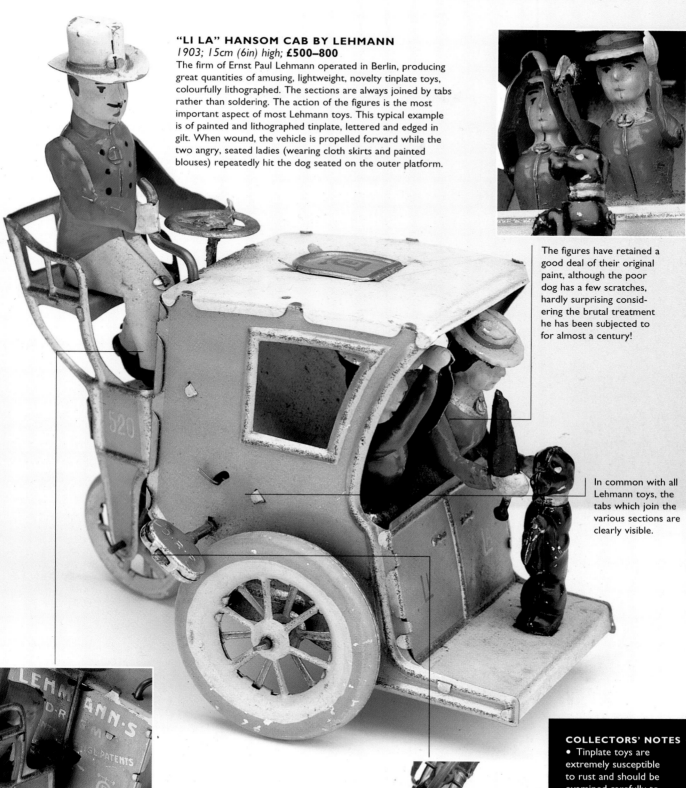

The figures have retained a good deal of their original paint, although the poor dog has a few scratches, hardly surprising considering the brutal treatment he has been subjected to for almost a century!

In common with all Lehmann toys, the tabs which join the various sections are clearly visible.

The Lehmann trademark, which is in the form of a spindle-press, shows quite clearly here. The stylized "e" is made up from the letters E, P and L – the initials of Ernst Paul Lehmann.

There is no need to guess the date of manufacture of this example as the gold lettering states unequivocally that it was made on 12 MAY 1903. The clockwork mechanism is also visible here. The key is an integral part of it and remains in the vehicle as it moves.

**COLLECTORS' NOTES**
• Tinplate toys are extremely susceptible to rust and should be examined carefully to see if they have been repaired and/or repainted.
• Look to see if all the paintwork matches exactly and that no areas have a "fresh"appearance.
• On Lehmann toys, make sure that the tabs holding the pieces together are intact and have not been replaced by rods.

# Early Diecast and Lead Toys

The toy soldier, the most typical and popular type of lead figure, has enthralled both adults and children since the first commercially manufactured examples were produced by the French company, Lucotte, in the 18th century. Although military figures, along with their vehicles, weapons and animals, dominated the market, many representations of a more peaceful existence, including zoos, circuses and farms, were also made.

These figures were made of solid lead until William Britain of the Britains Company in England developed the hollow-cast lead figure in 1893. By pouring lead alloy into an engraved mould, fully rounded figures with a hollow centre were created and required only half the metal of their solid predecessors. The innovation seriously challenged Continental imports and although other companies took up the process, Britains continued to dominate the market.

The earliest diecast toys, formed in a metal mould under pressure, were also made of lead, but in 1934 a safer magnesium and zinc based alloy known as mazac was developed and is still used in the manufacture of diecast toys to this day. Most are in the form of cars, lorries and aircraft, made in such huge numbers that most boys growing up at any time during the last 50 years had several of them to play with at any one time.

What gives so many of them such high value, however, is that they were so loved and played with that many have been destroyed. Pre-war boxed sets are extremely rare since most little boys bought vehicles individually. The retailer received the sets in trade boxes and sold them one at a time wrapped in a bit of paper. As he sold the last example in a set, he often gave the box to the customer. It was only a very privileged child who was given an entire boxed set during this period.

◄ **BRITAINS FARMYARD**
*1920s; average standing figure 5.5cm (2½in) high;* **£500–700**
After the bloodbath of the First World War, the public desired less militaristic playthings for children and Britains cleverly exploited this by launching their farm, circus and zoo figures which have proved ideal pocket-money toys ever since. The pieces shown here are in particularly fine condition. Single figures from this period can still be bought at antiques fairs for £2–5. If this collection was worn it would be worth no more than £150.

▼ **BRITAINS PONTOON SET 203**
*1920–25; pontoon 35.5cm (14in) long;* **£350–450**
A pontoon is a flat-bottomed boat which, together with the planks attached to it, was used to support a temporary bridge. This example, being dragged by four splendid horses, depicts British troops on campaign at the end of the 19th century. The horses are wearing heavy harnesses, which helps to date the piece as pre-1925, as after this date, lighter harnesses began to appear.

▼ **BRITAINS MEDICAL CORPS SET 145**
*1906–20; ambulance 26.5cm (10½in) long;* **£250–350**
Once again, the dating of this horse-drawn ambulance is helped by the type of heavy harness worn by the horses. These horse-drawn teams are much sought after by collectors who like to build up large quantities of figures – which should be of the same sort of scale and manufacture to look good together.

**▲ BRITAINS MONOPLANE AND CREW SET 434**
*1932–5; plane 15cm (6in) long;* **£300–400**
Britains aircraft were not made in great quantity and therefore
have a certain rarity value. They tend to be of very high quality.
The boxes are even more of a rarity because they were designed
to be cut up by children and made into aircraft hangers. If this
example had retained its box it would be worth £500–600.

**COLLECTORS' NOTES**
• If you are buying a diecast
vehicle, it's worth spending the
extra money to buy something
in its original box.
• When buying vehicles, choose
a period of cars and lorries that
you like and build up a selection
of objects within that time span,
even, perhaps, sticking to one
manufacturer or type of vehicle.
It will be a much more cohesive
collection than one which incorporates bits and pieces from
different eras.
• Buy a good model price guide
magazine, available from book-
shops, and find out where swap
meetings are being held. Going to
those, and to auctions, will give
you a good feel for prices when
you first start out.
• Avoid buying repainted pieces.
One of the best ways to spot new
paint is to put the item under
your nose and inhale sharply. Any
whiff of paint is a good clue that
restoration has occurred.

**COLLECTING TIP**
Good diecast toys from the 1950s
and early 1960s are an excellent
investment and mint and boxed
Matchbox toys from the late
1950s and early 1960s can still be
purchased for reasonable prices.

**▲ DINKY NO 36 (MEDIUM) MOTOR CARS**
*1936–40; box 37 x 10cm (14½ x 4in);* **£10,500–12,500**
The vehicles belonging to the No. 36 set, sold with drivers,
passengers and footmen, are still widely available and can be
collected one at a time, but it is the box which makes this
such a rarity. Since most pre-war Dinky vehicles were sold
individually, few boxes survive and this one represents literally
three quarters of the value of the set.

**▼ DINKY (MEDIUM) SUPERTOY TANKER**
*1947–52; 18.5cm (7¼in) long;* **£80–120**
The Supertoy range launched by Dinky in 1947 answered the
prayers of many children who hungered for new and exciting toys
after the long war years. They were larger than previous vehicles
and remained unique in the market place. This is a very typical and
standard model of a Foden 14-ton tanker. Condition is everything
when it comes to assessing the value of these toys and the box can
represent 50–80 percent of the value.

**▼ MATCHBOX A.E.C. Y TYPE LORRY**
*1957; 7cm (2¾in) long;* **£400–600**
"The Models of Yester Year" series launched by Matchbox in
1956 has become more collected internationally than possibly
any other range of toys. Matchbox aimed to undercut Dinky
toys by marketing small diecast toys in a matchbox-type box.
Most that survive are of low value, but a few were made in rare
colours, such as this mid-blue Osram Lamps lorry made for
only one year. In the common light grey it is worth £80–100.

**▲ TWO EARLY DINKY VEHICLES FROM 28 SERIES:**
**KODAK (MEDIUM) FILM VAN**
*1934–5; 84mm (3¼in) long;* **£500—800**
**PALETHORPES SAUSAGES VAN**
*1934–5; 84mm (3¼in) long;* **£500–800**
It was Frank Hornby, the inventor of Meccano and the name behind
Hornby trains, who launched the Dinky range of vehicles in 1934.
The first examples of Dinky toys were designed to be used along-
side the O-gauge railways. These two vans advertise Kodak Film and
Palethorpes Sausages. Condition is very important with these pieces
since pre-Second World War metal becomes brittle with age.

# Later Diecast and Modern Toys

The great advantage in collecting modern toys is that most of them are still affordable because they have survived in large quantities. Added to that, they were made within living memory of a lot of new collectors who cherish fond memories of playing with them as children. Many of these toys, as in the more distant past, reflect the developments in science and technology which were taking place at an increasingly rapid rate after the Second World War. The Vauxhall car tells the story of British car design at the beginning of the 1950s, and the Japanese battery-operated robot encapsulated the excitement of the space race and new atomic age.

Many of the most sought-after post-war toys are film and television related and this is an area that continues to grow as ever more ingenuity is spent finding ways to fill increasing leisure time. New products are constantly being manufactured, which is what makes the modern toy such an uncertain and exciting area for the collector. Buying new toys could be a wise investment for the future, but you must think in terms of delayed reward. Most of the items in the shops now will have only second-hand value for at least 30 to 40 years. There are a few exceptions. Fast food toys have become highly collectable and certain objects which have proved unpopular with the burger generation have been withdrawn quickly and, in bagged and unused condition, are now changing hands in the United States for as much as $1,000 (*see* p.213).

### ▲ VICTORY MODEL VAUXHALL VELOX
*1951; 25.5cm (10in) long;* **£70–90**
With every new Vauxhall car bought in a six-year period during the 1950s, one of these promotional model cars was given as a gift. Some were battery-operated, some remote controlled. Made in plastic to a 1:18 scale, these cars need to have survived in good condition with the box to be worth anything. This dark blue colour is quite rare. Those in light blue are more common and worth £40–50.

### ▼ TRI-ANG OCEAN LINER
*1950s–60s; 52cm (20½in) long;* **£40–60**
Before the advent of early morning children's television, nothing gave a young man greater pleasure than to be taken to the nearest piece of water by his father on a Saturday or Sunday morning to sail his boat. Boats have always been popular toys but few early wooden or tin plate ones survive. There is no reason for this battery-operated plastic boat not to last forever now that it is in permanent dry dock.

### ◄ SUPER SPACE EXPLORER ROBOT
*1960–70; 20cm (11in) high;* **£50–80**
A good late 1950s or 1960s robot made in Japan in a combination of tinplate and plastic complete with box can make up to £1,000 at auction. These robots were very much of their time, when the exploration of space captured the imagination of both adults and children. They continued to be produced into the 1970s. This example is quite late and made purely of plastic which is why it is still so affordable.

### ▼ CORGI *CHITTY CHITTY BANG BANG* CAR
*1968–72; 12.5cm (5in) long;* **£60–80**
Television- and film-related toys were made in huge quantities by Corgi and Dinky, including those inspired by *Thunderbirds*, *Batman* and *The Avengers*. This car appeals to film and television fans as well as collectors of cars, and many of these items have increased in value rapidly in recent years. If this had its box, it would be worth £120–140.

## HORNBY DUBLO LOCOMOTIVE

*1959–64; engine and tender 26.5cm (10½in) long;* **£100–130**

Finished in smart matt green, this electric, diecast A4-class British Rail locomotive was made during the period after 1953 when Hornby had nationalized the liveries on their trains and the factory was turning out large quantities of good-quality, diecast locomotives. The first Hornby Dublo trains were made in 1938, and sold in pale blue boxes printed with date codes. These early examples are prone to metal fatigue in common with all early diecast models. Hornby trains in plastic were made during the second half of the 1960s and during the 1970s, but the demand for diecast meant that production restarted and these locomotives are still being made.

This shows that the locomotive was made during the period before Meccano was taken over by Tri-ang

The wheels on earlier models are iron-disc types without spokes. These are nylon-disc and spoke wheels typical of the period.

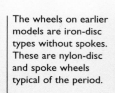

This is a Peco coupling featuring vertical bent hooks for easier coupling and un-coupling of coaches. Pre-war examples had horizontal hook-and-eye couplings

GOLDEN FLEECE

60030

20741

60030

Behind the wheels is a tiny contact wire which touches one of them to pick up the electricity from the track.

---

**COLLECTORS' NOTES**

Condition is even more important a\_\_\_ than in many others

- The current buyers of toys made post-1950 are the Baby Boomers who now find themselves in a

- "One for play and one to keep" is the attitude of many modern toy collectors who have small children –

**COLLECTING TIP**

When collecting trains from post-war period make sure

# Carpets & Textiles

Textile art is history through the eye of a needle, as more than one pundit has noted. It is also, for the most part, women's history. Many skills and crafts and the tools associated with them have been dominated by men. Both sexes have taken up the pen and the paintbrush, but with a few notable exceptions, men have never regarded the needle as a worthwhile creative instrument. The fruits of the loom, too, have traditionally been women's, with techniques and patterns handed down from generation to generation.

What separates textiles from most other areas of antiques is that they tell stories, charting not just the development of great industries and the transportation of materials by land and sea, but the work – of enormous complexity and beauty as well as great simplicity – being done by women at home. The best stumpwork and crewel work of 17th-century England, with panels of sumptuous embroidery worked in silks and gold and silver thread, was done by rich, intelligent women with a driving need to express themselves and plenty of time on their hands. For many, however, skill with the needle was a route to a regular if meagre income, and many a pair of shining young eyes grew dim through years of bending over the light of a flickering tallow candle.

The collector must choose to specialize because the field is so wide and varied. Pity the general expert in an auction house who takes in and values everything from printed 19th-century handkerchiefs to early tapestry fragments and everything in between, including quilts, silk pictures, samplers, lace, braid, ribbons and costume. Carpets and rugs are always treated separately from other textiles, by a different team of experts who spend many years studying the subtleties of design of rugs and carpets made from silk, wool and cotton by people from Armenia to outer Mongolia, as well as the output of European carpet manufacturers and the work of American Indian tribes.

You may come to textiles by looking at the history of cloth and the trade in cotton, flax, wool and silk over the centuries. A fascination with the scientific development of synthetics may lead you to collect more modern examples of fabric or weaving, or the complexities of lace might absorb you to the exclusion of all other textile art. Whichever area you choose, you will be surprised at how reasonably priced many antique textiles still are. You may have to pay several thousand pounds for a fabulous Chinese robe in pristine condition, but a pretty embroidered picture, or several pieces of costume or lace can still be bought for under £100.

*Clockwise from top left:* English framed sampler worked by Jane Brooker, 1825; 20th-century Kashan wool rug; Scottish woven wool shawl, c.1870; Chinese embroidered silk coat, c.1910; English Honiton lace fragment, c.1880; English quilt, c.1850.

# Where to begin

The joy of collecting in this area is that your purchases can often be used as well as looked at, but think carefully about what you want from a piece before you begin: 18th-century costume is not likely to be worn, but an old quilt will look lovely on a bed or draped over a sofa, and antique carpets can be hung, or laid on a floor.

## CARPETS

Always consult a reputable dealer or an expert at a leading auction house before investing in a rug or carpet. Many general antiques dealers and the experts at small, local salerooms don't usually have the knowledge to advise you properly. Understanding rugs is not insurmountable, but it takes time and experience to be able to tell the difference between one that will wear well and bring you pleasure for years and one which will quickly disintegrate, although it may look sound. Instinct and feel are the best guides, and the ability to spot a mechanical, stiff looking design which lacks balance and artistry.

### Looms

The size and sophistication of looms, which are either vertical or horizontal, depend purely on the circumstances of the weavers, but the type of loom used has no bearing on the fineness or overall quality of the finished rug or carpet. Nomadic people tend to use small, horizontal looms which can be staked to the ground and easily assembled and disassembled. This limits the size of the rugs they can produce, whereas the vertical looms used by settled peoples can be much larger. A loom is constructed in such a way as to provide the correct tension as the weaving grows, with the shedding device pulled down to pass the wefts through the warps.

### Construction

The foundation of rugs and carpets consists of the warp and the weft, onto which rows of knots are tied to form the upright pile. The warp, usually of strong, tightly spun, dark coloured wool, but sometimes of silk or cotton, runs along the length of the carpet and must be kept at an even tension throughout the construction of the piece. The fineness of the finished weave depends on how closely the warps are placed together and the density of the knots, which vary from 16 to 500 or more per square inch. The ends of the warp become the fringes which are usually either braided or tasselled. The weft, which passes from left to right is also generally wool, but sometimes silk or cotton. The weft is passed between each row of knots to secure them.

### Knots

The two main types of knots are the "symmetrical" Turkish or Ghiordes knot found on rugs and carpets made in Turkey, Turkestan and the Caucasus, and the "asymmetrical" Persian or Senneh knot found on those made in Persia, India, some parts of Turkestan and Egypt. To form a "symmetrical" knot the piece of yarn is wrapped around two warps with the two ends brought back between them. An "asymmetrical" knot is wrapped around one warp with the two ends divided and lying either to the left or right on the surface.

### Dyes

Vegetable dyes produce the subtle, harmonious tones of colour across a rug or carpet which are so desirable to collectors; chemical dyes are harsher and prone to fade more quickly. Beware of dating a rug by the type of dye used, however. Synthetic dyes were introduced in Russia in the 1870s, but a rug made in 1920 can still be vegetable-dyed. The variations in colours produced were dependent not only on the types of dye used but on the quality of the wool and the water. An expert is therefore able to associate particular colours with specific areas. The madder and indigo plants produced red and blue; other berries, fruits, barks and fungi produce a range of primary and secondary colours. The scarlet produced by using cochineal is only found in rugs made from the late 19th century, and was used mainly in Turkoman rugs.

### Dates

Rugs and carpets made in Muslim countries before the beginning of this century often incorporate inwoven Islamic dates. Some late 19th- and early 20th-century dates are known to have been tampered with to make them appear older than they are, so take good advice before buying. Later Caucasian carpets often have the Islamic and Christian dates side by side. The Hejira is the term for the beginning of the Muslim calender, the date, AD622, when the Prophet Muhammed fled from Mecca to Medina. In order to convert rugs dated from the year of the Hejira, divide the Hejira year by 33.7, subtract the result from the original date and add 622. Alternatively, for an approximate analysis, add 583 to the Hejira date.

### Care and Maintenance

Specialist dealers will often undertake cleaning and repairs, but never buy a badly stained or damaged rug without first finding out if the problems can be rectified. The cost of bringing it back to a good state may be more than the original purchase price. At home, a vacuum cleaner can be used with caution, but only in the direction of the pile, never against it. Far preferable is to hang the carpet and beat it from the back. A mild detergent diluted in warm water can be rubbed on and then off again with a sponge or soft brush, but take care never to soak the rug. Don't expose antique carpets, especially silk ones, to heavy wear or to long periods in strong sunlight. A certain amount of even wear is more desirable than one heavily worn area of the pile, so change their position at regular intervals.

## TEXTILES

When buying antique textiles you will most commonly come across pieces made of the following materials:-

**COTTON** This grows on bushes and is gathered after the ripe seedcases burst. The seeds at the centre of the fluffy balls are removed and the rest spun into fibres before being woven into cloth of varying quality. Some of the best early cotton was produced in India and Egypt. Syrian cotton was imported into Europe during the Middle Ages, after which cotton manufacturing industries were established all over Europe, reaching England in the 15th century. The United States became a major producer in the 19th century.

**LINEN** These fabrics are made from the bark or bast fibres of the flax plant, grown in damp soil. The fibres are separated from the rest of the stem after it has been pulled from the ground before the seeds fully ripen. The best early linen was produced in Egypt from earliest times until the end of the 13th century. Holland became an important centre of linen manufacture from the 15th until the 18th century. Stiffer than cotton but naturally very strong, it continued to be handwoven after cotton began to be woven by power-operated looms. The linen power loom was not introduced until the 1850s.

**WOOL** This is spun from the fleece of sheep which is cleaned to remove the natural oils, and then either carded or combed before spinning. Combing the material into long fibres gives an even, harder yarn known as worsted. The short threads, when spun, give a softer textured wool. Wool was much favoured by the Scandinavians during the Bronze Age, and by the Greeks and Romans later on. It is one of the oldest surviving industries in Europe, flourishing from the Middle Ages, with the preparation and finishing processes improving as the centuries passed.

**SILK** The silkworm secretes a combination of fluid and gum which forms its cocoon. When unravelled, several filaments are twisted together to form a single, silk thread. The earliest silk was made in China with fragments surviving from the 2nd millennium BC. It is the finest and yet strongest of natural fibres, taking dye well. Silks have been excavated from Chinese tombs dating from 475–221BC, embroidered with sophisticated designs in many colours. Silk found its way overland via the Silk Road to the Eastern Mediterranean with the Romans doing brisk business with the Chinese. The European trade flourished after the Renaissance with Venice being one of the main ports of entry. During the 18th century, Lyons in France became a principal centre of silk manufacture, as did Spitalfields in London.

## Care and Maintenance

Becoming a collector of antique textiles is an awesome responsibility since they are all, by their very nature, in the process of decay and disintegration. The way you treat them will directly affect how rapidly that process advances. Be wary of buying badly damaged pieces thinking they can be restored, because, as with carpets, the slow, painstaking work of restoration can easily cost more than the purchase price of the item. It is important, however, to make sure any trace of dust or pest is removed from your pieces before you add them to your collection. Specialists use tiny vacuum cleaners to remove the invisible larvae which can wreak havoc, and will do a number of colour tests before possibly carefully washing an item in de-mineralised water.

Light, damp and the human touch are all highly destructive. Never display textiles for long periods of time and not even for a short time in a south-facing room since ultra-violet light (sunlight) is the most damaging. You can buy a range of products which absorb ultra-violet rays, such as plastic window blinds, glass varnish and acrylic sheets, but all of these need regular checking as their absorbing properties don't last forever.

Most types of artificial light, apart from fibre optic lighting, generate heat and should not be placed anywhere near textiles. The salt in the sweat on your hands is also potentially damaging so wear cotton gloves when handling pieces. The best material for storage chests is metal, but cedarwood and mahogany are also relatively safe. Large pieces should either lie flat or be carefully rolled in unbleached calico. Smaller items can be wrapped in acid-free tissue paper and stored in cellophane bags. Hanging can pull and strain fragile fibres, but some costumes can be hung so long as well-padded hangers are used and heavy skirts are supported.

# Carpets

The first carpets were woven as a natural progression from using hides on the walls and floor of caves and huts to provide warmth in cold weather. Accounts of carpet-weaving in Ancient Egypt exist, but unlike ceramics or glass, rugs and carpets rot and few early pieces survive.

Historians have to rely on records and on studying patterns passed down within tribes. One of the earliest relics, the Pazyryk Rug, was found in 1947 and dates from the 5th century BC. It is woven in exactly the same way as rugs produced from the 16th century onwards, with a central field surrounded by borders. Fragments from the 13th and 14th centuries exist too, but there are greater gaps in knowledge in this area than in many others.

Weaving was one of the most basic and the most highly regarded of skills all over Turkey, Persia and across the great Russian steppes, through Afghanistan into India, Nepal and China. Henry VIII of England ordered great quantities of Turkish carpets; the Shahs gave finely woven rugs as gifts and commissioned pieces for their palaces, yet woven articles were also among the most basic necessities of nomadic tribes who used woven saddlebags to transport possessions between camps.

Great rulers set up court workshops where the finest work was carried out, but experts agree that traditional tribal village and nomad rugs are, in many cases, just as good as the work done at court. Nomads used the wool from their flocks and went to oasis towns to barter wool for dye. It is a romantic world where collectors can steep themselves in the history of the old overland trade routes and the tribes which journeyed along them.

▲ **ERSARI CHUVAL**
*1860; 96.5 x 53cm (3ft 2in x 1ft 9in);* **£800–1,000**
A chuval is the largest of the storage bags used by the Turkoman nomads (in this case the Ersari tribe), who for centuries wandered over Russia east of the Caspian Sea towards China. The bags were hung on the sides of animals during travelling periods and stored inside the tents once camp had been established. This is the face panel of one, piled just like a rug. Generally, the backs of the chuvals were flat woven in either plain colours or horizontal stripes but these backs are usually removed from examples on the market in Europe.

▲ **KARATCHOPH KAZAK RUG**
*1880s; 2.57m x 1.57m (8ft 5in x 5ft 2in);* **£6,000–7,000**
Made in the south west Caucusus (Russia), Karatchoph is a particular design type and relates to a village in the area. Kazak rugs usually have a thick woollen pile and were used by the shepherds during the winter months when they brought the flocks down from the mountains and remained in the villages until spring. Flatter, lighter kelims were taken on the journeys to return the animals to the pasture grounds in warm weather.

▲ **CHINESE NINGHSIA RUG**
*1880; 2.24m x 1.5m (7ft 4in x 4ft 11in);* **£1,000–1,200**
Made in the west of China, this rug's decoration features traditional Chinese dragon motifs within a characteristic sky, land and earth border. In the middle are the heavens, bordered by the sky, the land and beneath it the earth. A 19th-century Chinese rug will feel quite floppy when handled. By the 1920s they had become heavier and more rigid and were being woven for a European market. At this point many mythical motifs were replaced by more commercially viable bamboo shoots and such like. This rug is quite worn. In top condition it would be worth £2,000.

▲ **SILK FEREGHAN PRAYER RUG**
*1870s; 1.88m x 1.13m (6ft 2in x 3ft 11in);* **£3,000–5,000**
Fereghan refers to the place where this piece was made in the west of Persia (now Iran). It has been very finely woven on a silk foundation with a silk pile. Persian rugs of this type are naturalistic in design as opposed to the often more geometric motifs used on rugs made by nomadic tribes. The foundation of silk rugs is prone to drying out and cracking, referred to as "churuk." Such a rug will have a brittle feel, whereas one in good condition will feel soft and supple. Collectors like Persian rugs to be in mint condition as "churuk" greatly affects value.

## LADIK PRAYER RUG

*1920s; 2.03m x 1.27m (6ft 8in x 4ft 2in);* **£800–1,000**

In common with many Turkish rugs, the design on this example is named after the village in which it was made, and based on the rugs produced at the Ottoman court of Suleiman the Magnificent in the 16th century, a period of great innovation in rug-making. These Turkish village rugs are always worked in wool on a woollen foundation and the town of Ladik is well known for its prayer rugs, often in yellows as well as reds and blues.

The entire blue section of the rug is known as the Mihrab or prayer arch. The pointed section is placed pointing towards Mecca during prayer.

Much has been made about the significance of the number of bands around the border and the symbolism of the motifs, but in fact the border is purely decorative. It contributes to the overall balance of the rug, which should be examined as a whole.

Here you can see the woollen weft (the shoots of tightly spun wool which separate each row of knots). On other rugs these can sometimes be of cotton, jute or even silk.

The tulip has no special symbolic meaning in Turkish rugs. It is purely a pleasing motif, but this panel sometimes appears at the top of the rug rather than as a base panel.

The fringes of a rug are the warp threads which make up the foundation of the rug. Fringe condition is not important as long as the wear has not in any away eaten into the pile and affected the design. Nice plaited, knotted or brocaded ends are common among tribal rugs and if they have been removed it can affect value slightly, but it is not always easy to tell whether this has happened unless there are some tell-tale remaining remnants.

### COLLECTORS' NOTES
• Condition is very important. Repairs can be extremely costly, but an actual hole is much easier to rectify than overall wear.
• Big, decorative room-sized carpets sell well, but many of the tribal artefacts such as saddle bags, covers and storage pieces sell for very little unless they are particularly good examples.
• Kelims are very good value at the moment, having dropped in price markedly since the mid-1980s. You can buy a good 19th-century kelim for around £1,000.
• Don't buy rugs on holiday, buy from reputable dealers at home.

### COLLECTING TIP
19th-century rugs which have a slightly worn pile but will serve you for many years to come can be bought relatively cheaply, for around £300–500, unless they are of particular interest from a collector's point of view, in which case the price will soar.

# Needlework

Needlework has been done all over the world throughout history. The ancient Egyptians and the Chinese produced embroidery referred to in the Old Testament Book of Exodus. Varying in style and technique as fashions changed, it is as much a document of daily life as furniture, plate and ceramics. Little early work survives, as it often decorated costume which wore out with use, but between 1250 and 1350, high quality ecclesiastical garments were made in England and exported in great quantity. By the time the standard of this work declined at the end of the 16th century, secular embroidery in England had reached new heights. Cushions, hangings, panels for caskets and other furnishings were richly worked in silks and metal threads inspired by lavishly illustrated books and tended gardens full of colour.

Flemish tapestries were worked in great detail in the 17th century, and the influence of the Renaissance in Italy was felt all over Europe during the same period. The French king Louis XIV was a great patron of embroidery, and in Spain the Moorish influence was felt in the all-over patterns of their black and white work.

Some of the best needlework samplers came out of orphanages where children learnt skill with a needle to help find future employment. By about 1850 many forms of needlework fell victim to industrialization and much of what has survived is now valued by collectors.

### ◄ FINE STUART SILKWORK PICTURE
*c.1650; 40.6 x 40.6cm (16 x 16in);* **£2,500–4,000**
The name of the skilled embroiderer, Mary Spencer, appears in the top left and right hand sides of this picture depicting part of an Apocryphal story. Worked in coloured silks and couched metal thread, it displays a variety of stitches including French knots and satin and split stitch. The picture's design incorporates raised work pea pods and textured hillocks.

### ◄ ENGLISH NEEDLEWORK SAMPLER
*1841; 33 x 29.75cm (13 x 11¾in);* **£350–450**
Worked during the golden age of English samplers, this example consists mainly of cross stitch designs, showing birds and animals. The foundation is linen, edged with a running design, and, at the top, the letters of the alphabet. The final section of the verse reads, "Sarah Dowsett is my name and by my work you may see the same and by my work you may see what care my parents take with me...."

### ▲ FINE EMBROIDERED PANEL BY ANN MACBETH
*c.1905; 48.5 x 17.5cm (31½ x 19in);* **£2,500–4,500**
Ann Macbeth taught needlework at the Glasgow School of Art and worked alongside other well known women of the period, such as Jessie Newbery and Margaret Macdonald. This study of a girl with doves, in the Arts and Crafts tradition, in 1905 was illustrated in the British Studio magazine and exhibited at John Baillie's Gallery.

### ◄ PETIT POINT EVENING BAG
*1900; 25.5 cm (10in) wide;* **£200–250**
*Petit point* is the same stitch as *gros point* (one half of the cross of cross stitch), but worked on either a finer canvas or over one thread instead of two, giving the detailed effect that can be seen on every aspect of this evening bag. Made in Austria, it shows Esther in her finest robes entering the King's chamber. The central shell cartouche in the border is embroidered with the name "Esther." The chain handle is stamped "Austria."

---

## COLLECTORS' NOTES
- Early silkwork pictures should be displayed in a dimly lit room, a hallway, for example. Samplers, too, should not be exposed to strong sunlight.
- With unframed pieces, it is worth hunting around for a frame of the correct period. An unsympathetic frame can ruin a good example.
- Never attempt to clean a piece of antique needlework yourself because the colours can run so easily. A dirty piece should be cleaned, however, because moths can get at it, so invest in the skill of a good restorer.

## COLLECTING TIP
Embroideries from the 1870s onwards are underpriced. Bead or later silkwork pictures can be bought for as little as £40, but search for ones in good condition.

# Lace

The main lace-making areas from the late 16th and early 17th century were France, Italy and Flanders. Most lace items at that time were made in the form of ruffs, collars and borders for smocks and other garments. Since it could take a professional lace-maker several months to make one good piece, the wearing of lace was a luxury.

Fine antique lace is a joy to look at and very good value considering the work involved in making it. All lace was hand-made until the middle of the 19th century. It falls into two main types, needle lace – made with a needle working a fine, detached buttonhole stitch to a specific pattern – and bobbin or pillow lace which is worked on a lace-maker's pillow using lace bobbins.

The industry did not take off in England until the early 18th century, when it centred around the town of Honiton in the West Country. It was a cottage industry, making bobbin lace. A large piece might involve several people working on different sections. Queen Victoria's wedding veil was made at Honiton. Blandford in Dorset was another centre of production, as was Ayrshire in Scotland where whitework, a mixture of embroidery and lace was made during the 19th century.

**▶ DRESDEN KERCHIEF BORDER**
*c.1750; 152cm (60in) long;*
**£250–350**
Fine threads of muslin or cambric pulled together with fillings composed of intricate patterns characterize Dresden lace. It was used mainly for lappets, baby caps, half kerchiefs and waistcoats, with designs drawn professionally or at home.

**◀ VENETIAN *GROS POINT* NEEDLE LACE PANEL**
*17th century; whole panel 380cm (149½in) long, 30cm (11¾in) wide;* **£1,200–1,800**
This exquisite piece of early lace displays raised work and padded outlines of flowers and leaves, known as cordonnets. The overall design is baroque in flavour with asymmetrical details. The main lace was laid onto parchment and the fine threads added to join one raised piece to another. Venice was a great lace-making centre at this time.

**◀ AYRSHIRE CHRISTENING ROBE**
*c.1850; 109cm (43in) long;*
**£150–250**
During the 19th century, you could buy a panel of lace and have it incorporated into a garment, as has happened with this christening robe. It was a type of work devised by Mrs Jamieson, the wife of a cotton agent in Ayr, and was based on a baby robe from France. Many purists do not regard it as true lace, but as a type of cutwork embroidery on white muslin with lace fillings in the cut-out spaces. Much was exported to the United States, but the Civil War there badly affected trade. Development of Swiss machine embroidery sounded the death knell for Ayrshire work.

**▲ MIXED BRUSSELS LACE HANDKERCHIEF**
*1870; 35 x 35cm (13¾ x 13¾in);*
**£100–150**
**▶ FRENCH VALENCIENNES HANDKERCHIEF**
*1870; 36 x 34cm (14¼ x 13½in);*
**£100–130**
The Brussels handkerchief consists mainly of bobbin lace with small inserts of needle lace to give a rich and intricate border. Valenciennes is a fine lace incorporating simple, spriggy designs and was often used for edging baby clothes. It was made throughout the 18th and 19th centuries. It is often possible to buy several handkerchiefs like these at auction for a very good price.

**▶ HONITON BONNET**
*c.1860–80; 31cm (12¼in) diameter;* **£50–70**
Nature was the inspiration for much Honiton lace, which was used mainly for bonnets, wedding veils and lappets. In the trade, badly worked Honiton lace is known as slugs and snails.

**COLLECTORS' NOTES**
• Examine the fillings on Ayrshire work. Each one between the main design should be different if the piece is hand-made. The greater the intricacy of the fillings, the more desirable and valuable the piece will be.
• Condition is important. As a rule don't buy damaged lace because it costs a great deal to get it repaired.

• Lace is best kept in a drawer rolled up in acid free tissue paper away from direct light.
• Wash lace very carefully in warm de-ionised water with some pure soap flakes.

**COLLECTING TIP**
Brides-to-be can still pick up an antique Honiton appliqué lace wedding veil for around £300–400 at auction.

# Quilts

To provide warmth rather than adornment was the primary objective for creating the first quilted garments and bedcovers. A sandwich created by laying one piece of material over another with some wadding between, held together with rows of stitching, proved an effective method of warding off chilly draughts.

Although small numbers of 18th-century quilts survive, the art of quilt-making really came into its own in the 19th century and most of those on the market today were made in the United States and the British Isles. In general terms, American quilts are appreciated for their overall visual appeal and colour, while collectors of English whole cloth quilts are drawn to the intricate patterns achieved by the stitching.

Early American settlers lived lives of great hardship, but once the first established communities on the Eastern Seaboard began to acquire a few more comforts, quilts of great beauty began to be made in patterns given names which evoke those settlements. The great westward migration meant that names changed, so that Indian Trail became Kansas Troubles, Lemon Star and Lemoyne Star, and what was Hand of Friendship in Philadelphia became Bear's Paw as its exponents hit the trail.

The concept of groups of women getting together in a "bee" to produce quilts was not as strong in the United States as myth has us believe. For many women in small isolated cabins, it was more a question of setting up a frame on the back of four chairs and working when they could, perhaps using a pulley to take the quilt up to the ceiling when more pressing duties called. In England, though, the poorest women did club together to buy materials to make quilts which were then sold to bring in much needed extra income. The miners' wives of Durham, Northumberland and Wales were responsible for producing some of the most intricately stitched quilts still in existence, often composed of only one colour.

**◄ ENGLISH STRIP QUILT**
*late 19th century; 2.44 x 2.54m (8ft x 8ft 4in);* **£80–120**
Remnants of ginghams and flowered furnishing chintz have gone to make this simple, warm strip quilt. Without any attempt at sophistication, pieces of varying widths have been sewn together until two sections large enough to make both a front and a backing have emerged. A layer of wadding separates them with lines of visible stitching to hold the sandwich together.

**► ENGLISH HEXAGON PATCHWORK QUILT**
*c.1860; 2.47 x 1.98m (8ft 1in x 6ft 6in);* **£200–300**
Plain, flowered and striped scraps of fabric have been used to create this colourful early 19th-century quilt. This is very much the product of long hours of hand-piecing and was made as a cover for home use rather than sold to make money. The hexagon is one of the most widely used shapes in patchwork. In various configurations it offers different effects, creating patterns known as "Grandmother's Flower Garden" or "Mosaic."

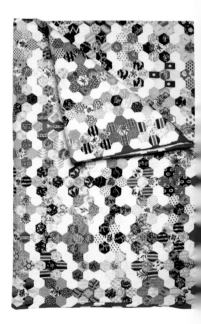

## COLLECTORS' NOTES
• Some collectors like to see still visible on the cloth the pencil marks that were put there to guide the quilters as they stitched the layers together.
• On English quilts, the paper templates still remain sewn into the shapes of the pattern (squares, hexagons, diamonds, and so on) and can be used to date a piece, as they were often made from old household bills, calling cards or envelopes, all of which carry dates marked on them.

• Don't be put off buying an antique quilt because of the maintenance. Believe it or not, some solid-colour quilts can be machine washed. They are both tough and practical, so if you can find a launderette with a large, industrial washing machine, put your quilt through a very low temperature cycle.
• Bear in mind that a strongly patterned and coloured quilt really changes the character of a room. They need to be set off against plain walls and carpets. If you are

deeply attached to the wallpaper or curtains in your bedroom, think very hard before buying a quilt because you will almost certainly need to make some changes as a result.
• Antique quilts which may have had heavy use should be examined very carefully for signs of wear and discoloration. Take your time doing this before committing yourself to buying, because it can take a few minutes before the thin areas of a heavily patterned quilt become apparent. Browns tend to

corrode very easily so look very closely at those patches.

## COLLECTING TIP
Quilts are often still very reasonably priced at auction in England, although in the United States they are generally more appreciated as an aspect of folk art and can therefore sell for a great deal of money. At an English auction, you can still buy a 19th-century quilt for a little over £100; in the US prices start at around $250.

**AMERICAN DRESDEN PLATTER QUILT**
*1930s; 1.6 x 1.88m (6ft 3in x 6ft 2in);* **£200–400**
This quilt was made in a traditional design by Clara Reimart Wagner in Pennsylvania during the 1930s when, despite the Depression, cotton dress fabrics could be bought for as little as 15¢ a yard. The overall pink colour, made up from many scraps of material, is very common on American quilts of this period. The iron mordants (metallic salts which fixed colours in fabrics made during this period) cause some colours to change with exposure to light and washing, so green fades to khaki and certain reds fade to pink. This quilt is a family heirloom, currently owned by the maker's grand-daughter who intends to hand it on to her children.

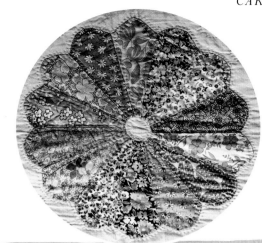

This was the era of bright, clear colours and flower prints. The remnants used here would once have been dresses, home-made from plentiful cheap cottons. The platter decoration, like this one shown, was pieced together in its entirety before being laid onto the cream-coloured background and stitched into place. The hole in the centre has been left vacant, but a coloured circle of fabric was often also stitched into place.

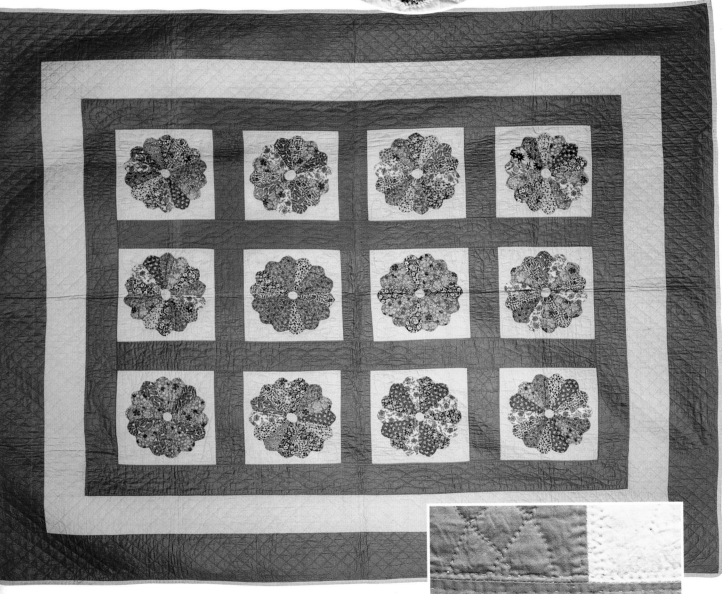

Once all the decoration was in position, it was time to complete the quilt by sewing together the three layers of the sandwich. Various patterns were used to do this.

A pencil was used to mark the lines to be followed and a little running stitch was then used to fix the layers, the quilt being held in a frame while the work was carried out.

# Costume

From the grandest ball gown to the simplest hand-embroidered smock, the clothes and accessories that have covered the human form throughout history provide a fascinating insight into its changing needs and desires. So much costume survives that many pieces can be bought for small amounts and do not fluctuate widely in value.

Garments and accessories made in Europe and the United States show a startling rapidity of change from the 18th century. However, in many other parts of the world, such as China and India, fashions have remained unchanged for centuries, almost to the present day.

In 19th-century Europe and America, women's fashions sprinted from the high-waisted Empire line to the crinoline to the bustle. Accessories changed too, and it is possible to build a colourful and varied collection of hats, gloves or parasols without breaking the bank.

Some garments, such as early embroidered waistcoats, or gentleman's caps, can make hundreds or even thousands at auction if they have been well cared for. An 18th-century brocaded silk open robe in top condition can fetch several thousand pounds; but with so many other interesting items on offer it is worth seeking them out rather than settling for a lesser example of the prized pieces. 20th-century costume is now widely collected. A 1960s French couture garment can be bought for a few hundred pounds. Many canny fashion victims who kept their 1980s Vivienne Westwoods and the lovers of classic style who have invested in designers such as Jean Muir, will not live to regret their purchases.

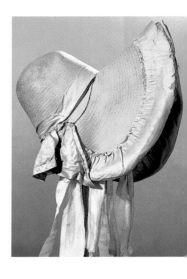

▶ **STRAW BONNET**
*1830s; 37cm (14½in) from top to bottom of brim;* **£150–200**
The young lady who was once the proud owner of this straw bonnet would have regarded it as one of the finest of her summer accessories. She is quite likely to have bought the ribbon separately from a draper and either trimmed it herself or employed a seamstress to do it for her according to the latest fashion. A bonnet was often treated to several trimmings during its lifespan.

◀ **BLACK TAFFETA DRESS AND BODICE**
*c.1880; 120cm (47¼in) long;* **£200–300**
The official period of mourning, a year and a day, was taken very seriously during the 19th century, and many women were constantly dressed in black. Consequently, these black taffeta dresses, in this case with a bodice and trimmed with velvet and lace, have survived in great numbers and can still be bought for quite a small sum.

▼ **18TH-CENTURY SHOE**
*c.1780s; 23cm (9in) long;* **£1,000**
18th-century shoes such as this one are often sold singly, having rarely survived in pairs. They are bought mainly by collectors and shoe museums.

◀ **GEORGE II GENTLEMAN'S LONG-SLEEVED WAISTCOAT**
*c.1740; 94cm (37in) long;* **£500–1,000**
This splendid coat of green ribbed silk was made for a gentleman of means, and richly embroidered on and around the pockets and borders. Styles for men at this time were more streamlined, as this example shows. Although not rare, it is a collector's piece and likely to get snapped up at auction by a museum.

▶ **BLACK SILK PARASOL**
*c.1880; 91cm (35¾in) long;* **£60–80**
Before the suntan became fashionable in the 1920s, it was quite unacceptable for a lady to expose her skin to sunlight. A parasol was indispensable. Many black examples survive as they accompanied the ubiquitous black mourning dress. The fabric is often worn, and collectors are more interested in the knops, which can be highly decorative and of silver, ivory or carved wood.

**◄ GENTLEMAN'S SILK TOP HAT**
*c.1870; 19cm (7½in) high;* **£100–200**
The top hat, introduced around 1780, had by the 19th century become the most popular type of hat worn by gentlemen as they went about their daily business. Top hats were first made of polished beaver and then of silk plush, and those that survive with an accompanying case are much sought after. In America they were referred to by different names according to their height, including High Stovepipe (5¾in), Chimney Pot (7½in) and Kite High Dandy (7¾in).

**► PAIR OF LIBERTY BLACK LEATHER SHOES WITH DIAMANTE BUCKLES**
*1920s; 26cm (10¼in) long;* **£40–60**
Shoes have become of enormous interest to collectors of costume over recent years, with early 18th-century examples studied for the materials and workmanship which went into making them. Dealers, shoe museums and private collectors compete to buy them and judging by current fashion, today's designers find styles of the past an inspiration. Some shoes are suitable only for display, but later examples, such as this pair, can be worn with many of the retro clothes now on sale.

**▲ PAIR OF CREAM KID GLOVES**
*c.1910; 54cm (21¼in) long;* **£30–50**
A new pair of gloves of this quality and length would be difficult to find today and prohibitively expensive. One of the most enjoyable aspects of buying antique costume is that pieces like these English Edwardian kid gloves, in perfect condition, with popper fastenings, can still be worn and are still affordable. They are often bought to wear at smart race meetings with an equally impressive hat.

**► JAPANESE IVORY FAN**
*19th century; 22cm (8½in) long (unopened);* **£1,500–2,500**
Now one of the most widely collected accessories, the fan was originally used not only to create a breeze, but as a tool of courtship. With leaves of silk, satin, gauze, lace or paper and sticks of wood, mother-of-pearl, ivory and tortoiseshell, the variety is endless. Delicately painted earlier examples fetch large sums of money, but paper fans given away as promotional items and overprinted with advertising are affordable.

**◄ HERMÈS KELLY BAG**
*1950s; 27cm (10½in) high;* **£600–800**
The Kelly bag is a design classic. The genuine article was created by Hermès in 1935, but it has been copied by every major manufacturer of accessories and produced in many materials including plastic. It was renamed in 1955 to mark the wedding of Prince Rainier of Monaco and Grace Kelly who was never without the bag, a favourite accessory. Early genuine examples are sought after.

**◄ CHRISTIAN DIOR EVENING DRESS AND JACKET**
*1962; dress 154cm (65½in) long;* **£350–550**
There is a growing interest in haute couture. A beautifully hand-finished garment by a leading designer can still be bought from a dealer or an auction house for a fraction of its cost when new, and the timelessness of classic design means that collectors have the bonus of not only owning, but being able to wear, their investments. Pieces are usually numbered and carry labels which identify the year and season of manufacture. This sumptuous Dior dress and jacket in gold brocade with a fur collar carries the number 116975 and was produced for the Autumn/ Winter Collection of 1962.

**COLLECTORS' NOTES**
• 18th century garments which have survived in their original state are at a premium and are often snapped up by museums.
• Inevitably, antique clothes have often led a hard life and it is better to avoid those which are stained or marked because it is often impossible to bring them back to their original state.
• The lady of the house often passed her dresses onto her maid. Clothes were handed on and altered as a matter of course.
• What appears to be a garment for a little girl may well have clothed a succession of little boys, as boys were very often dressed in exactly the same manner as their sisters during the 19th century.
• Shawls were popular in the mid-19th century, worn over voluminous crinoline skirts which were too full to be covered with a coat. Many of those made in Britain were copies of the original Kashmir shawls hand-woven from the hair of mountain goats.

**COLLECTING TIP**
19th-century country wedding dresses are still very good value. A seamstress made the dress in white or gold silk, and it would have gone on being used as a day dress. They can still be bought for around £70 in good condition.

# Art Nouveau & Art Deco

The graceful sensuality of Art Nouveau lasted a mere 20 years between the 1890s and the outbreak of the First World War. After the guns fell silent in 1918, the seeds of modernism, sown before the war, were able to take root and flourish. The style of the 1920s and 30s became known as Art Deco, an abbreviation of *L'Exposition des Arts Décoratifs et Industriels Modernes* (The Paris Exhibition), which took place in 1925.

Both were reactionary movements, Art Nouveau against the staid traditionalism and revivalism of the late 19th century and Art Deco against the curvaceous excesses of Art Nouveau. The former was probably the last great decadent style and the latter the first trumpet call of the truly modern age.

Whereas Art Nouveau took organic forms and used the writhing, sinuous shapes of plants, flowers, insects and birds as its inspiration, the straight, stepped, soaring lines and geometric shapes of Art Deco mirrored the exciting post-war developments in technology and mass production techniques. Art Nouveau designers worked with wood, glass and clay, as had their predecessors, but their counterparts of the 1920s and 30s took advantage of the new materials such as tubular steel, plate glass, concrete, plywood and even plastics.

Both styles found a following during the 1960s and both were initially derided by serious collectors of antiques, until first Art Nouveau and then Art Deco were given credibility when the top auction houses in London, Paris and New York began to devote sales to them. The market developed rapidly during the 1970s and is now an established area of collecting.

Although prices can be very high, both styles are still accessible to those on a more restricted budget. An Art Deco bronze and ivory figure by Ferdinand Preiss may be worth £3,000–4,000, but a small bronze figure of a dancer by Lorenzl (another good name) can still be bought for £300–400. Cymric silver (the silver designed by Archibald Knox for the British firm, Liberty) has spiralled in price over the last ten years, yet the Tudric (Liberty's pewter range) wares, also designed by Knox, are still affordable. You might have to pay £3,000 for a Cymric clock, as opposed to £600–800 for some Tudric examples.

*Left: left to right* French bronze and ivory dancer by Alliot; French lamp by Emile Gallé; English "Lotus" jug by Clarice Cliff; Iridescent "gooseneck" vase by Loetz of Bohemia; French ridged vase by Lallement.

# Metalware

Silver and gold have always been held in high esteem, but during the Art Nouveau period designers and craftsmen began to accord the same respect to pewter, cast iron and other base metals. This gave the flagging fortunes of the British and Continental pewter industry a considerable boost. Formerly, the staple products had been basic domestic and tableware, but by the 1890s the metal was being twisted and contorted into the glorious organic forms of Art Nouveau objets d'art.

The success of companies such as Kayser & Sohn in Germany encouraged Arthur Lazenby Liberty in England to introduce his Tudric range of pewterware alongside the already established Cymric silverwares.

In Germany, the most prolific manufacturer of metalware, usually with an electroplated finish, was the W.M.F. (Wuttembergische Metallwarenfabrik) factory. In the United States, the products of the Roycroft

Workshops, Californian copper worker Dirk van Erp and the Gorham metalworks of Rhode Island have left a rich legacy for the American collector. During the Art Nouveau period, the French specialized in small bronze pieces such as pin trays, night lights and door furniture.

In Vienna, distinctive geometric, pierced vases and baskets, sometimes in silver or in painted metal were typical products of the Wiener Werkstätte, and the same elements are evident in the work of the German silversmiths of the Bauhaus school in the Art Deco period. In France too, companies such as Christofle and Puiforcat produced tableware and tea and coffee services in strong, geometric forms. In the United States, the geometric emphasis eventually gave way to a more streamlined interpretation of Art Deco by designers such as Norman Bell Geddes and K.E.M. Weber, which reflected the American passion for aerodynamic design.

◀ **W.M.F. SILVER-PLATED TABLE CENTREPIECE**
*c.1905; 25.4cm (10in);*
**£500–700**
This is just one, very typical example of the vast range of goods manufactured by W.M.F. during the Art Nouveau period at prices that could be afforded by the masses. The centrepiece is cast in the form of a winged nymph standing before two wide lilypads supported on slender, sinuous stalks. Figural subjects are always the most popular with collectors.

◀ **GALLIA SILVER-PLATED SALT AND PEPPER POT**
*1925; 5cm (2in) high;* **£150–200**
This enchanting salt and pepper pot are cast in the form of a stylized monkey and squirrel with distinctly cubist lines. The French produced a great deal of electroplated useful and decorative wares at this time and stylized animal forms such as knife rests and cruets are quite common.

▼ **SILVER-PLATED ART DECO TEA AND COFFEE SERVICE BY ERCUIS**
*c.1930; coffee pot 25.4cm (10in) high;* **£300–400**
This banded geometric form with macassar ebony block handles closely resembles the work of Puiforcat, but the estimate for an example of his work would be a good deal higher. This was probably made in an attempt to undersell him and is very representative of the French approach to tableware design in the Art Deco period. The British tried to follow the clean, stepped, geometric shapes but usually failed. This service would originally have sat on a tray of canted rectangular shape with macassar ebony block handles.

◀ **TUDRIC CLOCK**
*1904; 23cm (9in) high;*
**£1,000–1,500**
Of all the Tudric wares (produced by Haseler's of Birmingham who also manufactured the Cymric range), the clocks are the most desirable, especially those like this that incorporate colourful enamel work. This design has been attributed to Archibald Knox. The entwined stem and entrelacs are indicative of his fascination with Celtic art, the source of which was scattered across his Isle of Man birthplace. The bases are stamped with a series of three or four numbers; the lower the number, the earlier the piece.

## CYMRIC BELT BUCKLE
*1901; 10cm (4in) wide; 5cm (2in) high;*
**£800–1,200**

The Cymric range of silver was launched by Liberty in 1899. It proved a huge commercial success because production was on a much larger scale than the one-off pieces made by the leading members of the Arts and Crafts Movement, and objects were consequently cheaper to buy. Everything from bowls and tea services to clocks, buttons and brooches were manufactured for Liberty by the Birmingham firm of W.H. Haseler. This is a typical belt buckle, fashioned in a stylized plant form with whiplash stems and brightly coloured enamel insets of blue, green and yellow.

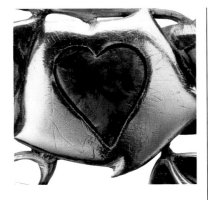

The heart motif seen here was a popular theme in most areas of the British decorative arts in this period. The large flowerheads below denote a definite Scottish influence. Liberty was strict in not allowing his designers to sign their work and the attribution of objects is therefore a subject of excited debate among collectors. This piece is almost certainly the work of Archibald Knox, the only designer who was occasionally allowed to break this rule.

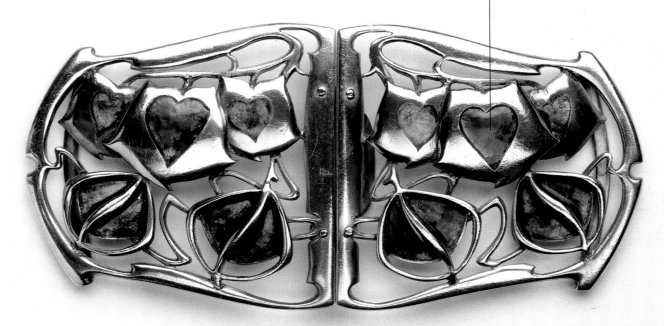

The construction of these buckles was a fairly labour intensive affair, requiring a good deal of hand finishing. As a result they were more expensive when new than many of the pendants, brooches and earrings which were die-stamped and could be made in larger quantities, often with enamel decoration being offered, as an extra, at greater cost.

Here you can see the hallmark for the retailer, Liberty & Co., the anchor mark used by the Birmingham assay office, the lion passant which confirms that the piece was made from Sterling silver, and the "D" which represents the date. Although Haseler's of Birmingham made the piece, their mark does not appear. Larger pieces are often also stamped "CYMRIC." You can also see from the back how the buckle has been assembled from several pieces.

### COLLECTORS' NOTES
Be careful when buying Liberty Tudric and Cymric enamel pieces. Plain wares have sometimes been embellished with modern enamel and original enamel wares have been restored and repaired. Restored examples are worth considerably less than those in original condition. Those incorporating modern enamel are to be avoided at all costs.

English hammered pewter teasets of cubist inspiration from the 1920s and 30s are relatively inexpensive, but their form and design are usually uninspiring and despite appearing good value, they have little to recommend them and are best avoided.

Good French Art Deco electroplated teasets can still be found at prices that compare well with a modern day equivalent.

### COLLECTING TIP
Considering Kayser & Sohn were the pioneers of German art pewter, their work, which is often highly organic in form, can still be found at prices which compare very favourably with that of their Tudric counterparts. The name of the company appears within an embossed oval pad found on the base of pieces.

### LIBERTY DESIGNERS
*As well as the famous leading designer, Archibald Knox, other important Liberty names include:*

Rex Silver

Oliver Baker

Fred Partridge

Jessie M. King

# Glass

The versatility and potential of glass as a sculptural material was explored in new and innovative forms at the turn of the century, particularly in France and the United States where the creativity of Emile Gallé and Louis Comfort Tiffany respectively, resulted in pieces which easily merit the status of works of art, and which have prices to match in today's market.

Cameo glass is the most representative of the period; this incorporates two or more differently coloured layers of glass on novel forms such as canoe-shaped bowls or slender cylindrical vases. The strongest inspiration was nature, with flowers, insects and landscapes faithfully depicted on vessels. The pieces often had trailed, etched, embedded, or wheel-cut decoration, or were given simple, metallic iridescent surfaces.

The Loetz factory in Austria and Tiffany in the United States were leading exponents of iridescent glassware. Other Bohemian and German manufacturers tried to emulate them but few were able to match their standard.

After 1918, the glass designer's art was dominated by the former top Art Nouveau jewellery designer, René Lalique, whose fascination with glass production had begun before the war. The mass production techniques employed by the Lalique glassworks enabled exquisitely designed glass to be manufactured in hitherto inconceivable quantities and amazing variety. Literally millions of pieces were produced by Lalique and his contemporaries such as Marius Ernest Sabino.

By contrast, the output of Maurice Marinot and the makers of *pâte-de-verre*, Gabriel Argy-Rousseau, Almeric Walter, François-Emile Décorchement and Albert Dammouse, was on a much smaller scale, with Marinot, particularly, overseeing every piece and treating each as an individual sculpture. In the creation of *pâte-de-verre*, different coloured glass powders were packed in moulds and heated until the glass fused, resulting in a dense, multicoloured vessel. *Pâte-de-cristal* used the same technique, but the addition of lead oxide gave the finished product a semi-translucent appearance.

Enamelled glass continued to be made in France and Czechoslovakia during the 1920s and 30s, with the French glassmakers Marcel Goupy, Delvaux and Jean Luce leading the field.

► **LALIQUE "SOURCE DE LA FONTAINE" STATUETTE**
c.1925; 58.5cm (23in) high;
**£6,000–8,000**
This figure was made in several different styles and sizes. Originally, one was positioned at each of the four corners, in several tiers, around an illuminated fountain on display at the 1925 Exposition. This example, probably made at a later date, was fitted into a polished mahogany plinth. In other versions the figure may be illuminated from beneath. A 5cm (2in) high version was used by Lalique in the centre of a small, circular ashtray. Despite the high price of this piece, smaller, less famous pieces of Lalique can be bought for as little as £50.

◄ **LOETZ IRIDESCENT GLASS VASE**
1900; 10cm (4in);
**£500–700**
Loetz glass is often thickly walled, with a ground, polished pontil mark on the underside. Many pieces are unsigned, but those marked "Loetz, Austria," are post-1891 and were intended for export. This type of trailed and feathered decoration is the most appealing to collectors. Loetz also provided lustre-decorated glass shades for light fittings, especially the figural creations of Gustav Gurschner.

▼ **ARGY-ROUSSEAU *PÂTE-DE-VERRE* NIGHTLIGHT**
c.1925; 15.2cm (6in) high;
**£1,500–2,000**
Argy-Rousseau produced a large variety of wares in both *pâte-de-verre* and *pâte-de-cristal*. His extensive range of bedside lights is particularly desirable; pieces featuring human or animal subjects are considered the most important. The thickly-walled body and simple, wrought iron base are typical, and the incised-cast signature can be seen beneath the lowest flowerhead.

▲ **GALLÉ MOULD BLOWN VASE**
c.1900; 30.5cm (12in) high;
**£3,500–5,000**
A small number of Gallé's cameos are mould blown vases, so called because the overlying glass was blown into the deep recesses of the mould prior to the underlying coloured glass being blown in. The process, using pneumatic air pumps, gave an overlay in high relief of a type extremely difficult to emulate. This vase was made in various colours, red and blue versions being of the highest value.

## DAUM CYLINDRICAL VASE

*c.1900; 20.3cm (8in) high;* **£500–800**
Internally decorated, acid-carved and colour-enamelled, this particular type of decoration upon thickly walled vessels was favoured by the Daum factory, which concentrated on floral and landscape decoration, especially seasonal woodland scenes. Auguste and Antonin Daum worked initially with Emile Gallé before setting up their own glassworks in Nancy. On this vase, the orchid decoration is faithfully depicted and coloured, the outlines having been acid-cut in relief against the surrounding frosted and textured surface.

The detail here shows the skill and dexterity of the enameller, who painted on the flowers with carefully selected colours, using various tones to achieve an almost three-dimensional realism.

Daum signed their glassware in a variety of ways. Acid-cut enamelled glassware usually bears an acid-cut signature. In this case, the "Daum, Nancy" signature, in the centre of the back of the piece, incorporates the cross of Lorraine, which on other pieces may be found wheel-cut into the base, rim or underside, or simply applied in black enamel or gilt to the underside of bases.

The internal, mottled decoration shows up well in this section. The dark colour is impregnated into the translucent glass, with the stalks of the flowers acid-cut and coloured in relief, giving the effect of a two-colour cameo.

### COLLECTORS' NOTES
• Beware of pieces which have been reduced in height as a result of polishing or grinding out chips on the rim or foot rim. If the cameo decoration is missing in areas, or disappears at the rim, it is a sure sign that the piece has been altered in this way.
• Lalique glass made during his lifetime nearly always carries the initial "R" before the "Lalique" signature. Collectors should beware of pieces which carry a shaky or poorly executed initial, because it may well have been added to something made much later than 1945, the year he died.

### COLLECTING TIP
Although pieces by the top makers of French cameo glass can command hefty prices, those by lesser makers such as Auguste Légras and Muller Frères are often good value for money. Sabino glass is still regarded as the poor cousin of Lalique. Admittedly the firm produced some objects of dubious merit, but they also made some worthy ones in both opalescent and coloured glass which are affordable in comparison with Lalique.

# Ceramics

A fresh vigour and innovation characterized the ceramics industry on the Continent at the end of the 19th century, as new glazes, colours and forms swept away many of the revivalist wares which had dominated the scene before 1890. The Austrian factories of Reissner, Stellmacher and Kessel, Ernst Wahliss, and The Royal Dux factory of Bohemia produced prodigious amounts of stylish Art Nouveau pottery and porcelain.

The Sèvres factory continued its tradition of excellence by commissioning work from top designers, such as Taxile Doat. In Holland, the Rozenburg factory produced wares by such designers as Theodorus Colenbrander and Juriaan Kok. The wafer-thin, hand-painted ivory bodies of pieces in exotic shapes much influenced by Japanese wares, are considered by many collectors to be the finest and most desirable examples of Art Nouveau ceramic design.

In Hungary, the Zsolnay factory manufactured designs which often incorporated female figural motifs and tree silhouettes covered in green, blue and deep red lustre glazes, and in Germany, the work of the architect Max Lauger found great favour at home and elsewhere. His slip-trailed decoration combined with elegant forms compared well with the designs of William Moorcroft, who was then developing his range of Florianware for the firm of James Macintyre in Staffordshire.

After the First World War, designs changed radically. The new woman is typified by the figural subjects produced by the Austrian Goldscheider factory, the German Katzhütte factory and Lenci in Turin, Italy. In Britain, Royal Doulton also manufactured figures in bone china depicting the contemporary woman dressed in the costume of the day. The "Bizarre" wares of Clarice Cliff introduced vibrant colour combinations on geometric forms while the designs of Susie Cooper adopted a more sober approach which incorporated a more visible balance between decoration and form.

Also in Britain, Keith Murray's designs were perhaps the most valuable contribution made at Wedgwood, while the Poole Pottery introduced its range of white-glazed stonewares embellished with formalized hand-painted decoration.

In the United States, the Rookwood Pottery in Cincinnati provided the American public with a range of wares that kept pace with contemporary American interior designs.

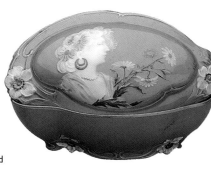

▶ **LIMOGES CASKET AND COVER**
c.1900; 17.8cm (7in) long, 5cm (2in) high; **£200–300**
The cover of this piece is decorated in a *pâte-sur-pâte* technique with the profile portrait of an Art Nouveau maiden, against an underlying pale olive green reserve. The name of the factory is marked in gilt on the base and the name of the artist appears on the cover.

▶ **KATZHÜTTE FEMALE SHOT PUTTER**
c.1935; 23cm (9in) high; **£200–300**
Athletic subjects were popular in Europe and the United States between the Wars. Many of these figures depict the Aryan ideal, an indication of the influence of fascism in Europe at this time. The Katzhütte factory produced a wide range of cream-coloured earthenware figures inspired by the factories of Rosenthal and Goldscheider. They provide a relatively inexpensive alternative to the bronze and ivory sculptures of the same period.

◀ **POOLE POTTERY VASE**
c.1930; 20.3cm (8in) high; **£80–120**
This colourful vase is typical of the wares of the English south coast pottery at this time. The factory started life in 1873 as Carter and Co., and became Carter, Stabler and Adams in 1921 when they began to manufacture this range of distinctive art pottery alongside their tablewares. They did not officially trade under the name of Poole Pottery until 1963.

◀ **GUSTAVSBERG ARGENTAWARE DISH**
c.1935; 23cm (9in) diameter; **£200–300**
Designed by Wilhelm Kage, this dish is from an extensive series of wares, including vases, boxes with covers and wall plaques, by the Swedish pottery of Gustavsberg. The silvered decoration is applied by an electrolytic deposit technique, prior to hand-finishing. In this instance the subject has a Far Eastern influence, though often human or animal figures were depicted in a stylized neo-classical manner.

## CLARICE CLIFF CONICAL SUGAR SIFTER
### c.1935; 10cm (4in) high; £250–350

Clarice Cliff is recognized as one of the foremost British ceramic designers of the 1920s and 30s. This sugar sifter in the Delecia Pansies pattern was produced at the A.J. Wilkinson Pottery where she worked. Its geometric form is typical, although the decoration is of a more traditional type, of flowers painted in pastel colours, than the geometric designs or landscapes in bold primary colours which most people associate with her work. The mark on the base indicates that it is from the "Bizarre" range of wares. Other ranges include "Fantasque" and "Appliqué," the last being the most desirable among collectors, as the decoration is applied without the use of any outlining. Early outlining was applied by brush and so is relatively thick and irregular, whereas the outlines made from 1932 using an ink pen gave finer, more uniform lines.

Looking at the base of this piece is the best way to examine the even honey glaze which covers the body, characteristic of the Wilkinson Pottery and of all Clarice Cliff wares.

This runny glaze was used on many Clarice Cliff patterns as a most effective decorative device. The flower heads are skilfully hand painted, as can be seen from the obvious brush strokes on the petals.

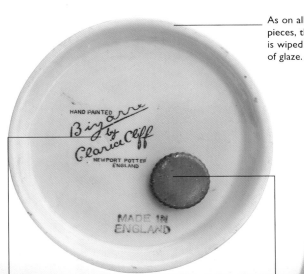

As on all these pieces, the rim is wiped free of glaze.

Two types of mark were used on these wares, the earlier one applied with a rubber stamp which gave a slightly imprecise definition, prone to smudging, and the later one of a smaller, transfer-printed mark which resulted in a crisper, better-defined image. On later wares, the rectangular outline of the transfer can often be detected. The "MADE IN ENGLAND" mark beneath the stopper here is under the glaze whereas the transfer-printed mark is on the glaze.

If you're really lucky you will come across a Clarice Cliff sugar sifter with its original stopper, a circle of claret-coloured enamelled tin covering the cork bung. It adds to the interest of the piece if the stopper is still intact.

### COLLECTORS' NOTES

If you are interested in Poole Pottery, familiarize yourself with designs produced during the 1920s and 30s. Later pieces decorated with similar designs and using the same palette are often covered with an ivory glaze less prone to crazing than the earlier wares and as such are less desirable. The later pieces (post-1963) have a glaze which covers the base and a printed stylized mark.

Many Clarice Cliff fakes have surfaced recently. The glazes are thin and pale compared with the rich honey glaze of the original, and the foot rims are shallower and slightly irregularly trimmed. The first fakers completely misinterpreted the colour enamels used at the factory, but the more recent copies show a better understanding of colour and design and are harder to spot, so always buy from a reputable dealer or saleroom.

Although expensive, the finest wares produced during both the Art Nouveau and Art Deco periods undoubtedly emerged from the Sèvres factory. Most pieces carry a wealth of information printed or incised on the base which credits not only the decorator but occasionally the designer as well. The factory called upon such eminent Art Deco designers as Emile Ruhlmann and Henri Rapin.

### COLLECTING TIPS

Although Rozenburg eggshell porcelain is prohibitively expensive, the company also made hand-painted earthenware, elaborately hand-decorated and well-coloured which has been overlooked and is still relatively affordable. Pieces are often much larger than the porcelain equivalents, which, because of their fragile nature, were made only for the cabinet. You might pay £400–600 for an earthenware wall charger, whereas the same money would not buy you a cup and saucer in eggshell.

Figures by Rosenthal of Bavaria still represent good value for money.

# Sculpture

Until the 19th century, sculpture tended to be large and was bought only by those with houses big enough to accommodate it, but the invention of reducing machines in the 1840s resulted in the production of perfectly scaled-down versions of full-size sculptures. As the century progressed, the popularity of smaller bronze pieces grew as they became increasingly affordable.

The trend continued into this century with large numbers of stylish figures manufactured during both the Art Nouveau and Art Deco periods either as purely decorative objects or as light fittings. During the Art Nouveau period, particularly in France, series of table lamps were produced by both Raoul Larche and Agathon Léonard, and, later, the tradition was carried on by Max le Verrier and Albert Cheuret.

The female form was the most common subject during both periods, with the mystical, ethereal and somewhat tortured heroines of the Art Nouveau period giving way to the stronger, more independent post-World War One woman. The dreamy eyed Art Nouveau maiden, trapped by her swirling hair and draped costume and imbued with symbolism was followed by her athletic and liberated younger sister, depicted playing sport or reflecting the world of entertainment.

**▲ PAIR OF GILT AND PATINATED BRONZE AND IVORY FIGURES BY ROLAND PARIS**
*c.1930; 30.5cm (12in) high;* **£2,000–3,000**
The elegant figure of the lady holding a fan which appears as an extension of her costume is being serenaded by her suitor playing his guitar. Roland Paris figures include a minimal amount of ivory, in these examples it forms only the hand and facial features. The posture of the human form is emphasized, with strong facial expressions and simple, tastefully patinated costumes. The bases are often, as here, contrasting marble and slate, with the signature engraved on the marble. Paris is also known for his series of Pierrot figures.

**▼ HAGENAUER BLACK PATINATED BRONZE FIGURE OF AN AFRICAN DANCER**
*c.1930; 15.2cm (6in);* **£250–350**
The Hagenauer workshop was established in Vienna in 1898, by Carl Hagenauer and passed on to his sons, Carl and Franz. The factory is still in production. This slender, minimalist figure, full of graceful movement, is very typical of their style. Her face is mask-like, with her grass skirt and brass hairpin the only suggestions of detail. The sculptures were of silver, brass, chromium-plated bronze, black-patinated bronze, as here, and sometimes carved and polished wood. Any decoration tends to be carved or included in the main structure rather than being applied; simple, unbroken lines convey the movement. Many functional and elegant pieces were produced including bookends, lampstands and candelabra.

**► PATINATED BRONZE FIGURE OF A DANCER BY JOSEPH LORENZL**
*1930; 35.5cm (14in) high;* **£700–1,000**
The Austrian sculptor Joseph Lorenzl fashioned a variety of nude and scantily clad female dancers, although in this case, the young lady with fashionably bobbed hair is dressed in a short pleated skirt with a tight-fitting bodice, a crimped collar and matching cuffs. His figures have long, slender legs and are often modelled standing on tiptoe with arms held aloft in a dancing pose. The bases are usually small and circular, or, as in this case, octagonal and of a variegated marble cut in an architectural design.

**► GILT BRONZE FIGURAL TABLE LAMP BY AGATHON LÉONARD**
*c.1900; 30.5cm (12in) high;* **£2,500–3,500**
This is one of a series of beautifully modelled table lamps by the Art Nouveau sculptor Agathon Léonard, which showed stages from a dance and was inspired by the famous American actress and dancer Loïe Fuller. Her celebrated routine, involving the use of flowing silks combined with ingenious lighting effects, entranced audiences as she became, in turn, a lily, butterfly, bird, fire or night. The light bulb is concealed within the billowing drapes she holds aloft. The figure embodies the magic of the early days of the electric light bulb. Charles Korschann and Leo Laporte-Blairsy also produced high-quality lamps and decorations in gilt bronze.

## FERDINAND PREISS BRONZE AND IVORY FIGURE
*c.1933; 23cm (9in) high;* **£2,000–3,000**

The famous German Art Deco sculptor, Ferdinand Preiss (1882–1943), produced many athletic Aryan subjects, with exceptionally well-proportioned and anatomically correct facial features and limbs, manufactured at the Preiss-Kassler foundry in Berlin. On rare occasions, the original embossed and gilt paper labels applied by the foundry survive, but the most usual mark is the "PK" foundry monogram and the signature, "F. Preiss". This figure of a seated young woman has been patinated and silvered and would have been made in an edition of several hundred, with many craftsmen involved in her production. The body was cast in one piece with the ivory arms and head fixed to the torso by screws.

The face has been exquisitely carved from ivory, the realistic detail enhanced by a subtle and carefully applied wash of paint to give a lifelike appearance. The head was the last piece to be secured to the figure. Her little waistcoat with its stand-up collar hides any evidence of the construction.

The bronze section of the figure has been cold painted, after casting, in blue and brown, but reds and greens were also used. The legs are either silvered, or gilt as in this example. The torso was trimmed and chiselled after casting and the colour then applied before the ivory sections were screwed on.

From looking at the detail achieved in this small area, the enormous skill of the craftsmen involved in producing a figure like this is immediately apparent. The proportions of the wrist and hand are anatomically correct in every detail and beautifully constructed down to each little fingernail.

The precision cut and polished pedestal base of Brazilian green onyx bears the engraved signature "F. Preiss" on the reverse. Signatures could equally be incise-cast on metal bases, and, on occasion, both types of signature are found.

---

**COLLECTORS' NOTES**

Beware of the large number of simulated bronze and ivory figures which have flooded the market in recent years. Most are of poor quality with badly finished bases often featuring artificially rusted nuts and rods. Familiarize yourself with the real thing and look for grain in the ivory of limbs and faces. Fakes often have excessive dirt rubbed into the crevices and are of patinated metal not bronze. Usually for sale at bargain prices, they can bear spurious signatures of well-known sculptors of the period.

Splits and staining in the areas carved from ivory detract from the desirability of a piece.

**VALUE POINTS**

• Bases cut in innovative architectural forms using marble of various colours can add value, but not to the extent that you should focus your attention on the base rather than the figure. It is better to look for a good quality figure on a simple base than the other way round.

• Value is usually determined by size, condition and attribution to a particular sculptor.

• Lorenzl figures still offer reasonable value for money in comparison with the work of other Art Deco artists. His output was prolific, but avoid examples polished by overzealous previous owners.

# Posters

The development of poster art during the last years of the 19th century came about as manufacturers began to realize the enormous benefits to be gained from pictorial advertising, rather than relying on pure typography as a method of selling products. And there were new and exciting products to sell, such as bicycles, corsets and cigarette papers, which lent themselves magnificently to the skill and imagination of such artists as Henri de Toulouse Lautrec, Jules Chéret and Alphonse Mucha.

The lithographic printing process revolutionized the art of poster making. The new technique involved the use of a flat stone onto which the design was drawn in wax crayon which acted as a resist. The stone was then washed with a powerful acid which ate away those areas unprotected by the wax. The remaining raised design was then inked and the poster printed from it. The stones were thick enough to be rubbed down and used again.

The boulevards of Paris in 1900 resembled an open air art gallery, with every available surface plastered with colourful advertising posters. They became instantly collectable, with desperate aficionados stopping at nothing to acquire the very latest examples, even sponging them down in the dead of night to remove the glue and carry them away.

The fantasy maidens and good-time girls of Toulouse Lautrec and Chéret disappeared after World War One, when the Modern age heralded another revolution in poster design. The preoccupation with speed and new, fast, comfortable methods of transport, such as the train, the ocean liner and the aeroplane were reflected in the work of designers such as A.M. Cassandre and Paul Colin. Women too, became sleek and sophisticated, liberated and conscious of their new role in society.

Art Nouveau and Art Deco posters are still avidly collected on both sides of the Atlantic. Collectors tend to concentrate on one period or the other, buying examples which compliment other objects in their homes such as furniture, metalware and ceramics.

## COLLECTORS' NOTES

During the past 20 years, both Art Nouveau and Art Deco posters have been reproduced and retailed through various high street outlets. You should familiarize yourself with the different types of paper that were used as well as the printing techniques, so that you can tell the difference between the original and the copy. Examine a copy closely and you will see thousands of little dots, a sign of modern printing techniques.

Collectors like the margins of their posters to be intact. If you are considering buying an example that is framed and the margins are not clearly visible, ask for the frame to be removed so you can be reassured they are still there.

### AVOID
• Posters that have been fixed to boards or panels, although those fixed with animal glue can be removed by a specialist restorer.
• Losses, which would have to be repainted. Tears can usually be put together and creases smoothed out in the restoration process.

### COLLECTING TIP
Many of the classic posters are far beyond the pocket of the average collector, but contemporary with the period, many albums were made containing faithfully reproduced reductions, sold as "Maître de l'Affiche," and individual prints from these albums can occasionally be found for around £100.

▲ "LA TROUPE DE MADEMOISELLE EGLANTINE"
BY HENRI DE TOULOUSE-LAUTREC
*1890–96; approximately 62 x 80cm (24 x 31in)* **£14,000–16,000**
Lautrec lives on as one of the legends of poster art during the Art Nouveau period. His immediately recognizable style owed much to Japanese art, employing large areas of flat, bold, contrasting colour. He focused on the theatre and the actresses who nightly kicked up their heels in the Pigalle area of Paris, without making any great attempt to depict them as beautiful, graceful figures.

▲ "PALAIS DE GLACE" BY JULES CHÉRET
*1900; 249 x 89cm (98 x 35in);* **£1,000–2,000**
The vibrant and lively girls depicted in Chéret's work are captured in bright colours and clever tonal shading. The typeface used on this poster is peculiar to the Art Nouveau period. Chéret set up his own printing firm, and with new machinery produced larger one-piece posters than any made before.

**▲ "THE FLOWERS: CARNATION; IRIS; LILY; ROSE"
BY ALPHONSE MUCHA**
*1900; 44.5 x 61cm (17½ x 24in);* **£3,500–4,500**
The work of the Czech Alphonse Mucha is so synonymous with
the Art Nouveau movement, that even at the time he was working,
many contemporary items were described as being in the "Style
Mucha." The young women he depicts are typically shown within
naturalistic settings, strewn with flowers or surrounded by them.
Their expressions are dreamlike, their ethereal qualities imbued with
symbolism. His name will always be linked with that of the famous
actress Sarah Bernhardt, for whose productions he designed many
posters. This series of flowers is one of his most famous works.

**▶ PAL BICYCLE BY
JEAN DE
PALEOLOGUE**
*1895; 147.5 x 107cm
(58 x 42in);*
**£1,500–2,500**
Jean de Paleologue
(1860–1942) was a
commercial artist
whose work does
not come up as often
as that of other better
known posterists of
the Art Nouveau
period. In this adver-
tising poster, he has
used a decadent young
woman clad in a
diaphanous, floating
garment and carrying
a Japanese lantern,
to sell Pal, a bicycle
manufactured in
France by Fernand
Clement & Cie. In a
clear example of the new approach to advertising,
he promises future owners in possession of this
vehicle previously undreamt-of freedom and
excitement. Paleologue's style has more in
common with Chéret than it has with Mucha.

**▲ CYCLES DILECTA BY G. FAURE**
*c.1930; 119.5 x 80cm (47½ x 31½in);*
**£2,000–2,500**
In contrast with the Paleologue poster
advertising bicycles, this stylish Art Deco
image of streamlined speed and strength
owes much to the enormous influence of
cubism on many commercial artists during
the 1920s and 30s. The eye is drawn to the
vibrant red and yellow streak of lightning
through the centre of the poster, and then
to the geometric, controlled rider, bent
intently over the handlebars.

**▲ *ÉTOILE DU NORD* BY CASSANDRE**
*c.1930; 105 x 75.5cm (41 x 30in);*
**£2,000–3,000**
A masterful use of perspective is probably
the strongest element in Cassandre's work.
His best known posters are those showing
the liner *Normandie* and the *Nord Express*
railway service. This design for the pullman
service, *Étoile du Nord*, shows an abstract
interpretation of railway lines with the feel of
strength, speed and distance pulling the eye
toward the star in the distance. Stark and
forceful images of the types of transport
which came to prominence during the Art
Deco period are typical of Cassandre's work.

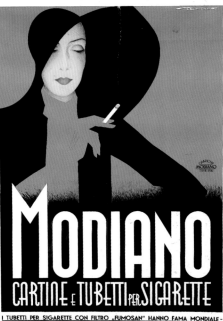

**▲ MODIANO CIGARETTES
BY FRANZ LENHART**
*c.1920; 151 x 99cm (59½ x 39in);*
**£1,000–1,500**
This elegant young woman is the epitome of
the liberated woman of the Modern age. She
was to be found in the smartest cafés and
had all the qualities of the Hollywood stars
she sought to emulate. And of course she
engaged in one of the most desirable and
sophisticated pastimes of the age – smoking.

# Furniture

As in so many other areas of the decorative arts, the French excelled when it came to interpreting the Art Nouveau style in furniture during the closing years of the 19th century. In the hands of such artists as Louis Majorelle and Emile Gallé working in Nancy, wood became an almost fluid medium, bent and twisted with the same inventiveness as clay or glass. In Paris, the same sculptural qualities in furniture were further refined in the work of Edward Colonna, Eugène Gaillard, George de Feure and, most celebrated of all, Hector Guimard, who designed entire interiors so that not only the furniture, but the light fittings, lockplates and fire surrounds all formed an aesthetically pleasing whole.

In Scotland, Charles Rennie Mackintosh was a true pioneer whose genius was not fully acknowledged until after his death. His radical approach, using the interplay between horizontals and verticals, rather than the sinuous contortions used by his counterparts in France, had a great influence on the Viennese Secessionists, whose key members, Josef Hoffmann and Koloman Moser, went on to form the Wiener Werkstätte in 1903. At the same time in the United States the Greene Brothers, Gustav Stickley and Frank Lloyd Wright combined elements of Arts and Crafts and Art Nouveau.

Again, it was the First World War which provided the break in furniture design between the romantic and the stricter, more formal approach which made use of radical new materials such as tubular steel and laminated plywood. The German Bauhaus school of design which enfolded architects, designers and artists was formed in 1918 to expound the modernist style, perhaps best summed up in 1923 by the French modernist architect-designer Le Corbusier, who declared that "A house is a machine for living." It was the United States which eventually benefitted from the talents of its leading exponents Marcel Breuer, Walter Gropius and Mies van der Rohe, when they fled there during the 1930s as the Nazi movement advanced in Germany. Despite Le Corbusier, French designers relied more on traditional cabinet making, using exotic woods and elaborate inlays. The work of Jacques-Emile Ruhlmann is often considered the ultimate in French Art Deco design.

**◀ CARVED MAHOGANY VITRINE DESIGNED BY HECTOR GUIMARD**
c.1900; 2m 19cm (7ft 2¼in) high, 1m 66cm (6ft 5½in) wide, 40cm (15¾in) deep; **£70,000–90,000**
In comparison with Emile Gallé's, Guimard's work is relatively scarce. He famously designed the cast-iron entrances to the Paris Metro. This magnificent piece illustrates well his sculptural approach, combining strong, organic elements which lend an asymmetrical emphasis to an otherwise standard form. Although it is beyond the reach of most collectors, it is worth seeing as an example of French Art Nouveau design at its very best. The pedestal shelf shows how effectively the outswept bracket creates the asymmetrical lines of the vitrine and gives the piece its feeling of movement and growth. The skill and subtlety of the carving, which depicts details of lilies of the valley, shows up beautifully. Rather than using marquetry inlay, Guimard has incorporated a pair of panels in the lower section carved in low relief with a flowing design of tendrils.

**▲ GALLÉ REVOLVING BOOKCASE**
c.1895; 91.5cm (36in) high; **£2,000–3,000**
This decorative, small and useful piece of furniture is in need of some restoration and cleaning to revitalise the marquetry inlay so typical of the furniture designs of Emile Gallé. The top features a large poppy flowerhead and leaf design, signed "E. Gallé" on one leaf. The shape is not overtly Art Nouveau, but the treatment of the spindles, which terminate as seed pods, and the formalized fretwork grilles, are absolutely of the period.

**▶ TUBULAR STEEL, METAL AND CANVAS CHAISE LONGUE DESIGNED BY LE CORBUSIER**
*1932; 159cm (62¾in) long;* **£12,000–15,000**
Le Corbusier is regarded by many as the most prominent personality in modernist design in the world. His pavilion at the 1925 Paris Exposition created such controversy that a huge fence was erected around it. In the creation of this chair, with its chromium-plated seat and original tan canvas upholstery, Corbusier worked closely with his friends and colleagues Pierre Jeanneret and Charlotte Perriand from as early as 1922. This example was manufactured by Embru in 1932 as model No. 2072.

**◀ BLACK LACQUER AND GILT WOOD PART SALON SUITE DESIGNED BY PAUL FOLLOT**
*c.1925; sofa 138.5cm (54½in) wide, 81.5cm (32⅓in) high;* **£4,000–6,000 for the full salon, including two chairs**
Paul Follot was a furniture designer who worked in the traditionalist way, using tried and tested materials. The shape of this chair and sofa echoes the designs of the French early Empire period, but the uprights in the form of slender, fluted cornucopia topped with clusters of Art Deco flowers, are very much of the Deco period. The ebonized and gilt wood frames provide the shape and strength, but the eye is drawn towards the strong, patterned upholstery.

**▲ EBONIZED WOOD SIDE CHAIR AFTER A DESIGN BY CHARLES RENNIE MACKINTOSH**
*c.1905–10; 71.5cm (28¼in) high;* **£2,000–3,000**
The geometric construction and perpendicular elements in the back rest of this chair are typical of Mackintosh's work, although the back is much lower than his famous series of tall-back chairs. Sometimes the ebonized finish on the tall-back chairs was substituted by white or natural oak grain. An original Mackintosh chair would carry a far higher estimate. This may have been made by William Douglas, a decorator colleague of the designer contracted by him on several commissions.

**▲ IVORY INLAID AMBOYNA AND MACASSAR EBONY COIFFEUSE "MOREL" NO. 1522 DESIGNED BY JACQUES-EMILE RUHLMANN**
*1920; 141.75cm (55½in) high, 50.75cm (20in) wide;* **£10,000–15,000**
This elegant coiffeuse illustrates the designer's preference for combining exotic woods with ivory inlays. Ruhlmann also produced larger, more heavily designed armoires, sideboards and bedheads. His work always combines the finest materials with first class craftsmanship. Later, he turned his attention to the new materials of tubular and stainless steel.

**▲ TUBULAR STEEL AND CANVAS MR 534 ARMCHAIR DESIGNED BY MIES VAN DER ROHE**
*c.1933–35; 76cm (30in) high;* **£10,000–15,000**
Van der Rohe practised his craft as a member of the German Bauhaus before fleeing the Nazis. This cantilevered chair is a good example of his ideals in which form follows function, allowing for no extraneous decoration. Designed by van der Rohe in 1927 on mathematical principles, the chair, known as the Weissenhof, has an almost clinical appearance. This example was manufactured slightly later by the firm of Thonet, famous for their bentwood furniture designs.

**COLLECTORS' NOTES**
In England, tubular steel designs that incorporate canvas seating are quite often discarded because the canvas is torn. Restoration is usually possible: pieces can be rechromed and the seating replaced. Look for applied metal labels signed "P.E.L." (Practical Equipment Ltd), "Isokon," or "Frank Brangwyn for Pollard and Co."

Art Deco tubular steel designs have continued to be manufactured to the present day, often with the patents being sold by one factory to another. Quite often it is literally only the nuts and bolts and other slight structural details which separate the originals from the later examples. A label or some corrosion of the metal is often the clue to an original.

Mackintosh furniture is exceptionally rare and is usually offered for sale with a provenance, but a large quantity of good quality oak furniture, contemporary with Mackintosh was retailed by Liberty's of London. Prices are relatively low because pieces are not attributed, but they are otherwise very desirable.

**COLLECTING TIP**
Armchairs and sofas produced during the 1930s with scallop-shaped backs and armrests, referred to today as "cloud suites," can often be bought for around £800, a lot less than a modern three-piece suite. Examples in red or blue leatherette are more desirable than those upholstered in a patterned fabric. Sections of seating are often veneered in pale wood which is usually damaged and missing. Examples which have lost substantial amounts of veneer should be avoided.

# Collectables

O ver the last twenty years, the antiques market place has undergone some radical shifts in attitude. There has been an evolving and continuous re-evaluation of areas which used to be considered unimportant in collecting terms. This process has been helped by the growing media interest in collecting, with new magazine columns, television programmes and reference books devoted to the subject multiplying rapidly, with more new ones every year.

Today, it is no longer considered valid only to consider collecting objects that fit strictly within the term "antique," meaning something which is over a hundred years old. The major auction houses and specialist dealers now take seriously entire categories of pieces produced as late as the 1950s and 1960s. If you had suggested to an expert in the field of antiques at the beginning of the 1970s that the memorabilia of the rock and pop industry or representations of contemporary design would be making serious money at auction a mere twenty years later, your comments would have met with derision. Yet this has come about, and a great deal more besides.

Time was when collectors who chose a subject outside conventional bounds were considered eccentric. This is no longer the case. To announce a devoted interest in airline cutlery or beer mats scarcely excites comment these days, and many a happy hour is spent pursuing objects that may never be worth a great deal of money but bring a good deal of pleasure, especially to those on a strict budget. In fact, one of the most attractive aspects of collecting within some of the categories on the following pages is that so many things are still affordable.

Certain types of African art can still be bought cheaply, as can costume jewellery, propelling pencils and printed ephemera. These are now considered established areas, but as this century draws to a close, much thought is going into what will become collectable in the future. A good tip is to seek out objects that were the first of their kind in a particular area. The Japanese battery-operated space toys of the 1950s and 1960s, which reflected the excitement of the post-war space race, are a good example. Progressing laterally, the first electronic calculators, disposable cameras and mobile telephones could be important antiques of the future, just as the first one-piece moulded plastic furniture and tableware is being seriously collected today. Concentrate on respected, well-known designers and manufacturers and you may be on to an appreciating asset. Exactly what will be most sought after as representative of our lives today excites such interest that a section of this chapter is devoted to some creative guess work.

*Left to right:* Alessi kettle, 1984; early 20th-century French dial telephone by Thomas Houston; British "Ecko Radio" by E.K. Cole Ltd of Southend-on-Sea, c.1930s; Kodak box Brownie camera, c.1930s; Italian Avem glass vase designed by Ansolo Fuga of Venice, 1958; ABS orange plastic drinking beakers and jug by Pierre Cardin, c.1970.

# Tribal Collectables

There are few better ways of learning about the customs and beliefs of some of the lesser known peoples of the world than by building a collection of tribal art. The field encompasses every continent but most collectors specialize in artefacts from a particular region or tribe.

The great museum collections of tribal art were gathered, for the most part, during the 19th century when anthropologists made the first contacts with many of the tribes. The criterion then was simply to collect as many curiosities as possible. It was not until artists such as Picasso began to take an interest in African masks and to draw inspiration from them, that the emphasis began to shift towards seeing tribal pieces as art in its most uncorrupted form. Collectors now tend to fall into two categories; art collectors and those who appreciate the wide range of more utilitarian items.

Africa provides the largest variety of objects, from the bedouins of the north, the massive Yoruba tribe of Nigeria or the Akan tribes of the Gold Coast, to the Zulu tribe in the south. In North America, the range is equally diverse, and pueblo Indian art and other native American artefacts attract many collectors. Australasia and Polynesia are also popular, with collectors happy to buy an early boomerang, Maori canoe paddle, or maybe a simple, elegant, polished Cook Islands wooden stool.

Artefacts range from simple, domestic utensils carved from animal bone, horn or wood which can still be bought for around £50, to Benin bronze mask heads from West Africa which have fetched many thousands at auction. It can be very difficult to date these items, and in most cases, quality is the more significant factor.

**◀ EASTER ISLAND CARVED WOODEN FIGURE**
*47cm (18½in) high;* **£35,000**
Easter Island is the most remote of the group of islands known as Polynesia. Artefacts from this area are enormously fashionable at the moment, and good, rare pieces like this carving in toromiro wood (a dense, tropical hardwood) sell for a great deal of money. The supply of timber ran out on this barren island and these standing figures, known as Moai Kavakava are no longer made. He has eyes inset with a glass-like material made from lava and known as obsidian and a fine, chocolate brown patina.

**▶ YORUBA BEADED SHOWPIECE**
*92.5cm (36½in);* **£8,000–12,000**
This richly beaded showpiece, possibly made by the Nigerian Yoruba tribe, incorporates two important elements of their ideology, the royal women and the ancestors. It shows a kneeling female figure carrying a child, standing on a Janus (the Roman god with two faces) helmet mask. Most African beadwork was done in Nigeria and Cameroon. The Yoruba are known for their wooden sculpture as well as beaded panels, crowns and figures like this.

**◀ MAORI GREENSTONE NECK PENDANT**
*17cm (6⅝in) long;* **£28,000**
Made of nephrite jade (generically known as greenstone) these carvings are referred to as Hei-Tiki, Hei meaning neck and Tiki the name of the mythical imp which appears in much Maori art. Made in varying sizes these pendants can sell for anything from £500 to £50,000. Hugely valuable in Maori culture, they were worn as talismans and passed from chief to chief, becoming more precious with each generation.

**▶ SELECTION OF PLAINS INDIAN BEADWORK ITEMS**
*Two pairs of moccasins; 26cm (10¼in) and 27cm (10½in) long,* **£300–500 each pair**; *Two pipe bags; 66cm (22in) and 74cm (29in) long,* **£400–600 each**; *Belt; 99cm (39in) long,* **£600–800**
The vast area of the North American Plains encompasses the lands of many Native American tribes including the Sioux, the Cree, Blackfeet and Crow. All are known for their decorative beadwork, which now forms a strong market for collectors. Prices started to climb steeply after the release of the film *Dances With Wolves* (1990) when people began clamouring to buy genuine beaded shirts and jerkins, as well as smaller pieces like these.

**COLLECTORS' NOTES**
• Be wary of wooden items whose patina appears to be even all over although the piece would have been handled in only a small area. The patina may have been faked to suggest greater age.
• Old is not necessarily valuable if the piece has a dull appearance. Objects which have a good patina and a vibrancy, even if made this century, may be more desirable.
• The most desirable objects are those which relate to the time known as Pre-Contact; that is, before the West made the great journeys of discovery and took over many civilizations.

**COLLECTING TIP**
Because of the prevalence of fakes, collectors are wary of West African artefacts, but some new markets worth examining are Tanzania, Zambia, Mozambique, Uganda and New Guinea.

# Antiquities

In the West European marketplace, an object must be at least a thousand years old to qualify as an antiquity. South American antiquities are referred to as pre-Columbian.

The collecting of antiquities is a pastime as old as some of the artefacts themselves. Even the Romans collected ancient Greek objects. More recently, rich young gentlemen in the 18th and 19th centuries visited Italy as part of their education and bought ancient statues and other pieces of interest which found their way into many of the grandest houses of Europe. Once excavations uncovered evidence of the ancient Egyptian civilization, collectors fought over the relics of a society of extraordinary sophistication. The Stone Age of the 3rd Millennium BC also yields up a range of flint implements which are widely collected. Roman glass is another popular area. The Romans made large numbers of utilitarian glass bottles, often bluish-green or light green in colour, which replaced ceramic containers as the most practical way of storing oils and liquids.

There is a strong international market for antiquities. The vast majority have been in circulation for many years, but there are still discoveries to be made. Occasionally a gardener or building worker makes a lucky find of a few Roman coins or a piece of jewellery quite by accident. Most serious collectors prefer to take a more academic approach to the field and are prepared to pay large sums of money for a particular figure of Venus, for instance, or an ornate carved section from a tomb. It is still possible, however, to buy small pieces of glass and pottery for as little as £50.

**▲ BRONZE FIGURE OF PTAH**

*Late Period after 600BC; 18.6cm (7¼in) high;* **£3,000–5,000**
Here, Ptah, one of the Egyptian gods, is shown in his role as a priest, dressed as a mummy wearing a close fitting workman's cap and Broad Collar, his hands protruding from his enfolded cloak. He is holding a sceptre, a sign of power. The bronze is set on an integral plinth, with an inscription to Ptah around three sides.

**COLLECTORS' NOTES**
• If you are new to collecting in this area, tread warily. Seek guidance and always buy from a reputable dealer or auction house where you can ask questions about objects and advice on where to start.
• Restoration, as in many areas, can be very difficult to detect. A nice looking terracotta figure, intact and in good condition, may be heavily restored. Again, buying from reputable sources is the only way to avoid this pitfall.
• Provenance is very important: always ask where a piece has come from and who has owned it previously.
• It's sensible and rewarding to keep a record card listing all your purchases and the details of each piece so that you can build up a picture of the period or the area that most interests you.

**COLLECTING TIP**
There is still quite a range of individual items that can be bought for under £200. They include small, Roman terracotta heads, small pieces of Roman glass such as bottles and phials, little Egyptian amulets, undecorated black Greek pots and Stone Age flint implements.

**◄ ROMANO-BRITISH BRONZE STATUETTE OF CAUTOPATES**

*c.1st Century AD; 6.3cm (2½in) high;* **£5,000–6,000**
This is a very rare Romano-British piece found near the Roman fort of Rudchester in Northumberland and thought to be the only example of its kind ever found in the British Isles. Cautopates was one of the two torch-bearers of Mithras, a cult god worshipped by the Romans. He is wearing a Phrygian cap (Phrygia being the ancient name for the region which is now Israel), tunic, trousers and cloak, and holding a hunting stick in his left hand and the characteristic down-turned torch in his right.

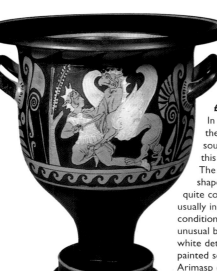

**◄ CAMPANIAN RED-FIGURE BELL KRATER**

*c.340BC; 40cm (15¾in) high;* **£5,000–6,000**
In the Hellenistic period, the area of Campania, in southern Italy, produced this type of red pottery. The Bell Krater is a bell-shaped two-handled vase, quite commonly found, but not usually in such good complete condition as this one. It is also unusual because of the added white detail and the interesting painted scene showing an Arimasp (a man with a griffin helmet) in combat with a large griffin with spread wings.

**► GALLO-ROMAN BRONZE APPLIQUÉ ROUNDEL**

*2–3rd century AD; 12.7cm (5in) high;* **£8,000–9,000**
Made in the area which is now France, this roundel has been cast with the bust of a female, her hair held in a narrow diadem (a crown or headband worn as a sign of sovereignty), wearing a v-necked robe fastened on her right shoulder. Her features are still sharp which is desirable to collectors, and it is likely that she was once part of a larger object, although of what type is not clear.

# Architectural Antiques

Twenty years ago, the term architectural antique had yet to become part of the vernacular of the antiques world. Such items as Victorian fireplaces and chimney pieces, cast-iron jardinières, wrought-iron gates and garden seating were available in great quantity at low prices and generally came under the heading of salvage. But with the passion we now have for recreating the past, all these objects have acquired value. Architectural salvage has become very big business and collectors are prepared to pay large sums of money for the right piece.

One of the main reasons for buying these objects is to install them in houses and gardens which have suffered a series of "improvements" during the 1950s and 60s, and are now being passionately restored to their original glory. Buyers are paying not only for the craftsmanship of the past, but for age and wear. The genuine patina of a section of oak panelling, the original paint on a garden seat, the moss and lichen on a stone urn and the original chains and drops of a chandelier are all desirable qualities in this market. In fact, fine carved wood and marble fireplaces have become so expensive that they are now the target of some particularly determined teams of burglars who hack them right out of the wall.

▶ **COADE STONE FIGURE**
*1802; 108cm (42½in) high;*
**£6,000–8,000**
Coade stone garden statuary is much sought after now. Named after a Mrs. Eleanor Coade, who invented this clay-based artificial stone at her factory in London in 1769, it looks rather like limestone but is durable and less prone to wear. This piece is in the form of a hooded woman emblematic of night, standing on a circular plinth and draped in loose clothing, holding her cowl in her left hand and her right hand outstretched. Originally, she probably held a lamp in her right hand. The piece is marked "Coade & Sealy, London 1802."

▲ **PAIR OF STAINED GLASS PANELS**
*c.1880; 223.5cm (88in) high, 76cm (30in) wide;* **£600–800**
This is a very typical piece of 19th-century ecclesiastical stained glass, taken from the window of a church. There was a tremendous revival of stained glass making in Europe during this period, with many studios devoted to its production. Pieces by top English designers such as William Morris and Edward Burne-Jones and Americans Tiffany and John La Farge make very large sums today.

▶ **LIPSCOMBE STONEWARE GARDEN URN**
*19th century; 64.5cm (25½in) high;* **£300–500**
Originally one of a pair, this elegant, classically inspired garden urn was made in the English town of Chesterfield which has a tradition for producing salt-glazed stoneware. The campana form (an inverted bell shape) is lobed around the base and has a flared rim decorated with an egg and dart pattern. The mask handles are intact and the body sits on a spreading circular foot and rectangular plinth.

## ▲ WALNUT BREAKFRONT CHIMNEYPIECE

*c.1860; 173.5cm (68¼in) wide; 119cm (46¾in) high;* **£800–1,200**
This rather grand walnut chimney piece would need a similarly well appointed room to show it off to full effect. It has been well carved in a typically 19th-century mish-mash of styles, with husk garlands and stylized strapwork carved in low relief. The figural subjects in the form of caryatids on either side of the blind fret-work topped with Ionic capitals and ending in paw terminals, make the piece highly desirable.

## ▼ BRASS FENDER

*c.1830–50; 122cm (48in) wide;* **£150–200**
The fender made its first appearance during the 18th century when houses began to be built incorporating standardized fireplaces rather than the large inglenook spaces of former times. This example is brass, elaborately pierced and chased with a pseudo-gothic frieze, and follows a style found in the late 18th century. Other favoured materials were steel and toleware (painted tin). Fenders can often be dated by examining the decoration, which usually reflects the taste current at the time of manufacture.

## ▼ CAST-IRON JARDINIÈRE

*c.1890; 91.5cm (36in) long;* **£300–500**
These cast-iron jardinières were intended primarily for use in a conservatory as they tend not to wear well in the garden. On occasion, they are still found with their original paint, but the burnished steel effect, as shown on this example, is also very popular with buyers. Made by Ducel of Paris, it is of a rectangular panel form cast with floral decoration with an attractively shaped rim. The circular foundry mark can be found on the inner rim.

## ◄ CAST-IRON AND BRASS FIRE GRATE

*c.1880; 47.5cm (19½in) wide;* **£500–700**
Since open fires came back into fashion, fire grates of every style have been reproduced, from simple medieval to ornate Renaissance, classical Georgian to flamboyant Victorian, so always buy an antique example from a reputable dealer. This example is late 19th century, aping the Rococo style of c.1740. It has a foliate scrolled backplate above a serpentine railed basket.

## ► ORMOLU AND GILT BRASS CHANDELIER

*1910; 101.5cm (40in) drop;* **£700–1,000**
Many salerooms now devote entire auctions to lighting, an area which commands a great deal of interest among collectors and interior decorators. This is an elaborate chandelier in a relatively unusual shape, hung with faceted bead chains, the central section adorned with wreaths and torch and quiver motifs. Very much a product of the Belle Epoque at the turn of the century in France, the triple-branch electric lamp-shades heralded the new age of electric light.

**COLLECTORS' NOTES**
• The Coalbrookdale ironworks in England produced the cast-iron garden furniture and ornamental gates and hallstands which are most sought after today. Look for the foundry mark cast in relief on pieces, often with a registration number.
• In the area of stained glass, look for painted figural decor-ation, not the simple coloured glass set into patterns and used within door frames.
• Avoid stained glass that is cracked but don't be put off by loose leading as it can be mended quite easily.
• Wrought-iron gates incorp-orating elaborate designs can often be found at reasonable prices, lower than that of a modern replacement.

**COLLECTING TIP**
Early Flemish and German glass in small panels (say, 25 x 23cm/ 10 x 9in) from the late 16th and 17th centuries can still be bought for less than £1,000, but the best value for money is the English 19th-century ecclesiastical window glass which has never appealed to a wide range of collectors, espe-cially that featuring martryed saints or the body of Christ. Angels have greater appeal. If you can attribute a piece to a maker such as Heaton, Butler and Bayne or Edward Kempe so much the better. Pieces by Morris & Co. may be prohibitively expensive, but you may find a piece by either of the other two makers for around £400. The original artwork for stained glass designs is a growing market.

# Scientific Instruments

The scientific instrument market can be guaranteed to throw up its share of mystery objects. So many precision instruments were made to demonstrate a theory, or be used during one particular experiment, that it is quite common to come across something made to a fabulously high standard in the best materials without being able to deduce its original purpose. Laboratory instruments are the most plentiful, and because the lenses on a microscope, for instance, are so important, most were made by optical and instrument makers.

The best and most sought after of the 17th- and 18th-century pieces, often in fitted silver or shagreen cases, were made for rich patrons of the sciences at a time when great discoveries were being made and new theories formed on the position of the planets and the world's land masses. A gentleman of means with no call to earn a living met to discuss these matters on a regular basis with friends, and his treasured instruments were made by the best craftsmen and lovingly cared for.

### ▲ NEWTON MINIATURE GLOBE
*1818; 5cm (2in) diameter;* **£2,500–3,500**
Globes are widely sought after, the best ones commanding high prices – as shown by this Newton miniature globe with its imitation fishskin case depicting phases of the moon and the seasons. The most interesting are from the mid-18th century until the Napoleonic Wars because the level of scholarship at that time and a rapidly changing world view resulted in a fascinating legacy of globes showing large areas of the world as blank and unexplored.

### ▲ J.B. DANCER BINOCULAR MICROSCOPE
*c.1855–60; 37cm (14½in) high;* **£800–1,000**
Microscopes appeal to a wide range of people, from botanists and chemists to geologists and doctors, which has a very positive effect on their value. John Benjamin Dancer was working in England between 1835 and 1878 first in Liverpool and then in Manchester. He is best known for his development of the micro photograph, but was also known in scientific circles as an optician; he also made and sold microscopes, telescopes and barometers. He is generally considered to be one of the best provincial English makers and his distinctive paper label can be seen here on the inside of the door.

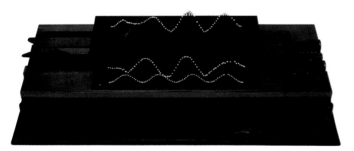

### ▲ WAVE DEMONSTRATION APPARATUS
*c.1870; 70cm (27½in) long;* **£3,000**
Made in France by Rudolphe Koenig, this is a piece of laboratory equipment of great appeal to collectors of more unusual scientific instruments. There is a lot of interest in demonstration apparatus made for a particular purpose. Some pieces were made for an exercise in solving a certain problem. This one shows the results of interference between waves and includes 16 mahogany wave templates fitted with white balls on the end of anodised brass sticks along with the complete instruction booklet.

### ◀ BRASS GALLON WEIGHT
*c.1850; 12.7cm (5in) high;* **£250–350**
Brass weights as well as instruments banded or mounted in brass are collected as much for their decorative appeal and the extraordinary degree of workmanship which went into making them as for their value as scientific instruments. This English gallon weight was an official standard used to check that retailers and wholesalers did not supply short measures. The weight sits in a protective brass cover with a screw top, enclosed in a brass-bound wooden carrying box.

## COLLECTORS' NOTES
• Make a study of the top scientific and medical instrument makers, as their products will always command a premium.
• Something in its original case is always worth more, because the cases are vital elements in protecting, say, a microscope or in keeping together a set of instruments which may work in conjunction with each other.
• Small is quite often valuable in this field, because such exquisite pocket-sized pieces were made as the playthings of rich gentlemen.
• Most brass instruments were originally covered in lacquer and such pieces are desirable if this is still in place.

## COLLECTING TIP
Don't imagine incomplete sets are valueless. A silver ruler or a set square from a drawing set, for instance, is likely to have been very well made and will be worth something to somebody.

# Medical Instruments

Antique medical instruments generally show more signs of use than scientific instruments. Designed as methods of diagnosis, destruction or repair, they were purely functional. Far fewer men played at being doctors than scientists in the 18th and early 19th centuries and early instruments have survived in fewer numbers. The market has traditionally lagged behind scientific instruments but there has been a huge growth in the last ten years since the care and craftmanship that went into making some of these pieces has become more appreciated. The appeal of scientific instruments encompasses collectors in many professions who may be interested in making use of the pieces today. Good quality antique medical instruments, however, appeal mainly to doctors and surgeons but, because of their scarcity and the relative affluence of the medical profession, prices tend to be quite high.

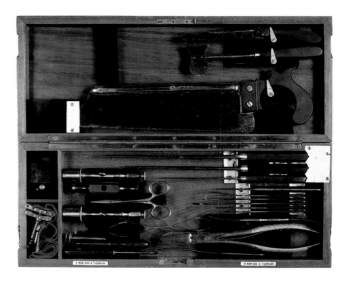

**▲ SURGEON'S INSTRUMENTS CASE**
*c.1870; 30 x 30cm (12 x 12in); £800–1,200*
Sets of surgeon's instruments date back as far as the late 18th century and were often taken into battle where emergency procedures were carried out on the spot. It is important to buy complete, boxed sets as any missing pieces are difficult to replace. This late 19th-century example contains, among other objects, a large bone saw, a finger saw, a double-headed skull saw, tourniquet, lancets and probes, all contained in a brass-bound mahogany case.

**▼ WALNUT HOMEOPATHIC MEDICINE CHEST**
*1880; 22cm (8¼in) wide; £300–400*
The medicine chest, in varying degrees of sophistication, was an essential part of many households in Europe, even during medieval times, when medicines were rare and expensive and treated with the same respect as other valuables such as jewellery. They began to be made in increasing numbers towards the end of the 18th century and became almost mass-produced by the 19th. Homeopathy reached Britain by 1830, and became widely practised. Chests like this walnut example were made to contain the remedies. They were light, with a drawer in the base and, in the main section, a thin perforated rack contained the many tiny, corked bottles of tinctures.

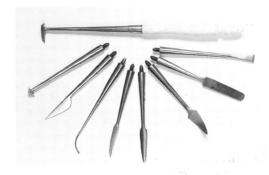

**▲ SET OF IVORY-HANDLED DENTAL SCALERS**
*c.1850; 8cm (3¼in); £150–250*
Dentistry was a gory and painful business before the advent of modern sterilizing methods and electrically powered tools. Dentists often doubled as general travelling physicians and dealt with the problems of animals as well as people. Sets of scalers, usually small, with different heads interchangeable on one handle were made from the 17th century in Europe and were often kept for use at home by their owner. By the time this sophisticated set was produced, technology had moved on and home dentistry had been superseded by the beginnings of the professional dentist operating from a fixed site.

**▲ SHOP DISPLAY SIGN**
*19th century; 91cm (36in) high;* **£1,000–1,200**
Shop display signs are popular with collectors and anyone with an interest in opthalmic antiques would want to own a piece like this, advertising the types and prices of spectacles available from the premises of a Henry Laurance, enclosed in a handsome, painted wooden frame.

**COLLECTORS' NOTES**
• Leech jars and drug jars are popular with ceramics collectors and are often more highly valued as examples of early ceramics than for their medical value.
• Good quality instruments often have "chequered" ebony grips because they are made from a high quality and expensive wood with a tight enough grain to decorate this way. The "chequered" grip also means an instrument is less likely to slip in use.
• Naval and military sets of medical instruments command a premium. They are usually recognised by their bullet forceps and probes.

**COLLECTING TIP**
Veterinary instruments are under-appreciated, perhaps partly as they are less elaborately decorated than many medical pieces.

# Coins and Tokens

The first coins were minted as a means of exchange in Mesopotamia c.600BC. Prior to this, bartering had been the most convenient form of trading, but once various economies began to grow and goods were moved over greater distances it was necessary to impose set values.

Coins survive in large quantities since many were buried and have been uncovered on archeological excavations. As architectural and anthropological evidence, they are invaluable, yet in commercial terms, many are still within reach of the collector on a budget.

Tokens also sell for modest sums. Introduced in England in the 17th century, copper tokens were produced by groups of local businessmen in order to give change to their customers when there was a shortage of low value copper coinage. They continued to be minted well into the 19th century and provide insights into particular companies and regions and the people who lived and worked in them. They were often used as an effective method of political propaganda, as well as an ideal form of commercial advertising.

**▲ VESPASIAN SESTERTIUS**
*AD69–74; 32mm (1¼in);* **£400**
Vespasian was legate to the Second Legion under Claudius during the invasion of Britain in AD43 and later, as emperor, started the Flavian Dynasty in Palestine in AD69.

**▲ ANGLO-SAXON PENNY**
*1066; 18mm (¾in);* **£600**
All Anglo-Saxon coins are pennies; this one was struck during the brief reign of King Harold II before the invasion of William, Duke of Normandy. When required, these coins were cut in halves and quarters to reduce their value .

**▲ DOUBLE EXCELLENTE OF FERDINAND AND ISABELLA**
*1474–1504; 28mm (1⅛in);* **£800**
This shows the Catholic Kings, Ferdinand and Isabella, whose marriage united the Spanish kingdoms of Aragon and Castile.

**▲ HENRY VII ANGEL**
*1507–9; 28mm (1⅛in);*
**£300–400**
The Angel illustrated here provided the bulk of England's gold coinage during the reign of Henry VII. Its value was bullion-related. If the price of gold went up, so did the value of the coin.

**COLLECTORS' NOTES**
• Concentrate on a particular area in order to avoid amassing a disparate and unsatisfactory range of coins. You can collect by monarch, country, denomination or type.
• Condition is all-important so buy the very best specimen you can afford. A collection of mediocre coins will not increase in value and a common coin in good condition is very often worth more than a rare coin in very poor condition. Dealers and auction houses classify coins' condition in the following way:
  FDC=*Fleur de coin* or perfect in all respects. Few survive in this state.
  Unc=Uncirculated or "mint" state.
  EF=Extremely fine
  VF=Very fine
  F=Fine
  VG=Very good. This can in reality mean that the coin is in quite worn condition.
NB All estimated values given on this page are for coins in "mint" condition.

**COLLECTING TIP**
Saxon pennies from AD700 to c.1150 are interesting and still good value. They can be bought from around £80–1,500, depending on rarity.

**▲ CHARLES II FARTHING**
*1675; 23.5mm (¹⁵⁄₁₆in);* **£200–250**
As a result of a shortage of lower denomination coinage in Charles's reign, unofficial trade tokens were issued. It was not until 1672 that the mint began producing copper coinage.

**▲ ADELAIDE POUND**
*1852; 22.5mm (⅞in);*
**£2,000–3,000**
Adelaide is situated in the state of South Australia which, prior to 1842, had been one of the six colonies. The first Australian coins were minted in very small numbers. Surviving examples are very rare and sought after.

**▲ U.S. $20 GOLD COIN**
*1898; 34mm (1⅜in);* **£300**
These $20 coins are not collectors' pieces, but are bought and kept for their bullion value alone.

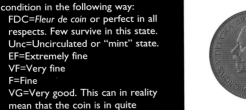

**▲ GEORGE V PENNY**
*1933; 31mm (1¼in);* **£20,000**
Only eight of these coins were minted in 1933 although some specimens were also produced. No pennies were needed during that year and the coins were struck purely as an exercise for the engravers.

**▲ JOHN WILKINSON'S "THE IRON MASTER"**
*1792; 28mm (1⅛in);* **£10–20**
John Wilkinson owned an iron foundry in north west England. Several tons of his tokens were struck, many are still available. This example is very worn, which is reflected in the price.

**▲ HULL HALF-PENNY TOKEN**
*1791; 28mm (1⅛in);* **£10–20**
This token, struck by tradesman Jonathan Garton of Hull, shows William III of Orange, a great Protestant hero. By minting it Mr. Garton was making a political and religious statement.

# Mechanical Music

If ever you get the chance to view an auction devoted to mechanical music, you won't need to ask the way to the relevant part of the building. You need only follow the cacophany of sound as collectors and dealers try out the various lots, from cylinder musical boxes to barrel organs and singing bird boxes.

Mechanical music grew out of the Swiss watch- and clock-making industry. Clocks and automata were fitted with musical mechanisms as early as the 17th century, but it was during the 18th century that the musical box, powered by clockwork or operated by a handle, came into being in its own right. By the 19th century it became established as an affordable form of musical entertainment. The sound is produced by a rotating cylinder with raised pins plucking a row of fine steel teeth in the form of a comb. As techniques improved, seven or eight tunes could be set on one cylinder.

In the 1870s, the first phonograph was produced by Thomas Edison which used a rotating cylinder and needles to record and play the human voice. Ten years later, Alexander Graham Bell developed the graphophone using wax cylinders. Around the same time, the gramophone was introduced, and with it, flat discs, a great innovation. At first, hand-cranking made the speed of the records difficult to regulate, but the development of a clockwork mechanism overcame the early problems. By the 1920s, electrical recording had been introduced and the world of mechanical music began to take on a new dimension.

**▲ EDISON GEM CYLINDER PHONOGRAPH**
*1901–5; 28cm (11in) long;*
**£200–250**
Thomas Edison first launched these appealing little machines in 1878. They work on the same principle as their successor, the gramophone, but with the sound cut into grooves on a cylinder rather than a disc. Thousands were made and are popular with collectors. Larger examples are most desirable.

**▲ BRITANNIA UPRIGHT DISC MUSICAL BOX**
*1910; 206cm (81in) high; discs 43cm (17in) diameter;*
**£2,000–3,000**
Made in Switzerland, this is the sort of machine you might have found in an arcade at a seaside town during the early years of this century. Although the base (a cabinet for storing the discs) and pediment are reproduction, the box is coin-operated, which makes it of great interest to collectors, as does the fact that it is large and takes big discs.

**COLLECTORS' NOTES**
• With many of these items, condition is very important. It could cost £60 or more to have one missing tooth replaced in a cylinder musical box, so avoid anything that is damaged.
• Beware of reproductions, especially gramophones made in India from old motors, but with reproduction cases and horns. The brass looks very yellow and people even go to the trouble of putting bogus HMV transfers on them.
• Rock stars and disc jockeys buying juke boxes sent prices soaring in the 1980s, but they have now come down to a more realistic level, in line with rarity and condition.
• Don't take the records out of a juke box and play them on a gramophone. The pressure of the arm in a juke box is so much greater that the records sound completely worn out on other machines.

**COLLECTING TIP**
Reproduction 78 rpms have started being made for record collectors unable to get hold of favourites, which is good news for gramophone collectors short of playing material.

**▲ MILLS "THE THRONE OF MUSIC" JUKE BOX**
*1939; 142cm (56in) high, 94cm (37in) wide;* **£2,000–3,000**
Providing the focus in diners and coffee shops worldwide, this American juke box played a choice of twenty 78rpm records. Mills had the most advanced sound system of all the juke box manufacturers, but because listeners couldn't see the mechanism working and the records turning round inside the case, this model didn't have as much appeal as some others.

**▲ OVERTURE CYLINDER MUSICAL BOX**
*c.1830; 40cm (15¾in) wide;*
**£3,000–3,500**
Cylinder musical boxes can be bought for considerably less, but this is an example of an early Swiss box still in good condition. The key inserted through the outside rather than being located beneath a flap is an indication of its early date. Examples from 1860 onwards also tend to have glazed covers.

**▲ SINGING BIRD BOX**
*c.1860; 10cm (4in) wide;* **£850**
These delightful singing bird musical boxes were toys of the rich, who amused themselves in idle moments by activating the on/off switch at the side, which caused the lid to flip open and the music to play. The box's mechanical aspect controls the flapping of the bird's wings and the wagging of its head. The creation of these boxes involved a high degree of workmanship, and some top quality examples can make thousands of pounds.

# Radios and Televisions

The first radio broadcast in the world was made in England in 1922. Wireless preceded it but was used mainly for military purposes. By the early Twenties, crystal sets were the commonest receivers, used in the home by enthusiasts who spent long hours making and operating them. Valve sets developed alongside them and by the Thirties, the radio was cased in wood or Bakelite. The first official broadcasting company, the BBC, was launched in Britain in 1922. It regulated the many companies manufacturing radios, and those that passed the rigorous inspections carried the BBC badge.

The television was a rare object in the home before the end of the Second World War. The first to be manufactured, in 1929, was a mechanical device, the Baird spring disc neon tube 30 line television. The first electrical high definition television was produced in 1936. Between 1936 and 1939, only 100,000 sets were made and sold in Britain, but during 1953, the year Queen Elizabeth was crowned, three quarters of a million sets found their way into homes across the country. The BBC reigned supreme in Britain, while NBC in the United States and Telefunken in Germany provided the bulk of their own domestic programmes.

▲ **AMERICAN SENTINEL RADIO 284 NI**
*1945; 30cm (12in) wide;* **£800–1,500**
You can see the similarity between the design of this radio, cased in marbelized orange cast phenolic resin, and the front of a car, which had become an indispensable domestic object by the 1940s in the United States. The yellow knobs simulate the headlights and the grille beneath them completes the picture. These Sentinel radios are quite rare, a marbelized blood red colour being the most sought after, and yellow the most common. To fetch this sort of price, the radio must be in mint condition.

▶ **EKCO RADIO, MODEL RS3**
*1931; 45.7cm (18in) high;*
**£300–500**
Made in Britain by one of the leading radio manufacturers and designed by J.K. White, this five-valve mains receiver is encased in moulded Bakelite in an Art Deco design which tries to mimic real wood. The decorative central grille is in antiqued copper with a design of trees evocative of the Art Nouveau period.

▲ **KENMAC RADIO LTD. CRYSTAL SET**
*1923; 11cm (4½in) high;* **£400–500**
The British radio company of Kenmac were jumping on the novelty bandwagon when they produced this delightful crystal set in the form of a book inscribed on the "cover" with the title "*The Listener* by E.R. Fone". There were five variations – red, green, blue and black leather and this most desirable tortoiseshell finish. The leather-bound examples are worth £200–300, but a premium can always be put on radios that retain their boxes and instruction booklets.

◀ **PHILIPS TYPE 2003 SPEAKER**
*1925; 48cm (19in) diameter;*
**£150–250**
To a radio enthusiast, this simple circle of mottled Bakelite can be as much of an attraction as any from the wide range of radios produced during this period, when modern radio technology was in its infancy. The 2003 was the first speaker made by the British company, Philips, to be manufactured in Bakelite and thus represents something of a turning point in the history of radio.

**▲ HMV 905 RADIO/TELEVISION COMBINATION**
*1936; 58cm (23in) wide;* **£2,000–3,000**
Despite the limited number of families who could afford to splash
out a prohibitive 35 Guineas (its original selling price) on anything
so luxurious as a television set before the Second World War, this
was marketed by the British HMV company as their cheapest and
most compact model of the time. It has a figured walnut cabinet
and Bakelite knobs and radio trim and might have been bought by
a prosperous shop keeper or professional middle class householder.

**▲ MARCONI 702 MIRROR IN THE LID TELEVISION**
*1937; 91cm (36in) high;* **£2,500–3,000**
To view this television, the prerogative of only a select minority as it
cost £85 when new, viewers looked at the lift-up mirrored lid which
was tilted at a 45-degree angle and had the screen reflected in it. The
television was still a novelty at this period, containing large tubes and
valves. After the war, the technology changed dramatically as a direct
result of the lessons learnt from radar, and sets became much smaller.

**▲ STEREOSPHERE TELEVISION BY JVC**
*c.1967; screen 30cm (12in) diameter;* **£150–250**
Formed in the shape of a spaceman's helmet, this black and white
television could be suspended from the ceiling or rested on a plinth
and was made in orange, white, yellow and turquoise with the words
"JVC Stereosphere" on the front. The Japanese manufacturers of
this model were quick off the mark in gauging exactly what would
appeal to the clamouring consumers of the West.

**COLLECTORS' NOTES**
• Check for damage on both
radios and televisions as condition
is very important and any chipping
or cracking of Bakelite cabinets
cannot be rectified.
• Televisions have only started to
make big money in recent years.
They have been collected by a
small and devoted band for many
years but are only now beginning
to command widespread interest.
• Check the perspex visors which
shield the screens of televisions
like the JVC Stereosphere shown
here, and avoid buying examples
which are crazed.

**COLLECTING TIP**
Pre-war televisions, like those
shown on this page, are getting
scarcer. If you come across one
(by Marconi or HMV in England,
Air King or ATC in the USA
or Lorenz or Telefunken in
Germany), buy it regardless of
condition – providing the price
is right.

# Household Collectables

The term "domestic bygones" encompasses items as varied as copper saucepans, pewter jugs, dairy equipment and wooden carpet beaters, but few individual collections include examples of every type of object that contributed to the running of a household. Many collectors of metalware, for instance, would not dream of buying treen (small domestic wooden objects) and a collector of jelly moulds would not necessarily seek out copper warming pans or smoothing irons. Collectors in the United States were probably the first to appreciate what is often termed folk art, attaching significance to the mundane but often beautifully made objects which tell us so much about how ordinary people went about their daily lives. The hand of the maker and the years of hard use so often evident in these pieces are now so thoroughly appreciated by collectors that prices have risen considerably in recent years, although bargains can still be found.

**▲ WHEELBARROW SALT**
*c.1780–1800; 11.5cm (4½in) long;* **£300–500**
This is an object that any collector of treen would love to own. The deep colour of the solid yew wood from which it has been carved and the polished surface make it most desirable. It begs to be picked up and handled and it is the tactile nature of so much treen that makes it attractive to so many collectors. It is a little novelty object of its day, designed to be filled with salt and trundled along the dining table.

**◀ FRUITWOOD SPOON RACK**
*c.1780; 38cm (15in) high;* **£800–1,200**
Spoon racks were made in all sizes and shapes, some to hold the large, wooden spoons used for cooking, and smaller examples, like this delightful solid fruitwood piece complete with drawer, for holding the spoons which the family used for eating. In buying something of this quality, the collector is paying not only for the decorative shape but for the patination of the wood, which helps to date it.

**▲ A FRUITWOOD AND A SYCAMORE MUFFINEER**
*(left and centre) c.1800; both 15cm (6in) high;* **£200–300 for both**
**PEWTER PEPPERPOT OR MUFFINEER**
*(right) c.1800; 18cm (7in) high;* **£150–200**
Known by a variety of terms including muffineer, pepper caster and dredger, the finest of these pieces were made in silver for the dining rooms of the smartest houses. Further down the social scale, pewter, brass and turned wood were the favoured materials, but all tend to follow the classical shape with a baluster base and elongated, domed top. The piercing is often generous as many were intended to hold sugar, much coarser in those days and broken off a big loaf with sugar nips before being ground in a pestle and mortar.

**▶ OAK WINE TRAY**
*c.1770; 28cm (11in) diameter;* **£400–600**
The greatest charm of this piece, apart from its wonderful rich and mellow patina, is that it has become slightly warped and is now a highly desirable decorative rather than functional object. Made from oak, it has been painstakingly fashioned by a craftsman and has coopered sides and raised lug handles. Both the ribbed banding which runs around the outside and the little out-turned feet are completely original.

### ▶ SMALL COPPER KETTLE
*c.1860; 12.7cm (5in) high;* **£60–80**
Copper items, cheaper and more hard-wearing than silver, tended to be made for use in the kitchen and include jelly moulds, saucepans and, most commonly, the copper kettle. In Victorian England, examples like this one, with a swan-necked spout and dovetail joints, were made in huge quantities and can still be bought for reasonable prices. They are sometimes fitted with glass, wooden or even porcelain handles. Copper must be tin-lined so that food and liquids do not become tainted. Most original tinning is worn, but occasionally it is intact, which adds to the interest, although not necessarily to the value, of a piece.

### COLLECTORS' NOTES
• If you want to display a collection of household objects, choose an area which works as a decorative theme in your home. A row of Edwardian vacuum cleaners may look out of place and take up too much room, whereas a good selection of copper jelly moulds might work much better.
• A nice pair of brass candlesticks can prove a good match for the more expensive silver counterpart.
• Reproductions have been manufactured in many areas. There is a lot of copperware which may have started life in a Middle Eastern bazaar not too many years ago. It lacks the precision of the European counterpart in the area of the joins, and swing handles are often crude and stamped with lattice decoration.

*front*

*back*

### ◀ SYCAMORE BUTTER PADDLE
*1884; 30.5cm (12in) high;* **£250–350**
Made in Wales, probably for use in a dairy, it is likely that this was originally one of a pair of paddles used to work and roll a quantity of butter. Once the pat had been formed into a circular shape, the printed handle was pushed down onto the surface. One side of this handle left an attractive pattern in the butter and the other side the words "VICTORIA MAY" and the date, 1884. Dated paddles are always at a premium.

### ▶ RUSH NIP
*c.1750; 25.5cm (10in) high;* **£400–500**
Early lighting devices like this one attract a devoted band of collectors. Rush nips were used to hold the bunches of rushes bound together and dipped in animal grease that served as candles in poorer rural households. This is a most desirable example since the original paintwork has survived intact. Many were made of wrought-iron sunk into wooden bases, and more of these survive than wooden ones, like the example here, many of which burnt.

### ▶ "HOG SCRAPER" CANDLESTICK
*c.1760; 32cm (12½in) high;* **£150–250**
The "hog scraper" candlestick was a great innovation when first introduced because the pusher (in this case shell-shaped) – an ingenious ejector system – allowed the used candles to be easily removed and either melted down or thrown away. This example is in tinware set into a turned beech-wood plinth, but variations also exist in brass.

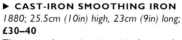

### ▶ CAST-IRON SMOOTHING IRON
*1880; 25.5cm (10in) high, 23cm (9in) long;* **£30–40**
This example retains its original enamel paintwork. It is hinged at one side and opens to allow the insertion of a firebrick, which heated the metal enough to make it effective in pressing clothes. Other versions took charcoal and these are often fitted with a funnel to allow the fumes to escape. Smoothing irons were made in a wide variety of shapes and sizes and for various functions from ironing newspapers to pressing linen. They are also still cheap to buy so a respectable collection can be put together without breaking the bank.

# Typewriters, Telephones and Sewing Machines

Early and unusual typewriters and telephones have been appreciated for many years, but will probably be of even more interest to collectors since recent technology has transformed methods of communication. The development of desk-top computers, electronic mail and the mobile telephone over the last ten years has lent even more of an antique appearance to the models on these pages. The first writing machines were developed to help the blind read and write, but it was not until typewriting speed could exceed that of handwriting that they began to be made in quantity. In 1873, Messrs. E. Remington & Sons signed a contract to manufacture the Sholes and Glidden typewriter, which was marketed worldwide as "The Machine To Supersede The Pen." This machine revolutionized life at the office and opened up an entirely new field of employment for women.

In 1876 Alexander Graham Bell transmitted the first recognizable speech through wires in Boston, Massachusetts. A Scot who had emigrated to the United States, he returned home to promote his invention, demonstrating the telephone to Queen Victoria in 1878. Connecting people with one another via a system of exchanges followed rapidly, and before long the telephone had become a method of international communication.

By 1860 there were 50,000 sewing machines in use in the United States. The first practical sewing machine was patented by the American, Elias Howe, in 1846, although devices invented during the late 18th century were able to carry out some of the tasks otherwise left to needlewomen. Isaac Merrit Singer is the man credited with taking the machine out of the factory and into the home, although his Perpendicular Action Sewing Machine, patented in 1851, was strictly an industrial model. Along with his competitor, Wheeler and Wilson, Singer monopolized the market in the United States, where the sewing machine was greeted with enthusiasm. Europe was slower to catch on, but by the end of the 1870s many homes found a corner for the machine and peoples' lives were made easier by its capabilities. Countless numbers of small companies made sewing machines during this period. Singer models, well-made and durable, still exist in great numbers and so are worth only modest amounts.

▶ **ODELLE TYPEWRITER**
*1890s; 25cm (10in) wide;* **£500–600**
Made in Chicago, this early example has a type-wheel mechanism. The paper is fed around the roller as usual. The crossbar moves along to shift the characters from left to right, but rather than pressing a different key for each character as with a conventional typewriter, the bar holds all the characters and the user moves the indicator along the bar and then strikes the required character.

▶ **NORTH TYPEWRITER**
*1892; 61cm (24in) high;* **£1,500–2,000**
This was the only model ever produced by the North Typewriter Manufacturing Co. Ltd. of London and as such is rare and desirable. It is a four-row single shift machine writing 76 characters, invented by George B. Cooper and Morgan Dunne. It was named after Lord North, a wealthy British aristocrat who bought the English Typewriter Company. The carriage is constructed with open ends so any width of paper can be inserted.

◀ **OLIVER NO. 9 TYPEWRITER**
*1916–20; 31cm (12in) wide;* **£40–50**
The keys on this typewriter are arranged in two banks, one on each side of the machine, and they hit the paper from the side. Machines designed in this manner were not usually popular but this one, invented by Reverend Thomas Oliver in the United States in 1888, was the exception. The Oliver Typewriting Company, founded in 1895, first produced this model in 1916. The fact that the piece is green rather than the standard black makes it more interesting.

### ◀ WOOD AND BRASS POST OFFICE TELEPHONE
*1920–30; 20cm (9in) high;* **£80–100**
This style of telephone was not designed for the home or the office, but thousands were installed in public buildings by the Post Office in England around this date.

### ▶ GENERAL ELECTRIC COMPANY GECOPHONE
*1933; 24cm (9½in) wide;* **£2,000–3,000**
Models of this telephone, particularly in this proto-type mahogany colour are extremely rare. This is one of a number of telephones made by GEC in the early Thirties for a famous golfing hotel in Scotland and finished in a metallic gold and silver to complement the lavish interior. They were discovered in a stock room in the 1980s, and when the silver veneer was removed, three of them were in this mahogany Bakelite.

### ▼ TWO PORTABLE COOKSON'S SEWING MACHINES
*1880; 30.5cm (12in) high;* **£800–1,200**
These two Cookson's machines both produce a chain stitch and are quite sought after by collectors, who enjoy inspecting the intricacies of the mech-anism and the design.

### ▲ REPLICA MODEL 162 TELEPHONE AND REAL MODEL 332 TELEPHONE
*1936; both 24cm (9½in) wide; left* **£80**; *right* **£200–250**
The red telephone above is a replica, made by using the parts of an old telephone and putting them into a modern case in a rare colour. Because they are made from a mould taken from the genuine article, the detailing is not as crisp as it should be. They are worth around £80, but some people have unfortunately paid up to £500 for them. The white telephone is the real 332. It was introduced in 1936 and is fitted with a "cheese tray" (the pull out section at the front). Designed with a built in bell it proved robust and popular. The early versions of the 332 had the side cord entry, as shown in the two telephones above, and examples are now very rare.

### ▼ NAUMANN SEWING MACHINE
*c.1900; 51cm (21in) wide;* **£20–30**
Made by Sidel and Naumann in Germany at the turn of the century, the style of this machine copies the Singer, which was hugely popular at the time. Cheap and virtually indestructible, like the Singer, it has yet to achieve any value to the collector. In fact, for those with an aversion to electric models, it is still a practical, working machine.

### COLLECTORS' NOTES
• Examine Bakelite telephones carefully, particularly the base and the handset. Cracks are very difficult to rectify and affect value.
• Beware of the many fake old telephones on the market.
• Some early telephones do not contain a bell or ringer. You will have to have a separate bell fitted.
• In the United States telephone manufacture has never been as tightly regulated as it has been in Britain. Consequently, in America there is a much wider range of collectable telephones from which to choose.
• Look out for early typewriters in a colour other than black. These are unusual and much sought after.
• If you buy a typewriter, make sure that the keys and the cast iron casings are intact, and that the gilt transfers are in good order. There is enough choice on the market to be able to avoid damaged examples.
• Completeness is equally impor-tant to sewing machine collectors who also like the gilt transfers to be in pristine condition. The shuttle of the machine should be intact because they were made in such a variety of size and thickness that they cannot usually be taken from one machine and put into another.

### COLLECTING TIP
Now is a good time to buy type-writers. There has only ever been a market for rare machines but it was a great deal more active, with higher prices, at the start of the 1990s than it is now.

# Ephemera

The term ephemera covers a wide range of items, which, in order to qualify being included in the category, must originally have been produced with a very limited period of survival in mind. Scraps, postcards, cigarette cards and greetings cards, paper dolls and food packaging all come under the heading, and many of these items have survived and can still be bought for very reasonable prices. Others have become so rare and sought after that they are now beyond the reach of those on a limited budget. A rare set of early cigarette cards can command £500, and a genuine set of Beatles' autographs, for instance, can fetch around £1,350. But it is still possible to find real gems at jumble sales and boot fairs, and searching out some longed for scrap can provide hours of happy treasure hunting. It can also be fun to try and spot collectable ephemera of the future.

**▲ "BEAUTIES WITH PLAYING CARD INSERTS" CIGARETTE CARDS**
*c.1895; 8.3 x 5.7cm (3¼ x 2¼in);* **£200–300 set of 52**
Sets of cigarette cards were printed and enclosed with most brands of tobacco from the 1890s onwards. Issued as a promotional device, they were always meant to be collected although, being made of paper and easily destroyed, no-one envisaged they would be around a hundred years later. Some of the rarer sets that survive are now worth a considerable amount of money. The very first sets were published in the United States and then issued in Great Britain by an American company. They covered the world of sport and entertainment, military and historical events and many other subjects, often with detailed information printed on the back. Collectors like clean cards which have never been stuck into an album, but kept loose in clear, plastic wallets.

**◄ RARE PAPER TOY**
*c.1840; paper doll 17.8cm (7in) high;* **£700–800**
Collectors both of dolls and paper ephemera would be enchanted by examples of paper dolls which are as unusual and have survived in as fine condition as this upright young man and his wardrobe. Entitled "The Boy's Doll With Eight Beautiful Dresses," it was made by the firm of Eigenthum in Germany, hand-coloured over a lithographed paper base and exported to England where it was retailed by Miller's Toy and Fancy Repository in Belgrave Square, London.

**▼ "HEROES OF THE VICTORIA CROSS" SCRAPS**
*c.1897; 94 x 24cm (37 x 9½in);* **£150–200**
Scrap albums from the 19th century are widely collected and those containing scraps with religious imagery published in Victorian England are currently finding great favour in Roman Catholic countries, particularly Spain and Italy. Scraps were bought by the sheet and pasted into albums. Many were manufactured in Germany for the British market. Today, those scraps which are in their original covers, having escaped the glue brush, such as this "Heroes of the Victoria Cross" set by the Bion Brothers, are at a premium.

**◄ ▲ THREE CALIFORNIA FRUIT CRATE LABELS**
*1900–1950; largest 89 x 74cm (35 x 29in);* **£15–20 each**
These beautiful and colourful American crate labels were designed and printed between 1900 and the early 1950s for the fruit producers of California. They were printed by a process, now obsolete, that involved the hand-separation of the colours. Skilled graphic artists were employed to produce labels of a very high quality. Originally pasted onto wooden crates, these are among a limited number left unused when, due to the rising cost of timber, cardboard boxes with pre-printed designs replaced wooden crates just after World War Two.

**▲ MECHANICAL GREETINGS CARDS**
*c.1905; from 15.2 x 7.5cm (6 x 3in) to 21.5 x 12.7cm (8½ x 5in);*
**£100–150 each**
Elaborate mechanical greetings cards which pop or fold out into a three-dimensional shape were a Victorian and Edwardian phenomenon. Those surviving in good condition, as these have, are very sought after. Valentine's Day cards pre-date Christmas cards and were made in great quantity from c.1850. Germany was a key centre for the printing of greetings cards – many were exported to England. In America, Louis Prang of Boston was pre-eminent.

**▲ CHROMOLITHOGRAPHED
BOX FOR MAZAWATTEE TEA**
*c.1910; 12.5 x 18 x 10cm (5 x 7 x 4in);*
**£200–250**
Food packaging attracts its own keen band of collectors, but this box is of particular interest because the original scene of the cats' tea party shown on it was painted by Louis Wain, famous British cat artist and first president of the National Cat Club. His pictures of cats were reproduced on postcards, calendars and in books. Some of Wain's later pictures appear in text books on schizophrenia as he went insane in 1924, dying 15 years later.

**COLLECTORS' NOTES**
• Condition is usually all-important in the field of ephemera. Despite being composed of items which might normally be thrown away, enough survives in most categories to enable serious collectors to be extremely fussy when buying.
• Because much ephemera is of a modest size, clear design is particularly important.
• Examples of printed ephemera from the late 18th and early 19th centuries with strong, fresh colours and in good condition will command a premium.
• Postcards are more interesting if they have been "postally used," but they must not have dog-eared corners.

Other collectable items include:
Theatre programmes
Advertising handbills
Posters (now a field of their own)
Packaging
Bubblegum cards
Trade cards
Catalogues/pamphlets

# Tins

A shelf or two stacked with colourfully lithographed tins which tell the story of the evolution of packaging, printing processes and advertising, form a delightful collection. The first hand-made biscuit tins were made as early as 1837 for the British company of Huntley and Palmer, whose name is synonymous with fine biscuits and whose products were exported all over the world.

Towards the end of the 19th century, the technique of off-set lithography had been perfected and it became possible to manufacture great quantities of brightly coloured tins in a variety of shapes and sizes. Chocolates and tobacco were also kept fresh in tins, but the majority of surviving tins on the market once held biscuits, and companies vied with each other to produce the most attractive and seductive designs.

In Britain, apart from Huntley and Palmer, the leading names included Macfarlane, Lang and Co., Peek, Frean and Co., Jacob and Crawford & Sons. In France, the Lefèvre-Utile factory commissioned famous artists such as Alphonse Mucha (*see* Art Nouveau posters, p.171) and Loir Luigi to design their tins.

▶ **BOOKS BISCUIT TIN**
*Late 19th century; 15cm (6in) high;* **£100–200**
Made in the form of a stack of books held securely by a strap, this proved a popular design of biscuit tin for Huntley and Palmer, who continued to market it for several years. Many of their tins were manufactured by Hudson, Scott & Sons, lithographic printers.

▲ **BOXED SET OF "CARAVAN AND MENAGERIE" TINS**
*1940s; tractor 16.5cm (6½in) long;* **£250–400**
This would form one of the star items in any collection of tins, especially as the original box is still intact and in good shape. The words "Chad Valley," "Harborne" and "Made in England" are on the base of the lithographed roller tractor, which has a hinged lid and yellow and black detailing. The colours are nice and fresh on the gypsy caravan and on the menagerie van with the red hinged top.

▶ **"BARREL ORGAN" TIN**
*c.1912; 16cm (6¼in) high;* **£800–1,200**
Some tins are rarer than others; few examples of this barrel organ tin survive, a fact reflected in its value. The words "William Crawford & Sons Ltd Biscuit Manufacturers, Edinburgh, Liverpool & London Great Britain" are on the inside of the lid with the registration number 594837 at the back. The tin has been lithographed to simulate mahogany with raised detailing of a monkey holding out his hat against a view of the Bay of Naples.

▲ **MACKINTOSH "ZOO CAGE" AND "THE ARK" TOFFEE TINS**
*c.1920; each 9.5cm (3¾in) high;* **£150–250 each**
Mackintosh's toffees were renowned world-wide, and a great number of delighted children would have received one of these brightly printed tins heavy with sugary promise for a Christmas or birthday present. The words "Mackintosh Toffee de Luxe" are printed on each lid. The zoo tin has a pull-out bracket at the front and the ark example has pull-out ends which simulate a deck above the waves.

▶ **"CORONATION COACH" BISCUIT TIN**
*1936; 23cm (9in) long;* **£200–300**
Issued by the British biscuit manufacturers, W. & R. Jacob, to commemorate Edward VIII's accession to the throne in 1936, this Coronation coach biscuit tin, in the form of a four-spoked wheeled coach, was one of the commemorative pieces which did not have to be discontinued after the abdication of the King, as it bore no likeness of him and could therefore be used for the next coronation.

**COLLECTORS' NOTES**
• Tins are lithographed so they are extremely difficult to restore if they become scratched and damaged.
• Avoid examples with rust unless they are in a design for which you have been searching for a long time, or which you find irresistible.
• Tins were mass-produced, so it is worth looking out for the more unusual pieces rather than settling for something very ordinary.

**COLLECTING TIP**
As Huntley and Palmer was one of the first companies to start marketing their biscuits in brightly lithographed tins, there are more early examples of their tins than any others and owning one enables a collector to form a collection covering a longer time span.

# Costume Jewellery

Pieces of jewellery made from coloured glass and base metals were produced as early as the 18th century. Surviving examples of these are highly sought after and fetch high prices. In the late 19th and early 20th century, glass beads and fake pearls were fashioned into pieces that were considered grossly inferior to those with real gems. During the 1920s, however, this changed and "costume jewellery" became popular with the liberated post-War woman, who now wore more informal clothes and wanted the casual jewellery to match. Parisian couturiers, including Poiret, Molyneux, Patou, Schiaparelli, and of course, Chanel, began to produce stylish costume jewellery which complemented their clothes. In 1927, *Vogue* magazine stated, "Fashion has decided that all we need ask of an ornament is to adorn us, and that neither our complexions nor our gems are to be natural."

During the 1930s, the focus of design switched to the United States, where costume jewellery was designed by top names, manufactured on a massive scale and had a great following.

Many pieces now sell for the same sort of price as precious gems, particularly if signed, but there are still bargains to be had. Pieces from the 1950s and 1960s are stylish and will rise in price, but the most important criterion when buying is to choose something you like, which complements your clothes and lifestyle, and then wear and enjoy it.

### ► CORO FLOWER BROOCH
*1940s; 9.6cm (3¾in) long;*
**£100–150**
It is easy to imagine this glittering base metal and diamante flower pinned to a black jacket or cocktail dress. Cohn and Rosenberger who founded Coro during the early years of this century in the United States, broke through many barriers of snobbery relating to costume jewellery. They made coloured stones and glitter available to a mass market, mainly of newly independent women who were beginning to earn a living and to enjoy a disposable income for the first time in history.

### ◄ COROCRAFT EARRINGS
*1930s; 1.7cm (¾in) wide;* **£40–50**
Whereas the pieces marketed under the name of Coro were mass-produced, Corocraft was the more exclusive side of the company, with items like these butterfly earrings usually made in limited editions. They incorporate glass "rubies" mounted in sterling silver.

### ►CHANEL BOW BROOCH
*1929; 9cm (3½in) wide;*
**£700–1,000**
Chanel costume jewellery is highly sought after. Seven years after Chanel's death in 1978, London salerooms sold her costume jewellery for similar prices to real jewels. Count Etienne de Beaumont and Duca di Verduci created many of her jewellery designs. Originally, her pieces were marked "Made in France." This diamante bow brooch is one of the first pieces to carry her signature instead.

### ◄ MIRIAM HASKELL EARRINGS
*c.1930; 5.3cm (2¼in) long;* **£250–350**
The American designer Miriam Haskell was highly successful from the start. She began working during the 1920s making innovative, limited edition pieces of high quality. These leaf-shaped earrings are entirely hand-made with each piece of diamante tied separately onto the base.

### ► PENNINO NECKLACE, BRACELET AND EARRINGS
*1940s; necklace 42cm (16½in) long, bracelet 17cm (6¾in) long, earrings 3.1cm (1¼) long;*
**£200–300 the set**
This base metal and diamante set carries all the hallmarks of Pennino – harmonious design combined with high standards of workmanship. Little is known about the company, who registered their name in New York in 1925, but before long their simple shapes which always complemented the fashion of the moment, gained a huge following.

### ▼ COPPER AND ENAMEL BRACELET AND EARRINGS
*1950; bracelet 17.5cm (7in) long, earrings 2.5cm (1in) long;* **£50–90**
This type of copper jewellery with splattered enamel decoration is particularly popular in the United States, where the estimate would be closer to £150. Stylish and typical of its time, this set was made by Matisse, an American firm of costume jewellery makers.

### COLLECTORS' NOTES
• Always examine a piece of jewellery carefully on the back to see if it has signature, paying special attention to clips of necklaces and earrings and the metal backs of brooches. American pieces are usually clearly marked with the name of the designer whereas European pieces may have more cryptic marks in the form of symbols or numbers.
• The best pieces by designers such as Haskell and Chanel have gone up consistently in price over the last ten years and will probably continue to do so, whereas examples by certain Sixties designers such as Paco Rabanne are still affordable and may prove a good investment.

### COLLECTING TIP
Never buy pieces which lack their large, unusual-shaped stones. The old coloured stones are becoming impossible to find, although gem wholesalers often keep some paste alongside their real gems, so small pastes can usually be replaced.

# Cameras

Camera is the Latin word for room, which goes some way to describing the very basic principles of photography. Using a lens, a small hole made in the wall of a darkened room will allow a two-dimensional image of what is outside the room to be projected onto the opposite wall. A scaled down version of this idea, the camera obscura (literally, dark room) was a box, used mainly by artists during the 18th and 19th centuries as a way of studying perspective, and as such, these objects can also be viewed as the first form of the camera.

The first photographic process was invented in the 1830s, with both Daguerre in France and Fox Talbot in England laying claim to the innovation. It was an idea developed at just the right time, and technology progressed apace so that by the mid-1850s, photography had become a craze for the masses and the development of the positive-negative process allowed numbers of prints to be produced of the same photograph. It paved the way for prints to appear in books and made the photographic portrait available to everyone.

The art of photography has never lost its glamour, and old cameras are widely collected for two main reasons. Firstly, they often still work and enthusiasts enjoy the skill required to use them to their best advantage, and secondly, most are beautifully designed with a great deal of workmanship going into their manufacture.

### ▲ CAMERA OBSCURA
*1800; 30cm (12in) long;* **£2,000–2,500**
The camera obscura focuses light onto a surface through the lens. The focal length is adjusted by sliding the lens in and out and the image comes into focus on a ground glass screen at the back. It was not until 30 years after this piece was made that the photographic plate was invented. Every camera collector longs to own a camera obscura. Made all over Europe, they are now rare, especially one like this which features the maker's plaque, W. & S. Jones of Holborn in London, a leading manufacturer of scientific and optical instruments.

### ▼ ADAM & CO. DELUXE HAND REFLEX PLATE CAMERA
*1900–10; approximately 10cm (4in) wide;* **£200–300**
This plate camera has a Kodak Aero-Ektar f2.5 7in lens. Adam & Co. were considered one of the best makers at this time and their cameras were generally the most expensive of their kind. They sold to customers directly, never allowing their equipment to be retailed through other outlets. If you had a passion for photography and money to spend, they would make a camera to your exact specifications. They remain one of the most sought-after makers.

### ◀ THORNTON PICKARD MAHOGANY AND BRASS TRIPLE EXTENSION HALF PLATE FIELD CAMERA
*1905–10; 22cm (8½in) high;* **£150–200**
### SANDERSON TEAK AND BRASS ¼-PLATE TROPICAL CAMERA
*1910–20; approximately 14cm (5½in) high;* **£400–500**
Both of these are good examples of cameras which are bought by collectors for their beauty rather than their useability. Thornton Pickard was a British company based in the north of England who produced this type of camera *(left)*, from the 1890s until 1914. They exude quality and the kind of classic camera design of the period which is now highly appreciated. Sanderson, also a British company, made this teak and brass camera *(right)*, specifically for use in the tropics. The wood is dense to withstand the high humidity levels, and the bellows were made of high quality leather to withstand rot. Because tropical cameras were made in small quantities, they are hard to find in good condition and command a premium at auction.

### ▲ NEWMAN AND GUARDIA BOX PLATE CAMERA
*c.1910–30; approximately 13cm (5in) wide;* **£250–300**
A special box plate camera with a Zeiss Protarlinse 224mm lens and two plate magazines, this product was made in Britain by the London-based company, Newman and Guardia, who were known for the high quality of their cameras. "Sybil" is probably their most famous range, but they also made stereoscopic cameras and early twin lens examples which are unusual and sought after.

### ▲ TEAK AND BRASS "SALEX" TROPICAL REFLEX CAMERA
*1910–20; approximately 15cm (6in) high;* **£300–400**
This was retailed by City Sale & Exchange of London who did not make their own cameras but retailed other makers' products under their trade name "Salex," an abbreviation of the company's name. This has a Taylor Hobson Cooke 6in f3.6 lens and tan leather bellows. In common with the example by Sanderson, it was made in dense teak with high quality leather bellows designed to survive the rigours of a tropical climate.

### ▶ "TICKA" CAMERA BY HOUGHTON
*1905–14; approx. 6cm (2⅜in) diameter;* **£150–250**
Collectors love novelty cameras and examples of the "Ticka" made to look like a pocket watch are widely collected. The version shown here was made in Britain under licence from the Expo Camera Company of New York, and is identical to the American Expo watch camera. It takes 25 exposures on a 16 x 22mm special cassette film. The little box, still intact, represents £50 of the value. Those which were made incorporating a watch face are worth £700–900 and the solid silver examples, £1,000–2,000 depending on their condition.

### ▲ LEICA (NUMBER 271255) STANDARD
*1938; 14cm (5½in) wide;* **£200–300**
These Leica cameras produced by the German company of Leitz are a gift to collectors who like to note down every minute detail relating to their pieces. The company's records were so meticulous that you can check the serial number and find out exactly what the model is and when it was made. This is one of a batch of 599 made in 1938. The company started in Wetzlar in Germany in 1849 and the first Leica was sold in 1924. They take 35mm film, making them easy to use today. This is slightly worn, but one in top condition might sell for £400, with 50% added on for those all in black.

### ◀ PHYSIOGRAPHE STEREO CAMERA
*1896–1920; approx. 17.5cm (7in) high;* **£1,000–1,500**
The Physiographe Stereo camera, made in France, was an early novelty piece, patented in 1896 and sold until the 1920s. It was designed to resemble a pair of binoculars, incorporating the deceptive angle view-finder in one eyepiece. The other eyepiece was used as a handle to slide out the plate magazine hidden in the case underneath. It was sold in England as "Watson's Stereo Binocular," and takes 45 x 107mm plates. The first two models used 5 x 12cm plates, with the earliest ones using a leather bag for plate changing rather than the magazine. These early models are highly sought after.

## COLLECTORS' NOTES
• Condition is very important. If you are buying to use, the camera must be mechanically and optically complete so avoid fungus and cracked lenses.
• If you are buying for display, avoid badly worn bellows and corroded metal.
• Daguerreotype and wet-plate cameras vary in value from £300 to tens of thousands. They are often hard to value because there are so few around to establish a regular price structure. Many are unmarked and/or have been modified over the years, so, with a little knowledge and a lot of luck it is possible to find a bargain.
• Stereo cameras are a very popular collecting field and will command a premium over other cameras of a similar age and maker.

## COLLECTING TIP
In the last few years, there has been increasing interest in early 35mm cameras by both Canon and Nikon. They are the new useable collectable.

# Pens and Pencils

The first practical example of a pen with its own reservoir for ink which would flow to the nib at a steady rate was designed by a mathematician at the court of Louis XIV in the late 17th century. Further improvements were made in the early 19th century. Advances in making ink and gold nibs led several people to develop a reliable modern fountain pen in the 1880s. L.E. Waterman and George S. Parker are the most famous of these pioneers today. People have collected both fountain pens and propelling pencils for many years but it wasn't until c.1980 that these collectors began to come together to form societies. It then stopped being a low key collecting area,

and pens and pencils became big business, with auction houses devoting regular sales to them.

The majority of propelling pencils on the market were made by the British company, S. Mordan and Co. Ltd., and a fascinating collection can still be put together for a reasonable amount of money. Sampson Mordan was born in 1790 and by 1822 had patented his first ever pointed or propelling pencil. He went on to manufacture many other useful items including bottles for scent and smelling salts, inkstands and cedarwood drawing pencils filled with Cumberland lead. At the bottom of the facing page are a few examples of his firm's enormous output.

◄ **GROUP OF PARKER DUOFOLDS 1927–1932**
*left to right:*
**JADE JUNIOR PENCIL £100–150**
**BURGUNDY AND BLACK SENIOR PEN £400–500**
**LAPIS SENIOR PEN £500–800**
**MANDARIN "LUCKY CURVE" SENIOR PEN £1,200–1,800**
**RED SENIOR PEN £300–400**
**DEMONSTRATION PEN £400–600**
**RED SENIOR PENCIL £100–150**
*Length of longest pen: 14cm (5¼in)*
The Parker Duofold pens and pencils were all made between 1927 and 1932 in two factories, one in the United States, in Jamesville, Wisconsin, and the other in Toronto, Canada. Straightforward, commercially successful pens, they are now highly collectable, mainly because they are still widely available and often affordable. The small ones are the least valuable and the yellow the most because it was the least popular colour at the time, prone to cracking and is nowadays the hardest to find in good condition. Lapis is also much sought after. All of the examples shown here retain their original paper price labels in gold and black around the pens and are therefore in mint, factory condition.

**COLLECTORS' NOTES**
• When buying Parker Duofolds, look for the Lucky Curve models, considered more desirable than the streamlined ones, although they are no rarer, and the Vest Pocket versions, introduced at the end of the life of the range.
• Top names to look for are Parker, Waterman, Mont Blanc, Sheaffer, Onoto by De La Rue and Dunhill Namiki from England, Kawecko and Soennecken from Germany and Conklin, Wahl-Eversharp and Le Boeuf from the United States.

**COLLECTING TIP**
Damaged pens are still the best source of spare parts, if they can be bought cheaply.

### ◄ PARKER SNAKE PEN

*1910; 14cm (5¼in) long;* **£14,500**

It is conceivable that there are as few as a hundred of these Parker snake pens in collections worldwide. For many, to own one means having achieved the pinnacle in their chosen field of collecting, but this is by no means the rarest pen in the world, nor was it the most expensive when it was made. The silver model 37 cost $10 when new, this gold plated example was $2 more. The design, depicting two glass-eyed snakes wrapped around the body, went on being made for several years. Snake pens made by L.E. Waterman between 1905 and 1918 are just as valuable, but those by other makers such as J.G. Rider or A.A. Waterman are much less popular as fewer people collect these brands.

### ▶ DUNHILL NAMIKI FOUNTAIN PEN AND PENCIL SET

*1928–30; 11cm (4¼in) long;* **£700–900**

This pen and pencil set, decorated with traditional Japanese lacquer work, is sought after by collectors all over the world. Namiki made high quality fountain pens in Japan which were marketed in Western Europe by their salesman, Wada, who sold to luxury goods stores such as Asprey and Dunhill. He made a deal with Dunhill and until Dunhill bought Mont Blanc, this was the only time Dunhill agreed to take on a product bearing the name of another company. The decoration varies from plain black to highly ornate, with every degree in between, and value today is closely linked to the amount of decoration on the pen.

### ◄ S. MORDAN AND CO. LTD. PENS AND PENCILS

*left to right:*

**ONE PEN/PENCIL THERMOMETER/ COMPASS COMBINATION**

*1860–80; 10cm (4in) long;* **£250–350**

This rare example enclosing both a dip pen and a pencil, has engraved yellow metal mounts and a compass on the top.

**TRIPLE DROP-ACTION PENCIL**

*c.1880–90; 8.5cm (3⅜in) long;* **£150–200**

This has three barrels with red, blue or black pencils released by buttons.

**YELLOW METAL EVER- POINTED PENCIL**

*1840s; 8.5cm (3⅜in) long when closed;* **£150–200**

The outer casing of this decorative and elegant pen is typical of the period.

### ▶ WATERMAN MODEL 20

*1905–15; 25.5cm (10in) long;* **£2,000**

Waterman specialized in extremes! In contrast to the tiny pen (*right*) this is their giant Model 20, advertised as the pen for the man with a bigger hand, but in practice bought and used by people such as postmen and court stenographers, whose jobs involved using a lot of ink and who didn't want the inconvenience of filling a pen at frequent intervals.

### ▲ WATERMAN "SMALLEST PEN IN THE WORLD"

*c.1910–20; pen 4.5cm (1¾in) long;* **£1,000–1,200**

Known officially as the Waterman Doll pen, this is a perfectly scaled down miniature which was manufactured purely as a display and promotional piece and is now sought after as a rare pen. Other companies such as De la Rue in England made small pens, but nothing to match the perfection of this one. To be worth this kind of money, the pen must be a perfect example, with no cracks or warping.

### ▲ S. MORDAN AND CO. LTD. PENCILS

*left to right:*

**DUCK PENCIL**

*c.1910; 29mm (1⅛in) long;* **£250–350.**

Mordan produced both this duck pencil and one in the form of an owl. This is rarer and in very good condition, although the price is slightly affected by the inoperative lead mechanism.

**HUNTING HORN PENCIL**

*c.1900; 9cm (3½in) long;* **£80–120**

Mordan made several novelty pencils, which are now eagerly sought after by collectors. This hunting horn has a coppered and silvered body and retains its plush lined, morocco case.

**YELLOW AND PINK GOLD PENCIL, SET WITH RUBIES**

*c.1850; 6.5cm (2in) long;* **£800–1,200**

Serious collectors of pencils would ache to add this to their collection. It is beautifully made with floral engraved decoration, set with three bands of rubies and a bloodstone finial.

**RULER SLIDE ACTION PENCIL**

*Early 20th century; silver case 17.8cm (7in) long;* **£100–150**

Useful for the affluent to use at home or at work, this novelty pencil holder is unusual in having both imperial and metric scales.

# Sporting Memorabilia

If you list every single sport you can bring to mind it quickly becomes clear that the collecting potential in this field is vast. Most people who have an interest in collecting sporting memorabilia concentrate on just one, or possibly two, areas. In each category, the most expensive pieces are usually clothing or equipment known to have belonged to a famous sports personality, and the least expensive are pamphlets, programmes and tickets relating to specific events, although many of these items are rare and sought after as well. Whether your passion is football or pigeon fancying, golf or billiards, you will find no shortage of objects waiting to be snapped up and treasured.

▲ **PHOTOGRAPH OF OLD COURSE, ST. ANDREWS**
*c.1865–70; 12.7 x 20.3cm (5 x 8in);* **£250–350**
Some golfing memorabilia items, such as rare antique clubs, are among the most expensive sporting collectables on the market, and anything relating to the home of golf, St. Andrews in Scotland, is particularly sought after. This Victorian photograph shows a player, surrounded by a band of loyal followers, about to putt on the 18th green of the renowned Old Course. It is a wonderfully evocative image and an early golfing photograph.

▶ **RARE ENGLISH PORCELAIN JUG**
*c.1818–50; 24cm (9½in) high;* **£3,000–4,000**
For lovers of cricket, this jug is a rare prize. Possibly made by Coalport, the titled view, "Cambridge Cricket Club," features early curved bats, stumps and a ball in front of a tent flying a banner and, in the background, the roof of King's College Chapel. The first recorded mention of the Cambridge Town Cricket Club is in 1816 when a feast was held at the Castle Inn by the townsfolk for their cricketers.

▲ **STAINED GLASS PANEL**
*early 20th century; 57 x 80cm (22½ x 31½in);* **£250–350**
Whether or not you are a tennis enthusiast, you could not fail to be charmed by this scene painted on glass showing a game of mixed doubles in full swing. Although it was done at the beginning of this century, it looks back to a much earlier time when men wore doublets and hose.

◀ **MOUNTED PIKE**
*1929; 137cm (54in) wide;* **£1,500–2,500**
A fisherman loves a trophy, and this is a magnificent specimen. This pike, inscribed "Old Charlie," was caught by one J.C. Newton of Dorset in England on 24 December, 1929 and weighed 18lbs 10oz (8.5 kilos). It has been particularly well mounted in a naturalistic setting with other smaller fish.

## ▲ RARE FOOTBALL MEDALS

*1961; 3cm (1¼in) diameter each;*
**£8,000–10,000 the pair**

The football fan has a vast pool of memorabilia to draw from, much of it still affordable because so many things are still readily available, from tickets and programmes to football shirts and rattles. Many collectors concentrate on one club and even one player within a club over a specific period. These rare F.A. Cup and Football League winners' medals are at the top end of the market, won by Terry Dyson of the English club, Tottenham Hotspur, for the 1960–61 season. Spurs were the first team this century to achieve the "Double," winning both the League and the Cup in the same season. Dyson scored one of the goals in the Cup Final.

## ▶ AMPHORA FIGURE OF A CADDY BOY

*c.1905; 27cm (10½in) high;*
**£400–500**

A great number of mass produced slip moulded wares were made in Bohemia and Austria at the beginning of this century. One of the best known companies, Reissner, Stellmacher & Kessel, was responsible for making a range of what were known as "Amphora" wares, among them this appealing caddy boy, still carrying his five original clubs and in very good condition.

## ◀ CRICKET PRESENTATION PIECE

*c.1910; 25.4cm (10in) high;* **£300–500**

Made as a shop presentation piece, this is exactly the sort of item that sits well alongside silver cups and other trophies in a display cabinet and is therefore desirable to any cricket enthusiast. The ball could also be interchanged with other favourite cricket balls in a collection. The cup is supported by three miniature cricket bats with three stumps between them and the whole piece sits on a circular base which was originally covered by a glass dome.

## ▶ BOBSLEIGH BRONZE

*20th century; 26.5cm (10½in) high;* **£5,000–8,000**

A product of the Austro-German school of sculpture, this dramatic piece skilfully captures the movement, tension and concentration of this dangerous sport, and shows a five-man bobsleigh taking a corner. It is identical to the bronze in the Kulm Hotel, St. Moritz, which is stamped with the foundry mark, Argenta-Wien, so we can assume this piece was also made there even though it has no mark.

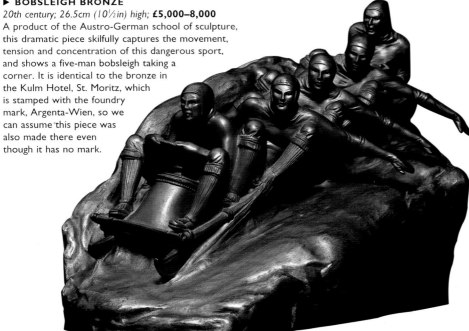

## COLLECTORS' NOTES

Pick your sport carefully before you start to collect, otherwise you will end up with a mish mash of things instead of a properly focused collection. The sporting world is your oyster, from hot air ballooning to tiddlywinks and everything in between.

Don't pay a lot of money for something supposedly antique just because it relates to your chosen sport. Check it is genuine. Reproductions abound and certain dealers are only too aware of how fanatical some collectors of sporting memorabilia can be! Carefully check the provenance of a piece too, especially of autographs and sporting equipment which is supposed to have belonged to a famous sports person.

The bigger the sport is internationally, such as cricket, football and golf, the greater the number of collectors there will be, compensated for by the volume of memorabilia produced. Baseball, for example, is only really collected in the United States or by Americans, so if you find baseball material outside North America it is likely to be under-appreciated. The more esoteric the sport, the fewer the collectors, but they will be chasing a very small volume of objects; prices can be high for quite obscure items.

Programmes can fetch phenomenal sums if they commemorate a special sporting event. The world record price for a football programme is £7,130, paid for one printed for the 1889 Cup Final between Preston North End and Wolverhampton Wanderers, when Preston became the first club ever to win the League and the Cup in the same year.

## COLLECTING TIP

Boxing memorabilia is under-appreciated at the moment in comparison with sports such as football and cricket, yet boxing has a long and honourable history. Many related items are very affordable.

# Plastics

Few areas offer such scope for the collector as the colourful, versatile world of plastics – the word coming from the Greek "plassein," meaning "to mould." Plastics were developed during the second half of the 19th century to supplement the dwindling supplies of luxury materials such as tortoiseshell, ivory, horn, lacquer, shellac and amber. By the 1930s they were being used to make everything from basic household goods to the most startling, innovative, state-of-the-art furniture, cars, scientific and medical equipment and clothes. Plastics suffered an image problem after the Second World War: the explosion in production, sometimes at the expense of design and quality meant that plastic goods were seen as "cheap and nasty." But designers, long appreciating the scope offered by plastics, fought back, with the result that some of the most exciting and well-crafted objects have been made in plastic, for plastic's sake, and new designs are still being created today. Some of these pieces become instant classics, changing hands for large sums of money. Others are on a slow burn, creeping up in value as time passes.

**▲ BANDALASTA BOWL**
*1927; 30.5cm (12in) diameter;* **£150–200**
Bandalasta, a pure synthetic officially known as urea thiourea formaldehyde, was made in England by Streetly Manufacturing in the form of mugs, cups, bowls and other household objects. The foot of this bowl unscrews from the main section because the technology of the day precluded making the item in one piece. Bandalasta was manufactured in many colours, often as picnic sets, this vibrant orange being the most desirable of all.

**▲ DUNHILL PIPE HOLDER**
*1930; 23.5cm (9¼in) long;*
**£300–400**
Dunhill made several versions of these stylized birds in England and the United States. Originally, they had a pipe protruding from their bottom, but some are so large that they may have been made for display purposes only. Bakelite and cast phenolic, of which this is partly made, are similar materials, the former compression-moulded and the latter poured into a mould.

**▲ INCOLOR MASTER COCKTAIL SHAKER**
*1935; 28.5cm (11¼in) high;*
**£200–300**
Made in Bakelite by Incolor in England, the Master cocktail shaker was marketed in seven or eight different colours, all stylishly mounted in silver plate. It was fitted with a recipe ring, which is revealed as the cap is turned to display the measurements for eight cocktails including Bronx, Sidecar, Tom Collins and Clover Club.

**▲ TABLE LIGHT**
*c.1970; 30cm (12in) high;* **£700–900**
This rare "Shrimp" light was made in white and pink by Superstudio, an Italian design group based in Florence in the 1960s and early 70s. The black knob at the side tightens and loosens the "shrimp" effect of the layers. Not many of these lights were made.

◀ **STACKABLE TABLES**
*1971; 43cm (17in) diameter;* **£140–180**
Unlike so many other examples of modern plastics, these particular tables are not easy to find, as they have always been considered objects of desire and retailed through expensive stores, even when they were first made. They were designed by the Italian Giotto Stoppino for Kartell, manufacturers of much plastic moulded furniture and other domestic objects.

▶ **DANSK VASES**
*1969; 23–30cm (9–12in) high;* **£80–100 each**
By the 1960s, the sculptural virtues of plastics were being exploited. These two vases, a purple double-sided injection moulded example and the brown/grey vacuum-compressed one beside it, were both designed in Italy by Enzo Mari for Dansk. The Italians have always been in the forefront of smart design and pieces like this are worth looking out for.

**COLLECTORS' NOTES**
**LOOK FOR**
Marks and logos – a lot of furniture and domestic objects carry moulded marks and company logos on the base.

**AVOID**
Major scratches and cracks, which affect value unless the object is extremely rare.

**COLLECTING TIP**
Take a second look at the things around you at home: many ordinary domestic goods are now collectable – for example:
• the Valentine portable typewriter designed in 1969 for Olivetti by Ettore Sottsass and sold in a red plastic box, now worth £100 (see p.204);
• the National Panasonic white plastic "Bangle" radio, now worth £30–50;
• a DAR fibreglass armchair designed by Charles Eames for Herman Miller in 1950, worth £150 or more;
• the "Grillo" telephone designed by Marco Zanuso and Richard Sapper for Ital Tel in 1965, worth £80;
• the "Teleono" light designed by Vico Magistretti for Artemide in red plastic with a white swivel shade, worth £40–80.

◀ **RADIO IN A BAG**
*1982; 28cm (11in) high;*
**£150–200**
Who said the parts of a radio had to be invisible and contained within a rigid casing? Daniel Weil designed his radio within an envelope of PVC as part of his degree course at the Royal College of Art in 1981. It was manufactured by Parenthesis in England.

◀ **MAXI STACKING DISHES**
*1964; tray 37cm (14½in) wide;*
**£80–120**
This bright red plastic stackable tableware has become a modern classic, embodying the 60s preoccupation with convenience and hygiene. Designed by Massimo Vignelli for Heller in 1964, it was included in an exhibition in 1972 entitled "Italy: The New Domestic Landscape."

▲ **WATER BOTTLES**
*1993; 30cm (12in) high;* **£140 the pair**
Even a plastic mineral water bottle is worth collecting, especially if it is one of the specially commissioned prize-winning Vittel bottles designed by Gaetano Pesce.

# The Fifties

In the early 1950s, after Europe and the United States had taken stock and assessed the impact of the Second World War, the general level of optimism began to rise. It was a dynamic decade, when architects and designers, their creative output on hold since 1939, set out to reshape society and carry it into the second half of the 20th century. Cities had to be rebuilt, so, in many senses there were blank canvases waiting to be painted. Materials which had previously been associated with industry such as aluminium, plastics and fibreglass, came into the home as never before and were used to make furniture and many basic domestic items.

In the United States, architect and designer George Nelson, wrote a book entitled *Tomorrow's House* which became a bible on contemporary living. It showed how entire living environments could be created out of the latest ideas. The "Britain Can Make It" exhibition of 1946 paved the way for the Festival of Britain in 1951 when the concept of light, colour, space and ease of living with open plan interiors, on show for the first time, began to transform the way people thought about their homes. The space race and the atomic age had begun, and both had an influence on design. Much as the heady excitement of the Art Deco period followed the First World War, so the Fifties seemed to hold out the promise of a better life for everyone.

▲ **"CAMPDEN" STAINLESS STEEL COFFEE SET**
*1957; pots 18cm (7¼in) high;* **£120–180**
Robert Welsh, the designer of this innovative stainless steel "Campden" range, was a leading light in the field of metalware during the 1950s in Britain. Many of his designs, including this one, were manufactured by the Old Hall factory who produced cutlery and other tableware. Robert Welsh's designs retailed through Heal's, one of London's top department stores, and this one became a design classic, transforming the image of stainless steel. It won a Design Council award in 1958 and pieces are stamped on the base, "Robert Welsh, Old Hall."

▲ **MIELE PRASIDENT VACUUM CLEANER**
*1952; 55cm (22in) long;* **£80–120**
Many products by Miele brought beauty and classic good German design into the home in the form of basic household gadgets. The idea was that an aesthetically pleasing object like this vacuum cleaner took the sting out of the drudgery of housework. Miele, along with AEG and Braun, have always employed top designers to work in their studios, resulting in a very high standard of industrial design.

▲ **COFFEE SERVICE "511" FOR SCHONWALD**
*1957; coffee pot 23cm (9in) high;* **£80–120**
The waisted form of the pieces and the elongated spout combined with *sgraffito* decoration make this service absolutely typical of late 1950s design. Designed by Heinrich Loffelhardt for German company Schonwald, it won a gold medal at the Milano Triennale XI in 1957. The price includes six cups and saucers. Some of the coffee pots have a base stamp stating that the design was a gold medal winner.

▶ **"ARIEL" VASE**
*c.1958; 12cm (4¾in) high;* **£800–1,000**
This rare vase was made using the so-called Ariel technique of trapping air bubbles within a thick wall of glass to create abstract motifs, made famous by Vicke Lindstrand at Orrefors. He designed the vase for the Swedish factory of Kosta, reflecting the new and exciting ideas of the decade. Scandinavian glass of the period is always evocative of the landscape. Fluid, organic shapes were inspired by ice, water and the domination of the rural over the urban.

### ▲ "DAX" CHAIR BY CHARLES EAMES

*1950; 87cm (34¼in) high;* **£250–350**

The definitive book on Charles Eames contains 15 pages devoted to discussing this chair, originally manufactured by Zenith Plastics. It was the first single-piece-seat chair ever produced in moulded fibreglass, a lightweight material which enabled the chairs to be stacked floor to ceiling at the factory, revolutionizing the process of assembly. Advertising in the Fifties showed families sitting comfortably on "Dax" chairs, either eating or reading, and they continue to be made today with subtle design variations. Early examples have solid steel rather than tubular legs, rubber and metal "glides" on the feet rather than nylon ones, and usually show some signs of wear.

### ▲ "NEPTUNE" CHAIR BY ERNEST RACE

*1953; 152 x 81cm (60 x 32in);* **£800–1,000**

Known as the stacking and folding deckchair, Race's "Neptune" was commissioned by the P&O shipping company for their Orient Line. His brief was to design a modern counterpart to the Victorian deckchair for use on board ship. After the first voyage, the laminate was changed from beech to mahogany. The chairs made for P&O are rare because of their small number, but Race later manufactured them with a birch veneer retailed through Ernest Race Ltd., his showroom. A leading name in British furniture design, he was responsible for the Springbok chair and tables arranged on every terrace at the Festival of Britain in 1951. These survive and are worth between £80–100.

### ◄ "GELTRUDE" VASE BY DINO MARTENS

*1954; 30.2cm (12½in) high;* **£5,000–6,000**

Dino Martens emerged as the leading glass designer in Italy during the Fifties producing unique pieces involving complex production techniques. The stylized form and bright colours typical of his work can be seen in this vase which incorporates *latticinio* work close to the rim and *millefiori* canes. His vases were produced in small numbers, each one an individual piece of sculpture in glass.

### ◄ AMERICAN DESK CLOCK

*c.1955; 13cm (5in) high;* **£150–200**

The Jefferson Electric Co. of Bellwood, Illinois, manufactured this plain, cylindrical desk clock which is very typical of the Fifties. With its stylized face and hands, much influenced by the space race and the atomic age, it sat well in an office or study furnished with pieces by leading American designers such as George Nelson and Charles Eames.

### COLLECTORS' NOTES

• In furniture more than any other collecting area, seek provenance before buying a piece because so many Fifties designs that became classics are still in production today and an original piece is clearly more desirable than a recent reproduction.
• Look for original paper labels or transfer stamps which still survive on many things. The Ernest Race logo, for example, shows a little white house within a green circle.
• Fifties textiles and tableware are still good value and lurk in attics and the back of cupboards in great quantities — but for how much longer?

### COLLECTING TIP

A good piece of Fifties design is an investment. By the year 2000, there will be retrospective exhibitions mounted (many are well into the planning stage) to look at this important decade

# The Sixties

If you sat on a moulded plywood chair sipping Vermouth in the Fifties, by the Sixties (if you were where it was happening), you were sprawling on plastic inflatable seating or bean bags, possibly smoking an illegal substance. The burgeoning youth culture of the Fifties was firmly in place by the Sixties. The music scene was hugely influential and touched every stratum of society, including those at the cutting edge of design, who used pop art, psychedelia and the various materials and advanced production techniques available, to shape the taste of consumers.

America gave us some of the great names in pop, including Jimi Hendrix, The Doors and The Grateful Dead, but it was London which became the centre of the fashionable universe during this decade when a small minority made not only enormous amounts of money but also the fashion statements which reverberated around the world. The growth of sub-culture and the seeds of rebellion were sewn during the Sixties, but the decade also gave us a wide range of products which are still readily available. Increasingly collectable, they are reminders of an extraordinary passage in our history.

▲ **VERNER PANTON TEXTILE**
*c.1968; 1.25m x 1.25m (49 x 49in);* **£200**
The textiles and living environments of the Danish designer Verner Panton are legendary. He designed this typically bright, repeating pattern, entitled Mira X Spectrum, for the company Mira X. Ahead of his time in his representation of psychedelia and alternative modes of living, he designed the first one-piece moulded stacking chair in plastic, and a freestanding tower which sat five people at different levels and angles.

▼ **"VALENTINE" TYPEWRITER BY OLIVETTI**
*1969; 11.4 x 34.4 x 35.1cm (4½ x 13½ x 13¾in);* **£100–150**
The launch of this red typewriter in Italy caused such a sensation that shop windows displayed them stacked floor to ceiling. Its creator, Ettore Sottsass, is one of the most feted designers of the 20th century. The "Valentine" provided the consumer with an affordable cult object and represented a complete rethink on the design of the portable typewriter with its new bright red plastic casing and the handle incorporated into the back rather than fixed to the elegant, loose sleeve cover. Olivetti are considered one of the finest manufacturers of typewriters and other office furniture and many of their products are now collectable.

▲ **BRAUN CK61 RADIOGRAM**
*1962; 58 x 24.5 x 29cm (23 x 9¾ x 11½in);* **£150–200**
Nicknamed Snow White's coffin, this radiogram represented the state of the art in sound equipment in Germany during the Sixties and became a cult object within a short time of its launch. Expensive when new, it combined beauty, function and form, and was designed by Dieter Hans Gugelot and Dieter Rams for Braun, the market leaders in product design.

### ◄ "TOTEM" COFFEE POT BY PORTMEIRION POTTERIES

*1963; 34cm (13½in) high;* **£80–120**
This is one piece from Susan Williams-Ellis's "Totem" coffee service for Portmeirion which became a cult design of the period. She takes the waisted, elongated shapes of the Fifties a step further, intending to evoke primitive beliefs and magic rituals with the long, totem pole-like shape and the moulded abstract motifs on the body. The pottery produced storage cans, coffee jars, vases and a tea and coffee service in blue, olive and rust brown. This white is the rarest and most sought after.

### ► "ASTEROIDE" LAMP FOR POLTRONOVA

*1968; 70cm (27½in) high;* **£2,500–3,000**
When the Museum of Modern Art in New York mounted its 1972 exhibition, "Italy: The New Domestic Landscape; Achievements and Problems Of Italian Design," this Ettore Sottsass lamp manufactured by Poltronova was selected as an icon of modern design. It became an instant classic, and whereas Sottsass's typewriter (*p.188*) was affordable, this was only ever within reach of the wealthier devotee of modern design. Produced in blue and pink, collectors now comb the world in search of one of each.

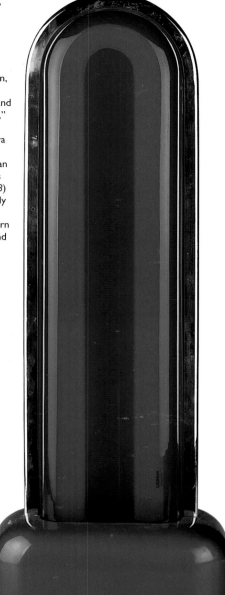

### ► "FIESTA" PLATE BY BARKER BROTHERS

*c.1962; 23cm (9in) diameter;* **£15–20**
Cheap, cheerful and available to all, this stylish range of ceramic tableware was similar to other ranges produced in the Fifties. It shows the type of tableware and cutlery that was fashionable during the Sixties. Much of it survives, having been packed away when it fell out of fashion by the mid-Seventies. It may be some time before prices rise.

### ▼ "CESTO" ITALIAN SILVER FRUIT BASKET

*1964; 15cm (6in) high, 32cm (12½in) wide;* **£150–200**
This elegant fruit basket by Lino Sabattini has a timeless elegance – the hallmark of excellent design – and could just as easily have been first produced in the 1980s as in the Sixties. Sabattini is considered one of the finest silversmiths and designers of his time, working over a long period from the 1950s to the 1980s.

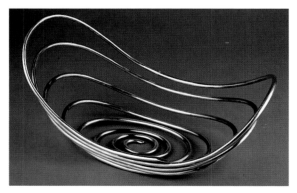

### COLLECTORS' NOTES

• Look at the condition of anything made of plastic. Little can be done to restore it if it is cracked.
• Much plastic of the period has mould marks showing the name of the designer and the manufacturer and sometimes the exact date of manufacture.
• Collectors of Sixties artefacts are often seeking to recreate whole environments and will not mix their cherished objects with anything from a different period. The same can be said of aficionados of Fifties design.
• The Sixties has a devoted following in Italy where much radical design took place. Collectors in the United States and the rest of Europe are now catching up and buying the best examples of Sixties design while it is still available.

### COLLECTING TIP

Look out for the wide and still affordable range of Joe Colombo designs in bright plastics with moulded marks on the base. A chair might cost you £100–150.

# Modern Studio Wares

Having achieved recognition and respectability during the latter part of the 19th century, the studio pottery of this century rapidly gained the status of a decorative art form on a comparable level with painting and sculpture. This was due mainly to the work of one artist – Bernard Leach. He travelled extensively in Japan, studying Japanese crafts, especially those of the potter, eventually marrying his knowledge of Japanese potting and glazing techniques with conventional Western drawing and etching skills to produce highly versatile and imaginative pieces. Perhaps one of the most significant meetings in 20th-century ceramic history took place between Leach and the Japanese potter Shoji Hamada in Japan in 1919. Their lifelong friendship resulted in many significant pieces being produced at Leach's St. Ives pottery, where Hamada worked for three years.

Probably the most important work in the early period following the end of the Second World War was carried out by Lucie Rie, an Austrian who moved to Britain during the 1930s. Her protegé was Hans Coper – acclaimed by many as the most original ceramic artist of the 20th century. Their output, among that of many others, makes the contemporary studio pottery market a fertile and thriving area which continues to attract new collectors. Much of the work, especially by young potters, is affordable. Providing you buy pieces you like, there is much enjoyment to be had from judging who may become the most highly regarded potters of the 21st century, and buying their work.

**▼ EARTHENWARE SALAD BOWL BY MICHAEL CARDEW**
*c.1935; 34.4cm (13⅝in) diameter;* **£4,000–6,000**
Michael Cardew became apprenticed to Bernard Leach at his St. Ives pottery in Cornwall in 1923, setting up his own pottery near Winchcombe in Gloucestershire in 1926. He concentrated on making domestic wares with slip-trailed decoration. This salad bowl is covered in a shiny ochre glaze, decorated in *sgraffito* with a bird. The impressed initials "MC" and the Winchcombe seals appear on the base, accompanied by a label in Cardew's own handwriting.

**▲ LARGE STONEWARE CHARGER BY BERNARD LEACH**
*c.1970; 34cm (13½in) diameter;* **£1,800–2,500**
Leach made this piece towards the end of his long working life. The wax-resist decoration depicts a bird in flight in the centre of the charger, and the entire dish is covered in a temmoku glaze. These black or dark brown glazes are found on 10th–13th century (Sung dynasty) Chinese stoneware. Japanese and Korean methods of decorating are very apparent in Leach's work – a result of the time he spent travelling and studying in those countries.

**◄ TWO STONEWARE VESSELS BY ELIZABETH FRITSCH**
*1974; 38cm (15in) high;* **£3,500–4,500**
*1976; 24.3cm (9½in) high;* **£2,500–3,500**
Created a Dame in 1995, Elizabeth Fritsch is one of the most highly regarded British potters working today. Born in 1940 in Wales, she studied harp and piano at the Royal Academy of Music in London, and weaves a sense of musical rhythm into her ceramic pieces. One critic declared that "her pots are almost to be viewed as still lives... ."

### ◄ BLACK CYCLADIC VESSEL FORM BY HANS COPER

*c.1975; 30cm (11¾in) high;* **£18,000–25,000**
As much works of sculpture as pots, Hans Coper pieces are usually referred to as "forms." This piece, mounted on a drum base and impressed with the "HC" seal, was included in his final exhibition at the Robert Welch Gallery in Gloucestershire in the west of England. Coper originally wanted to be a sculptor. After the war he met Lucie Rie who recognized his extraordinary talents. He became expert at potting, using clay to make both pottery and sculpture, uniting the two media. He continued to draw, paint and sculpt throughout his career.

### ▲ PORCELAIN BOWL BY DAME LUCIE RIE

*c.1982; 16cm (6¼in) diameter;* **£4,000–6,000**
The elegant work of Dame Lucie Rie constitutes some of the most recognizable of all studio pottery produced this century. She died in 1995 at the age of 93 having lived in Britain since moving there from Austria in 1939. She was much influenced by Bernard Leach and shared a studio for many years with Hans Coper. This deep emerald green bowl is flecked with manganese and has a runny golden band of thick glaze at the rim. It was fired to a critical temperature to achieve this effect.

### ▲ TEMMOKU STONEWARE POT BY SHOJI HAMADA

*c.1960; 20.5cm (8in) high;* **£3,500–4,500**
Strong, functional shapes and soft colours characterize much of Shoji Hamada's work. This can be seen in this stoneware pot with circular neck and feet, which has been cutsided and each corner embellished with rust brown vertical decoration. The work Hamada completed during the three-year period he spent with Bernard Leach is the most sought after by collectors.

### ► CIRCULAR EARTHENWARE VESSEL BY JAMES TOWER

*1983; 52.8cm (20¼in) diameter;* **£2,500–3,500**
Born in Kent in southeast England, James Tower studied painting at the Royal Academy school and The Slade school in London. He was associated with the Institute of Education group during the 1950s, where he developed the methods of tin-glaze decoration that can be seen so beautifully in this hollow, circular vessel with its deep brown and white painterly lines.

### ◄ THREE EARTHENWARE VESSELS BY CHRISTINE JONES

*1996; tallest 46cm (18⅛in) high; yellow 24.8cm (9¾in) high; blue slender 51.1cm (20⅛in) high;* **£350–550 each**
These coiled, plain, matt earthenware vessels are the hallmark of Christine Jones's work, although she sometimes applies linear decoration in constrasting colours to her pieces. Born in 1955, she works in Wales and examples of her work are exhibited at the Sainsbury Centre for Visual Arts in Norwich, East Anglia. Small pieces by her are still affordable.

### COLLECTORS' NOTES

• Equip yourself with a handbook of potters' marks and seals. Many potters impress their work with a monogram or initials, often within a small square or rectangular outline. More important pieces not only show the mark of the potter but of the pottery itself. Avoid buying unmarked pieces.
• Some studio pottery is both robust and useable. A cider barrel made by Cardew was intended to be a utilitarian item; a Shoji Hamada teapot was designed to pour tea and Lucie Rie liked to think of all her pots being used. Few collectors today, however, take the risk!
• Be wary of pieces signed "HC" as there are some Hans Coper fakes on the market. Bernard Leach's work has also been widely faked. The only way to be sure of what you are buying is to seek the advice of an expert.

### COLLECTING TIP

Inscribed pots dedicated to the original owner and signed and dated by the potter will always attract a premium.

# Rock and Pop

Two decades ago, a book like this would not have included any mention of rock and pop. The first sale devoted to memorabilia of the popular music scene took place in 1981 and heralded a vigorous new area in the world of collecting. Records, autographs, clothes, posters and musical instruments now change hands at regular auctions for large sums of money. Objects relating to the Beatles command the highest prices worldwide, with other major artists such as Elvis Presley, the Rolling Stones and Jimi Hendrix following closely behind. Pieces relating to the stars of the Sixties and Seventies are often prohibitively expensive, but an absorbing pastime is seeking out the pop collectables of the future by following the bands of today.

**▲ DEMO COPY OF THE BEATLES' "LOVE ME DO"**
*1963; 17.5cm (7in);* **£8,000–10,000**
This is the demo copy of the Beatles' first single, "Love Me Do," stored in the Radio Luxembourg record library until 1976. Radio Luxembourg was the only radio station playing "pop" music at the time. This actual copy of "Love me Do" was the first Beatles record to be broadcast on the radio. In the centre is the library reference number of the station, hand-written timings and Paul McCartney's autograph. Without the autograph, the 45 demo would still be highly prized, but it provides a fascinating extra dimension.

**◄ ELVIS PRESLEY BURNING LOVE STAGE SUIT**
*Early 1970s; 165cm (65in) collar to trouser hem;* **£70,000–90,000**
The king of rock'n'roll commands such a devoted following that an estimate of this magnitude on a significant item of clothing should not be greeted with shock. This was his only red suit, voted number one by his fans. A dark red wool-knit one-piece jumpsuit with a zipper front, decorated all over with gold metal stud-work, it was featured on the cover of his last chart-topping single, "Burning Love," and he can be seen wearing it in the film *Elvis On Tour*.

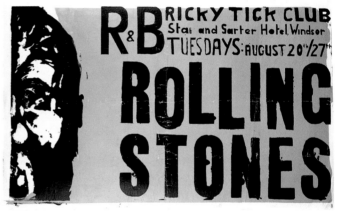

**▲ ROLLING STONES POSTER**
*c.1963; 51 x 76cm (20 x 30in);* **£800–1,200**
These early silk screen posters from the Sixties represent a new direction in poster making, with dramatic black lettering against brightly coloured backgrounds. These were the days when British bands like The Who and the Rolling Stones were still travelling about in bashed up vans and feeling grateful for every booking they got. The Ricky Tick Club at the Star and Garter Hotel in Windsor, Buckinghamshire was one of the main venues of the time.

**► CONCERT POSTERS**
*1967; both 38 x 76cm (15 x 30in);* **£250–450 each**
Psychedelia was a Sixties' inno-vation and thousands of concert posters used the technique to its best effect. These posters, produced by Hapshash and the Coloured Coat, are advertising bands playing at the legendary UFO club. On the left is a Pink Floyd poster, the one on the right lists forthcoming attractions.

### ◀ JIMI HENDRIX'S GIBSON FLYING V GUITAR NO. 932954
*1969; 105cm (41in) long;* **£50,000–60,000**

### JIMI HENDRIX'S ORANGE FLORAL VELVET JACKET
*1967; 86cm (34in) chest size;* **£30,000–40,000**

Jimi Hendrix memorabilia sells for staggering amounts of money, often to restaurants or large institutions involved in the music business who then display them to the public. He became successful only a short while before his premature death, but was one of the most significant figures in the Sixties rock scene. Whole books have been written itemizing his life in minute, daily detail and artefacts relating to him are highly prized. He was first photographed playing this guitar in Madison Square Garden in 1969, and the jacket was a well-worn favourite. Labelled inside, "Dandie Fashions, Inc., London," he was first photographed wearing it at Newcastle City Hall on December 4, 1967.

### ▶ MADONNA COAT
*1980s; 140cm (55in) long;*
**£3,000–4,000**

One of the most important aspects of rock and pop memorabilia is being able to authenticate artefacts, and a coat like this is so much easier to vouch for than some garments of indeterminate origin. Long, black and velvet, it was owned and worn on stage by Madonna. Her logo, the letter "M" in red velvet on gold, is applied to the back and the cuffs are decorated with crosses in the same colours.

### ▲ COPYRIGHT NEGATIVE
*1984; 35 x 35mm (1⅜ x 1⅜in);* **£80–100**

This is a copyright negative showing the progressive rock band Twelfth Night headlining an open air festival in 1984 that was subsequently used on the cover of their greatest hits CD released in 1991. Photographs and negatives with copyright are a growth area at the moment and still within reach of the collector on a budget. The demand for new photographs that offer fans something never seen before is becoming greater. Biggest sellers relate to the legendary bands, but all photographs relating to artists with a dedicated cult following are desirable.

### COLLECTORS' NOTES
• Good provenance, such as photographs, can add enormously to the value of an item. Without it many pieces are worthless.
• In costume terms, a garment that has been worn on stage or even in the recording studio, is more interesting than some favourite old jumper that has only been worn by the star at home.
• Beware of guitars signed on the scratch- or finger-plate. Ruthless autograph hunters sometimes get stars to sign a small piece of plastic and then fix it to the guitar and sell it for a fortune.
• It helps if musical instruments are relevant to the star – guitars belonging to guitarists, drum kits to drummers, keyboards to keyboard players, and so on. In general, microphones do not sell well.
• John Lennon and Paul McCartney memorabilia is more popular than George Harrison and Ringo Starr pieces.
• Unpublished lyrics by the major stars have risen greatly in value over the last few years. The highest price paid to date was £161,000 for John Lennon's "Getting Better."
• There has been a rise in prices for posters or period pieces such as merchandising for particular bands.

### COLLECTING TIP
The Hard Rock Café chain worldwide and the Hard Rock Hotel and Casino in Las Vegas house the largest and best collections of rock'n'roll and pop memorabilia anywhere.

# Collectables of the Future

Nothing is more satisfying than buying a piece which you like and enjoy and later discovering it has doubled in value. But what makes an item collectable?

Good design is probably the first criterion of collectability. Something that is stylish, well-made and suitable for its function, if it has one, will hold its value better than an ill-made or ugly item. If it has been made by a top designer, and is marked, so much the better. Objects which are very much of their time make good investments, just as many stylish Art Deco items have a strong market today, being so redolent of the 1920s. However, many items that fetch high prices today – for example, valentine cards, were inexpensive when made and never intended to last and yet are now highly sought-after. Predicting which of today's throw-aways or disposables will be collectable in the future is perhaps even harder than recognizing good design – but at least the investment is low.

The items on the first two pages of this section represent stylish but affordable design and may well prove to be excellent investments as well. On the other two pages are some very inexpensive – or even free – objects which you can enjoy now and which may have a good chance of increasing in value – it's anybody's guess.

#### ▲ ALESSI KETTLE
*1984; 24cm (9½in) high;* **current retail £90**
This charming kettle with its bird-shaped whistle spout was designed by Michael Graves and produced by Alessi as one of their most successful pieces. Although highly decorative, it has been designed for practicality – the body is of stainless steel; the handle-cover, knob and whistle are in heat-resistant polyamide.

#### ▲ JEAN PAUL GAULTIER PERFUME
*1994; 16cm (6¼in) high;* **current retail £46.50**
Gaultier's torso-shaped perfume and aftershave bottles caused a sensation when they were released in 1994. In this example, the outer dress comes off to reveal a clear glass bottle. Other versions are dressed in pop star Madonna's famous bustier! If you want yours to hold its value though, it will be a case of look but don't open.

#### ◄ DEAN'S TEDDY
*1995; 24cm (9½in) high;*
**current value £80**
Teddy bears have been the collecting phenomenon of recent years, with some older ones fetching hundreds of thousands of pounds – so look after yours carefully. This bear was made as one of a limited edition by the English firm of Dean's Rag Book Co. Ltd., established in 1903, and known for the high quality of their products. As well as the usual Dean's label on his right foot, he also has a tie-on label stating the number made and giving other details.

#### ▲ CAITHNESS PAPERWEIGHTS
*Left to right: 1996; 110mm (4⅜in) diameter;* **£795;** *1995; 78mm (3in) diameter;* **£50;** *1996; 78mm (3in) diameter;* **£34.50 all current retail**
The Scottish firm, Caithness, founded in 1969, are best known for their paperweights. The large "Neptune's Kingdom" is from a limited edition of 10; the inkwell weight, still made today, is very collectable; while the "Moonflower" weight is available in a variety of colours.

## ▶ WEDGWOOD LIMITED EDITION CLARICE CLIFF "AGE OF JAZZ" FIGURE
*1993; 20cm (8in) high;*
**current value £300**
Clarice Cliff was one of the most successful potters of the 20th century. This hand-painted dancing "Age of Jazz" figure produced by the top firm of Wedgwood in 1993, is a reproduction of a popular early design. It was made in a limited edition of 300 and comes with a certificate and box. Highly sought-after when first released, their value has already significantly climbed from the 1993 purchase price of £175.

## ▲ MISS SISSI LAMP
*1990s; 25.5 cm (10in) high;*
**current retail £49**
This electric blue lamp comes from a range of lighting by the top French designer Philippe Starck. It is made in a variety of sizes and colours, including yellow, orange, purple and emerald green, and has a time-less appeal that will ensure it remains fashionable for a long time to come.

## ▲ MOORCROFT VASE
*1996; 35.5cm (14in) high;*
**current retail £395**
This tall vase is the largest in the "Lamia" range designed for the Moorcroft factory by Rachel Bishop. A Moorcroft piece is a sound investment and there is no reason why a vase such as this should not appreciate in value in the future just as Art Nouveau pieces have in the past.

## ◀ "JUICY SALIF" LEMON SQUEEZER; *1988; 29cm (11½in) high;* **current retail £44**
With its super-modern form, this cast aluminium lemon squeezer, designed by Philippe Starck and manufactured by Alessi, has already become an icon of the 90s. Mass-produced but to a high standard, and very much of its time, this is the type of object likely to become even more collectable in the future.

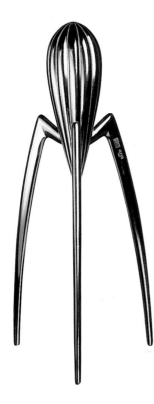

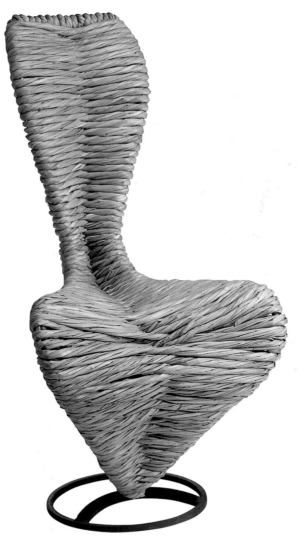

## ▲ THE 'S' CHAIR
*1987; 1m (39⅓in) high;* **current retail £950**
This sensational one-piece wicker chair was made by British designer Tom Dixon. They are now being manufactured by the Italian firm of Cappellini, who also produce a range in velvet upholstery. As a result those produced before mass-production have already increased in value.

# *More Collectables of the Future*

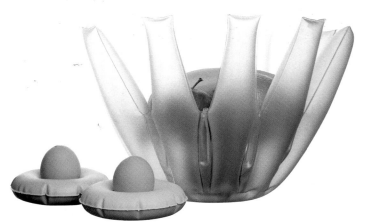

**▲ INFLATABLE FRUIT BOWL AND EGG CUPS**
*1996; fruit bowl 21cm (8¼in) high; £19.50; egg cups 11.5cm (4½in) diameter; £14.50 for four*
Today's designers are becoming ever-more ingenious. This unusual fruit bowl and the egg cups are made of inflatable plastic! They come in a range of colours and being stylish as well as practical, are bound to increase in value, especially once designs are updated in the future.

**▲ CHARM BRACELET**
*1995; 20cm (7¾in) long; £16*
Not all souvenirs are collectable, but this lovely charm bracelet has greater appeal than most. Still in its Warner Brothers box, it has eight charms showing different aspects of movie-making, from a film reel to a director's seat. This model sold out very quickly, something that could bode well for its future collectability. The company manufacture other charm bracelets but, at present, there are no plans for this one to be reproduced.

**◄ KINDER EGGS**
*From 1970s; 5cm (2in) high* **50p**
The tiny plastic toys that come in kit form inside these chocolate eggs are truly ingenious and may well rise in value over the years, especially as individual models are phased out.

**▲ KODAK DISPOSABLE "FUN" CAMERA**
*1990s; 7.5cm (3in) high; £9*
Many of the leading camera manufacturers have also produced a line of disposable cameras in recent years, in various degrees of sophistication. Some have a built-in flash. Others, like this one by Kodak, are waterproof. Most have a standard 27-frame film for colour pictures. When the film is developed some parts of the camera are saved and recycled. Those still in their original, unopened box will command a premium in years to come.

**▲ VIDEO GAMES**
*1990s; 10 x 6cm (4 x 2½in) £30–50*
Computer video games are very much a 90s phenomenon. Each in its way is a limited edition as they are updated regularly, making the previous version obsolete. The skill is in trying to spot which games will endure and buying the first edition of them. If you want to enjoy them though, buy two, one to play and one to keep.

## ▲ FAST FOOD CHARACTERS
*1990s; Winged figure 11cm (4¼in) high;* **free with food purchases**
These plastic toys were made by a variety of fast food chains, including McDonalds and Burger King. Some have a simple key-wind mechanism enabling them to move. Unpopular sets are quickly replaced, the small numbers of them made ensuring their popularity with collectors in the future.

## ▼ PHONE CARDS
*1990s; 5 x 8.5cm (2 x 3⅜in);* **in denominations from £2–20**
The earliest phone cards now fetch thousands of pounds at auction. Look for those promoting a specific event or product – and don't take them out of the packet if you want them to hold their value!

## ▼ FOOTBALLER FIGURES
*1996; 7cm (2¾in) high;* **£1.99 each**
These footballers can be bought individually or in sets, although only a few complete teams are available. Manchester United, shown here, won the 1996 Football Premier League and FA Cup, and as the winning team will be more collectable in the future.

## ▼ CRISP PACKETS AND TAZOS
*1996; Tazos 4cm (1½in) diameter;* **35p each**
Who would have thought that crisp packets could ever become collectable – but they are! And the small plastic toys and other give-aways are being avidly collected and swapped by today's younger entrepreneurs, who in the case of these plastic discs, can increase the value of their set by sending away for a special display album for them.

## ▶ JURASSIC PARK
*c.1995; 5cm (2in) high;* **£3.50**
The most popular films inspire a host of spin-off toys and other merchandise. *Jurassic Park*, a Steven Spielberg film, was an enormous success in 1993, setting box office records. This set of diecast metal dinosaurs also includes two collectors' cards, which build up into a full set. However, how much they increase in value over the years remains to be seen.

### COLLECTING TIPS
• Always keep any packaging and documentation that comes with your purchase, especially if they show confirmation of a limited edition as this is something which always puts the value up for collectors.
• The trick in collecting the collectables of the future is to be one step ahead of everybody else. Search for a new collecting theme with a ready supply at a reasonable price and avoid diving into a long established collectables market as there is little point adopting a collecting interest already pursued by the masses.
• Look closely at functional objects that blend into modern day interiors as these may well become collectable in the future.
• As with all collecting, it is most important that you like your chosen subject. The secret is to be bold, follow your own instincts and don't let others influence you.
• Remember, we live in the design label age, but only a few designers will stand the test of time. The fun is in acquiring what will eventually prove to be timeless design.

# Glossary

**Acanthus** The most widely used plant form employed as a motif in the decorative arts, based on the thick, scalloped leaves of the acanthus plant. Forms part of the capital of the Corinthian and Composite Orders.

**Air twist** Formed by twisting a rod of glass in which columns of air are trapped to produce a decorative stem. Used mainly in 18th-century English wine glasses.

**Annealing** The process of gradually cooling a completed glass object. The thick and thin parts cool at a uniform rate and the development of stresses within the vessel are thus eliminated.

**Apostle spoon** A silver spoon terminating in a handle modelled as one of the Apostles, made in England and Germany between 1490 and 1675. In sets of 13 incorporating a dozen topped with the 12 Apostles and the Master spoon, with the figure of Christ.

**Art Deco** The first truly modern style which made full use of mechanised production and new materials. The name derives from the first major exhibition of decorative arts held after the First World War in 1925, *L'Exposition Internationale des Arts Decoratifs et Industriels Modernes*.

**Art Nouveau** The new style, short-lived and excessive, which thrived between c.1880 and 1914. Characterised by curving, swirling, organic forms and, particularly, the whiplash motif, the name derives from a shop opened by Bing in Paris in 1895. Known in Italy as "stile Liberty," in Germany and Scandinavia as "Jugendstil" and "Secession" in Austria.

**Arts & Crafts** A 19th-century movement, led by William Morris and his artist and designer companions in England which sought to challenge increasing industrialization by re-introducing the medieval concepts of craftsmanship.

**Assay** The testing of a metal or ore to determine its ingredients and quality.

**Astragal** A small semi-circular moulding around the top or bottom of a column. Also used to describe the glazing bars of bookcases and other case furniture.

**Automata** Moving figures operated by a mechanical device, made as early as the 5th century BC, later used to decorate clocks and later still, in the 19th century, as toys for both adults and children.

**Bakelite** The trade name for the first truly synthetic resin, phenol formaldehyde or phenolic, developed by the German chemist Leo Baekland and patented in 1907.

**Baluster** An architectural term used to describe a short post or pillar, originally referring to one of the upright supports of a classical balustrade. Usually circular and undulating in shape, the word is also used to describe the shape of wine glass stems, furniture legs and coffee pots.

**Banding** Small sections or strips of *veneer* applied to furniture and other wooden objects. Cross banding is laid in short sections at right angles to the main veneer,

straight banding is applied in one long strip, feather or herringbone banding consists of two narrow strips of diagonally banded veneers placed together to give a feather-like appearance.

**Batch** Used in the glass making industry to describe the measured raw materials which, when heated in the furnace, become glass.

**Bergère** A wing armchair with filled-in sides which became popular from c.1725, with a caned seat and sides. Later examples were upholstered.

**Biedermeier** A German style, popular from the 1820s to 1840s mainly seen in furniture which is plain, solid and usually light in colour being of maple, cherry or apple wood. Based on French Empire, the style is plainer and less ostentatious.

**Bone china** A type of porcelain containing 25% china stone, 25% china clay and 50% ground cattle bones. Made extensively in England from the early 19th century and still produced today.

**Bracket clock** Made in England from the late 17th century, a type of portable clock designed to sit on a bracket fixed to the wall or on a table.

**Bracket foot** A simple bracket-shaped support for cabinets and chests of drawers used from c.1690 onwards.

**Breakfront or broken front** Furniture where the line at the front is broken or interrupted. Usually the central section projects slightly in front of the side sections. Most commonly found on bookcases and cabinets.

**Bun feet** In the form of a flattened ball, used on furniture from the late 17th century.

**Cabriole leg** An elongated "S" shape leg on furniture, often with a pronounced "knee" which is carved. Its origins may be a Chinese bronze altar vessel on three legs which first appeared at the end of the first millennium BC.

**Capital** The head of a column. *See Orders.*

**Carriage clock** A truly portable type of clock, designed to be taken on journeys. Made in great quantities in France in the 19th century and usually supplied with a leather carrying case.

**Caryatid** A decorative support in the form of a female figure, derived from Greek architecture and used since the Renaissance. The style was revived during the Rococo and Neo-classical periods and is found on English Regency furniture. Male caryatids are known as telamones.

**Cellaret** A deep box, usually lockable, in which wine was stored in bottles, first made during the 18th century. Either free standing or incorporated into a sideboard in the form of a lead-lined drawer.

**Celluloid** A transparent flammable plastic made from camphor and cellulose nitrate patented by brothers John Wesley and Isaiah Hyatt in the United States in 1869. Used

mainly to imitate tortoiseshell, horn and ivory in the production of cutlery handles, cigarette cases, combs etc, but also used for dolls.

**Chapter ring** The part of the dial of a clock or watch on which the numbers are marked.

**Chippendale** The generic term used to describe furniture in the style associated with the English designer Thomas Chippendale (1718–79) who published the first comprehensive book of furniture designs, *The Gentleman & Cabinet Maker's Director* (1754, 1755, 1762).

**Chronograph** An instrument for recording time with immense accuracy.

**Cire perdue (lost wax process)** A process used in casting bronze and in glassmaking. A model of the object to be cast is carved in wax and then enclosed in a clay mould which is baked so that the wax melts and is "lost." The mould is then filled with the molten metal. Once cooled, the mould has to be broken in order to retrieve the object.

**Claw and ball foot** Used on furniture, in the form of talons holding a ball. Oriental in origin, the dragon's claw was replaced in Europe by an eagle's claw.

**Cockbead** Small semi-circular section moulding applied to drawer fronts on mid-to late 18th-century English furniture, particularly mahogany and walnut examples.

**Commode** The french word for a low chest of drawers dating from the mid-17th century and made in various forms during the 18th century on the Continent, in England and in the United States. From the 19th century, the term was also used to describe a bedroom cupboard incorporating a portable latrine.

**Composition a.** A mixture of whiting, resin and size rather similar to gesso, which, while still pliable, was pressed into moulds and hardened. Thereafter it could be applied to surfaces to be decorated and embellished, such as picture frames and ceilings. **b.** A doll-making medium similar to papier-mâché.

**Crazing** A defect in ceramics resulting in the formation of a network of fine lines on the glaze caused by different rates of contraction in the body and the glaze during firing or because of an extreme change in temperature.

**Crewel work** A bold colourful type of needlework created by embroidering in wools on beige or white linen grounds, copying Indian designs. Used for bed hangings and curtains in the late 17th and early 18th centuries, the design is denser on earlier examples.

**Crisselling (or crizzelling)** The state of progressive deterioration in the chemical make up of glass caused by a faulty balance in the ingredients. Droplets of alkaline moisture form on the surface and a fine network of cracks develops.

**Cymric** The name given to the range of silver designed by top names such as Archibald Knox and Rex Silver launched by Arthur Lasenby Liberty in 1894 and made by the Birmingham firm of William Haseler.

**Delftware** Tin-glazed earthenware, first made in the late 16th century which takes its name from the Dutch town of Delft. The term is also used to describe the wares of this type made in England. (See *maiolica* and *faïence*).

**Devitrification** A state of deterioration which occurs when glass is cooled too slowly and becomes crystalline with a milky appearance. Not to be confused with crisselling.

**Diamante** Sparkling cut glass, often backed with foil, or a backing applied with powdered crystal, used to decorate costume and in costume jewellery.

**Dovetail** A right-angled joint on a piece of furniture in use by the end of the 15th century. The two sections are held together by the projecting tenon which fits into a corresponding cut-out section known as a mortise.

**Dowels** The pegs holding together the mortise and tenon joints in early furniture.

**Dumb waiter** First introduced around 1725, a piece of dining room furniture consisting of a central stand supporting, usually, three tiers of circular trays which was placed near the table and laden with food and drink to enable diners to dismiss the servants and serve themselves.

**Earthenware** A porous piece of pottery made from clay, lightly fired and still pervious to liquids. A glaze is needed to make it waterproof.

**Ebonized** Cheaper woods such as deal and pine blackened in order to imitate the expensive ebony native to Asia and Africa.

**Electroplating** A method of covering wares made with base metal with a thin layer of silver by the process of electrolysis, patented by G. R. Elkington in 1840 in England.

**Enamel** Powdered glass mixed with a flux to aid the melting process, and a metallic oxide pigment to give colour. Enamels have been used to decorate metals from very early times, applied in paste or powder form and fused to the body in a small kiln.

**Engraving** A method of decorating either a metal or glass object by cutting into the surface with a sharp tool or a set of revolving copper wheels. The technique dates back to ancient times.

**Entrelacs** An intertwining decorative motif used in the Art Nouveau period.

**Épergne** The term for a centre piece for a dining table consisting of a stand holding a single central dish and several smaller dishes for sweetmeats and fruit. Made from silver, Sheffield plate and sometimes glass.

**Escapement** The means by which the power which drives a clock or watch is controlled, allowing it to "escape" at regular intervals with the same time interval between each impulse.

**Escutcheon** The decorative metal plates which protect keyholes in cabinet furniture.

**Etagère** Originally a set of shelves, wall-mounted, used for displaying objects. During the 19th century, it began to be referrred to as a whatnot but the term is still often used by experts and dealers to describe free-standing display units.

**Etui** A small covered container, often with a fitted interior, which contained useful objects such as needlework accessories, which could be carried in a pocket or hung from a chatelaine.

**Excelsior** Soft wood shavings used for stuffing soft toys and teddy bears.

**Façon de Venise** Term used to describe Venetian style glass made in other parts of Europe, notably England, Holland and Germany during the late 16th and 17th centuries.

**Faïence** The French word for tin-glazed earthenware and probably derived from the Italian, Faenza.

**Fairings** Small, brightly painted and captioned porcelain figure groups, mass produced in Germany and originally sold at fairs and seaside stalls at the end of the last century and into this one. Cheap at the time, they are now much sought after.

*Famille rose, Famille verte* Describes the palette of enamel colours, the first dominated by pink and the second by green, which appeared on Chinese porcelain during the 17th and 18th centuries.

**Fauteuil** The French word for a chair with arms, which came into use in France in the second half of the 17th century to mean an upholstered chair with open arms either of plain wood or incorporating elbow pads with a curved or flat back.

**Favrile** The trade name given by Louis Comfort Tiffany of New York to his range of iridescent glassware.

**Federal Style** An American style, mostly seen in furniture, which came into being after the Declaration of Independence in 1776 and following the Neo-classical style in Europe.

**Feldspar** White china stone, a silicate of potassium and aluminium.

**Feldspathic glaze** Used on ceramic wares and made from powdered feldspar, lime, potash and sand and fired at a very high temperature to fuse it to the body.

**Flashed glass** A thin layer of coloured glass is applied by dipping a piece in a contrasting colour to the body of the glass.

**Flatbacks** Pottery figures and figure groups made for the mantelpieces of modest homes, designed to be viewed from the front only with unmodelled, undecorated flat backs.

**Flatware** In silver terms, cutlery, and in ceramic terms, pieces which are relatively flat such as plates, dishes and saucers.

**Fluting** Narrow, vertical, concave indentations often used as a decorative embellishment on furniture or on the shaft of a column. On glass, a cut pattern of round or mitred parallel grooves.

**Flux** An alkaline material which promotes the fusion of ingredients in a glass batch.

**Folding rim** Most commonly found on the foot of wine glasses, a double thickness of glass forming a narrow border around the edge to give strength and minimize the risk of chipping.

**Foot rim** Found on the bottom of glass objects, a slightly projecting rim on which the object stands.

**Forest glass** Also known as *verre de fougère* or *Waldglas*, glass made in wooded areas of Europe where the ash of burnt wood or ferns provided the alkali content of this greenish, brownish or yellowish glass of primitive quality.

**Fretwork** Decorative, open-work designs cut out of wood with a fret-saw or carved, geometric patterns of intersecting lines on wood, either pierced or in relief forming continuous bands.

**Frit** The cooled and ground ingredients of glass which are added to the other ingredients to facilitate the fusion of the batch.

**Gadrooning** Continuous convex curves or reeding on metalwork, furniture and ceramics, used to create a border or edging on a curved surface such as a rim.

**Garniture** A set of ornaments, usually vases, consisting of three, five or seven pieces, comprising an odd number of baluster vases and covers with an even number of cylindrical or waisted vases.

**Gather** In glassmaking, the blob of soft glass from the furnace on the end of the *pontil rod* or blow pipe before the object is formed.

**Gauge** Term used in metalwork to describe the thickness of a piece of sheet metal.

**Gesso** A type of plaster applied to carved wood as a base before painting or gilding.

**Glaze** The glass-like coating of varying colour, thickness and opacity which renders ceramic objects impervious to liquids.

**Gothic** An architectural style characterized by the pointed arch, the rib vault and the flying buttress. It originally flourished from the 11th to the 15th centuries but was revived subsequently, particularly between c.1750–70 and 1800–75.

**Hallmark** The complete set of stamps put onto a piece of silver or gold as a guarantee of its standard of purity.

**Hard-paste porcelain** Also known as true porcelain. Ceramic objects made from kaolin (china clay) and fusible feldspathic rock (petuntse).

**Highboy** The American equivalent of the English tallboy. See **Tallboy**.

*Humpen* Large, cylindrical German drinking

glasses, often lidded and decorated, made during the 17th and 18th centuries.

**Hunter-cased watch** A pocket watch with a hinged metal cover to protect the dial, so called because they were used during hunting on horseback. A half-hunter has a circular opening in the centre of the lid with a *chapter ring* engraved around it so that the time could be read without exposing the full dial.

**Imari** The Japanese porcelain painted in the distinctive palette of iron red, underglaze blue and gilding, first made in the late 17th century in Arita and shipped to Europe from the port of Imari.

**Incised decoration** Decoration which is cut into the body of an object with a sharp metal point.

**Intaglio** Incised decoration in which the design is sunk in relief below the surface. Seals are mostly commonly cut in this way.

**Iridescent glass** Glassware which is coloured in such a way as to give a rainbow effect when viewed from different angles and in different lights. Iridescent glass was first exhibited in 1893.

**Ironstone** A hard, white opaque stoneware, made by adding glassy ironstone slag to the ingredients for hard-paste porcelain.

**Iznik** Turkish pottery of red clay coated with white slip or tin-glazed and painted in bright colours, made from the 15th century at a group of factories in Iznik, around 60 miles southeast of Istanbul.

**Jardinière** A stand, usually ornamental, designed to hold flower pots in either wood, ceramic or metal.

**Kapok** The fine, fibrous cotton-like substance surrounding the seeds of the tree, *Ceiba pentandra*, used for stuffing soft toys.

**Kick** In glassmaking, the concavity at the base of an object where it has been pushed in by the pontil rod.

**Knop** The swelling in the stem of a wine glass or a decorative knob in turned wood, ivory or ceramic.

**Lappet** A small flap or fold of a garment.

**Lithography** The process of obtaining prints from a stone or metal surface treated so that the desired image can be inked while the remaining areas reject the ink.

**Loading** A metalwork term used to describe the pitch or resin added to the base of an object made of thinly gauged metal, often silver candlesticks, to add weight and stability.

**Longcase clock** A tall, narrow clock with a base which sits on the floor. Also known as a grandfather or, in the US, tallcase clock.

**Lowboy** The American term for an 18th-century dressing table or low chest of drawers often with high cabriole legs, made to match a highboy.

**Lug handle** A handle on an object which is too small to be of great practical purpose and therefore has more the appearance of a projection.

**Lustreware** A type of decoration on glass or ceramics achieved by depositing a thin film of metal onto the glaze in the form of silver, gold, copper or platinum.

**Maiolica** The tin-glazed earthenware of Italy produced from the 13th century. Not to be confused with Majolica.

**Majolica** The earthenware covered in bright, lead glazes produced in England and the United States during the 19th century.

**Marquetry** An ornamental pattern on the surface of an object created by laying together shaped pieces of coloured veneers or slivers of tortoiseshell or ivory, mother-of-pearl or metals.

**Matting** Creating a matt surface on a clock dial or on a piece of silver by punching it closely with small dots or circles.

**Ming** The dynasty which ruled China from 1368 to 1644.

**Monochrome** A term used by dealers and experts to describe pieces decorated in only one colour or in different tones of the same colour, or in black and white.

**Mortise and tenon joint** Formed by cutting a hole, or mortise, in one piece of wood into which is fitted a projecting section called a tenon, from another. The joint is then glued or held by a wooden dowel. In use since the 16th century.

**Neo-classical** The style which dominated Europe during the late 18th century, inspired by the architecture and ornament of ancient Greece and Rome following the excavations at Herculaneum and Pompeii.

**Nozzle** Detachable top part of a candle-stick which holds the candle and prevents the wax from pouring down the stem.

**Ogee** A continuous double curve in the shape of an "S" used for mouldings and to describe the bowl of a wine glass of a particular shape.

**Orders** The Five Orders describe the different styles of classical column – Tuscan, Doric, Ionic, Corinthian and Composite.

**Ormolu** The term used to describe bronze which has been gilded with an amalgam of mercury and gold. The piece was then fired to drive off the mercury, leaving the gold adhering to the bronze.

**Papier-mâché** A pulp made from paper mixed with glue, chalk and sometimes sand which hardens after moulding and baking and can then be painted and lacquered. It was first fashioned into objects during the 17th century in France and was a highly popular medium during the 19th century in England.

**Parcel gilt** The term used to describe a piece of furniture or metalwork which is partially gilded.

**Parquetry** The same technique employed in the formation of marquetry, but laid in a strictly geometric pattern created by using contrasting grains or colours of woods.

**Pate** A circular section which is placed just inside the hole in the crown of a doll's head, usually made of cork, card or composition, and to which the wig is subsequently fitted.

**Pâte-de-verre** Glass ground to a paste and wedged into a mould before being fired at a high temperature to create objects which have a sculpted appearance. Pieces were sometimes carved when cool.

**Pâte-sur-pâte** Meaning, literally, paste on paste. Designs and scenes are painted on unfired, unglazed porcelain bodies in liquid white slip, layer upon layer to build up a translucent, three dimensional effect in low relief.

**Patina** The changes which occur on the surface of an object, particularly wood, bronze and silver, as the result of the passage of time. Good patination raises the value of an object. Destroying it by cleaning or accident, adversely affects value.

**Pitch** The black or dark brown sticky substance made by distilling tar or turpentine, used to fill the base of thinly gauged silver candlesticks to give them weight and stability.

**Polychrome** The term used by dealers and experts to describe an object painted in a variety of colours.

**Pontil rod** The solid metal rod used to remove a blown glass object from the blowpipe so that the rim can be finished and any other shaping completed. Once the piece has cooled and solidified, it is knocked off the rod, leaving the pontil mark.

**Provenance** The history of an object. This might include when, where and by whom it was made and its previous owners. Good provenance can add interest and value to a piece.

**Prunt** A blob of glass pushed onto a glass object as a form of decoration, often pulled to a point or impressed with a pattern such as raspberrries or a lion's mask.

**Putto** A naked boy or a winged boy's head depicted in the decorative arts from the 15th century. The plural is *putti*.

**Raised work** See **Stumpwork**.

**Refectory table** The modern term given to the long, narrow dining tables, usually of oak made between the 15th and 17th centuries and also known as joined or long tables.

**Repeater** A clock or watch where the user is able to pull a cord, depress a lever or press a button to get the clock to repeat the strike for the last hour, and often the last quarter hour (quarter repeating) without having to read the hands.

**Reserve a.** The minimum price an object can be sold for at auction, reached in agreement with the seller. **b.** An area on pottery, porcelain or textiles which is left free of colour, ready for painting and free of the ground colour.

**Rococo** The decorative style which found its fullest flowering in France between 1720 and 1760, characterised by asymmetrical forms, "C" and "S" scrolls and the rockwork (*rocaille*) inspired by Chinese gardening. More diluted forms of the style travelled to other parts of Europe. The style was revived during the early 19th century.

**Roemer** A wide, traditional German drinking vessel with an ovoid bowl and a hollow cylindrical stem, often decorated with raspberry prunts, and a speading coiled foot. The form from which the English rummer developed.

**Runner a.** Oriental carpets which are longer than they are wide. **b.** The grooves running from front to back on a piece of case furniture along which the drawers run.

**Sampler** Panels of fabric, often linen or light canvas, embroidered with a variety of stitches sewn as a reference or to demonstrate the skill of the (usually) young needlewoman. They often incorporate the letters of the alphabet, religious texts or biblical scenes, the name and age of the embroideress, the date the work was completed and some figural work.

**Sconce** A candleholder, generally supporting two or more branches, made to be hung on the wall. The name can also be given to the section at the top of a free-standing candlestick into which the nozzle fits.

**Seal top spoon** The most commonly made style of spoon in England between the 15th and 17th centuries. The stem is hexagonal and terminates in a small disc cap.

**Serpentine** An undulating shape, usually used to describe the profile of a piece of furniture such as a chest of drawers with a convex centre and concave sides.

**Sgraffito** Literally meaning "scratched" in Italian, the term describes the decorative technique of scoring or scratching the surface of an object, usually pottery, through an unfired slip covering, to reveal the darker body beneath.

**Sheffield plate** The process, discovered by Thomas Bolsover of Sheffield in England in 1743, of fusing a sheets of copper between two sheets of silver and passing the resulting sandwich through a rolling mill to flatten it into sheet form from which objects could be made.

**Sheraton** Thomas Sheraton (1751–1806) gave his name to the simple, elegant and sophisticated style of furniture made in England at the end of the 18th century, characterized by straight lines, delicate forms and decoration, and satinwood veneers and inlays. Not a single piece has ever been identified as being made by him. His fame rests on his designs, notably in his books, *The Cabinet-Maker and Upholsterer's Drawing Book* issued in parts between 1791 and 1794.

**Shibayama** The Japanese technique of inlaying an object with a combination of mother-of-pearl, ivory and stones to create a pattern or scene, surrounded by lacquer.

**Slip** Liquid clay used to decorate pottery, which is then known as slipware, or to pour into moulds for creating hollow-ware, particularly figures. A stiffer slip, piped onto pots is a method known as slip trailing or tube lining.

**Soda glass** Glass made by adding sodium carbonate (derived from burning barilla plants found on salt marshes) to the dry mixture to give the alkaline content, rather than potash. *See forest glass.*

**Soft-paste porcelain** Also known as artificial porcelain, the mixture of clay, powdered glass and other materials including bone ash, flint and sometimes soap stone, which European potters developed in an attempt to copy the true porcelain produced in China and Japan.

**Spandrels** The triangular corner spaces between an arch or circle and a rectangle. In clock terms, the ornamental corners between the chapter ring and the dial plate. (See p. 121).

**Sterling silver** Objects made from sterling silver are 925 parts per 1,000 pure silver. In its pure state, silver is too soft to work and is generally alloyed with copper.

**Stoneware** A hard, dense, non-porous pottery made from clay and feldspar which, although not translucent or white in appearance, is often compared with porcelain.

**Strapwork** A decorative motif which originated in the Netherlands in the 16th century consisting of interlaced ribbon-like straps. It was used to great effect in Elizabethan England, and revived in the 19th century.

**Stumpwork** Needlework raised in relief by working stitches over a foundation of wool or cotton wool or by working buttonhole stitches one on top of another and applying seed pearls and other items to create a three dimensional effect.

**Swag** A Renaissance and Neo-classical motif in the form of a suspended loop of drapery, foliage, fruit or flowers.

**Tables: Console** – a form of side table supported by wall brackets with two front legs. **Drop leaf** – a progression of the gate leg, the leaves extend from the surface area and are supported on hinged legs, arms or brackets. **Gate leg** – introduced at the end of the 16th century in England, the leaves are held up by a structure like a gate which swings out underneath the surface. **Pembroke** – supposedly introduced by the Countess of Pembroke in the second half of the 18th century, these small occasional or breakfast tables have two hinged flaps for extension on either side of the surface. **Sofa** – introduced towards the end of the 18th century as a development of the Pembroke table and designed to be set in front of the sofa or along the back, they are about 150cm (60in) long and 60cm (24in) wide with drop leaves at either end with one or more drawers in the frieze.

**Taffeta** The name given to a variety of fine silk fabrics, usually plain but sometimes patterned. A gum-like substance was applied to some taffetas to give a shiny finish.

**Tallboy** One chest of drawers on top of another, first introduced at the end of the 17th century and known in the United States as a highboy.

**Tallcase clock** *See Longcase clock.*

**Tazza** The Italian word for cup. In antiques terms, it has come to mean a shallow dish raised on a central stem. Also known as a comport.

**Teapoy** Originally used to describe a small tray-top table with a central stem on a tripod support, it has come to mean a large tea caddy on a similar type of support.

**Temmoku glaze** The black or dark brown glaze used on early Chinese stoneware and revived by 20th century studio potters such as Shoji Hamada.

**Timepiece** A mechanical instrument for measuring time which, unlike a clock, does not strike.

**Tole peinte** A French term used to describe the wide range of decorative objects made from painted sheet iron from the second half of the 18th century in France. A similar range of goods produced in England is referred to as Pontypool ware after the place in Wales where pieces were originally manufactured c.1730.

**Treen** Small, domestic articles made of wood, either turned or carved such as spoon racks and butter pats. (See p.186).

**Tudric** The trade name given to the range of pewter wares retailed by the London store, Liberty, early this century, made to accompany their silver *Cymric* range.

**Turning** The shaping of wood, metals and ivory by turning the material on a lathe.

**Veneer** Thin layers or strips of usually very fine wood, such as mahogany, satinwood, rosewood and walnut, applied to a carcass of much coarser wood.

**Vinaigrette** Small boxes in a variety of shapes, sizes and materials which include gold, silver, enamel and mother-of-pearl, containing a piece of sponge soaked in aromatic vinegar blended with essential oils, the fumes from which escaped through the pierced inner lid to counteract the noxious smells on the streets.

**Vitrine** A glass fronted cabinet which was used to display silver, china and other objets d'art.

**Warp** The vertical threads which run from top to bottom of a tapestry or rug.

**Weft** The horizonal threads of a tapestry or rug which intersect the weft threads, passing alternately over and under them.

**Whatnot** A term first used during the English Regency period for a stand with shelves designed to stand against a wall and be used to display ornaments, books and curiosities. It grew in size during the Victorian period and is also referred to in the trade as an etagère.

# Auction houses, fairs and further reading

## Major Auction Houses

**Bonhams**
Montpelier Street
London SW7
Tel 0171 393 3900

**Christie's Manson & Woods Ltd**
8 King Street
St James's
London SW1
Tel 0171 839 9060

**Phillips**
Blenstock House
101 New Bond Street
London W1
Tel 0171 629 6602

**Sotheby's**
34–35 New Bond Street
London W1
Tel 0171 493 8080

## Antiques Dealers' Associations

**British Antique Dealers' Association (BADA)**
20 Rutland Gate
London SW7 1BD
Tel 0171 589 4128

**London and Provincial Antique Dealers' Association (LAPADA)**
Suite 214
535 Kings Road
London SW10 0SZ
Tel 0171 823 3511

**National Antique and Art Dealers' Association of America Incorporated (NAADAAI)**
12 East 56th Street
New York
NY 10022
USA
212 826 9707

## Major Antiques Fairs

**"Antiques for Everyone"**
National Exhibition Centre
Birmingham
Tel 0121 780 4141
held in April, August and December

**The British Antique Dealers' Association Fair**
The Duke of York's Headquarters
Kings Road, Chelsea
London SW3
Tel 0171 589 4128
held in March

**The Fine Art and Antiques Fair**
Olympia Exhibition Centre
Hammersmith Road
London W14
Tel 0171 370 8211
held in February/March, June and November

**Grosvenor House Art and Antiques Fair**
Grosvenor House Hotel
Park Lane
London W1
Tel 0171 499 6363
held in June

**Harrogate Antique and Fine Art Fair**
The Royal Baths Assembly Rooms
Harrogate
Yorkshire
Tel 01823 323363
held in February

**International Ceramics Fair and Seminar**
The Park Lane Hotel
Piccadilly
London W1
Tel 0171 734 5491
held in June

**London Ceramics Fair**
Cumberland Hotel
Marble Arch
London W1
Tel 01905 776 091
held every January and June

## Further Reading

### Furniture
Aguis, Pauline, *British Furniture 1880–1915* (1978)
Aslin, Elizabeth, *Nineteenth Century English Furniture* (1962)
Chinnery, Victor, *Oak Furniture – The British Tradition* (1979)
Collard, Frances, *Regency Furniture* (1983)
Edwards, R. and M. Jourdain, *Georgian Cabinet Makers* (1955)

### Ceramics
Godden, G. A., *Encyclopedia of British Pottery and Porcelain Manufacturers* (1988)
*Oriental Export Market Porcelains* (1979)
*Staffordshire Porcelain* (1983)
Halfpenny, Pat, *English Earthenware Figures 1740–1840* (1992)
Hayward, Leslie, and Paul Atterbury, *Poole Pottery* (1995)
Medley, Margaret, *The Art of the Chinese Potter* (1981)
Saville, Rosalind, *Sèvres Porcelain*

### Glass
Bickerton, L., *18th Century Drinking Glasses* (1986)

Hajdamach, C., *British and European 19th Century Glass*

### Silver
Bradbury, Frederick, *Bradbury's Book of Hallmarks* (1975)
Bury, Shirley, *Victorian Electroplate* (1971)
Clayton, Michael, *The Collector's Dictionary of Gold and Silver* (1985)
Culme, J., *Directory of Gold and Silversmiths 1838–1914* (1987)
Jackson, Charles, *English Goldsmiths and their Marks* (1921)
Pickford, I., *Silver Flatware*

### Clocks
Britten, F. J., *Britten's Watch and Clockmakers Handbook* (1982)
Cescinsky, Herbert, Webster, Malcolm, R., *English Domestic Clocks* (1976)
Loomes, Brian, *Early Clockmakers of Great Britain* (1981)

### Carpets & Textiles
Bennett, Ian, *Rugs and Carpets of the World* (1977)
Black, David (ed.), *World Rugs and Carpets* (1985)
Godden, G. A., *Stevengraphs and other Victorian Silk Pictures* (1971)
Hughes, Therle, *English Domestic Needlework* (1961)

### Bears, Dolls & Toys
King, C. E., *The Encyclopedia of Toys* (1978)
Miller, Martin and Judith (eds.), *Miller's Antiques Checklist – Dolls and Teddy Bears* (1992)
Pearson, Sue, *Bears* (1995)
Taylor, Kerry, *Letts Guide to Collecting Dolls* (1990)

### Art Nouveau & Art Deco
Knowles, Eric, *Miller's Victoriana to Art Deco* (1993)
Griffen, Meisel and Pear, *The Bizarre Affair* (1988)
Green, Richard and Des Jones, *The Rich Designs of Clarice Cliff* (1995)

### Collectables
Baddiel, Sarah Fabian, *The World of Golf Collectables* (1992)
Kay, Hilary, *Rock and Roll Collectables* (1992)
Lambrou, Andreas, *Fountain Pens Vintage and Modern* (1989)
Turner, Anthony, *Early Scientific Instruments* (1983)

### General
Miller, Martin and Judith, *Miller's Antiques and Collectables: The Facts At Your Fingertips* (1993)
*Miller's Antiques Price Guide* (1996)
*Miller's Collectables Price Guide* (1996)
Simpson, M. and M. Huntley, (Ed.), *Sotheby's Caring for Antiques* (1992)

# Index

# Acknowledgments

6 JJ/JH (glass jug) + JJ (pewter measure) + B (other items); 16 JJ/RCA (chest) + PC (chair); 22-23 PC (all); 24 B (tl, tr, bl), WDG (br); 25 B (tl, bl), S (tr); 26 B (all); 27 PC (all); 28-30 B (all); 31 B (t, l, r, bl), S (tr); 32-33 PC (all); 34 B(all); 35 B (tr, br), PC (tl), S (c, bl); 36-37 PC (all); 38-40 B (all); 41 PC (all); 42 B (tl, bl, br), WDG (tr); 43 B ( tl, l, r, br), S (tr); 44 B (l, cl), PC (cr, r); 45 PC (br), B (other items); 46 B (tl, bl, br), PC (tr); 47 PC (c), B (other items); 48 JJ/PC (all); 52 PC (all); 53 JJ/PC (all); 54 B (all); 55 JJ/PKA (all); 56 B (c), PC (bl, cr, r); 57 JJ/PC (all); 58 B (r), P (l), PC (b, l); 59 JJ/PC (all); 60 PC (all); 61 JJ/PC (all); 62-63 PC (all); 64-65 B (all); 66-67 JJ/LA (all); 68 B (c, br), PC (tr, bl); 69 B (r, tl), PC (tr, l, bl); 70 PC (all); 71 JJ/CS (all); 72 B (all); 73 B (tr, r, c), PC (tl, bl, b); 74 PC (t,r), S (b); 75 DR (bl), PC (tl, r, l , br); 76 JJ/PC (Bohemian candlestick) + JH (other items); 80-81 JJ/JH (all); 82 JJ/JH (tr, c, bl, br), S (tl); 83 JJ/JH (tl, l, br), S (br); 84 JJ/JH (all); 85 B (bl), JJ/JH (tl, tr, cl, cr); 86-87 JJ/JH (all); 88 PC (tr), JJ/JH (tl, l, r); 89 CMG (tr), JJ/JH (r, br,bl); 90 JJ/ELA (bl), JJ/JH (t, r, br); 91 JJ/JH (all); 92 JJ/JH (r, b), PC (tr, c); 93 JJ/PC (all); 94 JJ/PC (all); 100-101 JJ/PC (all); 102 B (tl, tr), PC (bl, br); 103 B (tl, tr, r), PC (bl); 104 B (all); 105 JJ/PC (all); 106 B (all); 107 JJ/PC (all); 108-109 B (all); 110 JJ/PC (all); 114 AM (br), B (tr, bl, b); 115 PC (all); 116 B (l, bl), PC (r, br); 117 JJ/PC (all); 118 B (l, r), PC (bl, br); 119 PC (all); 120 B (all); 121 JJ/PC (all); 122 B (all); 123 JJ/PC (all); 124 B (bl, r), PC (l, cl, cr); 125 B (tl, tc, tr, ttr, l, c, r), PC (tcl, ct); 126 JJ/SP (bear) + PC (other items); 129 CSK (l) ,MP/FAO (b), MP/SP (tr, r, c) ; 130-131 JJ/SP (all); 131 KW (tr - button); 132 GD/CSK (br), MW/SP (tl, bl), PC (tr); 133 GD/CSK (tl), MP/MrP (bl), MP/SP (bcl, bc, br); 135-136 MP/SP (all); 137 JJ/SP (all); 138 MP/SP (all); 139 MP/SP (tr, bl), PC (tl, t); 141 JJ/RYA (tr, r, br), PC (l);142 B (tl, bl), PC (tr, br); 143 JJ/PC (all); 144 B (all); 145 B (tl, bl, r, br), CSK (l); 146 B (all); 147 JJ/PC (all); 148 JJ/PC (all); 152 P (all); 153 JJ/PC (all); 154 B (l, bl), HM (r), PC (br); 155 JJ/LAL (all); 156 JJ/JGA (all); 157 JJ/AC (all); 158 B (bl), JJ/S+T (r, br), LM (tr), NM (bcl); 159 B (r, br), JJ/S+T (tr, l, bl), LM (tl); 160 JJ/PC (all); 162 JJ/PC (l), PC (r, br, bl); 163 JJ/VAG (all); 164 B (tr, r), PC (c, b); 165 JJ/PC (all); 166 PC (all); 167 JJ/PC (all); 168 B (br), PC (tr, bl, b); 169 JJ/PC (all); 170-171 RB/PC (all); 172 PC (r), CI (bl); 173 CI (all); 174 JJ/PC (all); 176-178 B (all); 179 B(tl, l, bl), PC (tr, r); 180-181 JJ (all); 182 B (tr, c), PAC (tl, tcl, tcr, l, r, bl); 183 B (r, b), P (bl), JJ/D (tr); 185 P (tl, tr), PC (l); 186 JJ/RYA (all); 187 JJ/RYA (t, r, l bl), PC (br); 188 B (tr, b), P (r); 189 B (r, tl), P (l), PC (b, tr); 190 B (all); 191 B (bl c), PC (l, tl, bl); 192 B (tr), S (tcr, r, br, l); 193 JJ/S+T (all); 194 B (all); 195 B (tl, tr, l, r), PC (bl); 196-197 B (all); 198 B (l, r, br, tr); 199 B (all); 200 B (br), JJ/D (bl, b, tr); 201 B (c, l, r), PC (tl, bl); 202 PC (all); 203 B (bl, tr), PC (t, br); 204 B (tr), PC (b); 205 PC; 206-207 B (all); 208 B (tr, r, br), B+B (l), 209 B (b); 210 JJ ( l, r), JJ/CG (br), JJ/PC (bl); 211 JJ (tl, bl), JJ/WM (c), JJ/Spa (br), PC (tr); 212-213 JJ (all).

**KEY:**
t=top; b=bottom; c=centre; l=left; r=right

## PHOTOGRAPHY:

| | |
|---|---|
| RB | Richard Barclay |
| GD | Geoff Dann (© De Agostini Editions) |
| JJ | James Johnson (© De Agostini Editions) |
| KW | with permission of Kunstverlag Weingarten/Germany from R.und C. Pistorius: Die schonsten Teddies und Tiere von Steiff |
| MP | Michael Pearson (© De Agostini Editions) |
| MW | Michael Ward (© De Agostini Editions) |

## COLLECTION:

| | |
|---|---|
| AC | Adelle Corcoran |
| AM | reproduced by permission of the American Museum in Britain, Bath |
| B | Bonham's |
| B+B | Butterfield and Butterfield |
| CG | Caithness Glass Ltd |
| CI | Christie's Images |
| CMG | The Corning Museum of Glass |
| CS | Constance Stobo |
| CSK | Christie's South Kensington |
| D | Decodence, Camden Passage, London |
| DR | David Rago |
| ELA | Eric Lynam Antiques |
| FAO | FAO Schwarz |
| HM | Hove Museum and Art Gallery |
| JGA | Judy Greenwood |
| JH | Jeannette Hayhurst |
| JJ | James Johnson |
| LA | Libra Antiques |
| LAL | Lunn Antiques Ltd |
| LM | courtesy of Luton Museum Service |
| NM | courtesy of Northampton Boot and Shoe Museum |
| MrP | Mr Punch |
| P | Phillip's |
| PAC | Peter A.Clayton |
| PC | Private Collection |
| PKA | Peter Kemp Antiques |
| RCA | Rupert Cavendish Antiques |
| RYA | Robert Young Antiques |
| S | Sotheby's |
| S+T | Steinberg and Tolkien |
| Spa | Space |
| SP | Sue Pearson |
| VAG | Victor Arwas Gallery |
| WDG | William Doyle Galleries |
| WM | W. Moorcroft |

The Author and Publishers would like to thank the following for their generous help in compiling this volume: Richard Barclay, Simon Bevan, Caithness Glass, Sarah Covelli, Nicholas Dawes, Roger Dixon, Tom Dixon, William Doyle Galleries of New York City, Hugh Edwards and John Moorcroft of William Moorcroft plc, Cyril Frankel, James Hammond, Jeanette Hayhurst, Beatrice Hosegood, Phillip Keith, Alison Macfarlane, Erica Marcus, Andrew Middleton, Emma Nicholson, Sue and Michael Pearson, Gad Sassower, Kevin Scott, Emma Thommeret, Tracie Vallis, Joanna Van De Lande, Thomas Ward, James Weedon, Mr and Mrs Robert Young.